Joey

JOEY

Donald Goddard

HARPER & ROW, PUBLISHERS
New York, Evanston, San Francisco, London

Portions of this book previously appeared in *New York Magazine.*

FIRST EDITION

Designed by Gloria Adelson

Library of Congress Cataloging in Publication Data

Goddard, Donald.
    Joey.
    1. Gallo, Joey, 1929–1972. I. Title.
HV6248.G28G6 1974   364.1′092′4 [B]   73–14262
ISBN 0–06–011570–X

To Joie

Contents

Joey

1

The Killing

On the eve of his forty-third birthday, Joey Gallo showed himself on Mulberry Street for the first time in ten years. The next night, he went there again, and they killed him.

With his eye for effect, he would never have picked Umberto's Clam House as the place, or his new wife and stepdaughter as the audience, or around five in the morning of April 7, 1972, as a suitable moment for his farewell gangster routine. Given a choice, he might have upstaged Don Rickles at the Copacabana some hours earlier, and made the morning papers. But when he felt it coming, he was too proud, too tired and probably too curious to put it off. Having done what he could to protect his companions, he defied his wounds long enough to die privately on the street.

New Yorkers loved it. Crazy Joe Gallo was all that Hollywood had led them to expect in a mobster. He was flamboyant, capricious and deadly—the saltiest racketeer since Prohibition, and darling of the show-biz set. His death fed their mournful pride in the special awfulness of city life. But among those who knew him, there were some who could not understand how the earth continued in its orbit.

One of them was Jeffie Gallo, his first wife. She had left him two months earlier and gone to California with their ten-year-old daughter, Joie. When a friend called her in Los Angeles with the news, she broke down in a rage of pain and despair from which she has never recovered. Twice married and divorced, she and Joey were as close as incestuous twins.

On Gallo territory in Brooklyn, his crew rallied around his brother Al, Kid Blast, on President Street, prepared for another gang war. The devotion Joey inspired in his followers had cooled in recent weeks with his apparent preference for Broadway society, but the killing had left a bewildering void for which his nine-year absence in prison had been no sort of preparation. The kingdom was now an embattled republic. Five more bodies would be found before Joey's was even buried.

Then there was Sina Gallo, married to Joey just twenty-two days, and her daughter Lisa, who, at ten, had at last found out what it was like to have a father. They felt his desertion cruelly. In the six months they had known him, Joey had remade their lives around his, and told them nothing. The idea of his being a notorious gang leader had seemed like a doubtful joke until they saw him shot to death.

His last day began around noon. After coffee and eggs, Joey and Sina left their apartment in the West Village together and then went their separate ways, she uptown to do some shopping, and he downtown by car with his bodyguard. He had two appointments, one with his accountant to discuss his 1971 tax return, and the other with Jerry and Marta Orbach's attorney to go over a draft contract with Viking Press for a biography he had been talking about off and on. After that, he planned to spend the rest of the day in Brooklyn working for Americans of Italian Descent, a civil rights group in which his older brother Larry, now dead, had once been interested, and which Joey aimed to take over. In the event, he canceled the meeting on the book contract—it was the fourth such appointment he had either broken or ignored in a week—and went to President Street instead.

On arrival, he stopped to pass the time of day with detectives of the Pizza Squad, the police detail assigned to monitor the comings and goings of the Gallo group and its rival factions within Joe Colombo's Mafia family. For twenty minutes, Joey talked to them about his plans for AID. He said he aimed to put together an association of reputable Italian-Americans—judges, senators and civic leaders—and run it "strictly honest."

The detectives listened politely. One of them had known Joey from the days when he was just a skinny kid making trouble in the neighborhood. "He was trying to hang on that stuff that he was going straight, going legit. And he believed it, you could see that. He had visions of grandeur, that he was going to become a respectable public figure. And here he is with all that, feeling he's on the right track now, he's really going to make himself something, and then turning around and doing the foolish thing that he did. Knowing he could get himself killed. Daring them to do something. I mean, how do you figure a guy like that?"

The cops had never been able to figure him out. All his life, Joey had made a point of being unpredictable, and not always from perversity. To do the expected was, for him, a dangerous abdication of will. Though his moods could change with unsettling speed, he rarely acted on impulse. He was a calculating man, and he had all the time he needed to weigh the risk of exposing himself that night on enemy territory.

The night before, he had gone down to Little Italy with two of the boys to eat at the Luna Restaurant, a favorite haunt of his in the old days, but now on Colombo turf. With a contract out on his life, this was either a spontaneous act of bravado or a deliberate provocation. To go there again twenty-four hours later was a deliberate act of provocation amounting to a conscious act of suicide.

The indications are that Joey hesitated for some hours before deciding to celebrate his birthday. Pete the Greek and Bobby Darrow brought him back from President Street at around six-thirty and drove away a few minutes later as though he had settled in for an evening alone with Sina. His stepdaughter Lisa, who had just opened on Broadway with Julie Harris and Richard Kiley in *Voices,* had already left for the theater.

At about ten o'clock, Joey's sister Carmella arrived at the apartment, but there was still no sign that he intended to go out. After about twenty minutes, she went uptown in a cab to collect Lisa at the stage door and brought her straight home. It was not until Pete the Greek, his date Edie Russo, and Bobby Darrow showed up about half an hour later that it became clear that Joey had finally decided on a night out at the Copacabana, but even this was unusual for he had no liking for nightclubs.

They drove uptown to Sixtieth Street in Pete's black Cadillac, which was plastered with AID stickers, and the Copa unrolled the red carpet. As far as Sina knew, it was Joey's first visit there for at least ten years, but everyone seemed to recognize him, from the maître d'hôtel on down to the busboys. They were led like royalty to a corner table on the mezzanine with a commanding view of the floor, and, after a few drinks, he began to mellow into something like his usual self, particularly when he spotted Marta and Jerry Orbach on the other side of the room entertaining Punchy Illiano. He was amused to see they had claimed one of the guys from President Street, presumably as a consequence of their friendship with him. He became more cheerful still when Lisa was asked to take a bow as one of the celebrities attending Don Rickles' opening night. This thrilled her, annoyed Sina and surprised the Orbachs, who, until then, had not known Joey was there. Rickles did, however, as he made clear with several mock-fearful allusions to the prominent Mafioso watching his comedy act.

When the show ended, Joey held court. His public appearances were always marked by a procession of callers who would choose the right moment to pay their respects, and the last was no exception. Comedian David Steinberg came over to arrange a dinner date for the following Monday; columnist Earl Wilson stopped by to introduce his wife and his secretary, whom Joey immediately co-opted as a date for Bobby Darrow, and they, in turn, were followed by the rest of the Copa's table-hopping crowd—except for the Orbachs.

Joey's only contact with them that night was by accident. On his way back from the men's room, he bumped into them as they were leaving. After a brief exchange, Marta Orbach and her husband continued on their way. Joey watched them go, then returned to the table. "Guess I took care of them," he announced as he sat down again.

After the second show, they were joined by Don Rickles, who put Joey in a reminiscent mood. In the old days, he and his brother Larry, who had died of cancer while Joey was serving his stretch for extortion, had booked Rickles into a club they owned called the Arpeggio. Once on the subject of Larry, one story reminded Joey of another until it was suddenly 4 A.M., they were the last customers in the place and Sina was nodding off. Lisa, however, was fizzing with high spirits, and Joey was hungry. On the sidewalk outside, he told Bobby Darrow to take Earl Wilson's secretary home, which he did reluctantly, and the rest of the party disposed itself in the Cadillac to await Joey's pleasure. Sina was praying he would settle for eggs at home, but when he climbed in the back between her and Carmella, nothing would do but Chinese food.

Pete the Greek dutifully headed downtown on the East River Drive, but Chinatown had long since closed for the night. Joey then told him to try the Luna, but that, too, was dark. Driving on along Mulberry Street, they noticed that Umberto's on the corner of Hester Street was still open, but passed by and around the block in search of something better. Drawing a blank, Pete brought them back to Umberto's and parked outside the main entrance. "Should be okay," he said. "A friend of mine runs it."

His friend was standing on the corner with three other men, and Joey recognized him at once as Matty the Horse. A member of the former Genovese family, Matty (the Horse) Ianniello had once employed Pete as a barman-bouncer at the Wagon Wheel on Forty-fifth Street. Almost certainly, Joey recognized one of his companions as well, although he didn't say so. He could hardly have missed the hulking figure of Joseph Luparelli, who had also worked at the Wagon Wheel as a muscle man, and at the same time as Pete. Since then, Luparelli had gone up in the world. He was now bodyguard and chauffeur to Joe Yacovelli, acting underboss of the Colombo family. With Vincent Aloi, who had taken over the leadership after Joe Colombo had been shot down in Columbus Circle, Yacovelli had issued a contract on Joey's life within a week or so of his release from prison.

Seeing Pete at the wheel of the car, Matty the Horse walked over to shake his hand through the open window. "Hey, how *are* you?" he said. "It's been a long time."

"Yeah," said Pete. "Howya bin? I got Joey with me."

Matty stepped back, and lost his tongue. Behind him, Luparelli and the other men looked at one another and drifted away.

Amused by Matty's reaction, Joey led the way into the restaurant, over the halfhearted objections of Sina, who didn't like the atmosphere at all. It was almost 5 A.M., but there were still a few customers inside: four men in work clothes at one table, an Oriental couple at another and a girl seated at the counter. Joey chose a table at the far end of the room, adjoining the side door onto Mulberry Street, and sat down between Pete, on his left, and Carmella. Opposite him, with their backs to the wall, were Sina, in the middle, Edie Russo, on her left, and Lisa, screened on her other side by a coat stand. Joey thus had Pete between himself and the side door, and Carmella between himself and the main door. By turning his head slightly to either side, he could see anyone entering or leaving the restaurant. Satisfied with this arrangement, he settled back in his chair and looked the place over, commenting, too audibly for Sina's liking, on its unpleasantly bright lights and the rather obvious decor of nets, floats and phony lifesavers.

A waiter brought bread and menus as Matty the Horse came in from the street. He walked slowly the length of the counter and perched on a stool at the end with his back to them. Joey watched him in silence. When the waiter returned to take their order, he twisted around in his chair, jerked his thumb at Matty, and said, "Let *him* order for us. He'll know what's good. Right, Matty? You tell them what to bring." Matty shrugged, and told the cook to prepare boiled shrimp and scungilli salad.

Luparelli, meanwhile, had arrived at 91 Mulberry Street, a local hangout for the Colombo group, where he found Carmine DiBiasi, also known as Sonny Pinto, drinking coffee with Philip (Fat Fungi) Gambino and two brothers whom he knew only as Benny and Cisco. A close associate of Joe Yacovelli's, Sonny Pinto had achieved star billing on the FBI's "most wanted" list in the fifties by blowing his partner's brains out, and then wounding a witness. After seven years on the run, he had turned himself in and confessed, but was subsequently acquitted on a technicality. Luparelli told them what he had seen, and Sonny Pinto went to the telephone to call Joe Yack. When he returned, he said, "Get some guns."

Half an hour later, armed with two .38 pistols and a .32, Sonny Pinto and the two brothers drove slowly down Mulberry Street and parked almost opposite the side door of Umberto's. Luparelli, following behind in the crash car with Fat Fungi, stopped just short of the intersection with Hester Street, and waited with the motor running.

By now, Joey had eaten his shrimp and scungilli and ordered more. Sina was still nervous, but nothing untoward had happened, and the others were kidding her about it. The cook, Salvatore LaMonica, remembered their mood particularly because "they were dressed up nice, and they were, you know, not loud—they were happy. Very happy." Before his second helping of shrimp arrived, Joey excused himself from the table and went downstairs to the men's room.

The basement area of Umberto's is unusually extensive for a restaurant of its size. An angled stairwell, then newly painted in black and white, leads down to a dogleg corridor with the door to a huge dark cellar on the right, and the men's and women's rest rooms tucked away to the left. At the end of the corridor is a staff locker room, and the vaultlike door to a walk-in refrigerator. Joey was gone a long time. After about five minutes, Carmella became restless.

"I wonder what happened to him," she said.

"That's right," said Sina. "What do you suppose he's doing down there?"

"Pete, why don't you take a look? See if he's okay."

"Ah, come on," he protested. "Leave him alone. Can't a guy even go to the men's room now, for Chrissake?"

"But why would he take so long? I don't like it, Pete. I think you ought to go down there."

"Listen, Cam, I'm telling you—leave him alone. I know what I'm doing."

As if to bear him out, Joey reappeared at that moment. But it was a very different Joey from the one who had left them. No longer smiling, he was taut and wary as an alley cat. It was a moment or two before he seemed to recognize them.

"Jesus, it's spooky down there," he said. "Like a tomb. You could hide a whole lot of bodies down there. It's got all kinds of rooms. All kinds of doors I can't figure out. And I heard noises down there that don't make sense."

Pete stirred in his chair. "What kinda noises?"

"I don't know, Pops. Like rustling. And whispering."

There was a silence. Then Carmella gave him a boisterous kiss on the cheek. "Well, happy birthday, brother," she said, but her voice tailed away because his skin was like ice to her lips. Sonny Pinto, Benny and Cisco were crossing the street from their car.

As though dreaming, Sina saw a chubby, middle-aged man appear around the coat stand with a silver gun in his hand.

"Motherfucker," he whispered, "I'll kill you."

He began shooting at Joey.

Lisa began to scream, over and over again, "Don't kill my daddy —please don't kill my daddy," and Sina caught her last glimpse of him alive. He was rising to his feet, eyes sightless, mouth jolted open from the impact.

The first bullet killed him. It smashed into his left upper back, about five and a half inches below the shoulder line and six and a half inches to the left of the spine. Piercing the scapula, it ripped from left to right, from back to front, plowing through the left lung, severed the right common carotid artery, one of the two main vessels supplying blood to the brain, tore through the right lung and came to rest under the collarbone.

He should have collapsed and died. Instead, he reared up, flinging out his arms, and sent Pete and Carmella sprawling backward, a considerable feat of strength for a dead man only 5 feet 6 inches tall and weighing 145 pounds. He then gripped the edge of the heavy butcher's block table in both hands and heaved it over onto Sina, Lisa and Edie in a tumbling avalanche of dishes, glassware, hot sauce and condiments that carried them out of the line of fire.

By now, he had been hit by a second bullet, which entered the left lower back about an inch above the buttock, drove through the organs of the lower abdomen, and rammed upward into the spine. Still refusing to go down, he turned away from the gunman and was struck a third time, the bullet passing through his left arm, slapping his chest and falling into the lining of his jacket. As he stumbled toward the front door, crashing into tables and chairs, two more bullets tracked through his clothes, but caused no further injury.

It had all happened in a very few seconds, although to Sina, the shooting seemed to go on interminably. Three guns were firing, people were diving wildly for cover, Carmella was screaming, and Pete was cursing like a madman as he struggled to free his own gun, a .25 caliber Titan automatic, which had caught in the lining of his pocket. So intent was he on getting into action that when one of the killers put a bullet through his backside as he rolled around on the floor, he didn't even feel it.

Matty the Horse, meanwhile, had ducked into the kitchen for shelter, and Salvatore LaMonica had dropped flat behind the counter. "It sounded like firecrackers," he said afterward. "So like I started to turn around to see what was happening, but I did a half-turn and something hit something that was on the counter, and the glass hit me, and I didn't bother turning all the way around, so I just hit the floor. I just kept down until the police came."

It was Lisa who broke Sina's trance. They had both jumped to their feet instinctively as the table came over on them, and were still standing there against the wall, frozen in each other's arms. "Everybody else was on the floor, and I thought they had all been shot. I was trying to hide Lisa's face, and I lost sight of Joey. I was sure that everybody in the place was dead, and that when they found us alive, they would kill us, too. So I remember telling Lisa to lie down on the floor and pretend like she was dead—I remember that vividly.

I covered her with my coat, and told her not to look up whatever happened. Then I started to crawl around on the floor looking for Joey, but he wasn't there."

Parked on the corner of Hester Street, Luparelli saw Sonny Pinto, Benny and Cisco run out of Umberto's. The door no sooner closed behind them than Pete opened it again a few inches and began firing at them, scoring several hits on Sonny's car. When the fusillade stopped, the three gunmen picked themselves up unhurt and drove off, followed by Luparelli and Gambino, to a prearranged hideout in Nyack, New York, where Joe Yacovelli was waiting for them.

With the empty gun in his hand, and still not feeling his wound, Pete looked around frantically for Joey, and caught sight of Matty the Horse hiding in the kitchen. Choking with frustration, he threw up the counter flap and stormed in after him, treading on LaMonica's hand as he lay on the floor. Too scared to cry out, or even raise his head, the cook heard a scuffle. Then Pete said, "Move, or I'll blow your head off," and dragged Matty out into the restaurant by his lapels. Jamming him up against the counter, and cursing him with every name he could lay his tongue to, he shook him till his head fell about helplessly.

"You motherfucking son of a bitch," he ground out, almost in tears. "What do you know about this? I'll kill you."

"Nothing, Pete—honest," Matty said earnestly, his eyes on the gun. "Jesus. In my own place? You gotta believe me."

Suddenly distracted by Carmella's relentless screaming from outside on the street, Pete dropped him and made for the door.

By some unfathomable act of will, Joey had refused to die with his enemies watching. His mind gone with the loss of blood to the brain, he nevertheless picked his way from one end of the restaurant to the other through an obstacle course of overturned tables and chairs. A walking corpse, he wrestled open the door, lurched across the sidewalk and leaned against Pete's car for a moment, as though to recover his strength. Pushing himself off again, he worked his way around it into the street, and out to the very center of the intersection before finally conceding he was dead. Folding gently at the knees, he rolled over on his back.

When Carmella reached him, he seemed to be sleeping. There were no signs of injury, for Joey had even bled privately. The autopsy a few hours later found three quarts of blood in his chest.

2

Joey and Jeffie

To describe Joey Gallo as a criminal is correct but unhelpful; as soon dismiss George Jackson as a convict. The two had no more in common than their prison experience, and would have felt little but contempt for each other had they met, but both were conscious enemies of society, and neither would submit to it. Beyond that, Jackson was concerned with his race, whereas Joey was concerned with himself—but he was not in crime for the money.

The rackets bored him. He died without leaving a penny. In his latter years, he was not even particularly convincing as a gangster, although he could act the part with terrifying ruthlessness if the situation called for it. Possessed of demonic energy, Joey was a man of action, a born warrior in an age when warriors were not only out of style but a damn nuisance. He enjoyed risky enterprises. He loved tumult and conflict and trials of manhood, especially against the

12

odds. Everything had to be acted out, every idea and fantasy, without constraint. Life was a game, a hugely absurd and pointless game played with live pieces, and the only object was to win. Society being infinitely corrupt, no other view made sense. Conscience was an alibi for losers. But winning excused everything, so he played his game with a killing intensity, aware but careless of its cost to those around him. If he admired professionalism in others, he could never settle for less than virtuosity in himself.

Not everybody loved him for it, of course, but those who didn't usually kept their mouths shut. In Joey's world, reputations were not lightly earned. Short, slimly built, with a bony face, thinning hair and a large mole on his left cheek, he was not an imposing figure. Only the eyes were daunting—pale, clear and direct. But he had learned early in life to offset any physical disadvantage by striking first, and with a crippling ferocity. Tangle with Joey, and he couldn't be stopped. You had to be ready to kill him. But if you were ready to love him and serve him, he would make you one of his people. You would belong. And on the streets of Brooklyn, to be one of his people conferred a respect—an identity, almost—that some could find nowhere else.

Joey was a criminal, but to him the term meant as little as the laws he broke. He refused to acknowledge a higher authority than his own, or to concede any claim on his life, made as of right, by anyone. South Brooklyn was his kingdom—disputed territory, but *his.* In the old days, when he walked the streets with his entourage, people came out of their houses to greet him, and not from fear: old women in black, who would grab his hand and kiss him, quarreling for a place at his side; the men standing in doorways and on tenement stoops, smiling, then bowing and nodding as they met his eye; their kids, the older boys hanging back to learn from his manner while the younger ones bummed his small change. Who, then, was going to tell Joey what to do?

Not the law. He saw it bought and sold like everything else. Laws were devised to keep the poor in order, and no society standing pat on a doctrine of self-help has any right to be surprised when people start helping themselves. Joey's kingdom coexisted with the "straight" world. It occupied the same territory, but obeyed *his* laws. He sought, not to escape his environment, as did most of the other Italian-American kids of his generation, but to master it. There was never a conscious decision to embark on a life of crime. He did what his nature had him do, knowing the "straight" world would try to prevent him or kill him for it. There was never an ambition he entertained that failed to bring him into conflict with a vested interest, and once battle was joined, he could never give in, win or lose.

At four, he rejected the inferior role of infant. Mary Gallo, who was very proud of his curly blond hair, found her son in the bathroom one day gashed and bleeding, a straight razor in his hand, the curls at his feet. At school, he rejected the inferior role of pupil. His attendance was bad, his achievement worse, and he dropped out after a year at the Brooklyn High School of the Automotive Trades, where he proved "defiant, uncooperative and in need of guidance." Joey could learn, but he couldn't be taught. At seventeen, he rejected the inferior role of Navy recruit. After six months, he was mustered out for "reasons of convenience to the government," on the grounds that he was "emotionally immature, egocentric and demanding."

Nearing thirty, he rejected the inferior role of buttonman in Joe Profaci's mob. With his older brother Larry as the only moderating influence, he set the stage for a revolt against Mafia authority that led on to the two bloodiest gang wars since the thirties. In 1959, Robert Kennedy described him as Public Enemy Number One—which was probably just as well, for Joey would never have settled for anything less. Found guilty of extortion in December, 1961—without benefit of counsel and on evidence that might seem less than conclusive—he rejected the inferior role of convict. Besieging the courts with appeals, he bucked the New York penal system from Attica to Auburn for nine years, surviving several attempts on his life, long periods of solitary confinement and the generally unremitting hostility of guards and inmates alike, and emerged—the same.

But the times had changed if Joey had not. Hemmed in by police and Parole Board supervision, at war with Profaci's successor Joe Colombo within weeks of his release, and dependent upon his people even for groceries, he rejected the inferior role of a toothless messiah. In his last two months, he moved in more fashionable circles, but again found nothing worth the cost to his pride. Brought face to face at last with a higher imperative even than survival, and sooner than deny his nature or the logic of his life, he then rejected the inferior role of a middle-aged mobster with nowhere to go, and died.

Given the standards most people live by, there was nothing commendable in this, unless consistency is a virtue even in willfulness. Though he possessed many of the qualities that make for success in the "straight" world—intelligence, imagination, intuition, charm, determination, drive, concentration and a persuasive tongue—to suppose, as some of his latter-day show-biz friends have hinted, that there, but for a quirk of fate, went the Italian John Kennedy is sentimentality. Joey carried the cult of individualism to its ultimate antisocial degree. Nothing took precedence over the instant gratification of his mildest whim. The primacy of self was absolute. And yet he was also capable of great tenderness and compassion. At a time when practically every investigation of a major crime in Brooklyn— from homicide and extortion to burglary and hijacking—led straight to the Gallos, the natural heirs to Murder, Inc., he would sleep every night with his head on his wife's belly so as not to miss the faintest stirring of their unborn child. In Joey Gallo, mobster, lived Joey Gallo, lover, friend, poet, painter, prince—and no one who knew the latter, including his two wives, could ever quite believe in the former, despite what they read in the papers. His life on the streets rarely intruded on the time they spent together. He never discussed it with them, nor did they, for their various reasons, ever ask him about it —not even Jeffie Gallo, whose life revolved around his for twelve years:

"I don't think anyone knew Joey better than I did. His brother Larry knew part of him. So did his mother and father. But I think I knew him completely—the total man. We used to lie around the house together for hours and days on end, just talking and making love. On occasions I would look at him and literally see light shimmering around him—I would have to blink my eyes. His skin was almost translucent. He was so *alive.* This incredible energy we always had between us produced a kind of electrical movement in the air.

"I never thought in terms of bosses or gangs. His business was *his* business. It wasn't real to me. I couldn't have been less interested in that world of hats. Oh, I'd say, when they called the house, the hats are coming. And when he left with them, he would never say where he was going or what he was going to do, and I never asked. I was only sorry that my time was up and he had to go. Someone would call, Joey would tell him to come over, and when he said that, I'd draw his bath and lay out his clothes. I kind of serviced him. I'd never done that for anyone before and I enjoyed it."

Domesticity had never been her strongest suit. When she met and fell reluctantly in love with Joey Gallo, Jeffie Lee was twenty-eight, voluptuously attractive, twice married and divorced, hounded by lovers and just back from another spell in Las Vegas as a showgirl. In those days, she was a Creole Marilyn Monroe, with wide eyes, the color of light jade, and a corn-crake voice from too much yelling and smoking. She had Monroe's luxurious figure, but near-black hair, as glossy as molasses, and skin so dark that Sammy Davis, Jr. once accused her of passing. When they saw her, few men were inclined to ask if she could cook, which was lucky for them, since her tongue was no less striking than her looks, and she had yet to boil an egg. A woman of powerful feelings and intractable will, Jeffie combined a gift for self-expression with the vocabulary of a mule driver, and suffered fools with so little patience that Joey once described her, not without pride, as the *real* hoodlum in the family.

Though a match in everything else, their backgrounds could hardly have been less alike. Joey's father, Albert Gallo, Sr., was an illegal immigrant who arrived from Naples in 1920, married a volatile Italian girl called Mary Nunziata, whom he confined to the kitchen, and fathered five children—Carmella, Lawrence, Joey, Albert, Jr. and Jacqueline—in the slums of Brooklyn. Jeffie's father, Frank Lee, was a rich Southern WASP from New Orleans who came to New York to marry Olga André, née Echeverria y Aguilar, a Ziegfeld beauty and daughter of the Belgian Consul to Costa Rica.

Installing her in the then very fashionable Apthorp Building on Broadway and Seventy-ninth Street in Manhattan, he stayed long enough to beget Jeffie before losing his money in a stock market crash and his wife in a divorce. Even if she *was* distantly related to Luis Echeverria Alvarez, now President of Mexico, his family disapproved of the match. Olga was not only a foreigner, she was also a chorus girl.

In her daughter's eyes, the Lees "were Scotch-English, social, old money, Presbyterian tight-lipped hypocrites, and mother had to go back to work. Being a very theatrical lady, in every sense, as well as a great beauty, that meant show business, and I didn't see much of her until I was about seven. She was in a touring show with Ed Wynn, and I had been left with the maid as usual. One day, she locked me in a damp closet because I'd been crying, and I got a mastoid. So Mother rushed home from Peoria or somewhere to be at my bedside, fell to her knees, wringing her hands like Lillian Gish, and wailed, 'Dear God, if you spare my daughter's life, I will never go on the road again.' Well, he must have been a pretty good theater critic, because I recovered and she went to work for NBC. And I fixed that maid pretty good. I hid the silver in the yard, and my mother thought she had stolen it."

At the National Broadcasting Company, Olga André became "the first voice heard over shortwave to Latin America," and was soon doing five shows a week of mid-brow music, poetry and interviews. Now living in an apartment on East Forty-ninth Street, she knew everybody in New York and invited most of them home to cocktail parties, which Jeffie had to attend. "At seven, I used to sniff cleaning fluid because I had to get stoned to hack it. I would sit in a big chair with a little glass of sparkling water, wearing a white dress with bows, because Mummy didn't want to look too old, you see, and people would say, 'And whose little girl are you?' And I would have to flutter my lashes, and say, 'I'm my mummy's little girl.' So before they came, I would try to get wrecked on Energine in the kitchen.

"Then my mother married the guy who ran her radio shows. I don't know why. She was a very naïve Ziegfeld girl. Very proper. She never went on to those Hearst parties after the show or anything like that. She was always kept virginal. In fact, I don't think she got laid four times in her life—she just knew that certain things were not dignified. And although I must have been going to school all this time—I was now about thirteen—I don't remember a day of it."

In 1944, NBC closed down its shortwave service to Latin America. Olga then divorced the producer, and left for California with her daughter to take a job with Warner Bros. dubbing soundtracks in Spanish and French. Now very poor, she rented a cheap apartment in downtown Los Angeles and entered Jeffie in junior high school, where she proceeded to rebel in classic Southern California teenager style, rolling garbage cans down the aisles of the auditorium and spending too much time on motorcycle pillion seats. Meanwhile, Olga was finding her social bearings. She began to write a gossip column for Latin-American movie magazines, and was soon being invited to all the previews and having her picture taken with all the stars. At sixteen, Jeffie was not impressed. When she wasn't busy with her boyfriends, she was ripping off Los Angeles department stores to the tune of $2,000 a week.

"I was a very angry person. I guess it was a textbook reaction. One day, I stole so many clothes I could hardly walk out of the store. I think I *wanted* to get caught—and I was. So they took me to the police station and called my mother. She made a tremendous entrance, wearing an enormous hat, turned to the desk sergeant and said—in a voice trembling with emotion—'I have just been named Cultural Attaché to the Consulate of Costa Rica, and my daughter —a *thief!*' It was such a great performance they let me go. And as soon as we got outside, she said, 'Now why would you steal clothes, dear? You must want clothes.' So she bought me clothes, in spite of my feeble attempts to explain that after stealing them for months I really didn't need any more."

A few months later, Jeffie married Joe Barreras, a short, slim, poker-faced Mexican-American a few years older than she who owned a green Buick. Had it not been for her mother, they might just have lived together for as long as it lasted, but Jeffie was now so angry with her that when Olga, rather surprisingly, suggested this course, she immediately insisted on marrying him. Predictably enough, they soon separated, but the experience gave Jeffie her first inkling of the virtues she would look for in a man. He was authoritative, saw that she got good grades and kept her out of bad company. After she graduated from high school, they worked together in a factory, putting eyes in rubber monkeys. Then the Korean War began, Joe was drafted into the Army and Jeffie was left alone. But not for long.

She had taken to spending Sunday afternoons in Hermosa Beach at a club called the Lighthouse, and getting to know the musicians who played there. She had also started going to City College, where she met an intense young man named Dick Bock, who worked as doorman at the Haig, then the best jazz club in Los Angeles and a favorite gig for top-liners. He introduced Jeffie to the pleasures of classical music, highbrow talk and $200 a week, mostly in tips, as a cocktail waitress. "Our relationship was very ascetic. It was one of those bread, wine and cheese numbers, and suddenly I was into the intellectual world. Before that, I don't think I'd had a conscious thought."

When Joe Barreras came home from the war, Jeffie decided she didn't want to be married any more. Too proud to argue, he divorced her, and the two have remained friends ever since. Bock subsequently started a record company called Pacific Jazz, which later became even more successful as World Pacific, and Jeffie met her next husband, at the Lighthouse.

"Gerry Mulligan had hitchhiked in from New York, and, like all the new guys, was playing just for his meals. It was a good way to get introduced. One Sunday afternoon, I was sitting there with a group of people and he came over from the kitchen with a cup of coffee in his hand and said to me, 'If you've got a nickel, I'll buy you a cup of coffee. Musicians can get it cheaper'—which I thought was sweet. So he brought me a cup of coffee and then he played, and he played his ass off that day. I was very impressed. He was gaunt, thin, tall and Christlike. Very pure. It was the same kind of thing I sensed later in Joey—a kind of innocence. They had a sense of themselves, a sense of their own being, apart from the world. Gerry brought out a protective quality in me. He had a kind of genius in those days,

Joey and Jeffie **19**

which no longer exists. So we got married. In about a month."

Mulligan quickly built a reputation. His quartet was booked into the Haig, where she still worked as a cocktail waitress, and Bock began to record them for his new Pacific Jazz label. Jeffie's main contribution to her husband's career was to persuade Chico Hamilton to leave Lena Horne. "He was very good for Gerry's quartet. They were a big, big success. But we weren't. As Gerry became popular and I got to know him, he began to talk *at* me. Then he started repeating himself, and it became a bit boring. Part of the problem, of course, was that Gerry was a junkie—although a very *good* junkie, very dignified and very angry. He had that dependency. He was always up with it. He was not a lame duck. In fact, I didn't even know he *was* a junkie till he told me he didn't want to be one any more. He thought we should go away somewhere so he could kick it. It only takes three days to kick junk, but you need somebody to tie you down. We went to Palm Springs, but I didn't know how to handle it, and he wasn't really cured when we went back to L.A. He started to connect again, so I decided to move on."

It was not quite that simple. Jeffie was pregnant at the time and taking ergot to abort herself—that was one complication. Another was the Los Angeles Police Department. The Mulligans were then sharing a house with Chet Baker, the quartet's trumpet player, and his wife, and one night they were raided. "It was a typical, sneaky L.A. bust. They only go after movie stars and such. They got into the house and found some grass, so they took us down to the club and arrested Gerry and Chettie right off the stand. It was all very camera-flashing, bust-bust time. After that, we went back to the house and Gerry showed them where his heroin was stashed. In fact, he took the blame for all the drugs—except the ergot, of course. One of the squad took a look at it and said, 'That's not ergot. That's Dolophene,' which is how I became known as the crazy lady of the police station. I used to go down there every day screaming for my rights. 'That's not Dolophene. That's ergot. Why are you *bothering* me?' Finally an FBI man saw how frightened and angry I was and told me not to worry. He said they knew it was ergot. It was just one of their little tricks."

Meanwhile, an ex-girlfriend of Mulligan's had arrived from New York and tracked Jeffie down to the Haig. "I guess Arlyn had heard rumors about Gerry and me because she asked if I had finished with him. If not, she'd get right back on the plane. I said, 'Oh boy! Am I ever! Thank you for coming.' So we became friends. I got aborted, an annulment, and went home to mother. Arlyn and Gerry got married, he did time on an honor farm, and they left for New York."

By then, the Haig had closed, and Jeffie was working at Jazz City. But she was tired of Los Angeles, and when her girlfriend Joyce suggested they should drive across country to try their luck in New York, she agreed at once. Jeffie makes few friends, but those she has are her family and stick for life, cheerfully submitting to her pitiless tongue, and lengthy periods of total neglect. On the face of it she might seem to ask more from them sometimes than she gives in return, but she repays their devotion in her own way—with passionate loyalty and spasms of near-suicidal generosity. Headstrong, temperamental and impulsive . . . there are no neutral moments in Jeffie's company. Joyce laughed and cried with her for a year in New York, then left to marry Al Lettieri, a tough young Italian actor struggling to get started in the movies. Whereupon Jeffie, who had been spending her days as a receptionist in an industrial-design office and her nights on the town with dates from the music business, packed up and returned briefly to California before embarking on her Las Vegas period.

It began like most of the other periods in her life. "I got up one morning and said, 'Shit. I got to get out of here.' So I went to Vegas, where I became a cocktail waitress at the Riviera Hotel. And through the sister-in-law of my first husband, I met a woman called Geri Nolan, who was the entertainment and publicity manager of El Rancho Vegas. She introduced me to the owner of the hotel, who said to her, 'Isn't she beautiful? She ought to be in the chorus.' So they put me in the line. I became a chorus girl, and I hated it. I was still an object. I was the only showgirl in Vegas who wore a trench coat and jeans and was contemptuous of mink, men with money, crap-shooting and all the things one is supposed to be a showgirl for. But I made good money and had a few laughs."

Some of them were with a wealthy Latin-American who fell madly in love with her and flew in regularly by private plane to see her. Others, though not so many, were with Norman Granz, the powerful, rather forbidding figure who managed Ella Fitzgerald, put on "Jazz at the Philharmonic," collected Picassos and dominated the music business as effectively as David Merrick controlled the theater. Jeffie met him through Billy Eckstine.

"I worked with Billy in a couple of shows in Vegas, and we dug each other as friends because we both had the dark skin and shit-color eyes. He and his girlfriend Nicole were going to L.A. one time, so I went with them and we stayed at the Garden of Allah, the old show-biz hangout. And I did the same exact take with Norman as I did with Joey later on, except that I was cooler with Joey. I was on my way out as Norman was coming in. I didn't know who he was —Nicole didn't mention his last name. But I remember leaving the suite to go to my car, reaching the car, then turning around and going back. He was not a particularly good-looking man, but there was this spark between us, and it floored me.

"We used to have dinner every night at Chasen's, and while I ordered everything in sight, he only ate hamburger, which I thought was a bit pretentious in a place like that. Then we would go to his house, where he had this enormous bed. I was terrified of him. He had such an overwhelming personality, and I wasn't used to people like that. Besides, he was the love of my life. I used to sleep in one teeny little corner of the bed, curled up so I shouldn't annoy him.

"He used to talk about me a lot with Georgia Brown. We'd become friends when she played the Mocambo. This was just after a Latin-American tour, and she was coming up fast. She told me, much later, that Norman once said to her, after we'd broken up, 'Ah, I should have married Jeffie. She really loved me.' And I really did."

Meanwhile, she continued slouching around Las Vegas in her raincoat, peeling it off for feathers and sequins at night and occasionally to put on a bathing suit for photographers. It was 1956. She was twenty-four, absurdly beautiful and miserably afflicted with migraine headaches. That summer, she sent a batch of bathing beauty pictures home to her mother, who by now had married for the third time.

"Hi there! Las Vegas Fabulous Girl," Olga wrote back. "What wonderful publicity they have given the glamorous Miss Lee. Mom is so proud of you. Some of the photos you sent us are just beautiful." Then, after a little family gossip: "Darling, if you haven't already sent the publicity to your Dad, I would advise you not to send it, for he would think the photos much too nude. You know how he is, and there is no need to have him rant and rant about it. Mother understands, but I don't think your Dad would."

Mother also understood about Norman Granz. A few months later she was advising her unhappy daughter "to sit down when you can be quiet and completely alone and THINK—THINK. You are so young and so beautiful—someday, sooner or later you WILL find the RIGHT MAN, I know. Use your HEAD. God has given you a very good one to THINK with. Try to detach your mind from the sentimental feelings you have for Norman. Look at him objectively and study him from all angles. Your natural desire for a home and children is entirely opposed to Norman's WAY of LIFE."

By July, 1957, when she opened at El Rancho Vegas in a show with Joe E. Lewis, Jeffie had reached the same conclusion. That fall, she returned to New York to share an apartment with Georgia Brown and to work for Patti Page on her TV show. "Keep up your dancing," advised Olga. "She might be able to use you on the line. Or a small part. Also keep practicing your typewriter. Instead of reading when you are not busy, take the typewriter with you to the studio and bang away at every free moment you have. You never know when opportunity will knock at your door, *and you must be prepared.* You are very intelligent, my Jeff. You have so much to offer, but you must buckle down to *serious work and not flit around from one thing to another.* You will get nowhere unless you *do.*"

As it turned out, she soon flitted on to a job as press agent with Eddie Jaffe, which also failed to please her, and then with Judd Bernard, who hired her in New York to work for him in California. In less than a year, she was back in Los Angeles. "As a press agent in L.A., you were really a servant to movie stars. You'd go around holding them up and getting their poodles dyed pink—it was really horrible. But through Judd Bernard I met a man who was business manager for a lot of Judd's clients. I was having lunch with him one day when I had a particularly bad migraine, and what with one thing and another, I guess I kind of flipped out and started to cry. So he asked me if I would like to meet a doctor who practiced Reichian therapy. This interested me because I had read one of Wilhelm Reich's books and wondered whether these headaches were maybe a physical manifestation of a psychological disorder. Anyway, we flew to New York and spent the weekend at his doctor's house. And I liked this doctor, so I said, 'Yes. I want to go into therapy.' But first I had to find the money, so I went back to work in Vegas as a showgirl and saved every cent."

By living in the hotel and eating all her meals there, she managed to salt away about $175 a week. Her faithful Latin lover, who was still flying in to see her from New York in his private plane, also chipped in discreetly by gambling for her at the tables, and, within a matter of months, she was back in New York, working for Raymond's Exclusive Telephone Answering Service, seeing her doctor twice a week and living in a fourth-floor walk-up at 63 East Eleventh Street.

Determined to settle at last, she wrote to her mother early in January, 1959, asking her to send on the family silver.

> The apartment is lovely—not yet finished, but very liveable. I have lots of heat, and the fireplace works beautifully. . . . I've been feeling very nervous this week, but as my doctor says, ups and downs are usual. And since I've been feeling so good most of the time, I shouldn't complain. Getting the apartment fixed is lots of work, and sans funds, makes it very difficult, but patience is one thing I must learn, and as you know, for me it's hard. Funny—until I got my little nervous spell, I didn't fully realize how well I had been feeling. To feel peaceful inside is something I never felt, and now I realize it's possible, I shall fight harder for it.

Olga responded by sending the silver and more maternal advice:

> Your letter was so warm and thoughtful. Mother is so very proud of her daughter. Never worry, darling, when you feel nervous, out of sorts or insecure. This happens to all of us at one time or another. I

always felt very nervous either before or after my menstruation period. This is quite natural and must be expected and taken in our stride.

Be sure, baby mine, to eat adequately before going to your work and throughout the day. When I don't eat properly, I always feel nervous. It is of the utmost importance for our physical and mental well-being to get the proper nourishment in our body.

Get some K cereal to eat for breakfast. It has all kinds of proteins and vitamins. Mix it with sugar and half and half—it is really delicious. Also have an egg or two daily. Scrambled or otherwise. Also celery, lettuce and tomatoes are very good for the health and nerves.

The Silver should reach you by Friday of this week. If you should not receive it by this time next week, *be sure to let me know. This is very important.*

Her dutiful, twenty-seven-year-old daughter did as she was told:

Dearest Mom,

Just a note to tell you silver arrived safely and I love it. Thanks, darling. Your 10 bucks really helped. You're an angel. Love and kisses to all,

Jeff

P.S. I used it for groceries.

Shortly after this, Olga's own health became a matter for concern. She was showing the first symptoms of a brain tumor that eventually would kill her. But she had recovered by the summer and was again exhorting Jeffie to improve herself. "Be sure to keep in mind the thought of taking a business course just as soon as possible. This is of the utmost importance in finding and holding a job. It is really the only way, baby mine. I know this by personal experience. So many good opportunities came my way, but I had to turn them down for lack of stenography and the touch system of typewriting."

Given the source of this advice and the crisis it was meant to solve, the prescription was hilarious. Jeffie ignored it, responding instead to a further inquiry about her eating habits. "My health is in great shape. My emotional state (which I could never convince you was important) leaves much to be desired. However, I'm positive I will have the world by the tail within the next year. I'm being helped beyond description by my doctor."

She was also being helped by a film producer, who took her to Europe with him in late September. Though they quarreled as soon as they left and scarcely spoke to one another for the rest of the trip, it led to a joyous binge with Georgia Brown in London that raised her spirits enormously. The sympathy that flows between Jeffie and her friends, their instant understanding without need of explanations, had always served to steady her. And on her return to New York, she was still further elated to hear that Joyce, her oldest friend, was coming back East with her husband to live.

They arrived in February, 1960, to stay with Jeffie on Eleventh Street while they looked around for an apartment of their own. It was natural enough, therefore, that Al Lettieri, who was no stranger to the city, should bring his friends home to meet her. One of them was Ali Hassan Waffa, whom everyone called Ali Baba, an affable, middle-aged, Egyptian seaman who was well known in nightclub circles for the prime quality of the hash he carried. He sat around with them one evening for a couple of hours, smoking and talking, and left early because Jeffie had to go to work next morning.

The following night, there was a knock at the door, and Jeffie, who was not expecting visitors, went down the long, rather dark hall of her apartment to open it. "Ali Baba was standing there in a black hat and coat, looking very swarthy, and behind him was another little guy in a black coat, wearing a gray hat with a band. I couldn't see him too well, but he had his eyes narrowed into slits and one shoulder hunched up. They looked very comical, and I started to laugh. I said, 'I haven't seen anything like you two guys in years. Except maybe on the Late Late Show.'

"Well, that didn't go down so good, but I asked them in and they preceded me down the hall to the living room, where Joyce and Al were. I was trying not to giggle because the second guy was still holding one shoulder higher than the other and sort of walking sideways. But then when we got in the light and I saw his face . . . There was a kind of instant energy exchange. I can't explain it. His electricity was vibrating in the air. I sensed it, and right away put it out of my mind, thinking, 'Jesus Christ, I'm in enough fucking trouble. If there's anything I don't need in my life, it's this funny-looking little character here.' He said his name was Joey Gallo, which didn't mean a thing to me. He sat down and we visited awhile, but as soon as I could, I excused myself and went to bed."

3

King Joey

Soon after his twenty-first birthday, Joey was judged insane. Then known as Joey the Blond in South Brooklyn, where he had already acquired the kind of reputation that silenced conversation when he came through the door of the Clinton Bar or the Ace Poolroom, he was picked up in February, 1950, by detectives of the 76th Squad on charges of burglary and possession of burglary tools. This was not by any means his first problem with the law. He had a record going back to March, 1944, when he was barely fifteen. But this time he behaved so disdainfully, with all the hauteur of a general officer captured by peasants, that the arresting officers concluded he was some kind of a nut.

The magistrate agreed with them. When Joey appeared before him, sharply dressed in his zoot suit, black shirt and white tie, and carrying a broad-brimmed gray hat with a band, he showed such an airy unconcern with the proceedings that even when he was sent to Kings County Hospital for a psychiatric examination, he greeted the decision with no more than the polite interest of a tourist in some quaint native custom. Obviously, he had to comply with the order, but it was all a misunderstanding. They simply didn't know who he was.

Nor did the examining psychiatrists. They found him "not imbecile," but "incapable of understanding the charges against him, and of making his defense." Diagnosing schizophrenia of a paranoid type, they gave it as their opinion that "Joseph Gallo is presently insane." This, of course, was just another absurd mistake, as Joey explained patiently, lucidly and to the complete satisfaction of the county court when his case came up in September. Having rebuked the psychiatrists for their patent error, the judge allowed him to cop a plea of unlawful entry, and handed down a suspended sentence. After that, people started calling him Crazy Joe, although not to his face.

Ten years, and a good many arrests, later, his indifference to the law and conventional restraints on behavior still seemed insane to those required to enforce them, but as far as Joey was concerned, it was simply not his fault if people failed to understand that the exigencies of war were not susceptible to ordinary moral judgments. He respected the law only in the sense that he respected every weapon used against him, and, indeed, most of his injuries had been inflicted by it. "They say I been picked up 15, 17 times," he told a reporter in November, 1961, just before going to trial on the extortion charges that put him away. "That's junk. I been picked up maybe 150 times, and they never make a record. I been worked over for nothing until my hat sits on my head like it belongs to some midget. I get picked up for vagrancy and for consorting with known criminals—my father and my brothers in my own house."

He was in Florida early in 1959 when he heard that a warrant had been issued for his arrest on charges of coercion and assault in Brooklyn. Sooner than risk being declared a fugitive, he returned voluntarily, and surrendered to the District Attorney of Kings County. "Two days later, they have me picked up and brought before a Kings County magistrate. I'm shackled, and the D.A. says, 'I'm afraid of this man.' And the judge says, 'I'm sitting behind this bench and I'm afraid, too.'

"They're afraid? Afraid of me in handcuffs? So they put me in this same nut factory again and I can't get out for 30 days. I get shown something with a lot of marks on it. 'What's it look like?' they say. 'It looks like somebody threw ink on it,' I tell them. '*What?* It looks like *something?*' So they say, 'Draw a house.' 'Draw a tree.' So I do what they tell me. Then they say, 'Would you like to live in a house like this?' 'Is this tree alive?' 'How old is it?' Jesus. If I could answer questions like that, I *would* be crazy."

Joey's attitudes had not changed after ten years of warfare, and his methods had become even more direct.

"So I spoke to this psychiatrist, and I said to him, 'You're appointed by the Police Commissioner, aren't you?' And he said he was. And I said, 'Look, I been accused of a lot of vicious crimes. It happens I know a lot of people who met violent ends, and that's my crime. And now they're trying to railroad me, and you tell me I got a persecution complex.' And I told him I had a large family and a lot of friends and if I was him I wouldn't let myself be used as a tool of the Commissioner and the D.A. and be the one to drop the ax on me. He asked if I was threatening him, and I said no, I wasn't. But the way it turned out, his finding on me was better than my own psychiatrist's, and I was judged sane."

Joey did not, in fact, *have* a psychiatrist, then or later, although he read extensively in the subject, copying down passages that seemed relevant to his state of mind. Not long before his death, he talked about it in the back of a cab going uptown with one of Jeffie's friends, Laura Lloyd, who was training to be a lay analyst.

"I had a book in my lap about schizophrenia, and he leaned over and picked it up. 'What are you reading?' he said. 'Let me see that book. What do they say there?'

"And I said, 'Oh, come on, Joey. It's a whole big book. What can I tell you?' I was a bit uncomfortable.

"So he looks at me with those clear blue eyes, and he puts on a very serious expression, and he says, 'Do you know what I am?'

"I said, 'No. What are you, Joey?'

" 'I'm a paranoid schizophrenic,' he says, and looks at me.

" 'I know,' I said.

"Laugh? It broke him up. *How* do you know?' he said. 'What do they say there?'

"Then I told him that although I was reading the book, I didn't really know what paranoid schizophrenia was or how to recognize it or anything.

" 'Then what *are* you learning in that dumb school?' he says, and I get annoyed.

" 'You wanna know what I learned?' I said. 'I learned that even though you want to do it, you're not allowed to do it. You want to kill? You can't kill. You can't pick up your hands—even though you're mad.'

"He says, 'Yeah? And what are you supposed to do with all the feelings inside? How do you get rid of *them?*'

" 'Scream them,' I said. 'Beat up a mattress. I don't know. But you can't do it.'

"He says, 'Is that what they teach you?'

"I said, 'Yeah.'

"He says, 'Is that what you're going to teach your kids?'

"I said, 'Yeah.'

"He said, 'Good.' "

Quite apart from the fact that no psychiatrist who valued his life could afford to become the repository of a gangster's secrets, Joey had no desire to be "cured" of his protective reactions. "Is it paranoid to be paranoid?" he would often ask. For Joey, playing his dangerous games against not only a police army of occupation but rivals as deadly as himself, it was the first law of survival. He had settled into a life that put him constantly at risk, and even policemen understood how easily it could happen. Raymond V. Martin, a former Assistant Chief Inspector in charge of Brooklyn South Detectives, wrote soon after his retirement:

A youngster in . . . South Brooklyn grows up under two flags. One is the flag of the United States, with its familiar institutions, traditions and culture. . . . [The other is] the syndicate flag . . . and its traditions differ from the American ones. On so many street corners in Bath Beach, in so many luncheonettes and candy stores in Bensonhurst, boys see the mob-affiliated bookies operate. They meet the young toughs, the mob enforcers. They hear tales of glory recounted—who robbed what, who worked over whom, which showgirl shared which gangster's bed, who got hit by whom, the techniques of the rackets and how easy it all is, how the money rolls in. What wonder is it that some boys look forward to being initiated in these practices with the eagerness of a college freshman hoping to be pledged by the smoothest fraternity on campus? With a little luck and guts, they feel, even they may someday belong to that splendid, high-living band, the mob. The legend in Bath Beach is that the underworld wields the real power in the land.*

Ralph Salerno, a former member of the Central Intelligence Bureau of the New York Police Department, holds much the same view:

The Gallo group was composed of youngsters who grew up in areas of Brooklyn where gang violence and the exchanges of power and control in years gone by was common neighborhood talk among them, and probably of much greater interest than their elementary school lessons which they were receiving at the same time. Although young, they had been well schooled, each of them having, in his late teens, embarked on their careers as bookmakers' runners, policy pick-up men, burglars, hijackers, and then ultimately progressing to strong-arm men and killers.†

Joey followed this progress, but with a difference. He was interested in power rather than dames and easy money, but the same rule applied. If you wanted it, you had to take it—and generally from someone who wasn't ready to part with it. To become a man of power and then survive among men of power, he needed a reputation, and while other kids were content to run errands for the guys in the black limousines and silk suits, Joey set about getting one, as methodically as some sought to qualify in accountancy.

He was encouraged in this by his mother, who was often said to be the steel in his family. It has even been suggested that Mary Gallo

*Revolt in the Mafia, Duell, Sloan & Pearce, 1963.
† The Crime Confederation, Doubleday, 1969.

brought Joey up as an instrument of revenge against a social order that shackled her to the stove of an Italian household, that through him she lived out her fantasies of rebellion, and of her five children, Joey was certainly the favorite. He was the sensitive one, the most like her in temperament. Jeffie recognized this years later, although she and Momma scrapped like stung viragos most of the time. "She's a bright, rather beautiful woman who got terribly bruised. I dig her. She hated her old man from the day she was sold to him by her mother, and finally left him after Joey and I got married. She's a heavy, and I dig her. Every time Joey would tell a story of being a tough guy, she loved it—'Ha! My Joey!' When he was soft, she hated it."

He gave her little enough cause to hate his early career. Nobody can quite remember now what his first arrest was for—he drew probation for "juvenile delinquency"—but the police celebrated his sixteenth birthday with an assault charge, and marked his graduation to adult criminal status at eighteen with an arrest for packing a gun. With his brothers, he had been running with the Garfield Boys, a street gang with a heavy reputation for violence and minor crime, that operated under license from Joseph Profaci, the old-guard Sicilian Don who exercised strict feudal control over this territory. Through his lieutenants, he kept a godfatherly eye on the rising generation, much like a pro coach keeping tabs on a college football squad. Besides the Gallos, the Garfield Boys also produced Joey's archenemies in later years, the Persicos, led by Carmine (the Snake) Persico, Jr., now serving a fourteen-year term in Atlanta Federal Penitentiary for hijacking, and lord *in absentia* of what was once the Profaci-Colombo family.

"They were a tough crew," according to Detective John O'Flaherty, one of the last two serving members of the original Pizza Squad set up by Inspector Martin in 1961. "The Persicos got to be runners for a policy bank and chauffeurs for some of the bigger guys down there, and this is how they moved up. The Gallos were runners, too, but you couldn't control them. Especially Joey, you couldn't. He had his own ideas. He would do almost any damn thing."

Detective James O'Brien, who joined the squad with O'Flaherty when it was formed, graduated from the Police Academy in the winter of 1946–47, and has spent his whole career on the streets of Brooklyn. "In the late forties, the Gallo brothers were just a source of irritation to us, like all the other wild kids in the neighborhood, but we quickly started hearing more and more about them as they got to be muscle men. Larry was the leader, but Joey was the more flamboyant. It seemed like there was nothing he wouldn't do or try. The first time I met them, they were on a corner, making a noise and milling around. In those days, we had standing orders to keep pushing them off the corners. That went for everybody—any group of guys gathering on a corner. You just moved them along. And they moved. No trouble. In fact, I never had any real trouble with the Gallos, although I knew they were behind a lot of the burglaries and gang fights that were going on at that time. But proving it was something else. Nobody wanted to offend Joey. If anybody offended Joey in any way whatever, he would hit them. He would absolutely cream them. He wasn't a big man, but it didn't seem to make any difference. He'd take on the biggest guy and whack him. And the mere fact it was Joe Gallo, they'd be cowed."

This also explained why almost all the charges ever brought against him, even in the beginning, were dismissed. No witnesses. Once people got to know that careless talk was liable to bring Joe Gallo around to remonstrate and maybe make his point with an ice pick, witnesses in Brooklyn became as scarce as woodpeckers. So did welshers. Once the story got around that Joey had gripped a defaulter's forearm by the wrist and elbow and broken it over the edge of a desk to remind him that his account was past due, the Gallos had very few cash-flow problems with their gambling, loan-sharking and protection business. Indeed, they became so proficient as enforcers that free-lance commissions were soon coming in from the other New York mobs when they wanted witnesses to lose their memories or complainants to change their minds.

The Gallos' steadiest source of income, however, was always from gambling, and they learned the business from a master, Frankie (Shots) Abbatemarco, a veteran Profaci soldier and ex-enforcer who ran a small but profitable policy bank grossing around $2.5 million a year. Albert, Sr. and Mary Gallo were then in the restaurant business with an all-night luncheonette called Jackie's on Church Avenue, near Beverly Road, and as this was close to the center of Frankie Shots's operation, it became a convenient headquarters for the Gallo boys. It was also convenient for the police, inasmuch as they now knew where to find them. Just before Joey's twenty-third birthday, he and his brother Larry were found there and subsequently arraigned with Frankie Shots, his son Tony Shots, Carmine Persico and five others on charges of operating the numbers. They were also held as material witnesses by order of a grand jury investigating crime and racketeering in Kings County, and it was now that Joey finally came to the conclusion that if he was going to run the risks he might as well run the territory.

Though he and Larry were both "made" men in the Profaci family, sponsored by Ottilio (Frankie the Bug) Caruso, Joey for one was not about to start kissing anybody's hand or bowing his head in the presence of the Don. "He was never an organization man," said a Police Department spokesman after one of Joey's several arrests for coercion. "He went off on his own hook. Soon he had enough guys behind him—real heavies like Joe Jelly—to go after what he wanted. A little numbers first, then an extortion or two, and finally the jukeboxes." He might also have mentioned Joey's floating crap game, which accounted for a number of court appearances between 1950 and 1957. These were the only "crimes" he ever confessed to publicly. "Lieutenant Kaufman used to knock us over all the time," he once told Gene Grove, of the New York *Post.* "He had the best stool pigeons in the city. He was so close, I think he used to sleep with me. So what am I going to do? Get knocked over all the time? I start bringing the guys to the game, wherever I'm running it, and nobody leaves until the game is finished."

Less easily settled was the question of image. Never doubting his superior generalship, his ability to outsmart, outfight and generally outclass the local opposition, Joey was still left with a problem of deportment. Besides a reputation that now preceded him from Boston to Florida, and a genial, unstudied contempt for authority, what else did he need before people would recognize him on sight as a natural big shot? What was the right kind of bearing for a new-style gang leader who, unlike the old Mustache Petes, was one of his men yet apart from them? What was the right blend of camaraderie and condescension, of informality and distance?

In his later years, Joey could hit the right note every time. When he chose to, he could rivet the attention of complete strangers, or exact instant obedience from his followers, without ever having to invoke his reserve powers. The habit of command had become second nature. But in those early days, his touch was less sure. There being no local models he wished to emulate as a kid of fifteen or sixteen, he would stand on a corner like George Raft, endlessly flipping a half-dollar and talking to himself without moving his lips. Later on, people began to notice similarities with Richard Widmark, particularly in the role of Tommy Udo in *Kiss of Death,* the movie in which he kicked an old lady in a wheelchair down the stairs, giggling insanely. Others claimed to see a touch of John Garfield or hints of the younger Cagney, but Joey was well into his Widmark period when Sidney Slater joined him in 1955.

Slater was a smooth, plump, well-manicured salesman with a confiding manner and a larcenous heart who could as easily have sold dresses as rental contracts for jukeboxes, shuffleboards and pinball machines. One morning, his boss said Joey Gallo had taken over, and he was leaving for Florida on account of his health. Next day, Slater was summoned to President Street to meet his new employer, who wore a white tie on a black shirt, reminded him strongly of Widmark, and increased his salary by $100 a week as a reward for mentioning it. Later on, after he had turned informer, Slater would insist, in an article he wrote with Quentin Reynolds for the *Saturday Evening Post,* that this was his first contact with the mobs, but if so, he showed a remarkable aptitude for the work. In addition to servicing the taverns on his route, he was soon doing all kinds of "little jobs" for Joey. "If someone owed him money, he'd send me to do the talking, and to back me up, he'd send along a couple of enforcers with guns. He was interested in all kinds of activities—some legitimate, most not. He was a shylock. He ran a numbers racket. He owned a few horse parlors and small nightclubs, and he had a few guns for hire. Joey liked to pick up small nightclubs and bars cheap, and he'd turn them over to me. I'd receive a percentage of the profits —if any."

One of these clubs was the Playboy, on East Fifty-sixth Street between Park and Lexington avenues in Manhattan. On the night of November 1, 1957, Joey came in, according to Slater, with four of his boys: Joseph (Joe Jelly) Gioielli, the lord high executioner of the Gallo court, Punchy Illiano, Ralph Mafrici and Sonny Cammerone. Joey was still dressing like Widmark, but the Gallo style had by now evolved into something of his own, an unsettling blend of power and confidence. Like all his men, Slater borrowed from it, and felt larger than life in his company. "When Joey walks into a club, it vibrates," he once said. "I've been with him. There's something about that guy that shakes people up. You feel it when he's in a room."

He felt it particularly that night. Joey seated the boys at his table with three of the bar girls and waved Slater over to join them. "We all had drinks, then Joey laughed and said something that made me freeze. 'From now on, Sidney,' he said, 'you can call us the barbershop quintet.' I just kept on sipping my drink, hoping that the girls were too dumb to catch on." Exactly one week earlier, Albert Anastasia, boss of Murder, Inc. and probably the most brutal killer in Mafia history, had been murdered in the barbershop of the Park-Sheraton Hotel on Seventh Avenue. Two gunmen had waited until his face was swathed in hot towels before strolling in, shooting his head to pieces and strolling out again. They were never caught.

The Anastasia killing set the capstone on Joey's reputation as an enforcer, much as a cannibal acquires his enemy's virtue by eating him. Though the police were never able to pin the murder on him, nobody connected with the underworld ever seriously doubted that Joey was responsible, and, indeed, Joe Valachi later confirmed it publicly. He also unraveled some of the threads of the plot that led up to the hit. Vito Genovese, Lucky Luciano's underboss and heir-apparent, returned from Italy in 1945 after a long period in exile to find Frank Costello firmly entrenched as acting head of the family. After a twelve-year campaign to unseat him, culminating in a botched attempt on Costello's life in May, 1957, he finally managed it, only to incur the displeasure of Anastasia, who, as boss of another powerful family, disapproved of such disrespectful behavior. Genovese then found a natural ally in Carlo Gambino, Anastasia's ambitious underboss, and a contract for Anastasia's execution was accepted by Joe Profaci, who had never particularly relished Anastasia's iron grasp on the Brooklyn waterfront. Profaci then turned the job over as a matter of course to his leading hit squad—the Gallo boys, Joe Jelly and, some say, an obscure young buttonman by the name of Joe Colombo.

Profaci and the other family bosses were very willing to employ Joey and his men as a kind of mobile strike force for these special assignments, but they were not about to cede him any territory of his own. Nor was he strong enough to take it. With a score or so soldiers under his command, plus a mixed bag of part-time irregulars based on President Street, he could hardly expect to defeat the other 250 or so members of the Profaci family. With Larry counseling patience, therefore, Joey turned instead for a closer look at the labor unions.

His first experience in this field had been as the muscle behind Carmine Lombardozzi, a well-known labor "consultant" whom Joey had met at Frankie Shots's policy bank. A suavely versatile front man for the Gambino family, Lombardozzi had stood in at the bank for Frankie while he and his son Tony were doing a little time for bookmaking. After that, he had been assigned by the Mafia's High Commission to organize the jukebox industry in New York, with occasional excursions on the side into other vulnerable businesses, and it was on one of these that Joey picked up his first indictment as a labor racketeer. He was accused with two others of inspiring an assault on a truck driver employed by a Brooklyn corporation involved in a labor dispute, and then receiving "several thousand dollars" from that corporation, as a representative of a bogus union, to provide protection against such incidents.

District Attorney Edward S. Silver told the court that the evidence he had collected between October, 1955, and November, 1956, showed that "real hoodlums of national repute are behind this operation. Because the inquiry is continuing, I am not in a position at this time to name the ringleaders." As it turned out, he never was in a position to do so, and the case was later dismissed—for lack of witnesses willing to testify.

With this relatively crude exercise in labor-management relations behind him, Joey went on to a far more sophisticated operation almost by accident. "I was running my crap game from the Okay Restaurant at Church and McDonald avenues in 1957," he once explained to Gene Grove of the New York *Post,* "and the guys that ran the joint were forced out of business because the union made them keep help they didn't need. They went to the union and told the guy that they'd have to pack it in if he don't ease up, and this union guy reaches in a drawer and hands them a lock for the door, and they had to wrap it up." Seizing this opportunity to become "a legitimate businessman," Joey bought the restaurant at a marshal's sale and set about solving its labor problems in his usual, direct style. "What am I going to do? This union drove my friends out of business. You got to have a union, so I got hold of a union organizer and we started a *new* union. Sure, the bosses liked it—it didn't make no oppressive demand on them. But it was legal and it kept the bartenders' union and the restaurant employees' union out. Anybody goes into business, they ought to start their own union."

The organizer he got hold of was Johnny Amalfitano, who had worked on the Brooklyn docks as a member of Tony Anastasia's local of the International Longshoremen, and quickly seen that there was more money in running unions than driving cranes. In the early fifties, he helped launch the Federated Service Workers Union, which proved very obliging when it came to granting charters to businessmen like Joey Gallo who wished to start locals of their own. To cover expenses, Amalfitano also fingered truckloads of merchandise for his own hijacking crew, who picked up $500,000 in this way before he was caught, but he lacked real muscle until he teamed up with Joey to operate Restaurant and Cafeteria Employees Local 26, FSWU.

Besides protecting his own business, Joey was anxious to share the advantages of his private union with other restaurant owners in the neighborhood, even if they couldn't quite see them at first. The proprietor of the Fra-Mar Restaurant on Avenue U, for example, chose to ignore Amalfitano and his pickets—until one morning he arrived to open up and found all his windows smashed. Faced with a repair bill of $1,200, he then saw the wisdom of signing with Local 26. By comparison, the dues were quite reasonable. Two other restaurant owners, who still preferred to remain anonymous ten years later when they appeared before the New York State Investigation Commission, testified that under the terms of the contract they signed with Joey's union they were each required to pay $5 a month for every employee, most of whom remained blissfully unaware of the fact that they had been "organized."

The established unions were not, of course, prepared to take this lying down. They sent pickets around to the Okay Restaurant, a step which almost destroyed Joey's faith in the free enterprise system. "I'm getting shook down," he told Gene Grove. "This isn't America —it's Germany. So I get three mugs and picket three of *their* locations. They got cops protecting their pickets, and I thought maybe I'd picket the police station, too." It wasn't necessary. Despite their police escort, the pickets lost heart when they saw the kind of customer who patronized Joey's place, and called off their demonstration. Local 26 was in business. And it did business no harm when a membership card was found in Joe Profaci's wallet after he was picked up at a mob leaders' summit conference in Apalachin in November, 1957.

The success of Local 26 gave Joey his first real sense of territory, outside of President Street. He took on authority of another, more benevolent kind. "It was the cleanest neighborhood in town," he said. "We kept the narcotics out, no thieves. And word got out that Joe Gallo don't give a damn for nobody, and I started getting a lot of little people with little beefs. The lamisters, they got a shylock after them. They'd come to me and I'd tell the shylock to blow. Cabbies, waiters, bartenders, longshoremen—I'm a clearinghouse for the beefs of the $2 bettor."

The cops noticed this, too. "People were very loyal to the Gallo boys down there," said Detective O'Brien. "Maybe some of it was out of fear—there's only so much protection the Police Department and the FBI can give. If they had to, they'd squash you like a bug, and people knew that. But a lot of it was genuine affection. Or misguided admiration. They were good to people in the neighborhood—little people. They never shook them down. When they went out for groceries, they always paid for them."

Besides building a constituency, Joey was also widening his share of the labor rackets. Encouraged by his experience with a restaurant union, he spread out, through his associates, into other promising small-business areas. He recruited Hyman Powell, secretary of the Jewelry Workers Union, as one of his lieutenants, and Sidney Slater became involved with the United Machine Office Workers of New York. But, having an ear for music, the field that really interested Joey was jukeboxes. He already had an interest in the business through his acquisition of Sidney Slater's old firm in 1955, and now, according to his own story, a moonlighting fireman named Norman Clark came to him with an interesting proposition. If Joey could use his influence to secure new locations for Clark's machines, he could have 50 percent of the business after the equipment was paid for. Aware of Carmine Lombardozzi's brief to organize this lucrative and traditionally mob-dominated industry, Joey readily agreed, but almost at once he ran into the same problem that had faced him in the restaurant business—an existing union.

"Three weeks, four weeks, we'd build up the business to five times what it was. Then the fireman comes to me and he says that they want him to join the union. 'Join it,' I said. Well, he says, that's not all. If you join the union, you got to join the owners' association that has the contract, the Music Operators of New York, and they're so tight they won't let us join unless we give back all the locations we jumped. What? Then we're out of business. So I get hold of the guy that organized the restaurant union and tell him my problem and another union was formed. But meanwhile the AFL-CIO has decided to run John Kennedy for President and they throw out the Teamsters. So this guy from the Teamsters calls and he says he wants us to join them. All the little jukebox operators come to me and say they want to go into Teamsters Local 266, and everything is legit.

Except now it really starts. Every city department starts checking all my locations for violations, and the cops start picking me up every time there's a beef."

It was not quite so simple as that. Early in 1959, Robert Kennedy, then Chief Counsel of the McClellan Committee—the Senate Select Committee on Investigation of Improper Activities in the Labor or Management Field—invited Joey and Larry Gallo down to Washington to explain their operations in a little more detail. In 1956, elections had been held for the presidency of the Teamsters Joint Council 16 in New York. On the eve of becoming president of the International Teamsters, James Hoffa had been at pains to secure the office for his nominee and friend, James O'Rourke, by the simple expedient of granting charters for new Teamster locals to Johnny Dio, Tony (Ducks) Corallo and other racketeers, who thereby acquired sufficient votes to make O'Rourke's victory certain. Although these gangster unions, of which Local 266 was one, existed only on paper, they could invoke the coercive power of 140,000 New York Teamsters in any squeeze play that took the mobs' fancy, and as Lombardozzi was then having trouble bringing some of the bigger coin-machine operators into line, the jukebox industry was the first to feel the weight of this highly effective new weapon. Any tavern owner reckless enough to dispute the right of Joey's Teamster Local 266 to choose his jukebox for him was liable to have his beer supplies cut off.

In the eyes of the McClellan Committee this constituted a thoroughly improper activity—one of many attributed to James Hoffa—and it came as no real surprise to Joey when he and his brother were summoned to testify. "When the hearings got around to the situation in New York," he said, "they had one purpose—to get Jimmy Hoffa. All New York was in a tumult because of my aggressiveness in certain businesses. I had incurred the wrath of unions and businessmen who ran the Democratic Party, and that's why they paraded us to Washington. I would have told them anything they wanted to know if they wanted to ask me in committee and grant me immunity. But they were more interested in getting me before the cameras to take the Fifth and make a show for them."

On February 17, 1959, he certainly gave them a show. All that remained of his Widmark period were the clothes; he no longer needed gimmicks or props. Joey was king of the enforcers, and nothing was out of reach. Secure in his powers, he felt himself to be the master of every situation, and in his own world he probably was. Most of the time, people played *his* game. If he was occasionally required to play someone else's, as in Washington, he would do so *his* way.

"The day [the Gallo brothers] were to appear before the Committee," Robert Kennedy recalled,

a man entered our reception room in Washington and started toward my office. Suddenly another man dressed completely in black sprang to his feet, approached the newcomer and searched him, running his hand professionally through all his pockets. The newcomer, flabbergasted, turned and rushed out.

Someone in the office asked the man what he thought he was doing. He replied: "No one is going to see Mr. Kennedy with a gun on him. If Kennedy gets killed now, everybody will say I did it. And I am not going to take that rap."

And he was probably right. The man was Joey Gallo, the brother of Lawrence Gallo, self-professed successors to Murder, Inc. Joey Gallo was one of the most extraordinary witnesses to appear before the Committee.

When he first strode into my office, dressed like a Hollywood Grade B gangster (black shirt, black pants, black coat, long curls down the back of the neck), he felt the rug and said: "It would be nice for a crap game."

Ten minutes later, he offered one of our secretaries a job, telling her that she could determine her own salary by "taking as much as you want from the till."*

Joey's own recollection of the meeting was slightly different. Describing it to Gene Grove nearly three years later, he claimed that Kennedy's assistant, John Constandy, had said that if he went along with them and helped get Hoffa, he would want for nothing. "So I told him that he must be crazy. I walk into Kennedy's office and he's got his sleeves up and his tie down and he says, 'So you're Joe Gallo

* *The Enemy Within,* Harper & Row, 1960.

the jukebox king.' 'What jukebox king?' I says. 'I haven't even got a suit of clothes. I had to get money from Constandy before I could fly down to Washington.' Then Kennedy got mad and told me, 'You're not so tough. I'd like to fight you myself.' I told him, 'I don't fight.' "

Grove was particularly struck by Joey's smile when he said that. And Jeffie remembers Joey telling her once that when Kennedy refused to let him testify in committee, insisting that he appear instead at the hearings, Joey agreed to answer all his questions in public if Kennedy would in turn agree to answer publicly, one for one, all the questions Joey would put to him about his involvement in Massachusetts politics.

Clearly, no such bargain was struck, for when he was called into the marbled splendors of the caucus room on the third floor of the Senate Office Building to sit, wearing dark sunglasses, under the chandeliers and television arc lights where J. Pierpont Morgan had once dandled a midget on his knee, Joey took the Fifth Amendment forty-eight times—even to such inquiries as "Are you married?" and "Have you a father and mother?" But if the answers were dull, the questions were interesting.

MR. KENNEDY: You had initially moved in on a man by the name of Clark, had you not, and taken over a part of his business?

MR. JOSEPH GALLO: I respectfully decline to answer on the ground it may tend to incriminate me.

MR. KENNEDY: And then you were operating these machines on a small scale and then along came local 1690. This was in the middle of 1957. Along came local 1690 and started placing picket lines in front of your various locations, is that right?

Local 1690 of the Retail Clerks International was bound by contract to the Music Operators of New York, an association of 160 jukebox operators who controlled about 8,000 machines producing a gross profit of around $11.5 million a year. Under the terms of their membership agreement, each operator registered his locations with the association and undertook not to poach on his fellow members' preserves. If he breached this rule or if an independent operator jumped a registered location, then the union was required to set up a picket line there. And to get over the rather odd sight of a union picketing on behalf of employers, the collective-bargaining agreement very sensibly specified that all employers should join the union.

Similar arrangements were in force with the Automatic Amusement Machine Operators of New York, a rival and much smaller association, whose members owned most of the other three thousand or so machines in the city.

MR. KENNEDY: You had no union at that time, so then the idea came to you that you would form Local 19, and form your own union. Isn't that what you did—you formed your own union?

Joey, of course, returned his now standard answer to this question, but he and Larry had in fact called a meeting at Jackie's, the Gallos' luncheonette, on November 23, 1957, to discuss the matter with Carmine Lombardozzi and John Amalfitano, who, as trustee of the Federated Service Workers Union, had readily granted them a charter, on October 22, for the formation of Cigarette and Coin Vending Machine Employees Local 19.

MR. KENNEDY: And at that time you had the backing of Carmine Lombardozzi. . . . You also got some of the coin operators to join your union, the Jacob brothers, for instance. Isn't that right?

Lombardozzi had by now made such a mess of his original assignment that one of the principal items on the Mafia High Commission's agenda at the Apalachin summit meeting had been what to do with him. Far from achieving a neat monopoly for the New York mobs, he had inspired nothing but confusion, a tangle of competing "paper" locals and rival associations of operators. Turning finally to a union with muscle, Lombardozzi threw in with the Gallos' Local 19, which had also commended itself to the brothers Herbert and Eugene Jacob, two ambitious AAMONY operators with a simple plan to control the industry: Herbert would organize one big operators' association, which would then sign a contract with one big union organized by Eugene.

King Joey   45

MR. KENNEDY: Then when the regular association would not join, the Jacob brothers and some of their followers walked out of the regular association and formed their own association, the United Coin Operators Association, isn't that right?

When Bert Jacob suggested to his fellow board members of AAMONY that they sign a contract with Local 19 to restore peace to the industry, at least half of them pointed out that it was Local 19 which had caused most of the trouble. A general meeting of the association was then called, and when the vote went in favor of negotiating with Teamsters Local 202, a legitimate union, as distinct from the gangster-run paper locals, Jacob walked out with around 40 percent of the membership. Joining up with a group of nonmember operators, they then formed the United Coin Operators Association, whose managing director turned out to be none other than Joey's front man, Sidney Slater.

MR. KENNEDY: Then it was decided in order to get even more strength, you would switch your efforts from Local 19, and this was after our investigation began, that you decided that you would switch your efforts from Local 19, which was an independent union, to a union which was well established, and that was the Teamster Union, Local 266?

Joey's Local 19 had run into problems that muscle alone could not solve. The power of the paper unions rested in their legal right to picket locations that were the subject of a labor dispute. But in the case of the jukebox industry, the location owners—the bar and restaurant keepers—were not a party to the dispute. The fight was between the operators, who leased the machines, and the unions, who were supposed to service them. Sooner than get dragged into it, with a consequent risk to their businesses, the location owners would invariably disconnect their machines as soon as the pickets showed up and insist that the operators remove them.

It was thus essential for the operators, particularly the smaller ones, to belong to the "right" union, and none was more effective than Joey's. When the Music Operators of New York obtained a permanent injunction restraining Local 19 from picketing its locations, Joey at once trumped this ace by setting up Teamsters Local 266, in association with Gene Jacob and one Joseph DeGrandis, who had now virtually succeeded Lombardozzi as the mobs' jukebox-racket coordinator. With 140,000 Teamsters ready to honor the picket lines of Local 266, individual operators, including the hold-outs at AAMONY, were helpless. Injunction or no, the location owners could in no way afford to offend a union which could cut off all their deliveries.

MR. KENNEDY: So through the efforts of the underworld in New York City, the jurisdiction of the regular Teamster Union which would ordinarily have been in this field, Local 202, was taken away by Mr. John O'Rourke in early 1958. The jurisdiction was taken away from them and switched to his gangster-run union of Local 266 of the Teamsters Union, is that right? And this was the union that you, Lombardozzi, DeGrandis and the rest of the gangsters in New York were backing at that time?

Having procured O'Rourke's election as president of the New York Teamsters Joint Council 16, James Hoffa, who had now succeeded Dave Beck as president of the Brotherhood, confirmed his friend in office by making him a vice president of the international union. Using this power, O'Rourke not only eliminated the honest Local 202 from contention, but became so closely identified with Local 266 that he was subsequently indicted, in June, 1959, by a Nassau County grand jury, along with Joey and fifteen others, on a variety of jukebox-racketeering charges.

DeGrandis, who had done time in Sing Sing for receiving stolen goods, for parole violations and for possessing an unregistered still, was a former president of Amusement and Concessionaires Local 413, Retail Clerks. He could thus claim some qualification for the presidency of Local 266, although inquiries showed that the only organizational work he had ever undertaken had been an attempt to unionize the staff of Willowbrook State School on Staten Island, where his wife was employed as an attendant. When the Retail Clerks revoked his charter in March, 1957, and sent their officials around to pick up the local's membership cards and records, all they found was a gun and a billy club.

MR. KENNEDY: Then what you did was you proceeded to work with the association. You went around and started putting pressure on the various tavern owners that they should belong to this association, which would then automatically make them members of Local 266 of the Teamsters, isn't that right?

Joey again felt that a responsive answer might tend to incriminate him, although this time Kennedy was wrong on a point of fact. The pressure Joey had exerted through Local 266 was not on the tavern owners but on the operators who leased them their jukeboxes. As soon as the contract with Bert Jacob's United Coin Operators was signed, Gene Jacob arranged for the union to start picketing locations served by the AAMONY holdouts, who capitulated almost at once. Indeed, they had no choice. With Teamster pickets outside cutting off their supplies, the tavern owners immediately unplugged their AAMONY machines and hid them in storerooms to await collection. Before long, all the remaining operators had applied for membership in United Coin, and AAMONY's records were transferred to the UCO office presided over by Sidney Slater. Whereupon, the association resumed its original title of the Automatic Amusement Machine Operators of New York, and United Coin was wound up.

Having thus captured a considerable piece of the industry, Joey now turned to the more difficult problem of enlarging it at the expense of the rival Music Operators of New York. Some caution was needed for they had already stopped Local 19 in its tracks with an injunction, and they were clearly prepared to try the same defense against Local 266 if all else failed. Indiscriminate picketing of MONY locations being therefore ruled out, he turned instead to rather more direct methods of encouraging tavern owners to specify AAMONY members' machines and, at the same time, of inducing individual MONY operators to switch associations.

As usual, when Joey wanted something, Joey got it. By the time he appeared before the McClellan Committee, the Music Operators had lost over sixteen hundred locations and many members. Delighted with his progress, the Jacob brothers had also brought his talents to bear on their operating problems in West Virginia, Pennsylvania and Ohio. But direct methods entailed direct risks, and by early 1959 the District Attorneys of Kings County and Nassau County were each preparing to indict him on charges of coercion.

MR. KENNEDY: Isn't it a fact that you are going to attempt, through these underworld connections, to gain control over all of these operations in this area? And if it was necessary, you would have somebody like Mr. Saul knocked on top of the head, or somebody like Mr. Green—isn't that right?

Sidney Saul and Milton Green were New York jukebox operators who resisted "unionization." In the summer of 1957, Saul had been taken to see Larry Gallo at Jackie's luncheonette by one Ernest (Kippy) Filicomo. When he declined to go into "partnership" with them, Filicomo flew into a rage and threatened to kill Saul, but Larry intervened and sent Filicomo away. A couple of months later, in October, Filicomo called another meeting, this time at the Wagon Wheel luncheonette, one of Saul's jukebox locations, at which he asked Saul, in a friendly enough manner, to see Larry at Jackie's and sign up as a member of Local 19. Saul said he would, but did nothing about it. Then, one evening in December, he received an anonymous telephone call from someone at the Wagon Wheel who said that unless he got down there right away, his machine would be smashed to bits. Thoroughly alarmed by this threat, Saul agreed to go, but before leaving he told his answering service operator that if he failed to call her again within half an hour she was to notify the police.

On arriving at the Wagon Wheel, Saul was greeted by two men he had never seen before, Charles Panarella and Anthony (Dutch) Tuzio, both of whom had long police records—Tuzio's including a conviction for murder. The three talked amiably about the music business for about twenty-five minutes, and then Saul suddenly remembered the instructions he had given his answering service and called to cancel them. When he returned to the table, Panarella reopened the conversation by making the same kind of partnership proposition that Larry Gallo had offered, and when Saul again declined it, Panarella slapped him across the face "pretty hard." He then demanded $500, without explaining why, and as Saul tried to convince him that he didn't have that kind of money, Filicomo walked into the luncheonette and joined them at the table. Whereupon Tuzio got up to feed coins into Saul's jukebox, Filicomo peeled off his jacket and, as the music commenced, began punching Saul in the face.

"I started pleading with them," Saul told the McClellan Committee, "and it didn't seem to have any effect. The only remark was that I was an excellent actor. They kept saying to each other, 'This fellow is an actor,' because I was pleading with them to stop beating me. He kept pounding away at my head and face and it got to a point where I was just barely able to keep my head up. Every time I started to plead, Panarella would lift a napkin holder, a commercial-type napkin holder used in luncheonettes, with the open face on both sides, about ten inches high—he lifted it in his hand and said he would bash my skull in if I said anything else. He kept pounding away and Tuzio kept saying, 'If you haven't got $500, give them $300. It is cheaper than buying a new set of teeth.'

"Finally, I was bleeding profusely from the right nostril and my mouth and he stopped punching me. I sort of felt I was losing consciousness and I was slumping over the table. With that, Panarella ordered some coffee brought to the table. So I wiped the blood from my face and I had the coffee, and I wasn't even finished when he started asking for the $500 again. Before I had a chance to look up, Kip was back at me, and this time it was really heavy, much heavier than he was before. I didn't know what to say, and I didn't cry, and I just went along and pleaded with them to stop beating me. This time I was bleeding from both nostrils and my mouth, and I felt myself going to a subconscious mind. Just as my head was slumping over, I could hear everything that was going on, and this Panarella said to Kip to stop, but Kip didn't stop. He was like a wild man, and he just kept punching away at me, and finally he jumped up from the table and he yelled something to him, 'Lascialo!'—which I later found out meant to stop in Italian—and with that Kip took his jacket and walked out.

"Then Panarella ordered some more coffee. At this stage of the game, my mouth felt like it was full of sand, and I was all full of blood, and Panarella reached over and he straightened my tie. He called for a wet towel, or he got up. He called for one and then he helped wipe the blood off my face."

By now, Saul was also bleeding from the ears, his eyes were closing up and his nose had been pounded out of shape. The luncheonette was full of people, but nobody had shown the least concern, much less attempted to interfere. "I couldn't open my mouth at all, and my jaws felt as though they were locked at the end, and I could hardly talk. Then he started the conversation again that he wanted to be a partner in the jukebox. Finally, out of desperation, I said I would take them in as a partner."

Saul was then allowed to go. Next day, he sent his truckman around to the Wagon Wheel to collect the jukebox, but the proprietor refused to let it go, saying Saul's "partner" had told him it had to stay. With that, Saul called a lawyer who took him to the District Attorney's office, where he told the whole story. Panarella, Tuzio and Filicomo were subsequently arrested, tried and convicted of felonious assault.

The attack on Milton Green was no less brutal and its consequences even more severe. He not only refused to join Local 19 but defied a warning to keep his mouth shut at an association meeting called to consider the advisability of signing up with the Gallo-DeGrandis union. On his way home, he told the committee, "they came out with steel bars and they split my skull open for me and I was taken to the hospital." He never completely recovered the use of his faculties, and no arrest was ever made in the case.

But if the penalty for defiance was a beating, the automatic sentence for treachery was death. When Joey's Local 19 was first formed, Biagio Latriano, a Brooklyn tavern owner, was appointed vice president in charge of correspondence. This was necessary because the union's office was "in Amalfitano's hat," and Latriano had an address to which letters could be sent. After six or seven months' experience of the racket from this privileged position, he was so impressed by its potentially rich pickings that he began to look into the possibility of forming a jukebox combine of his own. Around 4:20 A.M. on August 29, 1958, he was found on the sidewalk outside his home on Ocean Parkway with eleven bullets in his head.

MR. KENNEDY: But you wouldn't do it yourself, would you, Mr. Gallo? You would have somebody go and do it for you, wouldn't you?

MR. JOSEPH GALLO: I respectfully decline to answer, Mr. Kennedy, on the ground it may tend to incriminate me.

MR. KENNEDY: Do you find it is much easier to have a big man go and do it rather than a little fellow like you?

MR. JOSEPH GALLO: I respectfully decline to answer on the ground it may tend to incriminate me.

It was the last time but one that he used this stock rejoinder to Kennedy's questions. The committee had, of course, known in advance that Joey would take the Fifth, but the object of this otherwise sterile exercise was to enable Kennedy to read into the public record the substance of his investigators' findings. This done, Senator McClellan picked up Kennedy's cue and tried to taunt Joey into an unconsidered reply.

THE CHAIRMAN: Are you a physical coward?

Joey sighed with weary resignation and repeated himself for the forty-fifth time. As the star of a TV spectacular, he had overcome the monotony of his lines with a wealth of facial expressions and an eloquence of gesture that included knocking over two glasses of water and sweeping an ashtray to the floor. It was a performance with which he was well satisfied—indeed, it had made him the matinee idol of organized crime—and the chairman's attempt to provoke him inspired no more than polite interest. Joey had enjoyed the limelight, but he was as little involved in the proceedings in any personal sense as a Martian might have been. There was no common ground between them, and therefore no basis for taking offense.

After lunch, the first witness in the afternoon session was John Amalfitano, Joey's favorite union organizer. At the end of his testimony, in which he pleaded the Fifth Amendment fifty times, Kennedy told the committee that despite his lack of response, Amalfitano was "not in the same category as the Gallo brothers," who were "far worse than this man." Joey, apparently, thought this was "very fair." He told John Constandy afterward: "Mr. Kennedy is a better fellow than I thought he was. We really appreciate him saying that nice thing about Amalfitano."

"When Amalfitano came downstairs after testifying," wrote Kennedy, "Joey rolled up a newspaper, hit him over the head, and laughingly said, 'You damn labor racketeer, you gangster, aren't you ashamed of yourself?' " Then, as they were leaving for New York, he stopped by the office to thank Kennedy for treating him "very nicely." He said he would line up his people to support Senator John Kennedy, who was a member of the McClellan Committee, in his bid for the Presidency in 1960. "To prove this, he called five or six of his friends in and made each one pledge a vote for Senator Kennedy for President. I told him the second biggest favor he could do me was to keep his preference quiet—and the biggest favor would be to announce for my brother's opponent. He laughed and went merrily on his way."*

Twenty-one months later, Joey remembered his promise. He made Jeffie get out of bed to vote on election day.

*The Enemy Within.

4

Jeffie

My own life,

Should I write a thousand times the words "I'm sorry," would you know that I was? Looking back into life, I find a small boy, who knows much about the "dirty-filty" streets, streets are nothing, unless there are people. Some people look at his clothes that bear the stamp of the poor, they despise him for taking space, being in the deathly struggle to elevate from the degradation that envelops and makes men brutes. Being so little, so old is pain, that only the intelligent understand. To cry or whimper was stupid, not weakness. When other children cried, he felt the pain that freely flowed from their eyes—but remained in his tight belly, with no escape.

He traveled far, too fast, for all the rest. School was a continuous humiliation, because poverty, a condition that demands subservience and invisibility were foreign to his nature. He did learn to read and write—you see, those two subjects being taught in the very beginning

—when he thought the world was one—then it separated and he was alone. One teacher he never will forget took him to her home, gave him cookies, candy and let him wind the Victrola, listen to beautiful music—such a wonderful thing! A Victrola! Her name, Mrs. Lowenstein, the class 3A. All he ever learned was in her classroom—she cared, and he did not yet see his poverty.

The winter was mean, beating the body hard. The "Home Relief" —dried fruit, eggs and milk, powdered, "lumpy," and clothing that branded the wearer LEPER! NO MORE, no more.

"Who's this woman sleeping next to me? I'll blow smoke in her face, she's waked and smiling happy, do you want coffee?" "Give me the world—the universe." "Hey! Don't open that window, not yet." "Where did he go?" "He comes like a nomad, from nowhere and leaves in clouds of smoke." "Why do your eyes mist and body get sad?"

Ah, my Queen, the magic man is calling my soul, he waits alone, cold and far away. He comes to fill his heart—to be sure I feel his presence, then in soft smokiness he journeys toward Mecca. You cry inside, long till sleep brings release—your motion is searching and drawn Eastward. Now the sweet heavy odor is vivid. Close your eyes —follow me through space, your body has answered, No! Why are you angry? Oh! You little fool! I shall never leave you, my Queen, you are exactly little, like a child who pouts when her daddy caresses some other child.

It's you who should bring that memory back with love and laughter. It belongs to us, we own beautiful things, material and spiritual —a phase of life we shared tightly. Don't let me cry inside forever let me express the quality of my happiness with you, without a fear of your iciness. Come kiss and expand, the world at your command. Awake to a pleasant familiar odor, sweet and chocolaty.

"Ha! You know the medicine." "Did I take long to waken?" "No, very fast." "Who is this woman asleep beside me?" "Why ask me? She be there a long time ago." "Hey! Why do you purr and smack your lips?" "Because you are tasty and hard—don't move. Our bodies are magnetized. Stay horizontal till it goes."

The sun is strong—smoke whirls and colors in its rays, desert music, a flute and tambourines replace the mad mambo beat that rises from the flat below. Sweet smokiness everywhere, forms a soft cloud, wafting two souls upward into space, a rocket ignites, the random course is altered, its pounding rhythm increases, deafens and explodes! showering the cosmos with multi-color sparks and shimmering spangles, alighting briefly upon passing comets, zooming past brilliant stars, touching Venus, then descending slowly, dizzily, in a spiral, the souls are fused—the Latin beat returns—kiss and expand, the world and universe you command.

"Say! Who is this creole woman with emerald eyes and peasant legs, stirring beside me?"

"Why ask me? She be there long time ago."

My precious baby, it is very clear that I am not sorry for anything —I have felt your love always, from the sweet smokiness to this very clear and starry night. We were never far apart. And you *felt me also!!!* Poor Lepke used to try to snuggle between us. Jeffie, remember when the mirror crashed down? There was just the "four" of us and a trusty rifle, and at #63, when the evil spirits were chased by a wild man's cry that unearthly night some day.

Joey Gallo #18140

The letter arrived from Attica State Prison. Though addressed to his daughter, Joie was not yet old enough to read. He and Jeffie had lived a turbulent two-year lifetime, quite beyond the expectation, or even the desire, of either one. On sight, she had marked him down as an electric, half-comic, half-interesting little man she had no intention of getting involved with, and he, in turn, had made it clear he saw her as a threat to his independence. There was danger, he told her, in allowing anyone to influence his emotions. Even so, the first move had come from him.

On Sunday afternoon, a week after his skulking, slit-eyed debut in her apartment, he showed up again, without warning, with Ali Baba, to take her out for a meal. Jeffie was not particularly surprised, nor particularly pleased, but she got dressed at his bidding and they drove down to the Grotta Azzurra on Broome Street, where Joey proved an attentive, charming host and insisted on her trying all kinds of Italian dishes she had never even heard of before. The first time they met, Joey had hung back, trying to establish his own identity in a room full of strong personalities. This time, he was a figure of authority to whom everyone they met deferred, and he didn't seem comic at all. Nor did he seem like a suitor. There was none of the flirtatious byplay Jeffie was used to in male company. Joey was just making himself known to her. When he took her home, the nearest he came to arranging another date was to tell her he had a club called the Arpeggio, where she was welcome to drop in at any time.

Being Jeffie, she had heard of the Arpeggio—Carmen McRae had played there and Bobby Short—but not of Joey Gallo. She knew only that she had never met anyone like him before, not even in Las Vegas, and, somehow, that it would be impolitic to pry. She assumed vaguely that he was one of the nightclub crowd—a bookie, perhaps.

Jeffie and a girlfriend from Vegas, Jean Lerner, were then busy fixing up a place nearby that they planned to open as an after-hours joint serving champagne and crêpes Suzette. It belonged to Lucky Pierre, another friend of Al Lettieri's, who owned a restaurant where he cooked steaks with a blow torch, and where Joyce sang for his customers in the back room. After working late one night, Jeffie remembered Joey's invitation and dropped in at the Arpeggio with Jean to see if he was there. He was, and after that she got in the habit of stopping by on her way home.

"It was still just friendly. The first time Jean and I walked into the club, there was a good deal of scurrying about when we asked for him, and then we were led over to his table, where we had a couple of drinks and listened to the music. By the second or third time, I noticed some blonde was always ushered from the table and taken away to the bar as we arrived, which I thought was kind of amusing. But every time I saw him, there was a click at the back of my mind. Something was happening with this interesting guy. He was not coming on strong with me. We were playing a game, cat and mouse."

For a time, it was hard to tell who was which. If Joey had come straight out with the proposition she expected, Jeffie would have turned him down, but she was interested enough to feel glad he didn't force her hand. She also suspected that he knew how she felt, and, being the man he was, would hold off sooner than court the humiliation of being refused. But as the weeks went by, it became clear to both that something more important than either had bargained for was about to happen. Neither had so much as touched the other, but each was acutely aware, in the most physical way, of the other's presence. They listened to each other—and Jeffie had never really listened to anyone before. She found a mutual understanding, about life and people and music, which she had never expected to find, dimensions and depths she could scarcely comprehend. He began to absorb her, to the exclusion of everyone else. And still he held off.

Her friends did not entirely approve. "They all said, 'Oh, you have to go out more. You have to go to parties.' So one night, I went to a party given by Leo Shull, the guy who runs *Show Business* magazine. It was one of those New York parties that everybody should go to if they want to snag a husband or a bit part on Broadway or whatever the hell it is they go to these parties for. There were seven models, four stars, three directors, one writer, the token nigger and two analysts, and Leo had a new apartment with a lot of Cupids and things with water spurting out. But I said, 'Okay, that's what I'm supposed to do. I'm going to give it my all. I have to get out there and try to be a social animal instead of a loner. That's positive. And this funny little guy with his club is obviously negative.'

"So I tried it. They had these enormous couches, and I sat smackdab in the middle of one of them with people on my right and left, and made with the conversation. I passed some comment, I think about politics, and the man to my right turned to me and said, 'My dear. Isn't that rather *obvious?*' And I thought, 'Oh, holy *shit!* Let me out of here. I don't want to *be* with these people. I don't care what anybody says, I can't *stand* them. I'll never fit in. I can't *make* it. Help!'

"I called the Arpeggio and got him on the phone. I said, 'I'm at a party, and I don't want to be here. Come and get me.' Well, he didn't, of course. He sent somebody else, and it was like going home. We were alone at his table that night—I guess for the first time. And I remember looking at him, willing him to make the first move, but he wouldn't. Joey was king, and he wasn't going to have it that way. So in the end I said to him, 'Why don't you ever touch me?' Then he did. He held my hand. And after a while, he took me to Ali Baba's little penthouse out in Brooklyn and we spent the night alone there.

"Next morning we got up early because he had to go to court. That was the first I knew that he was on trial, and he asked me to go with him. It was his way of saying, 'This is who I am.' So I went—which was my way of saying, 'Come in. It's okay.' "

Joey was standing trial with John O'Rourke, president of New York Teamsters Joint Council 16, and fifteen other codefendants on charges of extortion, coercion and conspiracy, arising out of attempts by Local 266 to take over the jukebox industry in Nassau County. As far as Jeffie was concerned, he was just a union guy in some kind of trouble that didn't seem to worry him unduly; if he was convinced he could handle it, she had more pressing things to think about. There had been a shocking openness about him the previous night, a wholly unexpected vulnerability that, for the moment at least, had left her in charge of their relationship. She now knew it couldn't be light. They either had to end it there, with no real harm done, or go on in the certain knowledge of a loss of freedom that each might easily come to resent. It was up to her to decide.

When court adjourned for the day, he went home with her to the apartment on Eleventh Street, and never really left her after that. "I knew he would be completely consuming—I accepted that. And I always knew, right from the very beginning, that it would be stormy. We didn't agree about many things, but the exchange was fascinating. He was into Nietzsche and Machiavelli, and I was into Wilhelm Reich, but we each respected what the other had to say. Life narrowed down very simply to him and to me. I gave up the supper club idea. Joey made it very clear that he wanted me at home with him, not working, and that was fine with me. It got so that I didn't even see my girlfriends unless he was going to be out, and as I never knew when he was going to be in or out, it meant I hardly ever saw them at all. Not that he ever told me *not* to see them. I just knew that that was what he wanted. And I didn't mind his possessiveness. I got a very strong sense of protection from it."

In their first few days together, Ali Baba called at the house each morning to take him to court, and in the evening they would dine out somewhere before going on to the club, where she met his brothers, Larry and Kid Blast. Like the rest of the family, they were very friendly. Joey had always had a woman, and while they might have preferred him to stick with Italian girls, they had no reason then to suppose that Joey was any more serious about Jeffie than he had been with any of the others.

"But this was very different from anything either of us had ever experienced. I had never really trusted anyone with myself before, and nor had he. I guess I began falling really in love with him. And while this was happening, my doctor left for California, which was another big turning point in my life because he had made me very aware of my needs. Dr. Albert was Daddy. Southern. Gentile. And now Daddy was leaving again. It was very hard. All the things that therapy might have done for me stopped, and I focused everything on Joey. Poor bastard."

Then the trial ended. After twenty-three hours' deliberation without sleep, the jury convicted three "officials" of Local 266, found O'Rourke and twelve others not guilty, for lack of evidence, and failed to reach a verdict on Joey. The case against him was dismissed. That night, he and Jeffie threw a big celebration party at the Arpeggio. She was very happy, and so, she believes, was Joey, although he lived at one and the same time on so many different levels that she could never feel entirely sure.

"We talked endlessly—for days on end. Not so much about personal things but about attitudes to life. Philosophies. He was reading a lot of male-supremacy, warrior-type books that I would always take exception to—I remember we used to discuss things like the basic homosexuality of large male-buddy groups—and we were both kind of immersed in exploring each other. We became friends. We really got to trust each other. It was the first time Joey had ever discussed things like that with anyone—he wasn't exactly surrounded by great intellects. And I don't think he had ever been in love before. But we were both aware of the private part in each other, and how vulnerable it was, so we took care of it in each other.

"We talked about the difference between taking and giving. I insisted you couldn't really take where love was concerned, but he thought that that kind of love was a liability. He maintained he had to be in control of my love or he wouldn't be safe. There was danger in allowing one's emotions to be controlled by someone else. And I agreed. If he planned on living the kind of life he had had before, that was probably wise. But in that case, what were we doing there? If he wanted my love, he couldn't have it unless I gave it to him freely. But if he liked to walk around *thinking* he was in control, then that was all right by me. In those days, Joey was really living out the role of prince in his own domain. He talked in terms of kingdoms and princes. I'd never met anyone before who thought in that way."

Much of the princely ceremonial was conducted in restaurants, and particularly at the Luna on Mulberry Street, where a round table was permanently reserved for him in the back by the bar. In those early months, while Jeffie was still entranced with her combined role of handmaiden, geisha and queen consort, she would prepare him devotedly for these public occasions, often at the expense of her own appearance. She would draw his bath, lay out his clothes, make sure the ribs of his black socks matched, and then, when he was ready at last, have no time left to do more than drag a comb through her hair and throw on a shirt and jeans before following him through the door. Princes waited for no one.

"Dinner was always a grand occasion. It was about the only social life we had. He would order all kinds of different things to be prepared for us, and he'd taste and have me taste them. Usually, we'd have about two hours alone, and then he'd lean back in his chair and look around and other people would start coming to the table. I used to sit there beside him for hours, well into the morning, watching them come and go. They'd talk, the Strega would be poured and I would never speak. I just knew I was his woman then, and he was showing me his world, he was including me. They were moments that I cherish. Then the hookers would come in and the crap games would start, at five or six in the morning, and soon he'd be ready to go home. I would be very content. I felt fulfilled and rewarded by sharing those times and those moods. There were months of nights like that, when I was completely entertained, just sitting quietly at his side."

There were also less tranquil moments. One night they arrived at the Luna with Ali Baba and Hyman Powell to find his usual table occupied. The waiters were distraught. Volubly apologetic, they explained that they hadn't known he was coming in, but of course they would have the interlopers moved and would he do them the immense kindness of sitting at another table until this could be done? Joey graciously fell in with their suggestion, and ordered a plate of shrimp for Jeffie, who was ravening for food. But it soon became clear that the people at Joey's table, in the middle of their meal, were not taking at all kindly to the waiters' attempts to move them. Nor were they much impressed by the magic of Joey's name, because one of them got up, came over and proceeded to abuse him roundly for trying to disturb them. Jeffie cannot remember what Joey said in reply—she was too busy wolfing her shrimp—but the man then swung a punch.

"The next thing I know, Ali Baba has rushed into the kitchen and is now chasing this guy through the Luna with a great big knife. With everyone yelling and screaming, he chases him into the street, and Joey, bleeding slightly at the mouth, goes over to the other table to apologize for the inconvenience he has caused them. Very dignified. He was never visibly thrown by anything. He wasn't going to fight. He had people to do that for him. But I was hungry that night. Hy was sitting at the table with me, and he says there was not a break in the movement of fork from plate to mouth. Anyway, the people at his table now decide they've finished after all, and go look for their friend in the street. Ali Baba comes back, hands the knife to the waiter and takes Joey home to change his shirt. The problem is nicely resolved, the table is vacant and I'm ready for the next course."

Being two of a kind when it came to defending their rights to self-expression, there was no lack of incident in their domestic life either. At the same time, there were few difficulties between them that defied a solution in bed. Joey had a sexual charge that challenged almost everyone, an aura to which people responded, sometimes against their will. Jeffie saw it work with women, old as well as young, men, children—even dogs. One of his nieces, from the age of three, would go rigid the moment she was touched. But Joey would take her in his arms and hold her tightly, stroking her back, rocking her, soothing her, until she unclenched and snuggled against him, content. He was the only one who could do that, and he did it for Jeffie, too.

"There was a complete union, an ability to give up ourselves without restraint. When we lay together, even without making love, he would cleanse himself of everything else. Joey was always an extremist. As tough as he was supposed to be, he was also that tender. He had a great sensitivity, a great need for touching. He would give to me totally, and I would respond, and everything else would melt away. That's really what held us together. There was never anything else. And neither of us found it easy—this giving up of self. When the moment passed, I think he resented it almost. I think he resented having been out of control, having given me something I might use against him. But always, through good, bad and indifferent, there were always those times when we were absolutely a world unto ourselves."

There were also times when he would retreat into a world of his own, and she quickly learned to recognize the signs. They would be alone together in the apartment, generally late at night, talking and playing records, and she would sense a restlessness in him, a feeling that he had to go from her but didn't want to. Watching his face, she would see his expression change, lose animation, turn somber, and his eyes, clear and alert until then, seemed to film over. Then a ritual would begin that never varied, a ceremony of departure. He would play Arabic music on the phonograph, the heavy, rhythmic music of a pipe, drums and tambourines, insistent and unsettling, and stand by the window in his robe, watching the street. His manner would be calm and peaceful—quite without tension—but Jeffie knew he was preparing himself for something he had to do alone in the world outside.

"It was as though he saw all of life for an hour or two. He saw it, accepted it and accepted the responsibility he had in it. There was no weariness. It wasn't an effort, and yet it entailed an effort. It was something that went against the Joey that wanted to be, but he had to acknowledge the Joey he was. This ceremony was to reconcile the two. It was only in the mind, but the mind shimmered through the house. You could feel it. After he put the music on, I would just watch him and never talk. I would just be with him. I knew that he was sad, but I knew I couldn't help him or even go near him. There was something that had to be done. I have no idea what, but it had to be done alone. Nobody would come for him. At these times he always left by himself. I never wanted to know where he was going. That was his affair. It didn't matter. I had been allowed to share in his ceremony, but then I could go no further. That was the end of my time. And the experience was always of such intensity that afterward I just felt the movie was over and went to bed."

Jeffie was never aware of what triggered these moods, which came on him perhaps once or twice a month. If anything in particular was preying on his mind, he never showed it. Nor was there any pattern to his absences. Sometimes he would be gone for a few hours; at other times, he might be away until the following afternoon. But when he returned, he always behaved as though nothing had happened, and life went on exactly as before. Except that quite suddenly, on June 20, 1960, the idyll was over.

"He had to go to court for some minor thing. I remember we went there thinking it couldn't amount to anything. But they took him away to Rikers Island. He was found guilty. I couldn't believe it. He had had no suspicion that this was going to happen, and I was in a complete daze of loss. All I can remember after that is walking out of the courthouse in Brooklyn and he wasn't with me. I still didn't know any of his people very well. In fact, I didn't even know how to get home or which direction to take. I couldn't believe that all of a sudden he was no longer there. Finally, Larry sent me home in a cab—and I had only just enough money to pay for it. I never had any money. Joey had been paying the rent and the other bills. I used to take what I needed from day to day when he put his money on the dresser at night. I was broke. I went home and sat staring at the wall. I didn't understand what was going on, and I didn't know who to call or anything."

The "minor thing" that had taken Joey to court that day was a two-count indictment for attempted assault and coercion, and he had been less than candid with Jeffie when he led her to believe he had no suspicion of what might happen. Joey had surrendered on these charges on May 23, 1959, some three months after his appearance in Washington before the McClellan Committee. He was then under suspicion for the murders of Biagio Latriano and John (the Mortician) Robilotto, a middle-aged enforcer who had wound up with four bullets in his head after opposing attempts by Local 266 to enlarge its territory. The Kings County District Attorney's office claimed that Joey had entered Rocky's Bar and Grill on Bedford Avenue and told the owner, Rocco Supino, that Local 266 would be very unhappy if he insisted on returning a pinball machine he had rented from a company belonging to the Associated Amusement Machine Operators of New York. The members might even want to picket the place. Joey was said to have underlined this ultimatum with a large kitchen knife that he waved under Supino's nose. By the time Joey went to trial, however, over a year later, Supino had changed his mind about the knife. He thought Joey might have been doodling with it, and so the jury found him guilty of coercion but not guilty of attempted assault.

On September 9, 1960, he appeared before Judge Samuel S. Leibowitz for sentencing. Having heard the Kings County prosecutor describe Joey as "a hoodlum who, for over a decade, has thumbed his nose at the police, the District Attorney and the courts," Leibowitz handed down the maximum penalty, an indeterminate period of imprisonment for up to three years. "All we can do," he added, "is to keep our fingers crossed and hope this is the end of the line in his criminal career."

Jeffie was quite convinced it was the end of the line for her. After sitting around the apartment for a week, she had finally grasped the fact that he had gone. Using her show-business connections, she had then found a job, which relieved her anxiety about the rent, and, a day or two later, she heard from Larry that the lawyers were hopeful of getting Joey out in a few months on a certificate of reasonable doubt. Though she couldn't believe it, the news got her going again. In July, she wrote home to Olga:

> I'm fine and working hard with a personal manager getting some vocal groups together. As soon as they are organized, the work will let up a little. At the present, I'm at it 12 hours or more a day.
>
> My Joey is away and won't be home till September or October, and I'm lonesome as hell. No time for beach this summer. Seems the older you get, the harder it is to earn a living. Oh well, we must live for our occasional happy moments.

But Olga was more concerned about Jeffie's prospects than her emotional state. "Darling, why don't you get a typewriter?" she replied.

> It is of the utmost importance to have when writing business letters. What has happened to your handwriting? For a while, you had a very nice one, but your last note was up and down and all over the place. Why don't you get a copy book at the 10-cent store and exercise your handwriting when at work? For no matter what kind of work you do, it is important to develop a good handwriting.

Her priorities may have been right, for Jeffie's job with the personal manager was short-lived. The next time she wrote to her mother was on her birthday, November 1.

> How I wish I could spend Christmas with you all. However, I would have to give up my job, as that is their busiest time, so I will not be able to come. It's when all the shows are given for out-of-town buyers and they need me. I work in a fabric showroom. I have become very interested in the world situation. The false values that govern our society cannot survive (I hope). I see no basic difference between racketeers and politicians. . . . Joey still away, so I've been catching up on my reading.

Olga was very impressed—with her handwriting.

> I am in receipt of your beautifully written letter—what a difference from the last one you sent your Mom—it is just perfect. What you tell me about your work is very interesting. Remember, darling, no work is *easy*. We must find the kind of work we most enjoy doing and then *stick to it. It is the only way to get ahead.*

Before Jeffie could really profit from this advice, Joey was back. Toward the end of October, when she had been thinking quite seriously of joining Olga in California, he had called from prison, as though divining her intentions, and told her not to go anywhere as he would soon be home. He also said she was to see Larry, who, with Ali Baba, was then involved with another club called Joe Howard's. Still not believing in miracles, particularly as Joey had never once written nor asked to see her before this phone call, she stopped by the club one night, more out of curiosity than hope, and was quite astonished when Larry greeted her warmly, stuffed money in her purse and told her not to worry, that his brother had told him to take care of her expenses until he got home. Sure enough, on the eve of election day, 1960, Joey strolled in, hung up his hat, sat down on the sofa and demanded coffee as if he had never been away. He had also bought her a present—a wire-haired terrier called Lepke.

But things were never quite the same for Jeffie after that. She had had a taste of what life with Joey could mean, and a chance to think about it. Though still without any real knowledge of who and what he was, she had lost him once without warning, and common sense told her it could as easily happen again. But common sense had little to do in the abandon of their first few days together. They fell upon each other like loving wolves to repair the waste of time. It was only when the edge had worn off their appetites and he spoke of wanting a child that caution reopened her eyes. The idea frightened and excited her. She was being asked to make the same kind of total commitment as she had made before, but this time, knowing she might be left again, to fend not only for herself but also for a child. On the other hand, although he hadn't mentioned it, she knew that if he wanted a child, he probably had marriage in mind, for he was very Italian in family matters. Was she ready to go that far? Before she could really answer the question, Jeffie discovered she was pregnant.

She wrote to her mother in California, preparing her for the possibility of a third son-in-law. "Darling," Olga replied, "please don't think of marrying anyone before your Mom has the chance to take you to Latin America. There are some wonderful 'partidos,' that means eligible men, in those countries that would be just right for my beautiful girl. So please, darling, delay any plans that you may have for matrimony until the end of 1961."

Jeffie paid as much attention to this advice as she had to all the rest. But Joey's family was not particularly enthusiastic either, nor were the boys on President Street. Wives were wives, and girlfriends were girlfriends. The idea of his marrying a twice-divorced ex-Vegas showgirl could hardly have shocked them more than if he had chosen a Forty-second Street hooker. Furthermore, she wasn't Italian. Worse still, she couldn't cook. When the women went into the kitchen, she stayed with the men at the table. Later on, Mary Gallo took to calling Jeffie "the gypsy whore" whenever they had a difference of opinion, which was often and about almost everything, but out of deference to Joey, as he was clearly set on going through with it, she swallowed her reservations and, with the rest of the family, turned up at the Copacabana to give them a big send-off. They had decided to drive down South and get married in Florida. Jeffie was now three months pregnant and very happy about it. Joey seemed happy, too. For the first and only time in their life together, she managed to entice him onto the dance floor, where he behaved "as if he were going to be shot any moment."

Next morning, they set out from Eleventh Street like kids on a picnic, with Jeffie driving. He liked the way she handled a car, her dash and impatience, and on the way down, he taught her the basic rules for chauffeuring a gangster: Never stop alongside another car at a stop light. Never stop so that another car can come alongside *you*. Never take the shortest or most obvious route to anywhere. But in spite of all this, they made good time and crossed into Florida still in the best of spirits. Then they stopped at a gas station because he wanted to make a phone call, and Dr. Jekyll returned to the car as Mr. Hyde.

"Joey was literally another person. He was cold, hostile and angry —the first time I'd ever seen him like that. He even looked different. Pinched and mean. His whole physical presence had changed. He had gone to call some people to tell them we had arrived, and I've no idea what they said to him, but when he came back, he wasn't about to do anything but bite my head off or tell me anything except 'Get lost.' Whatever it was that upset him had blown the whole thing —me, the baby, getting married, the works. There was just no way of getting through to him, and I stopped trying. I was in shock.

"So I drove to the motel with this time bomb on the seat beside me, and I didn't know what was happening. I could feel his anger in the car like the heater was on, and I thought, 'Well, maybe it's me. Maybe he's changed his mind and doesn't want to get married any more.' Then we went out to dinner with some people and everything got cloak-and-daggerish. He told them we were living in some other motel and he was wary and suspicious of everybody, including me. I couldn't open my mouth but he jumped down my throat. And all I could think of was that the man I had been with and cared for and whose child I was going to bear had changed into somebody else. There was nothing I could do to please him."

After a day or two of this, her natural pugnacity reasserted itself, and she began to give as good as she got. All her earlier misgivings had revived and redoubled, her anger was rising to match his, and they were now as fiercely divided as they had once been fiercely united. She called Lyn Morgen, an older girlfriend of hers in New York, to ask if she could hide out for a while in her apartment. "I've got to get out of here," she said. "I've got a fucking maniac on my hands. I'm pregnant, and I want out."

Still convinced that the change in Joey had to do with his feelings for her and the prospect of marriage, Jeffie was not to know that the real reason for his rage was that a carefully laid plan to depose Joe Profaci and take over his empire had miscarried. Instead of grabbing him and his principal capos in one cleanly executed round-up, the Gallos had somehow tipped their hand. The Don and his powerful lieutenant Johnny (Bath Beach) Oddo had slipped the net—and Johnny Bath Beach was reported to be in Florida.

On the fourth day, Joey and Jeffie drove down to the Keys for want of something better to do. They were temporarily bored with abusing each other and were now fighting silently. "There I was with my belly and we were still not married. He was stony quiet and I was stony sulking. He hadn't talked for two or three hours, and then, out of a clear blue sky, he turned to me and said, 'If anything happens to me, I want you to go to my mother. With the kid.'

"I was jarred beyond belief. I said, 'Go to your *mother?* With *my* kid? You got to be crazy.'

" 'No,' he said. 'You go to my mother. I want my mother to take care of everything if anything happens to me.'

"And I said, 'Forget it. It'll never happen. Ne-ver happen. Go to your mother? I wouldn't go to *my* mother. I'm not having a kid for your mother. If you want your mother to raise a kid, go fuck your mother.' "

It was a fairly reckless suggestion to make to any Italian, let alone Joey Gallo. The next day, they flew back to New York. And, as soon as his back was turned, Jeffie borrowed some money from Lyn, left home and had an abortion.

5

The Profaci War

At about 8:25 P.M. on November 4, 1959, Frankie (Shots) Abbatemarco was shot to death in Cardiello's Tavern on Fourth Avenue, Brooklyn. He had arrived some fifteen minutes earlier, obviously to keep an appointment there because he kept looking at his watch and then out the window. After a couple of rounds of drinks, he evidently spotted whoever it was he had arranged to meet, for he buttoned his camel's-hair overcoat and left. But the door was still closing behind him when four shots were fired in rapid succession and he staggered backward into the tavern, bleeding from the head and neck, and fell heavily on his back. Joe Jelly and another man, both masked in red bandannas, followed him in with drawn guns and everybody in the bar dived for cover, upsetting chairs and tables in a pandemonium of fear and breaking glass.

Frankie Shots was still alive. He tried to sit up but fell back, his

71

head hitting the floor with an ugly thump. Joe Jelly bent over him, pulled a .38 Smith & Wesson from Frankie's shoulder holster, straightened up and emptied it into Frankie's head at point-blank range. The gunmen then looked at each other, nodded and walked out as casually as they had walked in, dropping Frankie's gun outside on the sidewalk.

Nobody moved for several seconds. Then everybody in the tavern stampeded for the door, pushing, shoving and cursing—everybody but Tony Cardiello behind the bar, who turned off the television set and gloomily tried to figure out what he would tell the police. When they arrived a few minutes later, Frankie was somehow still alive, despite nine bullet wounds in his head and neck. One eye was closed, the other staring sightlessly at the ceiling. He died later in the hospital without regaining consciousness.

Frankie Shots's death had been ordered by Joe Profaci for nonpayment of taxes. A run of bad luck had left him $50,000 in arrears with his payments to the Don from the proceeds of his policy bank. Going from bad to worse, it had then prompted Profaci to award the contract to the Gallos, who in turn passed it to their bodyguard and chief enforcer, Joe Jelly, who rarely bungled matters of this kind. But they drew the line at shooting Tony Shots as well. Tony was a friend of the Gallos, and they could see no justice in killing the son for the sins of the father, as the contract specified. Instead, they hid him out until the difficulty could be smoothed over.

This was not the first time that Joey had seen fit to question Profaci's orders. He and his brothers had always resented the levy that had to be paid to the Don on the profits of their various enterprises. They were also irritated by the $25 a month which they and every other "made" member of the Profaci family had to pay as dues —a custom long since abandoned by the other New York bosses. Nor had Joey forgiven the old man for ordering the deaths of two of his followers, John (Johnny Roberts) Robilletto and Jimmy (Bucky) Ammino, without even consulting him first. The shooting of Ammino had seemed particularly spiteful. When Profaci heard that a jeweled crown had been stolen from Regis Pacis Roman Catholic Church in Bensonhurst, he spread the word that he wanted it returned at once. Joey promised to see that this was done and ordered the reluctant Bucky to send back the crown by registered mail. He did so, but it arrived with three diamonds missing, and, being a deeply religious man, Profaci had Bucky shot by an out-of-town gunman. To Joey, this was petty and vindictive.

But most of all, he resented Profaci's nepotism. Instead of rewarding the men who ran his empire with fiefs of their own, the old man parceled out the rackets and revenues among his relatives and cronies, leaving his soldiers to fend for themselves. In *The Crime Confederation*, Ralph Salerno wrote of a conversation he had with Joey on the street around this time: "Some old *compare* greaseball comes over from Italy," he remembers Joey saying, "and Moneybags put up $15 G's to open a grocery store for him. The delivery boys in the store stole the business right out from under his nose and he goes bankrupt, and Moneybags backs him a second time. Me, I can't even get to run a crap game. Why? You need a college education to run a crap game? When you want somebody hit, we're good enough. But not good enough to come to the house."

Profaci had several houses, including a two-story brick fortress at 8863 Fifteenth Avenue in the Bath Beach section, a sumptuous villa in Miami Beach, and a fortified 328-acre estate with a private airstrip at Hightstown, New Jersey. Joey, on the other hand, was living at home with his parents at 639 East Fourth Street, and feeling the disparity acutely. Not that he set much store by possessions—a comfortable pad, a closet of clothes, his books and a piece of hash were all that he really needed—but the logic of being a leader required him to be *the* leader. To him, the only route to the top of the heap was the shortest and most obvious. You put a gun to the old man's head and told him he was retired. And if you could do it to one, you could do it to all, because force was what made the world go round.

Larry Gallo was more respectful, however. He leaned to the old school, as did Joe Jelly. Though critical of Profaci's greedy, cantankerous rule, they were still organization men, inclined to work their way up by earning favor and promotion rather than by trying to usurp established authority. Joey naturally found this frustrating, since he couldn't act without them. When the police bugged the phone in one of the Gallos' bars, they heard him lash out when someone remarked casually that Frank Costello had Louisiana. "Who gave Louisiana to Frank Costello?" he demanded. "Eisenhower? Any man who is strong enough to take something and hold it, he owns it. If he is not strong enough to take it and hold it, nobody can give him Louisiana or anyplace else."

Joey was all for applying this dictum to Brooklyn, and as the months went by and Profaci showed no sign of relaxing his grip on what the Gallos now felt was their rightful territory, Larry began to come around to his brother's view. For one thing, Profaci and his brother-in-law Joe Magliocco, who acted as underboss, had both been convicted of obstructing justice following their arrest at the mobs' Apalachin summit conference in 1957. If their appeal failed, they wouldn't *have* to be deposed—the family would be leaderless anyway. It was only prudent, therefore, to discuss the mechanics of taking over, and the more they discussed the idea, the less shocking it seemed, until at last their decision turned on how Profaci disposed of Frankie Shots's policy bank. If he gave it to them in recognition of their services, okay. But if he cut it up among his cronies, that would be the cue for a coup d'état. Though outnumbered on paper, the Gallos were the family's élite enforcers and would also enjoy the advantage of surprise.

In the event, the Profaci-Magliocco appeal was upheld, and the Don gave them no part of Frankie Shots's business. More humiliating still, he sent his bodyguard, John Scimone, around to President Street to warn Joey publicly to watch his mouth and behave himself. Joey considered this briefly, then spat in the gutter. With his brother and Joe Jelly still urging caution, he began to look for allies. In the early hours of December 9, 1960, the police broke up a meeting at the Luna between Joey, Anthony (Tony Bender) Strollo, Frankie (the Bug) Caruso, Joseph (Curly) Argone, Philip (Katz) Albanese and George Filipone. All were taken in on charges of consorting with known criminals—each other—and subsequently discharged when Tony Bender's attorney demonstrated to the magistrate's satisfaction that the police could offer no proof that the six had consorted together for an unlawful purpose. But the publicity was damaging. Everybody, including Profaci, now knew that Joey was talking business outside the family. Tony Bender was an old-time big shot—a capo in the Genovese family, Joe Valachi's immediate superior, and boss of the Lower Manhattan waterfront. Backed by Genovese and Lucky Luciano, he was out to take away the international narcotics racket from Profaci, so that an alliance with Joey was clearly in his interest as well as the Gallos'.

A few weeks later, the Gallos surfaced again, this time in the person of Joey's younger brother Al (Kid Blast), who was picked up in the company of Charles (Ruby) Stein and Nicholas (Jiggs) Forlano, the city's leading bookmakers and shylocks, Carmine Persico, Jr., Joe Yacovelli and nine others in a raid on the White Turkey at Second Avenue and Fifty-seventh Street in Manhattan. Ruby Stein had been using the restaurant every afternoon for weeks as a clearinghouse for gambling on basketball, football and baseball games. With Jiggs Forlano as a partner, he didn't need all this extra Brooklyn muscle. But did the Brooklyn muscle need *him?* For financial backing, perhaps?

Speculation was soon silenced by events. In February, 1961, though the element of surprise had been lost, the Gallos moved against Profaci—in Joey's diplomatic absence. Picked groups of his men grabbed Joe Magliocco and Frank Profaci, the Don's brother, from their homes, and Sally (the Sheik) Mussachio, a powerful capo, and John Scimone from a downtown social club. Each of the four was then taken to a separate Manhattan hotel and kept there under guard. But the old man himself escaped, despite his worsening health, and so did Johnny Bath Beach. The coup had failed—ruining more than just Joey's temper and Jeffie's Florida wedding. Profaci's obvious countermove now would be to ask the other New York families for help in putting down this mutiny, and no one knew better than Joey that he would probably get it. The old man's fellow Dons would like nothing better than a chance to demonstrate to their own young Turks the penalties for insubordination. The one hope he had of snatching something from the wreck was to react fast and decisively. He flew back from Florida with every intention of killing one of the hostages and demanding $100,000 in cash from Profaci as an earnest of good faith before sitting down to negotiate.

But his brother wouldn't hear of it. All his old uneasiness about the propriety of taking the law into his own hands had returned and redoubled. Larry was not afraid, but he would offer no further disrespect. Backed by Joe Jelly, he had decided to sit tight, hold on to the hostages and wait for Profaci to make the next move. He saw a good chance of the Commission upholding their grievances if matters were taken no further, but with Profaci alive and at liberty, to continue the revolt from a position of weakness was to invite certain disaster. And he was not to be moved from this, though Joey stormed, sulked, charmed and abused him by turn. Rightly convinced, as it turned out, that Profaci would never forgive the affront to his pride, Joey came close to staging a second revolt against his own brother, but in the end, when all arguments failed, took himself off to California instead to win back Jeffie, who had fled there after the collapse of their marriage plans.

On February 23, Profaci made his opening move, just as Larry had predicted. Two comparatively neutral emissaries arrived on President Street to open negotiations. They were Don Lorenzo, an elderly businessman who ran a linen supply company in Trenton, New Jersey, and Charles (Sits) Locicero, who owned a furniture factory. After an hour's discussion, they left with a full account of the Gallos' grievances and demands. Before the hostages could be released, Larry would require Frankie Shots's policy bank to be handed over to Tony Shots, free of claims for back taxes; the right to extend Gallo territory, both geographically and commercially, and $150,000 in compensation for all the heat and inconvenience. He also wanted a hearing before the Commission, which he got a few days later, with Carlo Gambino in the chair and Tony Bender sitting in for the absent Genovese.

Not surprisingly, Bender took the Gallos' part. They were wrong, but they were right, too. Profaci had acted unfairly. After an inconclusive discussion, the Dons took a neutral line: the dispute could best be settled by the parties to it. This was an internal, family affair, and thus immune, by tradition, to outside interference. The Gallos were jubilant. With Profaci sick and isolated, a powerful alliance with Tony Bender and a large loan from Ruby Stein to tide them over, they had merely to wait the old man out. Never mind if he kept his emissaries going back and forth, haggling over details—they were gathering strength every day. Their old friend Carmine Persico, Jr. threw in with them; then Salvatore (Sally D.) D'Ambrosio, another tough Profaci soldier, and even John Scimone, the old man's chauffeur and bodyguard, whom they had taken hostage. How could they lose? Dismissing Joey's continuing objections as sour grapes, Larry was so confident of playing a winning hand that when Profaci finally agreed to come to the conference table on condition the hostages were first released, he immediately turned them loose—except for Scimone, whom he held for another week so as to allay any suspicion in Profaci's mind that he might have changed sides.

Then nothing happened. No word came from Profaci, and Sits Locicero sailed for Italy aboard the *Leonardo da Vinci* to consult with Lucky Luciano and Joe Adonis, the near-legendary boss of Brooklyn in the thirties. The money from Ruby Stein ran out, the police and FBI were more or less permanently encamped on President Street, and the Gallos went broke. With all this official attention, it was impossible to carry on business as usual. On April 7, Joey was arrested for consorting with known criminals—his brothers—in the Café Espresso at Bond and Union streets, Brooklyn, where they had met to talk about Attorney General Robert Kennedy's new program against organized crime. A month later, on May 12, he was picked up with Ali Baba, Sidney Slater and two others on charges of attempting to muscle in on a bar and check-cashing business run by one Theodore Moss. It was the crucial arrest of his life, but at the time, as far as Joey was concerned, it was just one more nuisance to contend with. He had more important things to think about than the routine police dragnet that pulled him in every time the department had a crime it couldn't solve. It was harassment, that was all.

Among the other things he had to think about was Profaci's continuing silence. Larry's explanation for it was that the old man was trying to starve them into a compromise, but Joey had an uneasy feeling there was more behind it than that. Profaci was too proud, too unforgiving, too like himself to give up any part of his empire without a gun at his head. As the truce dragged on through spring and into summer, the more certain he became of this, until the only question left in his mind was when and where the Don would strike back.

The answer came on Sunday afternoon, August 20, at the Sahara Lounge on Utica Avenue, a mob hangout run by Charles Clemenza, an old friend of Profaci's. Sergeant Edward Meagher and Patrolman Melvin Blei happened to be passing in a prowl car when they noticed the side door ajar. As the Sahara never opened before six o'clock, the sergeant went to investigate and found Clemenza in the dark, busily polishing glasses. Assured that everything was all right, Meagher turned to go. But then, in the shadows, he saw what looked like a pair of legs sticking out from behind the bar.

"What's that on the floor?" he asked suspiciously.

"No," yelled Clemenza, and not at the sergeant. "Not here. I don't want no trouble."

Shaking off a long moment of paralysis, Meagher reached for his gun, but from out of the darkness, three men were on him before he could draw it, bundling him aside. They ran out the side door, followed by the sergeant's warning shout, and as Patrolman Blei scrambled from the patrol car, one of them fired into his face, the bullet piercing the cheek and lodging under his nose. The three then threw themselves into a waiting white Cadillac that took off with a screech of burnt rubber.

The legs belonged to Larry Gallo, who was only just alive. When Sidney Slater heard about the murder attempt on the six o'clock news, his immediate reaction was to wonder what had happened to Joe Jelly, who had hardly left Larry's side since the failure of their February coup. It was the first question he asked when he reported to President Street for orders.

Nobody knew for sure, but the previous Friday night, a dead fish, wrapped in Joe Jelly's coat, had been thrown out of a passing car into the doorway of his favorite hangout, a candy store on Avenue D. The message seemed clear enough, especially to Joey. "Joe Jelly called me last Wednesday," Joey said. "He told me he was taking the day off to go fishing with Sally D. They went fishing out of Sheepshead Bay on Sally D.'s boat. Carmine Persico, Joe Yacovelli and John Scimone went along for the ride. I guess they all came back except Joe Jelly." Sally D'Ambrosio and Joe Jelly were like brothers. They had grown up together, and served in the Marines together.

Larry himself told Slater what had happened at the Sahara, his voice still hoarse and his neck still ringed with purple from the garotte. "Scimone called me and told me he bet on a horse and it came home and paid a big price. He said he wanted to split the winnings with me. So I met him and he handed me a C-note. So I said to him, 'Let's go someplace and have a drink.' And he says, 'Okay. Let's go to the Sahara Lounge. Some of the boys will be there.' So we go to the Sahara, sit down at a table, order a drink, and then Sally D. comes in the joint with Carmine Persico. Which is great—until they pull guns.

"Then one of them says to me, 'Larry, you got to go. There ain't enough room in Brooklyn. You guys are muscling in on things you got no right to. Joey gets it next. Then Kid Blast. Then the others.' Then they slip the rope over my head and start to pull. And the more I fight, the tighter it gets around my neck. And they keep on talking to me. They tell me how they dump Joe Jelly in the bay, and about then I start to pass out." He omitted to mention that they had used the garotte instead of their guns for a reason. They had hoped to choke him into calling Joey down to the Sahara so that he could get his, too.

When he recovered consciousness, Larry found the bar full of cops. Scimone was there also, nursing a battered face. He had been found four blocks away lying alongside the abandoned white Cadillac, having apparently fallen out while it was still moving, although he insisted he had been thrown out by the would-be killers after they had abducted him at gunpoint. "I didn't see *anything*," he kept telling the police, dabbing at his bleeding left cheek with a handkerchief. "Larry's my friend. I was buying him a drink. I went to take a leak. I didn't *see* anything." Nobody seemed to take this very seriously, however—although he had, in fact, left the table just before the cord was looped over Larry's head.

The Profaci War 79

True to the code, Larry hadn't seen anything either, despite being done so close to death that he had lost control of his bladder and bowels. He told the police he had no idea who might have wanted to kill him, nor could he identify his stranglers. After cleaning himself up as best he could in the men's room, he was taken to the hospital and arraigned next morning in front of Judge Samuel S. Leibowitz as a material witness, along with Clemenza, Scimone, Alphonse Cirillo, a Profaci soldier who owned the getaway Cadillac, and Arnold Nong, a cook working at the Sahara, whose life, said Judge Leibowitz, "would not be worth a pretzel" unless he was held in protective custody. Joey, who had been at home with Jeffie at the time of the attack, was also arraigned by the Kings County District Attorney on the grounds that he was next on Profaci's murder list, but the judge ruled that the court had no power to hold him on bail "just because somebody wants to murder him."

Joey really appreciated this, understanding as well as anyone that the D.A.'s concern for his safety was rather less compelling than his desire to lock up one of the two commanders in what promised to be the bloodiest gang war New York had ever seen. Bail had been set at an impossible $100,000 for Larry, and the same had been asked for Joey. Now vindicated by the turn of events, exhilarated by the prospect of action and bent on revenge, to the exclusion of almost everything else, he could hardly contain his high spirits. Taken to see Larry in the hospital, he bounced into the room, grinned at the cops still questioning him at his bedside and told him he ought to sell his house and give the money to the Patrolmen's Benevolent Association for saving his life.

Not much more than twenty-four hours later, he withdrew the suggestion after an early-morning police raid on President Street. Acting on an FBI tip that the Gallos were assembling an armory there, several squads of detectives under Assistant Chief Inspector Martin combed the block but found nothing except two perfectly legal shotguns and a supply of shells on the flat roof of No. 51, the headquarters of Joey's Direct Vending Company. Whereupon, he rather lamely arrested Joey, Al, Poppa Gallo, Amando Illiano—better known as Mando the Midget—and seven others on the now familiar charge of consorting with known criminals and took them off for a hilarious reunion with Larry Gallo and Tony Shots at the Raymond Street jail.

A few hours later, they were released on bail, and walked from the Magistrate's Court into a bedlam of reporters and TV cameramen. Working through the crush to Joey's side, Gabe Pressman thrust an NBC-TV microphone under his nose and asked him if he was not afraid of the mob forces now arrayed against him. "Afraid?" said Joey, encircling Mando with his arm. "How can I be afraid when my bodyguard is with me?" And even the camera shook with laughter as it panned down to the dwarf's intimidating scowl.

The next evening, Joey sought out an astonished Judge Leibowitz at Cafiero's Restaurant near the Kings County Courthouse.

"What are *you* doing here?" the judge demanded, somewhat disconcerted at being seen in public with the notorious Joey Gallo, who, besides his television appearances, had also made the front pages every day since the Sahara incident.

"Listen, Judge, I want to thank you for letting me go home to my wife on Monday. I want you to know I really appreciate that."

"Don't thank *me*," said Leibowitz bluntly. "I had to do it under the law."

Joey laughed, and turned to the judge's dinner companion, Assistant District Attorney Louis Ernst. "I love this man," he said. "You know why? Because he's a tough man."

"He's a tough man with tough people," said Ernst, looking around uneasily.

"How did you know I was here?" asked Leibowitz.

"You're on my territory, Judge," said Joey, smiling as if he owned the restaurant. "I asked where you were and they told me. So I came here to show my friends I could sit next to you."

He stayed long enough to make them both thoroughly uncomfortable, then excused himself with a charming smile and left. Next morning, he turned up in Leibowitz's court and passed a message to the bench saying he would like to see him. On his own territory this time, the judge surveyed the room and spotted Joey sitting with Jeffie in the spectators' section. "I understand that a distinguished gentleman by the name of Joe Gallo is in the court and wants to speak to me," he said, in a mildly sarcastic tone. Joey got up as though taking a bow in a nightclub and came forward to the bench. "Good morning, Your Honor," he said. "I got to thinking about it, and I guess I owe Your Honor an apology for approaching you last night. I didn't mean to embarrass you."

The judge glanced at the reporters. "Never mind the apology," he said coldly. "What do you want?"

"I want permission to attend that hearing in the hospital tomorrow," said Joey. The wounded Patrolman Blei had identified Tony Shots Abbatemarco—wrongly, as it turned out—as one of the men who had escaped from the Sahara, confusing him with Sally D., who was not unlike him in build and general appearance. He and John Scimone had each been held on $100,000 bail pending a magistrate's hearing ordered for that morning at Blei's bedside in Kings County Hospital. Like Larry, who had already vehemently denied that Tony Shots had had anything to do with the attempt on his life, Joey was anxious to get this confusion of identities cleared up.

"There will be no such hearing," replied Leibowitz. "The matter is being presented to a grand jury right now. If you want to appear as a witness, go to the grand jury room and report to Assistant District Attorney Benjamin Schmier, who is handling the matter. Do you want to appear as a witness?"

Having spent most of his adult life trying to avoid invitations of that sort, Joey backed off, holding up his hands in mock surrender. "I'll have to see my counsel about that, Your Honor," he said. "And I think he's in Florida." Honors were about even.

A week after his arraignment as a material witness, Larry himself appeared before Judge Leibowitz—on a motion to reduce bail from $100,000 to $25,000. Assistant District Attorney Schmier thought "he would be a moron if he walked the street. If I were in his shoes and my bail was down to only $25, I'd stay in jail. But if he wants to walk the streets, that's his business." The judge agreed, but urged the police to keep him under observation at all times. "I didn't see a cop tailing Joey Gallo the other day when I saw him in the restaurant," he added severely.

That night, according to Sidney Slater, Joey threw a party for Larry "the likes of which Brooklyn had never seen. It began in Mama Rosa's, a very good Italian restaurant, but the crowd was so big that it overflowed into the street, and dozens of hoods sat on the curb drinking out of wine bottles."

Next morning, the brothers settled down to discuss their war strategy. To everyone but Joey, the situation left a lot to be desired. The long delay had given Profaci all the time he needed, not merely to break up the coalition ranged against him, but also to set the former allies at one another's throats. Carmine Persico, Jr., having been won back with the promise of rewards beyond anything the Gallos could offer, was now in charge of the opposing army, with Sally D. in close support. Ruby Stein and Jiggs Forlano had also clearly seen the light, their wavering loyalties to Profaci no doubt stiffened by the Gallos' inability to repay their loan. Only Tony Bender remained, and he was much too fly a bird to commit himself to more than promises while the issue remained in doubt. In any case, an inconclusive struggle between the two sides suited his purpose as well as if not better than a clear-cut victory. Outnumbered and outgunned, therefore, the Gallos had no choice but to settle in for a siege.

In this, they were assisted by the police, who could easily have dispersed the gang from President Street had they wished to do so and given Profaci's men every chance to pick them off one by one. Instead, they very sensibly decided to keep the Gallo camp intact and under continuous observation by the Pizza Squad, so that any further hostilities on either side would have to take place in plain view. Though critics of this policy complained that the department, in effect, was providing police protection for a gang of practicing criminals, in fact, the cordon around the neighborhood and the daily rollcalls on the block made it virtually impossible for them to practice at all. The Pizza Squad detectives were as much their jailers as their protectors, and what they couldn't see or hear for themselves, they could now learn from Sidney Slater, who had cracked under the threat of a fourteen-year sentence for being Joey's coconspirator in the pending extortion case and turned informer. Besides his restaurant interest, Slater was now acting as a collector for Joey, visiting jukebox operators and numbers brokers with two armed bodyguards and bringing in about $1,000 a week. For the next six months or so, he was to keep the police supplied with a daily bulletin on the Gallos' war plans, earning Assistant Chief Inspector Martin a reputation for powers akin to clairvoyance. Time and again, his detectives would raid 49 and 51 President Street at exactly the right moment to forestall Joey's carefully prepared offensives.

"Martin gave me an unlisted telephone number and told me to use the code name Sam every time I called," Slater explained later, after Frank Hogan, the Manhattan District Attorney, had blown his cover by making him testify against Carmine Persico, Jiggs Forlano and Dominic (Donny Shack) Montemorano for assaulting him at the Copacabana. "I filled him in on everything that had happened the past few years—the murder of Joe Jelly, the ones who really tried to kill Larry Gallo—and I told him Sally D. had shot Patrolman Blei. I gave him the answers to four or five other killings as well.

"I helped stop a lot of that trouble on President Street. I tipped them when and where to hit, so that when they picked up somebody, the shotguns would be right there. There was six or seven who died, and I felt it my duty to stop the killing. It might have run into hundreds the way it was going. Joey was a wild man, and he made his men wild. He's a strong and dominating personality. The raids made him madder than hell, and I was scared to death. It was like living in a foxhole. But he never suspected me. I'd take the arrests with everybody else when they came. Sometimes I'd be at a meeting place, and the cops would raid the joint just to get me out in one piece."

Frustrated at every turn, Joey and Larry set about overhauling their defenses. The Gallo block of President Street, down by the livid waters of Gowanus Creek, is set in a dying slum of low, brick tenements, boarded storefronts, vacant lots and rusting Fords. The people who lived there were always poor, but now that the Italians are moving out and handing over their stoops and walk-ups to the Puerto Ricans, the neighborhood has taken on a curious, leftover air, like an old, abandoned social experiment cut off from the rest of the city by a moatful of traffic on the Brooklyn-Queens Expressway. Accessible by only four streets and a footpath, and with a friendly local population to warn them of strangers approaching, the Gallos' turf was practically immune to surprise attack, even without police surveillance. Nevertheless, two Profaci cars did manage to slip through the cordon in the first few days after the attack on Larry, and so 49 and 51 were converted into a fortress.

At that time, Joey could probably have mustered an army of 250 for a full-scale campaign, but while the siege was on, the sleep-in garrison rarely exceeded the top twenty-five on Carmine Persico's target list. With Poppa Gallo cooking for them, and Larry dividing the domestic chores among them, they slept on cots and mattresses in a second-floor dormitory with chicken wire nailed across the windows to keep out grenades or sticks of dynamite. Detective O'-Brien of the Pizza Squad remembers somebody telling them that the IRA used to tie fishhooks to their grenades so that they would catch on the wire, and next day work parties were out fixing storm screens. Floors were swept daily, and once a week the premises were scrubbed out with pine disinfectant, a sanitary precaution that probably owed as much to the gang's experience with their legendary "lioness" Cleo as it did to Larry's fastidious nature.

Cleo, who still survives in a New Jersey private zoo, was in fact an ocelot cub acquired in a typically unguarded moment as a Gallo mascot, but inevitably the story got around that Joey had bought her to frighten his shakedown victims. He would throw her a piece of meat, it was said, and her growl of appreciation would immediately end all resistance. In reality, the principal sufferers were Mando the Midget and his Doberman pinscher. When the novelty wore off, Cleo was confined to the cellar of Mando's social club at No. 74 while the gang tried to find someone to take her off their hands. "And Jesus, the *smell!*" said Detective O'Brien. "It stank like a zoo down there. Mando told us the other day, he says, 'That cat,' he says, 'he took some swipe at my dog. He took some chunk outa him.' "

The hard core of the garrison, all of whom had criminal records, included Vincent (Vinnie the Sicilian) Gugliaro, the late Joe Jelly's silent partner, who had taken over as principal enforcer; Jimmy (the

Bat) Cardiello, so named in his youth for his skill in fracturing limbs with a baseball bat; Ali Baba; Punchy Illiano; Tony Shots; John (Mooney) Cutrone; Big Tony Regina and his brother Chico Regina; Joe (Little Lollipop) Carna, who weighed in at over two hundred pounds, and Larry (Big Lollipop) Carna, who was much smaller and got shot in the ankle by Carmine Persico on Union Street when he went out to buy house paint at Pintchik's; Nick Bianco, a dapper young soldier who later switched sides; Louis (the Syrian) Hubela; Hyman Powell; Peanuts Sorrentino; Tony Gargulio; Joe Magnasco and Joseph (Joey T.) Tomasello, an accomplished hand with a paint brush, who lined the hallway and stairs of No. 51 with lettered signs reminiscent of World War II: "DON'T TALK—THE LIFE YOU SAVE MAY BE YOUR OWN."

The cultural tone of President Street was also upheld by Larry Gallo, who whiled away the hours between court appearances and bouts of do-it-yourself improvements to the building by playing his collection of operatic records loudly enough to be heard at each end of the block. Assistant Chief Inspector Martin relates in his book how Larry one day explained his devotion to music: "Mr. Martin," he said, "I ain't going to be doing what I'm doing for the rest of my life. You may not think so, but life is made for finer things. One day, I'm going to retire. I don't want to be like so many fellows I know who retire and they can't do nothing. When I retire, I'm going to be cultured. I'm going to sit back and enjoy, enjoy, enjoy."

Right from the start, relations between the Pizza Squad and the Gallo gang had been imbued with a grudging professional respect, which, in certain cases, shaded into something close to affection. They played the game by the rules. "They're a peculiar mob, they really are—they have such characters," says another squad spokesman still on the street. "The other side, they came on heavy. They gotta convince you they're tough guys, and you know they're nothing but shitheads. Especially the kids—they're nothing. With them, it's 'Hey, what do you guys want? Fuck you. I'll get my lawyer.' But the Gallos, they didn't do that. They knew what we had to do and they weren't going to question it. They treated us like gentlemen. This don't make them good guys, but they have a little more savvy. It was like 'Why stir the pot? If you're going to be down here, let's make it pleasant for both of us.' It's a game. If you get caught, you get caught.

"The Gallos used to tell our boss, 'You come in here to search our place, right? We know that if you find something, you found it—that it was there when you came in.' They had that much trust in us. They knew we were not going to flake them. One time we had word they were supposed to be loading up with guns, so all the bosses started calling up. 'Go down there. Search the place.' And they had an outside crew come in, but the Gallos said, 'No good. You produce a warrant before you come in here.' Then Joey called our lieutenant and said, 'If you want to come in with your men, I'll take you right through the place,' and that's the way he solved it. And the place was clean.

"It's the same today. If we want to talk to some guy, we'll call up on the phone and say, 'Come in. We want to talk to you.' And he'll say, 'Okay, I'll be right in.' And you sit there and he'll come in. He won't tell you anything, but he'll be there. Try that with one of the Persicos and he'll come on heavy, which shows you what assholes they are."

The romantic potential of the President Street siege was not lost on the press. With the sugar-coated worldliness that characterizes so much New York journalism, even at its most censorious, the tabloids and television were soon depicting the Gallos as a gallant band of Runyonesque folk heroes returning their enemies' superior firepower with volleys of wisecracks. Letters from admirers began to arrive on President Street from all over the world, some containing money, others proposing marriage or looser arrangements, and a few with offers of specialized assistance from Army-trained automatic-weapons experts. The Gallos enjoyed these attentions hugely, especially Joey, who acted as principal spokesman by virtue of accessibility as well as rank. Too proud, and too comfortable on Eleventh Street, to submit to confinement in Brooklyn, he had Jeffie drive him back and forth from Manhattan every day. Blissfully unaware that the streets were patrolled by cruising Profaci gunmen, she would drop him off and pick him up on President Street as casually as a suburban matron shuttling her commuter husband to and from the office.

Unimpressed by this new public image, and under pressure from Attorney General Robert Kennedy, the FBI, the Police Department and the District Attorneys of Kings County and Manhattan stepped up their efforts to take Joey out of circulation before he could engineer any serious bloodletting. First on the list for questioning in any major homicide case, he was pulled in almost every time a body was found in Brooklyn. Then, on August 30, the first moves were made to separate him from his codefendants in the extortion case with the idea of bringing him up for an early trial. Three days later, Judge Leibowitz revoked the bail granted pending an appeal against his conviction in the jukebox coercion case and returned him to Rikers Island to complete the remaining two years and nine months of his three-year sentence. In fact, he served only four days, until September 6, when his lawyers, David Price and Joe Iovine, an uncle by marriage, managed to get him out again on $5,000 bail and a certificate of reasonable doubt from an Appellate Division justice.

On September 12, three immigration officials from the Department of Justice struck morale a low blow by arresting the garrison cook, Poppa Gallo, for illegal entry—forty-one years after the event. "Don't worry, Pop," shouted Joey as they drove him away. "We'll get you a lawyer." In truth, he was in greater need of one himself, for the Teddy Moss extortion case was now being ominously stacked against him, but he was much too busy trying to get his long-delayed offensive under way to worry about that. Hurting for money, he had decided to snatch Ruby Stein and hold him for ransom. As the shylock knew all his boys by sight, he brought in Fat Jack Camposito and Lefty Castiglione to handle the job, two Los Angeles hoods whom he had met on his trips to California earlier that year to win back Jeffie. As neither had seen their quarry before, Joey sent them out with a chauffeur-fingerman, who eventually spotted Ruby in Manhattan going into the El Borracho Restaurant on East Fifty-third Street. When he emerged a couple of hours later, the two grabbed his arms and started to hustle him toward the waiting car, but Ruby wasn't anxious to go. He screamed and yelled and struggled and fought, and the wrestling trio were soon ringed three-deep with interested bystanders. Inhibited by all this attention, Fat Jack and Lefty then dumped Ruby on the sidewalk, sank their alligator pumps into his ribs a few times and fled for the car, which made off, pursued halfheartedly by two foot patrolmen who had run around from Park Avenue to see what the screaming was all about. To avert possible reprisals from the muscle end of the Stein-Forlano partnership, an attempt was made shortly after this to assassinate Jiggs outside his home in Astoria, Queens, but this, too, miscarried in a rattle of poorly directed gunfire.

On October 4, the President Street garrison lost its first man to the enemy, in a skirmish at Fourth Avenue and Union Street at five o'clock in the afternoon. It was quite unpremeditated. Chafing from inaction, Joe Magnasco, a hot-tempered cousin of Tony Shots, persuaded the Regina brothers and Punchy Illiano to join him for a cruise around town. They were unarmed, for Joey had issued strict orders that no one was to take any unnecessary risk of getting picked up and put away for violating the Sullivan Law. They had gone barely a mile from President Street when they saw Harry Fontana and his bodyguard standing on the corner. Fontana was Profaci's capo in charge of the Red Hook district, and the Gallos had long felt he should have supported them in their claims for a better deal.

Magnasco told Punchy to stop the car. He jumped out, stormed over to Fontana and began to berate him furiously for his shortcomings. Punchy, Chico and Big Tony looked at each other, shrugged and climbed out to join him. Getting no response from Fontana beyond a bored stare, Magnasco grabbed him by the lapels to underline his complaint, but Fontana's bodyguard obviously mistook his intentions because he backed off a pace, pulled a .32 from his coat and, in full view of sixty or seventy people, shot Magnasco three times, through the shoulder, chest and leg. He then pointed the gun at Punchy and his companions, who prudently turned tail, ran for their car and drove off in a hurry. Satisfied they now had the field to themselves, Fontana nodded to his bodyguard, who threw the gun over a fence and disappeared in the crowd, and then drove away in the opposite direction.

By a wild coincidence, Tony Shots's wife Lucille came up from the subway entrance on the corner at that moment and saw Magnasco on the sidewalk, his face masked with blood from the chest wound. "My God," she said. "It's Cousin Joe." When the police arrived, they could find only one witness, who later changed her mind. Nor did they learn much more on President Street, for the news had traveled fast. When Inspector Martin arrived with his men at No. 51 barely twenty minutes later, he found Joey, Larry and nine of the boys seated around a table with their lawyer, waiting for him. They were taken in for questioning.

The pace was warming up. Next day, Carmine Persico, Jr. pleaded not guilty to the attempted murder of Larry Gallo and was released on $25,000 bail. Oddly enough, he had just been convicted with Joe Magnasco and others of a hijacking rap, and the week before had received a fourteen-and-a-half-year sentence for it from Brooklyn Federal Court. Since he was then let out on bail pending an appeal, it was clearly Joey Gallo's continued liberty rather than Persico's that most worried the authorities, and from that moment on, until he finally went to jail on the extortion charge, Joey was to spend more time in court or under questioning than running the war.

At 9:30 A.M. on October 10, the police raided President Street for the third time in seven weeks. Acting on another tip from Sidney Slater, they were looking for guns. (Joey, however, wasn't there. He had been picked up the previous evening on Eleventh Street in anticipation of the raid and held overnight on a technicality.) The twenty-five officers broke down the door to find Larry still in bed, Tony Shots in his underwear and the rest sitting around drinking coffee. No one seemed very surprised. After examining their warrants, Larry helped the police search No. 49 as well as 51, even pointing out a loaded shotgun which they had missed under one of the beds in the dormitory. This and two rifles of .30 and .22 caliber, a .30 carbine and a closetful of ammunition—including dumdum bullets, according to the officers—constituted the entire haul. Nonplused, because these weapons afforded no grounds for arrest, the inspector who led the raid took them in to Bergen Street police station for questioning on charges of consorting. There they were joined by Joey, and that evening the whole group was arraigned as material witnesses for the grand jury investigation into the murder of Joe Magnasco and the attempted murder of Larry Gallo.

"Undoubtedly, a blazing rifle battle between the Gallo mob and their avowed enemies has been averted," said a spokesman for the Rackets Bureau, with more fervor than plausibility. "We heard they were going to war, and we didn't want a Saint Valentine's Day massacre in Brooklyn." Judge Hyman Barshay agreed. Complimenting the Police Department on its peacekeeping, he set bail at the impossibly high figure of $25,000 each, which meant that all thirteen would have to spend the night in Raymond Street jail awaiting their appearance before the grand jury next morning.

Joey, as imperturbable as ever in public, was in good form. "Hey, detective!" he yelled across court as the judge withdrew. A sleepy-looking member of the Homicide Division held up his hands in mock surrender. "How many days you been working, huh? You watch. Everybody on the homicide squad is going to wind up getting divorced." Coming from the man responsible for most of his workload, this drew a weary smile. He was used to Joey, who, as always in court, behaved as though the proceedings had nothing to do with him. When his name was called, he went up to receive his grand jury subpoena, folded it carefully and poked Assistant District Attorney Walter Buchbinder in the chest with it. "Walter," he said, "someday I'm going to give *you* one of these things. I've had about a hundred from you, and you haven't solved a crime yet."

Next morning, he was a good deal less talkative—at least in court. He refused to testify without being offered immunity to prosecution and his appearance lasted just one and a half minutes. As soon as he left the grand jury room, however, he conducted one of his now famous press conferences for the waiting crowd of reporters. "Gang war?" he said, with elaborate scorn. "Dumdum bullets? Ha! It's all made up. They made up a big story about a gang war. There's no gang. There's no gang war. There's nothing. You guys are making up something out of nothing, and I want to tell the truth."

The prospect of this so disturbed his attorney, David Price, that he grabbed Joey by the nape of the neck and shook him, shouting, "Goddamnit—you shut up."

"No, wait a minute, counselor," he said coldly, throwing him off. "This is my life. Let me say what I want to say. I want the reporters to get the right story. The police are harassing us. It's an election year, right? Everybody wants to get into the act."

One of the reporters then asked him what they were doing with rifles, a carbine and a shotgun if everything was so peaceful in Brooklyn. "Jesus, they're not *murder* guns," he said, as if humoring a mental defective. "They're *hunting* guns. We use them for hunting deer." With dumdum bullets? "There was no such thing—no such thing," he said sharply, turning to Buchbinder, who had just left the jury room. "You, Walter—you know damn well we know nothing about the murder." Pained to learn that the D.A. had offended the code by serving subpoenas on the wives of the men holed up on President Street, he was then led away to spend another night in jail.

Next morning, he redeemed his promise to Buchbinder. As soon as he entered the Supreme Court Building in Brooklyn, he started calling for him. "Walter! Where's Walter? I need Walter. I want to see him." Alight with hope for some dramatic new breakthrough in the case, Buchbinder hurried down to where Joey and his men were waiting. "Well?" he said expectantly. "You wanted to see me?"

Joey winked at the reporters standing by. "Here, Walter," he said, thrusting a paper in his hand. "Try this for size." It was a subpoena ordering Walter Buchbinder to appear before the grand jury. Joey had stolen a blank form from the D.A.'s office the previous day.

When his audience regained its composure, Joey went on to explain to the reporters that he and his partners were running a legitimate business and all this publicity was having a bad effect on it. "These men working with me are all ex-servicemen and heroes who've been wounded in battle. Joe Magnasco was with the Fourth Marines in the Pacific. He got four wounds and four decorations. If I knew who killed him, I'd tell the police. Maybe he was fooling around with someone's wife—he was a fellow who went for the girls. There *is* no gang war. There is as much gang warfare in Brooklyn as there is a dangerous Communist Party in this country."

Asked about his feud with Joe Profaci, he denied all knowledge of it. "He's a kind and religious man," he said, without a hint of a smile. "He was all shook up when he was told about the assault on my brother Larry. He's not even our competitor. He's in the olive oil business. My partners and I are just trying to make a living. The District Attorney checked with all the people we do business with to see if we used any coercion or strong-arm methods. None of them said we carried out strong-arm methods. The police are harassing us, and my relatives are running out of bail money.

"You fellows have been calling us hoodlums, gangsters and racketeers," he added reproachfully. "If anybody on the street would call me a hoodlum, I'd punch him in the nose. But when the District Attorney calls me that, what can I do?" He thought the D.A.'s action in calling the wives was an outrage. "These girls will have to go on home relief," he said, "if their husbands aren't let alone to go back to work."

Unmoved by his plea, the police took them back to jail for the weekend owing to their relatives' lack of bail money. Joey was getting increasingly restive under this treatment. He had never taken kindly to confinement. One of the detectives working on the Manhattan extortion case recalled that, after the arraignment in May, when Joey had spent twenty-one days in the Tombs while his lawyers tried to get his $100,000 bail reduced, he had emerged "not looking so good. He does what they call 'hard time.' He missed a meal a couple of times and had trouble shaving once or twice. He was just another prisoner, and it was tough for him to keep his so-called status. More than anyone else, this guy reminds me of Legs Diamond. Legs was crazy, too, and wouldn't play ball with any of the other racket guys. Eventually he got shot down. That's what'll happen to Joe Gallo, too."

Meanwhile, the law was closing around him like a fist. He was flat broke, his attorney, David Price, was away sick in Florida, and still Joey was too busy to work on his defense. "That's legal business," he would say to Uncle Joe Iovine, Price's partner, and Robert Weiswasser, their firm's newly qualified assistant. "Attend to it. Go away. Don't bother me." And they would go away to do their best to stave off the inevitable, arguing for a change of venue on the grounds that all the unfavorable publicity surrounding their client was prejudicial to his chances of a fair trial, and then, when that failed, for a post-ponement on the grounds that counsel of his choice was sick and not available. Joey was still supremely confident that neither the law nor his enemies could touch him. When he appeared in Manhattan's General Sessions Court with his attorneys on October 30 to attempt yet another delaying maneuver, the now ever-present reporters drew his attention to the elaborate police arrangements—at least twenty officers were posted in and around the courtroom. Did he think he was in danger?

Joey smiled tolerantly. "I have never been in fear of my life," he said. "I have nothing to fear. The only guy I'm afraid of is Khru-shchev. This fallout business—I think he's nuts." Breaking off re-peatedly to greet people he knew, policemen and friends alike, as though he had stopped by on a courtesy call, he said he thought the security precautions made "good reading before an election. I just wish the cops were on the street where they belong, getting the rape artists and crooks."

Two weeks later, on November 14, 1961, Joey went to trial before Judge Joseph A. Sarafite with a court-appointed lawyer he refused even to talk to.

6

Charlie

Joey and Charlie were born in the same place, within a few months of each other. They grew up on the same streets. They went to the same schools. They got into the same kind of trouble as kids. They knew each other slightly, and understood each other perfectly. Joey became a famous gangster; Charlie, an unknown dancer. When the unknown dancer heard the famous gangster had gone to jail, he wrote a poem for him and called it "Next Time."

There lived a man
so sure,
that he forgot all
the things he knew.
Somebody said, "Remember,"

And so he tried—
but forgot was all
        he could remember.

When all alone
        the truth was true,
"Don't try it's yours
        or not."
"I know," said man
        as proud and pure
As sure as he could
        be.

But, and that's a
        But,
This man forgot that
        he was free.
                Not Me.
I won't forget.
        The pain that brings
is not for me.
                Not Me.
                Remember—
Don't be the man
        that forgot to
        Remember.
He knew, you know
        It's True.

And who's to say you're
        not?
So by yourself you sit
        and wait
With all that room to
        Contemplate.
Of course you're right.
There's not one man
        who isn't.
But all alone it doesn't
        matter,

Whose records did
     you shatter?
Do you believe in
     Next Time?
Can dreams one pain
     erase?
Do you believe in
     Next Time?
Are you really in your
     Place?

Wish that you were
     fat, not skinny?
Been born a Hebe and
     not a Guinea?

Then you believe in
     Next Time
'Cause now is here,
     see it?
     What's to fear?
Be you, that's right,
   no more, no less,
     is asked.
Just you, alone, God
     threw away the
     Cast.

Not one mind moves
     in time with yours.
You've proved you're right
     Now who believes?

What misery erased?
     Your world, the
one you hear, is made
     of thoughts and paste.

Make one deed worthy
     every chance,

Like some boy scout or
        lover;
            Dance, just
            Dance
Even if you're alone, take
        a chance. Just Dance.

But if you throw away
        the rule book,
you'll surely come in
                Last.
Learn the game, It's the
                same.

            It's the same.

This game of life, from
        here it's not that fast.

Say nothing, is the same?
        It's just the game.
This life that dies,
            in spite of us,
        Reaching for a name.

Don't play this game
                with fools.
Use your wit, drink
            some wine.
Don't be asking, "What's Mine."
Smile a smile, Be Cool—
And This Time's moment
            Now,
        Is it yours or mine?

            Next Time?
                Z.

   "When I was a kid and I wanted a bicycle, I got a can of paint.
You want a bicycle? Go get a can of paint. You can steal a can of
paint in your pocket. You can't steal a bicycle in your pocket. So first

the paint. Then you go riding by the guy you stole it from on a pink bike.

"I threw the brick through the window, too. But the difference between Joey and me is that I never had to be better than anybody, or in competition with the other fucking clowns on the block. I *was* better. I didn't have to prove it by being tougher or smarter in school, I *knew* I was better. My mother gave me that. My personal proof was being able to spell all the big words. I didn't have to prove it on the street. That's the importance of this Momma syndrome for the Italian, this poor fucking greaseball that's brought up with a tough father and a smart, all-knowing, loving mother. It's really hard if she makes you pay your dues. There's no retreat. No retreat. You got to give it all, no matter what. And if she rewards you for hanging around with the tough guys on the block . . .

"Listen, I could fight with any of them. Fuck, I'd go onto the street and I used to beat up Tony the Iceman and all those fucking guys with the chains. I'd come home with battered fucking eyes and all that shit. But you want to know the difference? The thing I fought for was not fulfilling. The fulfillment had to be inside. But if you don't have a solid dinner table, if everything is cat and dog at the fucking dinner table, if you don't have that solidness, you have to look for it outside, see. I've done it. I used to sneak out the bedroom window and shinny down the fucking rainpipe at eleven o'clock at night to go to gang meetings. I could have been captain of the gang. All you had to do was beat up the boss. But to be captain of the gang meant you had to be there every night. There was no fulfillment in that. But Joey got rewarded for it. No good.

"One time my mother was walking down the street and this guy at the corner spit at her. When she came home and told me—it was the only time in my recollection that she made me her attack dog, and I can understand this feeling, see. Right away it comes to my head. I was maybe fifteen years old—and a *good* fifteen. I mean, a solid, thick fifteen with lots of fucking moves behind me. And this kid that spit at her was a member of that gang over there on the next block, the Clover Street Boys. So we went and we *got* them. It made the papers—'COMANCHE BOYS GO GET CLOVER BOYS.' They don't know why, but *I* knew why. This guy spit at my mother and hit her on the sleeve. He didn't know she was my mother. She was just an old lady walking down the street, right?

"But after that happened, there was no more. Once you've been sicked on and you go, you got to make up your mind whether you're going to be an attack dog or not. Who are you going to protect? You ever seen a guy hit over the head with a two-by-four? They end up ding-a-ling, right? Ding-a-ling. I got two square feet that I take up as I'm walking down the street. I make it my business not to infringe on *your* two feet. Now if you come and infringe on *my* two feet, I'll use every fucking thing I know to maintain my two feet. But in the meantime, I'm not going to antagonize you to want mine. I'm not going to flaunt mine and say, 'Hey, you. Come over here. Yeah.' No. Fuck that shit. For what? For your two feet? Fuck you and your two feet. My two feet are *better* than your two feet. I got all I need, all I need. Now who gave me that? My mother.

"If Joey could have had that . . . Never mind all the fucking luxuries and all the bullshit and adulation and love of your fellow men—your fellow man can't perceive who you are. I knew what it was to be respected when I was a kid, respected for myself. I got it from my mother and my father, just from being there. Not only that, I was six feet tall and weighed two hundred pounds. . . .

"But when you're a kid, when you're seven to fourteen years old, it really doesn't matter how big you are. It matters how much balls and heart you got. I was very young when I met Joey, and even as a kid he looked strong. I stayed very far away from him. He was trouble. And who needs trouble? Why get your name in the paper? I can steal just as much and live just as good without getting my name in the fucking paper. The secret of being a good crook is for nobody to know you're a crook. I'm a crook. I'm not a fucking gangster. Fuck them. They're always looked down on. Anybody that wants to be famous is not a good criminal. He should be in Hollywood, an actor, so they can give him an Academy Award. If a gangster is an actor, what's his prize? Jail? A coffin? A big funeral? No thank you. A good actor belongs in Hollywood making movies

—not shooting people or hurting people or collecting money from people.

"Listen, suppose you had a sausage and peppers stand on the corner, and five guys came up to you and said, 'Hey, Louie. You're going to give us five sandwiches a day, every day. We don't care when we show up here—you're going to give us the sandwiches.' And you're Louie. You're really struggling to make a living, right? You're selling thirty-five-cent sausage and pepper sandwiches. You're just a dumb greaseball on the corner with a pushcart. And you say, 'Bullshit! I work hard for my fucking money. Fuck you guys.'

"So the first move they do, they come driving around the corner real fast and they catch your wheel with the front bumper and your cart's a fucking mess. Not only did you blow five sausage and pepper sandwiches, you blew your whole day's receipts. Plus the damage. Okay. What was the number of the car? Who the fuck knows? He didn't even see that. All he was watching was to get out of the way. That goes on. If it goes on for two days, that's a long time. Once is usually enough.

"Now they got five free sausage and pepper sandwiches every day. That didn't take much imagination. Do you know what takes imagination? Being able to digest them. If you ask me how they do that, I can't give you an answer. The sausage and pepper sandwich is the symbol of the whole fucking thing. How do you get it? Will you stoop to that to get it? Do they ever go after the big guys? No chance. That's what's wrong with gangsters. You got to have a better goal. You got to know there's bigger things. Like how many Jews there are in Rome. Like knowing how to draw a map of Portugal when you're seven or eight years old. Joey never got that—never got an intellectual word in his life until it was too late, until he was trapped in it.

"Even in jail, who did he have to talk to for nine fucking years? Niggers? Would some fucking smart greaseball go up to him and talk about the niceties of human existence? Did those conversations happen? Bullshit. Prison's got to do with straight-out basic survival. If you deal with it twenty-four hours a day, day in, day out, you've got nothing else to think about—just the every-fucking-day brutality of survival. Those are the kind of people you're dealing with—brutal people. No chance. Not your fault or my fault or society's fault—it's got to do with the self-fulfillment these guys never had. They can only get gratification through an outward act, not an inward act.

"Is that too nebulous? It's the difference between a gangster and a good criminal. Gangsters *love* to see their pictures in the paper. That used to amaze me. They used to buy the paper—I mean, come with the fucking papers. Clippings. Scrapbooks. 'Look at me. This is show biz, baby.' Bullshit. It's funny, but it's tragically funny. People are really suffering and dying for it. I wrote about that, too:

> The world is filled with
> sounds of despair, but
> none can compare
> with the clang of the
> closing steel door
> that separates a man
> from the living.
>
> Somebody dies all the time.
> I hope it's never me.
> They got to go, I guess,
> So things that were will be.
>   Z.

"I always watched these guys from afar. The dues I would have had to pay even for the knowledge of what they did would have been too high for me. I never hurt anybody, so why would I want the reputation of hanging out with guys that did? I'm the dancer, remember? I like to have a good time.

"An Italian is very noticeable, whether he's blond or bald or blue-eyed or brown-eyed. You can tell an Italian. They move different. When they're trying to explain something to you, they move different. People nail you right off the bat, that you're a dumb greaseball. So you carry it past that. It's not enough to be a calm greaseball gangster. You really have to be a showy greaseball gangster.

"A Jewish gangster can do it with a pair of glasses, a pinstripe suit and a briefcase. He can go rip off jewelry companies by writing orders. Send it to this address. Give me thirty-day billing. Fifteen days he's gone. Good Jewish boys have been doing that forever. But if a greaseball tries to do what a Jewish boy does, with the same words and the same attitude—oh boy! I used to have Jewish partners, man. They'd be in the joint, they'd have the fucking jewels on the counter, they'd be showing them the jewels, and then *I'd* walk in, right? And right away they're shoving the stuff in the safe and closing it up. 'Hey, wait a minute, Mr. Solomon,' the guys would say. 'This is our partner.' 'No deal. No deal. It's no deal.' It got so the Jewish guys would look at me and say, 'Listen, kid. Don't come in no more. We'll cut it up, maybe eighty-twenty, but do us a favor—don't come in no more.'

"You got to be a hard-rock gangster. You can't be the suave, con-man type. I'm supposed to be sinister—almost an Arab. It's back-alley. People will always look at Italians as back-alley. Walking into a fence with a hot piece of merchandise, you're still going to get the shitty end of the stick because you're a fucking greaseball. Italians are back-alley unless they play the game completely by the rules and are very obsequious and nice subservient people. If they play the game very tight, they can work their way up to be bank president. But I can't be a sneak. Fuck you. And I can't be a con man, so I got to do hard-rock crime. It comes easy because you're pushed there. There's a necessity to slip and slide because you're disdained from both ends.

"That's the reason for organized crime. These people are understood by their own. It's a way to go. Clean—amongst your own people, see. But it's the same job. You still got to work your way up and show respect. The parents of Italian kids keep it going. They're intrigued by any story about the mobs. They buy magazines about it. They'll avidly read about killings. 'Oh, look at this—another guy found in a trunk in the Bronx, Dad. Hey, do you know this guy? Found with his pockets turned inside out and his eyelids slit. What does it mean when the eyelids are slit, Dad?' The kid is exposed very early. Joey was. Joey couldn't be happy inside himself, so he got trapped.

"But Joey was different. With him, there was no braggadocio about it. There was no forcing you to like him or overpowering you with his charm. It was almost like he overpowered you with his humility. 'Hey, nice to see you. How are you?' Meanwhile, what's going on in his brain—'I got to talk to these fucking assholes'? They're not around any more, guys like him. He looked after his people. He had the aura of a winner. He had their respect because they knew they were in the presence of somebody who would win if they challenged him.

"The best place to learn about that is when you get locked up in a canary cage. Nobody knows you, and you got twenty-five cells on your tier. When they open up the cell doors at eight o'clock in the morning, you got nothing to do but sit in your cell or walk up and down your fucking tier for the twelve-hour period while the doors are open. You got to know right then and there whether you're a winner or a loser. And *they* know it. It's the way you walk. It's the way you handle yourself. It's the way you walk up to a guy and say, 'Hey. You got a cigarette?' You got to do six to eight months inside before you know whether you can do time. Jail is made for those who are comfortable there, just as hell or heaven is. If you're not comfortable, don't do anything to get yourself into a spot like that. Break the law, sure, but leave a margin for safety, because once you go past five years, you're a dead duck.

"When I heard Joey was coming out, I just knew there was going to be a great problem in adjusting to what had happened all the time he was inside there. It's just like me going to the mountains and becoming a hermit and sitting by the side of the stream and thinking the world is peachy and creamy and everything is beautiful. All you have to do is agree with somebody and get something going for you and catch a fish every once in a while and throw it in the frying pan. . . . But that ain't the way it is. He fought horrible battles inside there.

"I told Jeffie there was no way he could get away, no way. The world progresses at the same rate when you're in jail, but you don't.

You're a dead man. You lie dead in there. You lose all contact with reality. Jeffie became nonexistent. His mother, brothers—everybody became nonexistent. The only important thing was getting out of there. So the world really stops for you. Everything outside is peachy and creamy. Everything out there is beautiful. But what happens? He gets out after nine fucking years and finds he's lost his place on the shitpile. He can't find it and doesn't want it. So he gets himself shot.

"And what happens when you're shot? You're the maddest motherfucker in the world. There ain't no motherfucker in the world that's going to do that to you and get away with it. So he won't go down. There are those that are hit and don't fall down. He's dead, but he keeps going. He's getting away from the humiliation of being dead. He wouldn't let the motherfuckers see him laying down. Not for a minute. No chance.

"So I wrote a poem for him:

> Whatever happened to what's-his-name?
> You know the one I mean—
> The guy who ran that funny game.
> He always had a scheme—
> From running numbers to becoming one.
> Best of all, it looked like fun.
> Nobody liked this what's-his-name,
> So strong his search for fame.
> He played and stayed just long enough.
> He took from those who gave.
> A man remembered always—the slave.
> A tie of white with shoes of alligator—a slave.
> To what? To scheming.
> Good-bye to what's-his-name.
> At last I see him clearly, somehow, even dearly.
> Better not to ask, What's his name?
> Forget it. A mask, that's all. A mask.
> Z."

7

Jeffie

After her abortion, Jeffie went to lay up with Joyce and Al Lettieri on West Thirtieth Street. This was natural enough, for Joyce was her closest friend, and her apartment was the first place Joey would try if he wanted her back. But she also needed to rest. The pregnancy had been four months advanced, and she was still bleeding heavily.

Joey found her in a matter of hours. First, he telephoned, but Jeffie refused to speak to him. Then he told Joyce he was coming over to talk to her, and Joyce, pregnant herself and alone in the house with Jeffie, nervously phoned Al to come home.

Joey arrived ahead of him, none too pleased that Joyce, whom he also counted as a friend, had taken Jeffie's part against him. Ignoring her warnings that she didn't want to talk to him, he insisted on going into the spare room to see her, thereby touching off one of Jeffie's more spectacular displays of temperament. She screamed and howled, accused him of making her lose the baby—even afterward, she never dared confess to the abortion—and generally worked herself up to such a pitch of bawling fury that he retreated for fear she might do herself an injury. Returning to the living room, he sat down and waited for three days, while Joyce passed messages back and forth.

On the third day, he won. She packed her bag and went back with him to Eleventh Street. But it was only a partial victory. Although she loved him, she could see no future for them together, and told him so. It was a question of self-preservation. She wanted him out of her apartment, and when he refused to go, they fought bitterly. Then an incident occurred at the Arpeggio which confirmed all her fears and she ran away again, this time subleasing the apartment to jazz singer Annie Ross, who happened to be in town for a three-week nightclub engagement.

Joey had taken her to the Arpeggio for a big family get-together. About twenty people sat down at a long table in the middle of the room for a loud, jovial evening of eating, drinking, stories and conversation that went on until around 5 A.M., when the club closed. Everyone was a little drunk by then, including Jeffie, who carefully negotiated the stairs to the cloakroom and there found one of the boys, in even worse shape, struggling to get into his coat. Having sorted him out, she then allowed him to help her on with hers, which resulted in a tangle that reduced them both to tears of laughter. "Jesus," she gasped, brushing the hair out of his eyes. "You're *really* smashed." Then she went down with him to rejoin Joey and Ali Baba, and they all drove home together in the same car. When it stopped outside their building on Eleventh Street, Jeffie got out, expecting Joey to follow, but instead, without looking at her, he told Ali Baba he would wait for him while he took her up. Though disappointed at this anticlimax to a thoroughly enjoyable evening, she went upstairs obediently and straight to bed.

Some time later, she woke to find him sitting by her feet in his hat and coat. He looked sad and remote, but she was too sleepy to think about it then. "Jeffie," he said, and his tone also puzzled her when she thought about it later, "Jeffie, do you *really* love me?"

"Of course I do, baby. Come to bed."

"Listen, Jeffie. Do you think I'm crazy?"

"Sure—a little. Why not?" She went back to sleep.

Next day, he didn't talk to her. She figured he was in one of his moods. The day after that, he didn't talk to her either. He went out and came back, very late, without a word. By the third day, the silence was getting on her nerves. "What's the matter?" she demanded. "Is something wrong? What did I do now?"

"You don't know?" he said coldly.

"No. I don't know."

"*You* know. Think about it."

She thought about it and, by the fourth day, was decidedly angry. "Listen," she said. "I've had it with this silent treatment. Have I done something? What have I done? If you don't want to talk, rap once for yes, twice for no."

He looked at her seriously for several seconds, and she was suddenly frightened, not *of* him, for there was nothing threatening in his expression, but, in an unaccountable way, *for* him.

"Jeffie," he said quietly. "You know what you did."

"No. Honestly, baby. What did I do?"

He shook his head. "Then you must have been very drunk the other night."

"What?" She was genuinely taken aback, for that had seemed to be one of their good times. "Well, yes, I guess I was—a little."

"It's not only me," he said. "My whole family saw you."

"Saw *what*, baby?"

"Saw you kiss that guy in the cloakroom. In front of everybody."

He seemed to be beseeching her to give him an explanation for it that he could accept so that he could forgive her and forget about it, but her surprise was so great that this, too, only dawned on her afterward. "*What?*" she said. "*That* greasy pig? *Kiss* him? I never —I—I—what are you *talking* about?"

With that, his expression turned bleak and closed again. "Okay," he said. "If that's the way you want it. But my mother saw you. And my brother saw it. So don't tell me you don't know what you did."

It was some time before she recovered sufficiently from her astonishment to piece together an explanation for this extraordinary occurrence. Though she had certainly taken a good deal of wine that evening, she remembered the cloakroom incident very clearly, and, drunk or sober, nothing in the world could ever have induced her to embrace the man in question. He was very unattractive. Equally clearly, she recognized that Joey was no less convinced that she *had* done so. It was not a question of his making up this story simply to torment her; he truly believed he had seen it happen. That was frightening enough, but as the days went by and he continued her punishment by silence, she began to realize that more hung upon the outcome than simply establishing the truth of the matter. She had no doubt of his love for her even now, but, at the same time, she knew he resented his feelings of dependence on her. Could his delusion, then, be some kind of unconscious device for branding her as a tramp and justifying his getting rid of her? Maybe even killing her? And having had this delusion, was it necessary for him to believe in it absolutely or else know himself to be insane?

To Jeffie, the fact that Joey hadn't killed her proved that his love outweighed his resentment, and this was a source of pride in spite of her fear. But there was no way around the second question. If she was right, to convince him of his delusion would be to prove he was crazy, and even if that were possible, she loved him too much to do it. So she "confessed." Yes, she *had* kissed the guy. It hadn't meant a thing. It was a drunken impulse when he made her laugh, but she was deeply ashamed and could he ever forgive her? He forgave her at once, although she had a hunch he knew she was lying. He became as warm and loving as he had been cold and aloof only moments before. It was as though the siege had never been. But Jeffie now needed time to think, and the first chance she got, she fled. Swearing Joyce and Jean Lerner to secrecy, she hid out with Lyn Morgen in her apartment a few blocks away on Eighth Street.

When Joey realized she had gone again, he again did the rounds of the people she knew, and, drawing a blank, made snap visits after that in the hope of catching her unawares. For a man involved in the opening phase of a gang war and harassed more or less continuously by the police, he seemed to her friends remarkably patient in dealing with this latest aberration. One evening, he called at Joyce's apartment and found Jean Lerner there. After both had denied all knowledge of Jeffie's whereabouts, he stayed on to chat for an hour or two, sharing a piece of hash, and eventually took Jean home, where he spent the rest of the night on her sofa as it was snowing too heavily for him to make it back to Brooklyn. Next morning, Jean was awakened by the telephone, and found Joey had gone. Picking up the receiver, she was roundly harangued for several minutes by a furious Jeffie, who had learned from Joyce that Joey had taken her home the night before and had instantly assumed the worst. Unconvinced by Jean's indignant denials, Jeffie slammed down the phone and stamped around from Lyn Morgen's apartment to her own on Eleventh Street, which Annie Ross had just vacated. Ten minutes later, there was a ring at the door, and when she opened it, Joey walked in, furious at having had to waste so much time and effort finding her.

Jeffie was angry, too, but also upset, because in that ten minutes Olga had called from Los Angeles to say that her beloved Ralphie, Jeffie's latest and favorite stepfather, had died. Overwhelmed by the shock, by Joey's sudden appearance and all the painful confusion of the previous weeks, she crumpled up and cried. At this, Joey took charge, shifting moods, as always, from one extreme to another without so much as a pause for breath. He would go with her to California and take care of everything. All she had to do was pack their bags while he made the arrangements.

That night, he stretched out on the bed beside her with his hands behind his head staring at the ceiling. They were due to leave for the airport in a few hours, but neither could sleep.

"Say, listen—you remember that guy at the club?" he said, breaking a long silence. "The guy you were fooling around with?"

Jeffie propped herself up on one elbow. "Now don't you start with me," she said warily, although he had sounded casual enough. "We're all through with that. I don't want to hear about it."

"No, listen—he's dead. I forgot to tell you."

There was a moment before she could speak. "He's what?"

"Yeah. Last night," he went on chattily. "He had a terrible accident on the bridge. His car went out of control."

Now she knew why he had spent the night with Joyce and Jean. The dead man was nothing to her, hardly worth a thought. When guys like him killed one another, for whatever real or mistaken reason, that was the name of their game. What terrified her was that her "confession" had not been enough. Though Joey had forgiven her, it had left his delusion intact, and, consciously or not, sooner than doubt his own sanity he had acted it out to the last. The devil had had to be exorcised. She fell back helplessly. "Are you satisfied *now?*"

"What are you talking about?" he said. He sounded genuinely puzzled. "That's a terrible thing. He was a nice guy."

Now Joey again wanted to marry her, and they wrangled about it all the way to California. Though she felt she would never again be free of him emotionally, Jeffie was determined to end it somehow. She now knew she was dealing with a man she could never hope to live with on equal terms. If they stayed together, she would have to yield to him as men had always had to yield to her, and she knew herself well enough to know she could only submit when it suited her. Stiffened by her new understanding of Joey, she made up her mind to wait him out in Los Angeles, knowing that sooner or later he would have to get back to Brooklyn. With that resolved, she could almost look forward to the first encounter between Queen Olga and Prince Joey.

To her astonishment, they adored each other on sight. Indeed, Jeffie felt almost left out. "From the moment he came into my mother's apartment on Franklin Avenue, he just kind of took over and became the man of the house. She was very impressed with him. She saw his strength and found him very magnetic. I said, 'Ma, will you stop kissing him? He's killing me. Stop thinking he's so wonderful. He's not so wonderful.'

"She was a very lovely, dignified, soft woman from another century who had no idea of how to be a mother. Joey saw who she was at once and gave her credit for it, while I was only contemptuous of what I saw. They were both very gracious to each other and he chided me for my attitude toward her. They had a great understanding on what I considered to be a very unrealistic level.

"Then came the funeral. Natalie Kalmus was there, and all those wealthy, well-bred, social, Pan-American League ladies, and when he walked in, I thought, 'Oh God, it's coming in with that hat. I can't cope with the hat. What am I gonna do?' But he charmed them. This whole roomful of frilly ladies. This guy with the hat. He had them going pant, pant, pant. He *captured* them. I was walking around in a daze saying, 'I don't *believe* these people.' They were mesmerized. Not by his reputation or anything, because nobody in my mother's circle in California had ever heard of him. He just made them all flutter as women. And he's smiling at me one minute and choking me the next because now we have to go home right away and get married, and I don't want to get married.

"Meanwhile, he's sleeping in the living room and I'm sleeping with my mother in the bedroom because I didn't want to be with him. For three nights he let me stay with her, but finally he got sick of it, walked in and took me right out of my mother's bed. 'Come on,' he says. 'Come on. You come over here and sleep where you belong.' He made me go sleep with him on the floor of the living room. And my mother, who wouldn't know a prick if she was eating it with a knife and fork, absolutely accepted this. She was startled, but she knew we had been living together and couldn't understand why I was putting up all this fuss. She respected him. She recognized something in him I did not think she was capable of recognizing. She was very pleased that I had a strong man."

Olga was also impressed with Joey's evident importance around town. When he took her to dinner with Jeffie at the Quo Vadis, the management literally rolled out the red carpet for him and gave them the full, Hollywood-style celebrity treatment. And when he heard that Uncle Juan, the Cuban husband of Olga's sister Ilma, was out of work, he found him a job at another fashionable Italian restaurant, the Villa Capri. Aunt Ilma, who met Joey for the first and only time at the funeral, thought this was very nice, but did not consider him a suitable match for Jeffie, who was "so beautiful at that time. My sister had such hopes for her, for a good marriage to a man of position from a good family. But there was nothing to be done. Jeffie was so madly, madly in love with him.

"We had no idea at all of who he was. He didn't have the appearance of a tough guy. He was small and quiet, and very polite and charming at the funeral. He wanted to know all about the family and its background, and he was very impressed, as naturally he would be, a person like that. My father was a prominent diplomat, born in Costa Rica, educated in Spain and knighted with the Order of the Crown by the King of the Belgians. And so when we started reading about Joey in the papers, we couldn't believe it. The shock to the family was terrible. To this day I tremble when I talk about it.

"My sister was very brave, but I tried to warn her. I'm very intuitive—I'm a Libra, you see, and I don't make friends easily. I have to study a person before I extend them my friendship. On the day of the funeral, he went into the bathroom and left his jacket on the chair, and something came over me to look through his wallet. He had a driver's license in another name. This was very strange, I thought, so I told my sister."

Olga obviously did not find this sufficient grounds for ordering Joey out of the house, although she, too, was intimidated by Jeffie to the extent that she would often hide her true feelings rather than seem to interfere. But after a week of $50 or $60 phone calls daily to New York, Joey suddenly announced that he had to go back. He tried everything he knew, short of kidnaping, to persuade Jeffie to go with him, but she dug in her toes. No sooner had he left, however, than she was overcome with desolation.

Never a man to give up easily, Joey then called her every day from New York, wearing down her resolution, and two weeks later he was back again. She was at a friend's house when her mother phoned to say that he had arrived at the apartment, as usual without warning, asking to see her. This time, he was accompanied by Ali Baba, who, as soon as Jeffie saw him, served as a convenient lightning rod for all her pent-up frustrations. "I remember screaming, 'If I have to look at that man's face over the dinner table one more night, I'll throw up. Get him out of here.' Poor bastard. He looked so surprised it was comical. I guess I was getting at Joey as much as him, because if Joey loved anybody in the world apart from his brother Larry and me, it was Ali Baba. So once again we're into the usual silly kind of battles, and he and my mother are still being gracious to each other. He listens to all her radio-show tapes and wants to hear all about her aristocratic connections. In the end I told him, 'Why don't you marry *her* and leave me alone?'

"One morning, I went into the kitchen and there she was, cooking eggs, with him sitting at the table like he owned the place. Now she had never fed her husband—he died of a heart attack because he never ate—and here she is making eggs for a man I'm not even sure I want to be with. So I'm furious with both of them. I grab the frying pan out of her hand and throw it in the sink, and he looks at me like I've gone crazy. I'm screaming, 'Don't cook for him. You never fed me. You never fed your husband. Now all of a sudden you're going to start *cooking?*' I guess it must have spoiled his appetite because he went back to New York next day. And he never saw Olga again."

Though preoccupied with gang-war preliminaries, Joey kept up his daily barrage of phone calls. Finally, in an attempt to make her jealous, he threatened to marry some nice Italian girl if she didn't come home right away, and she hung up on him. A week later, she was back on Eleventh Street.

Jeffie now knew exactly what she was getting into. She could no longer blame him or, indeed, anyone but herself if it turned out badly. She had knowingly chosen to share the instability of his life and moods. "I had to accept who was boss and who was in power. Joey could always take over and manipulate anyone any way he wanted to, but my instincts told me that kings fall and nations crumble. I had to accept that, as he had been taken from me once before, he could also be taken from me again. This time, it really was with a full knowledge of what I was doing. I was going to take my shot, knowing I could be left alone at any time. I had finally made my commitment, the first and only one in my life.

"There was no advantage to either of us in being together except that we were right together. He once said to me, 'Jeffie, I was a virgin when I met you,' and I knew what he meant because I felt that, too. We had been born again in each other. Everything I was, he needed. Everything he was, I needed. Our neuroses matched perfectly. There was no money. I didn't need my name in the papers. I didn't need bloody bodies to my right and left, and I didn't need to be married to somebody famous. I've been around famous people since I was born and I'm not impressed—least of all by famous gangsters. But when Joey was playing the prince, he made me the princess. I was Cinderella. You had to experience him to know."

They were married at City Hall on April 6, 1961, Joey's thirty-second birthday. He had met her off the plane from Los Angeles the day before, and given her $2,000 as a wedding present. But now it was *his* turn for a display of temperament. Warm and loving, with all her decisions behind her, Jeffie found Joey increasingly cool and aloof as the hours went by toward the ceremony. They were staying overnight at Jean Lerner's apartment, but by the time they went to bed, neither had spoken to the other for some time. Still fully clothed, Joey silently stretched out on the bed and folded his hands behind his head. Jeffie eyed him for a moment, quivering with restraint, then laid herself down beside him, mimicking his attitude.

"So there we lay with our hands behind our heads and the corsage wilting in the fridge. All of a sudden he leaps out of bed and says, 'Give me some money.' So I gave him some money and he left. In the middle of the night. I went in to Jean and said, 'Jean, wake up. The groom has gone.' She says, 'Oh my God. What happened?' 'How the hell do *I* know?' I said. 'I'm only the fucking bride.' Then we tried to figure out what to do. In the end, I decided that I'd be ready, except that it wouldn't look like I was ready. Then if he came back to tell me the marriage was off, I wouldn't look like a total fool.

"We bit our fingernails all morning. Just as I've decided that he means to stand me up, in he comes with Ali Baba at about one-thirty. The wedding is at two. 'What's the matter?' he says. 'Didn't you think I was going to show?' 'Course I thought you would show,' I said, very calm and ladylike. 'I'll be ready in a minute.' And I was, but I could see he wasn't in a very good humor. So when Jean started gushing about, I said, 'Leave the fucking flowers in the refrigerator. This is no time to bring out the bridal bouquet.'

"We went silently downtown, and he ignored me through the whole ceremony. Afterward, he walked out with Jean and I walked out with Ali Baba, who had been the best man. Nobody else was there—none of his family nor any of the boys. Everybody disapproved of the whole thing, including me by this time. Anyway, we go to some restaurant, but nobody is celebrating anything—the marriage, his birthday . . . nothing. There are lots of guys around, but nobody talked to us the whole time. Everything was stony silence. Jean was looking at me, and I was looking at Jean and thinking, 'Holy *shit!*' Then finally this long, drab evening ended. When we came home to Eleventh Street, he turned to me and said, 'Well, now that you've got me, I hope you know it's an empty victory.' I started to laugh. Then we both fell about laughing and made love, and after that everything was marvelous."

Four days later, she was pregnant, and trying to mend bridges with his family. Jeffie maintains there was nothing personal in their boycott of the marriage, although nobody ever pretended to think that Joey had made a suitable match. It was just that the war had begun and they wanted him on President Street, undistracted by a demanding wife who had loudly proclaimed her intention of staying in Greenwich Village. Tony Bender, Joey's principal ally, who, to her delight, disappeared a year later in the hydraulic press of a New Jersey scrap-metal dealer's car-crusher, an engine of retribution she always gleefully refers to as a "Tony Bender Machine," had tried to dissuade him from marrying her by saying she had been a chorus girl in Vegas, as if that were unanswerable proof of depravity, and most of the boys had agreed with him.

The Gallo womenfolk, on the other hand, were less censorious, but they knew their place, which was at the other end of the room keeping their mouths shut. For weeks, everyone had sat tight, hoping Jeffie would go away, but once she was married, it was clearly no longer politic to ignore her, however much they may have disapproved of Joey's choice. A thaw set in. His grandmother, with whom he parked Jeffie when she drove him to President Street, was the first to hear she was pregnant, and from then on, she was more or less accepted as the maverick member of the family.

There were no such problems for Joey in joining Jeffie's circle. "He liked to be with my friends because he was free. Nothing was expected of him. Nobody thought he was a big deal. No one was impressed with his reputation. All his labels disappeared when we were out socially. If he could be himself, he didn't have to be in the center of everything. If somebody else was impressive, he would applaud longer and louder than anyone. Joey was a marvelous listener. When you spoke to him, he really listened to what you said. And there was nothing you couldn't say to him. You could attack him intellectually or even talk about insanity and he would never get angry. He enjoyed debate. If you could make your point, he would light up. If you could give him a new idea, he was excited by it. He really liked my people—he enjoyed knowing them. He was never forbidding. He was never Joey Gallo, tough guy. Our life together was very good again, just as it had been in the beginning."

Good, in Jeffie's terms, did not necessarily mean serene. Though she had yielded to Joey as the dominant partner in their marriage, it was a highly qualified surrender. She would abide by his decisions only if she approved of them. Mutual respect was her watchword, and if, on minor matters, she did sometimes give way against her better judgment, she would always make it clear to him that this was without prejudice. She was doing it, wasn't she? She didn't have to agree with him, too. Fortunately, they were of one mind about the raising of children.

"I was into Reich, and very aware of the difference between freedom and license. I was going to treat my child as I would treat any human being that I had respect for, and Joey was with me one hundred percent. We didn't believe in circumcision. We didn't believe in pinching babies, like the Italians do. People use children like toys. Both he and I had been manipulated since birth so we were in complete agreement. When the cord was cut, we would have another person in the house whose needs were as important as ours. I was going to nurse her—I thought that was important—and we were going to live on the basis of mutual respect. Without pinching. That was a big thing with Joey. He kept telling me, 'Don't let them pinch the kid.' Italians pinch babies until they're purple. While they're raving, 'Ah, my little darling,' the kid's screaming with pain. It's their way of showing love. And their way of teaching a kid how to survive is to put it up on a ledge, hold out their arms and say, 'Jump, bambino, jump.' When the kid jumps, they let it fall on its head. 'Ah! See? Remember. Don't trust nobody.' But Joey and I were going to have a nice, free human being that came from both of us, free of all the shit that we'd been stuffed with.''

This rejection of family convention came much easier to Jeffie, of course, who had been in open rebellion since childhood, than to Joey, whose background was narrowly conformist in everything but religion. For him, it required a conscious effort, first to become aware of the early conditioning he had undergone, and then, harder still, to rid himself of its effects. Living with Jeffie inevitably speeded up the process. "One of the people who used to join us at his table at the Luna was a priest named Brother Richard. He must have been a monk because he wore dresses. We used to tease him a lot and have fun with him, and he liked Joey. Joey was not religious, of course, because *he* was the superior spiritual being, but one night I'm sitting there with my belly having dinner and out of the blue he says, 'We got to baptize the kid.'

"I nearly choked. I said, *'What?'* He said, 'Yeah. We got to do that.' I said, 'What do you mean—baptize it? What for?' And he said, 'Well, you know, you got to have a paper to say your religion. Everybody's got to have that.' *'Why?'* I said. 'Who says so? You mean, when you go to jail? Well, forget it. If I have any control over it, I will never in a million years allow some schmuck to take my kid and dump it in water.' 'No,' he says. 'We got to have it baptized.' In his world, there were certain things you had to have before you could be respectable, and one of them was a baptism certificate.

"So I said, 'Joey, you've got to be putting me on.' 'No. It's got to have a paper.' 'Well,' I said, 'there must be a way to solve this. Why does it need a paper? Because it's going to hell if it dies?' 'No.' 'Because you want it to be Pope?' 'No.' 'So basically, what you're saying is you want a piece of paper that says Baby Gallo is a Catholic, right? That what you want?' 'Yeah,' he says. 'That's what I want.' 'Okay. Then call Brother Richard. He'll give you a paper. We'll give him $50 and a bottle of booze and he'll give us a paper—okay? Why do I have to put the kid through a dumb ceremony?' 'Oh,' he said. 'All right.' He thought that was a reasonable compromise, and it was the last I ever heard of it. I know how these things are. I was brought up a Catholic myself. I had a bar mitzvah and everything."

The first sign of real trouble came in May, when Joey was arrested on the extortion charge and held for three weeks in the Tombs while his lawyers tried to make bail. This brought the precariousness of the life she had chosen into still sharper focus, but he treated it as casually as a parking ticket and she allowed him to calm her fears. Indeed, the only time she ever saw him show any concern about what was happening in his own world, away from Eleventh Street, was when the Profaci mob tried to kill Larry.

"We were going to his sister Jacqueline's house that Sunday afternoon, and we were halfway down the stairs when I remembered the electric kettle we were supposed to be bringing her as a gift. We went back up to get it and the phone was ringing. It was Larry warning Joey to get out because they would try to kill him, too. Anyway, as we left for the second time, the cops were coming up the stairs and they took us to the 6th Precinct station in the Village. He told me to wait in the car while he went inside with them, and later on, somebody came out and drove me home. They were going to hold him as a material witness, they said, but next day Leibowitz let him go. And now Joey wasn't playing any more. This was serious. They'd touched his family, and he had to get even for that."

Jeffie still knew no more about his affairs than what she read almost every day in the papers. He was obviously in danger, but as there was nothing she could do, either to alter the situation or influence him, she preferred not to think about it. The only difference she felt personally was that he now spent a little less time with her. Apart from that, life went on as before, with neither of them taking any special precautions. He kept a loaded rifle in the bedroom and never traveled alone, but Jeffie came and went as she pleased, unescorted, and they continued to dine out most nights on Mulberry Street.

"Joey was able to use every moment of his life to the fullest. After the attempt on Larry, winning the war became the most important thing in his life, and yet he was still able to cut it off and be with me and in love, into the baby and into loving. I could have eight hours a day of that. He never gave up our life together—he was totally consumed by it. That didn't mean that twenty minutes later he couldn't be totally consumed by something else, but I knew that now. If he was moody when he came in, I knew it had nothing to do with me, and I could always get him out of it."

Even so, his awareness of the danger they were in ran always close to the surface. One night, as he reminded Jeffie in the letter from Attica, a mirror fell off the wall of their bedroom and smashed to the floor while they were sleeping. "Joey sprang from the bed right out of the window—in one leap. I couldn't quite understand why anybody would do this, but it seemed that if somebody was breaking in to attack you, the best thing to do was to attack them first and throw them off balance. So he went zooming right out of the window onto the fire escape—stark-naked. Can't imagine what the neighbors thought. And there was I, still sitting in bed with the covers pulled up. Typical movie scene. When I stopped being frightened, I thought it was kind of funny."

This was the only frightening moment Jeffie can remember in the three months between the attempt on Larry's life and the start of Joey's trial—apart from a general sense of foreboding that kept breaking through no matter how hard she tried to ignore it. At least part of the reason for this was that the police were now following them almost everywhere. "We'd usually tell them where we were going and then proceed to lose them, which would drive them crazy, but we'd always wind up where we'd said we'd be. At other times, they would come to the house and want to take him in for questioning. They'd ring the bell around noon, and I'd go into the bedroom and tell him so-and-so is at the door and what should I do? He'd say, 'Have them come in,' and I'd make them coffee while he got dressed. They were very polite. They would always stand up when I came in the room. He seemed to be on good terms with them, so it was all very nice."

By now, Jeffie was so conspicuously pregnant that she could no longer manage the four long flights of stairs at Eleventh Street. With Jean Lerner's help, she began looking around the Village for another apartment, and eventually settled for one with a garden and a rear exit into the mews, at 20 West Eighth Street. Jean also helped her move in, and Joey said he would, too. He broke off from the war and drove in from Brooklyn with Ali Baba and one of the boys to give them a hand. The three picked up one piece each of Jeffie's hi-fi equipment, carried it out and disappeared. When Jean tottered downstairs some time later with a carton of books, she found them leaning against their car, talking. "Crazy Joe?" she said breathlessly. "*Crazy* Joe? They ought to call you *Lazy* Joe."

Money was now very tight. According to Joey, his mother had mortgaged her house and sold off the furniture to pay for bail bonds and lawyers. There was certainly nothing to spare for interior decorators, even if Jeffie had wanted one, and so she fixed the place up for $100, humping her belly around the neighborhood auction houses for bits and pieces she knew would please him. "He loved all the little things I got. It just seemed that everything either of us did turned the other one on. We were closer than ever. But the trial was coming up, and I kept reminding him that fourteen years of his life were at stake and he'd better do something about it. But he just pooh-poohed it away. He figured the lawyers would take care of that end of the business. He didn't want to be bothered. He was going to do what his lawyers told him to do at each point. But they were in despair because he wouldn't give them the time they needed to prepare a proper defense. I knew it was wrong, but he wouldn't listen. He was much more involved with Larry and the group than he was with his own trial.

"Every night, he would go to sleep with his head on my belly, feeling the baby. We'd all be in the bed together—me, the baby, Joey and Lepke the dog. It was a lovely family. He made contact with his child that way. It made him very excited. We never discussed the future. Our future was hour by hour. We had no future."

8

Joyce, Jean and Lyn

Joyce and Jeffie were both nineteen when they met; both had a marriage behind them, and both were looking for answers before they had framed their questions. Not much given to introspection, but sensing the same dissatisfactions in each other, they teamed up, ready to try almost anything in hopes of stumbling across the good life. As fair as Jeffie was dark, and built like the torch singer she later became, Joyce had started out as a child movie actress, but her career had run down to occasional bit parts, which she eked out by working as a photographer at the Coconut Grove, almost directly across the street from the Haig, where Jeffie was a cocktail waitress and Gerry Mulligan the resident attraction. Joyce was then in love with his trumpet player, Chet Baker, and got to know Jeffie while hanging out there every night after finishing work around twelve. They saw each other through several crises, including the break-up of Jeffie's brief and inexplicable marriage to Mulligan, and then, still trying to discover themselves, set out together to drive across country to New York in their tiny Hillman Minx. When it broke down about a hundred miles out of town, they were delayed for a week by a fatherly mechanic with seven unmarried sons.

All went smoothly after that, however, and with a ready-made circle of friends from the jazz world, they settled in quickly. Before long, Joyce found what she was looking for—at the San Remo Restaurant in Greenwich Village, where Al Lettieri was working as a waiter while he tried to decide which he was, writer or actor. After going together for a couple of months, Al moved in and Jeffie moved out, still restless, still dissatisfied, and the two girls then rather lost touch with each other. Joyce and Al moved back to Hollywood, while Jeffie virtually commuted between Las Vegas, New York and Los Angeles. Arriving in California to spend the Christmas of 1959 with her family, she called Joyce, who was now working as a singer, and walked in "looking absolutely smashing in a beautiful gray Italian dress. I said, 'I love that dress.' And Jeffie said, 'Come back to New York and I'll give it to you.' So we went back to New York." She and Al were bored with Los Angeles, and looking for an excuse to leave. Joyce went on ahead to stay with Jeffie on Eleventh Street, while Al closed up the house and drove across country with their things.

Jeffie was then busy with Jean Lerner on the supper club project, and as Joyce and Al had both worked for Lucky Pierre in the past, she took Joyce uptown to reintroduce her. "He had this marvelous little place off Fifth Avenue. It was a restaurant in front, and in back he had a little room with a grand piano and couches and overstuffed chairs. There was no heat—he had Sterno in the corners—and Con Edison had disconnected the electric supply, so there were candles everywhere. But it had a marvelously intimate atmosphere, and when Lucky Pierre said, 'Do you want to go to work?' I said, 'Yeah.' I knew I wouldn't get paid, but at least you ate, and if you really needed twenty dollars, he'd give you twenty dollars. It was great."

Joyce and Al had previously met Ali Baba through Lucky Pierre, whose clientele ranged from "the highest strata of society to the biggest bums in the world. Ali had a real flair for the dramatic. He was very vital, very energetic and alive, and had a lovely glow about him. He once said, 'I've been everywhere on earth—I've seen everything—and New York is the greatest country in the world.' He would come visit us with pastries, because he knew I loved baklava, and we would sit and smoke and he would tell me stories. Once he took us to a marvelous hashish party up at a mad doctor's, who was very much into seaweed and who I heard later was doing bad things to people with adrenalin. It was a big, midtown apartment—very safe —and Ali put the bandanna around his head, set the big water pipe in the middle and blew to get it really going until the room was in a pall of smoke. He loved the ceremony. We enjoyed each other very much."

It was natural, then, that he should call at Jeffie's to welcome them back the night after Al arrived from California, and Joyce was only mildly surprised when he returned the next evening with a friend. "Joey came in first, with his big hat and his overcoat, his slicked-back hair and his mole. When he saw us, he stopped, kind of cocked his head and grinned. He had a funny kind of a mouth and a beaky, birdlike look. I didn't find him attractive at all. In fact, he looked peculiar—his mommy dressed him funny. But he had a sort of stage presence. He came on like an energy field that popples and crackles. It was strong and vibrant, very piercing and direct. And right away I knew he was a danger to Jeffie, because I sensed a change in her. He was someone she couldn't dominate. Jeffie's on top of most men she meets right away, but as soon as I saw him, I knew she would never be on top of Joey. Not that either of us had the least idea who he was, but he had caught her off-guard. She was flustered, and that doesn't happen very often.

"It was Ali, in his affection and warmth for us, who made the connections and brought down the usual barriers between strangers. 'I wanted my people to meet my people,' he said, and I could see he really loved Joey. You could tell by the way he looked at him, and he was so respectful. Anyway, Jeffie put on some records and made coffee, and Ali brought out a nice piece of hash and we started to smoke and talk about music and it turned into a very nice evening.

Joey understood music, he *felt* it, in a way that isn't usual, except among musicians. Then, all of a sudden, Jeffie retreated—which is something she does do. When she feels like going to sleep, she goes to sleep. But this time, I knew she did it because of Joey. There was something about him she couldn't handle. He unsettled her. She wasn't in control of the situation, and it wasn't because he was forceful. We had known many strong-willed, egotistical guys— Gerry Mulligan had thought he had the voice of Christ in his horn. It was just that Joey could see into her secret hiding places. He really scared her as a woman."

The next person to sense the current passing between Jeffie and Joey, well before either of them acknowledged it to the other, was Jean Lerner. One night, after working late at their would-be supper club, Jeffie took her in to meet Joey at the Arpeggio. "We went there in our dirty dungarees and dirty hair and dirty fingernails from all the hammering and painting and scraping and cleaning, and I was introduced to this man, and I said to myself, 'My God. Jeffie's in love. In the most feminine, romantic way.' Couldn't believe it. Jeffie wasn't that kind of lady. She was armored—nothing could touch her. But suddenly something *had* touched her and the transformation was amazing. She had turned into a mouse. And *he* was in love with *her,* that was obvious. I could have been dishwater for all the notice they took of me, which I rather resented. There was always this competition between me and Jeffie. To which dark lady do you go? This one had already gone. It's not unusual to see a lady go, 'Ahhhh . . .' But when you feel a man do the same thing, when a man doesn't see anything but the lady he's talking to, that's important. I was piqued, but happy for her.

"Jeffie had never been in love before. She didn't know about giving and relinquishing. She was not as heavy as she is now, but there was always a bit of the street urchin in her, the tough guy. And now suddenly for her to blossom into this flower, into the complete antithesis of what she had always believed herself to be . . . Couldn't believe it. She'd let it all go. He just had to say, 'Come along, little girl,' and that would be that. He was a knight in shining armor come to rescue her."

Now Jean had to find out who he was, this man with whom her very dear friend was in love, and the first clue was Ali Baba. She had met him years before she and Jeffie had worked together in Las Vegas, and formed quite the opposite opinion of him to Joyce's. In those days, Jean had been living with Gabriel Dell, one of the Dead End Kids, to whom "the freaks of the world seemed naturally to gravitate. I was an innocent, wide-eyed child until I met Ali Baba one day in a restaurant in Brooklyn. We took one look at each other, and he scared the life out of me. *'Who* is that ripe little, plump little, innocent little *plum?'* Gabe saw I was frightened, so I was never exposed to that world again, but after all those years, Jeffie drags me in to meet Joey, and there's Ali. And he's like Joey's uncle.

"Later on, when I got to know them better, he and Joey always made a big ha-ha-ha about how he had frightened me that time. But whenever I got Joey alone, I would say to him, 'What are you doing with that terrible man?' And he would say, 'Come on, Jean, leave him alone. This is my friend, my uncle, my father—don't you put him down.' But there was a guy I felt would do *anything.*"

Some of the things Ali Baba would do were described to the police by Sidney Slater, who seems to have shared Jean's assessment of his character, although, as an informer and, for a time, a codefendant with Ali in Joey's extortion case, he was hardly an impartial witness. "Ali Waffa wasn't very good with a gun or a knife," he said, "but he sure was good with his head. I mean he had the hardest head in the world. Sometimes when Joey was feeling good and if we were all at some friendly bar, he'd say, 'Get a hunk of two-inch plank. I'll bet three to one Ali can break it with his head.' There was always some sucker there who figured that Joey Gallo was loaded, and they'd put their dough on the line. Someone would dig up a plank of wood and damned if Ali Waffa wouldn't run at it and split it right down the middle with his head every time.

"I've also seen Joey give him the nod to hit some creep, and even if the creep had a gun in his hand, this crazy Egyptian would run at him, butt him in the belly with that iron head and the guy would be out like a light with maybe three broken ribs. Ali Waffa did a lot of dirty work for Joey but never got paid much. This dopey Egyptian really figured it was a great honor to work as Joey Gallo's body-guard."

Another one who regarded Ali as dangerous and contemptible—and Joey more so—was Jeffie's friend Lyn Morgen. She recoiled from Joey as her refugee parents might have recoiled from an invitation to Berchtesgaden. Gangsters were Fascists, lice on the body politic, parasites destructive of everything decent in society, and the fact that Jeffie had taken up with one caused her little surprise. "I loved Jeffie. She was like my sister—my disturbed, erratic sister who was always attracted to anything antisocial. Joey was a killer, but he was Jeffie's killer, and I figured everybody had a right to go to hell in their own way. I thought she was a lunatic, but I love her."

Twelve years her senior, Lyn had taken to Jeffie on sight. Eddie Jaffe, the Broadway press agent, had called her toward the end of 1958 to say that he was thinking of getting married to a girl he had met in Las Vegas, and did she have room to put her up for a while in her house on Eleventh Street? "I said, 'Sure, send her over,' and Jeffie shows up, very pretty and appealing, and also very funny. She explained that the real reason she wanted to marry Eddie was be-cause she loved the idea of being called Jeffie Jaffe. Adored her for that. Another reason was that she hated tall men. She couldn't bear to look up to any man. She had to meet them eye to eye, literally and figuratively on the same level, which I guess is one of the things that attracted her to Joey.

"Anyway, there was the future Jeffie Jaffe in our house, and now Georgia Brown moves in with her. I remember they used to sit around a lot, which made me mad because I was the only one working. Selling lamps. It was a stinking job, but somebody had to buy the food, and I was it. Once I cooked some chicken and left the dirty pot full of water because I had to go to work, and nobody touched it for three days. In the end, I threw it at Georgia."

Shortly after this, Lyn and her husband, Rick Morgen, had to sell the house because they couldn't keep up with the mortgage pay-ments, and moved to 63 East Eleventh Street, where, by chance, an apartment for Jeffie fell vacant at the same time on the top floor. To enable her to pay the rent, Lyn also found Jeffie a job as a night-shift

Joyce, Jean and Lyn **127**

switchboard operator at Raymond's Exclusive Telephone Answering Service, and for a time the two were, indeed, like sisters, sharing confidences and spending a good deal of time in each other's company. Then the Morgens moved again, to a house on Eighth Street, and although they heard about Joey over the telephone, they didn't actually meet him until he had moved in with Jeffie. Unlike her other friends, Rick knew exactly who he was, but he was still astonished.

"When I saw him, I said to myself, 'Oh my God—*really?*' Here was this little guy with the big mole on his face, a dese-dems-and-doser, and dressed like a freak. He was George Raft in a 1937 gangster movie—the white on white shirt, the white on white tie, the whole bit. Would have been laughable if he weren't so dangerous. But this one was a snake. He was a rotten little guy, and I sensed it right away. I never felt his famous magnetism. I never found him attractive or glamorous or interesting. Only boring, tiresome and frightening. He was a power-driven shrimp with a Napoleonic complex, and I don't like violence and strong-arm tactics. I don't even think he was capable of any real emotion. The world existed only for him. But he was Jeffie's guy, and Jeffie was my friend. If this is what she was so hung up on, then okay."

In fact, they had very little to do with him, then or later. Lyn saw him perhaps six or eight times in all, always in a crowd, and never long enough to get past her prejudgment of Joey to Joey himself. Had she done so, there would still have been no great sympathy between them, but she might have understood his fascination for Jeffie a little better. As it was, she had primed herself to meet a crude and illiterate hoodlum, and that was all she saw. Sensing her antipathy, Jeffie made only a halfhearted attempt to include her in their circle, and abandoned even that after a conversation she had with Lyn soon after Robert Kennedy's book *The Enemy Within* was published in 1960.

"I remember we were walking down University Place with Jean, heading for the bookstore to pick up a copy, and Jeffie said, 'You know, it's too bad Joey feels he's got to play Robin Hood. Those schmucks—what does he need them for? He was doing fine as a shylock.' And my back went right up. 'Listen, Jeffie,' I said. 'To me, shylocks are one of the biggest menaces we got in this country. The shylock's an exploiter and a thief and a cheat. I hate them. They prey on poor people.' But she didn't even know what I was talking about, so the subject was dropped. I didn't want to hurt her. If Jeffie didn't believe he was Robin Hood, she couldn't live with it. But to us, Joey was a caricature, and, knowing the way we felt, she didn't count us in after that when he was around. I never took offense because we had no desire to see him. In her head, I guess she thought we didn't understand or didn't relate to what was going on—we belonged to a different generation. So she surrounded herself with people who shared her fantasy, who wanted to see what *she* saw for *her* sake."

Though neither Jeffie nor Jean has any recollection of Lyn's attack on shylocks, Jeffie readily accepts her account of the incident, dismissing the remark that provoked it as a mild joke that misfired. If so, it was well in keeping with her wry, often self-wounding, style of humor—and she is not the sort, in any case, to draw moral distinctions between moneylenders. But she strenuously rejects the suggestion that her other friends allowed themselves to be deluded about Joey for her sake, and so do they, priding themselves on an almost hurtful honesty with one another, which they see as the truest test of friendship. Jeffie, Jean and Joyce share a consciously skeptical view of human pretensions; they are looking for people to fail. To falsify their feelings about Joey in order to abet Jeffie's self-deception would be considered not only a disservice to her but lacking in respect. To abandon an honest view would earn them nothing but contempt.

Besides, Joyce and Jean became friends of Joey's in their own right, often taking his part against Jeffie when they thought she was being unreasonable. Both of them reached a point where, like Jeffie, they simply could not reconcile the Joey they knew with the Joey they read about in the newspapers. For Joyce, the friendship began the second time they met, which was a few weeks after Joey's first evening in Jeffie's apartment. She and Al had now found a place of their own on West Thirtieth Street, and she was singing most nights at Lucky Pierre's.

"One evening, Joey came in with Jeffie, and I was halfway surprised about it because I didn't know she had been seeing him. It was cold in that little back room, so he kept his overcoat on, and I remember he made me nervous, just being there. It was the same as if a musician I knew had come in to listen to me—it was the kind of place where you couldn't hide anything. I didn't even have a mike. It was just me and my piano player and everything out in the open. You couldn't fake it. I was doing a set of heavy love songs, like 'Detour Ahead,' 'Blue Prelude' and 'The Thrill Is Gone,' and I felt him respond. I knew he heard me because I received back—you can always tell.

"I sat with them afterward, and I could see how much they were involved in each other, though they weren't touching. They enjoyed playing together, and having a good audience. And I responded to him right away. He had seen who I was and admired what he saw. He wasn't just being nice to his girlfriend's girlfriend. I could be *me,* without having to sell him anything or win him over, and that's rare —that instant rapport. After that, he came to the club a lot, got to know Al, came to the house and soon we were friends, good hangout friends making no demands on each other. When he came in the door, he would take his hands out of his pockets. He was safe there. There was nothing we wanted from him and nothing he wanted from us.

"Perhaps if I had gone to him and said, 'Joey, get me a job in the Persian Room. Do that for me, please,' he might have busted legs to get me what I wanted. But I never thought of him in that way because he never used that kind of stuff around me. He was egotistical, sure—but not evil. Never evil. There was never a sign of his outside life, even when I knew from Jeffie that he was up to his neck in something heavy. Joey could carry his load. We just talked and smoked and drank some wine. We had a good time together. With and without Jeffie. With and without Ali Baba. He dug me as a woman without thinking of me as a lay. Or if he did, as *more* than a lay. And I dug him as a man—not as a guy to buy me dinner or push weight around someplace.

"There was no smallness in him. He didn't look to change the truth to suit him. He never lied to make himself sound important. He never changed his attitude to suit the moment or the company.

He was himself all the time—whoever he was. Whatever he did, right, wrong or indifferent, he didn't hold back. If you could get something from Joey, Joey would give it to you. And he gave me recognition. They were good times—very intimate, very clean and totally out of context with his life. What he felt he had to do in the outside world had nothing to do with me. I didn't agree with it— I *never* agreed with it—but he couldn't get out. Being who he was, out there he had to be on top."

Joyce saw him on top, out there among his people, only once. By another of those odd coincidences that link the people who were close to Joey, Joyce also had a friend among the Dead End Kids, Huntz Hall, who looked her up while visiting New York in the early summer of 1960. "When Joey heard this, he decided to give the neighborhood a treat. One Saturday afternoon, he took this true character, this figure from American folklore, out to President Street. And it was like the Pope showing up at the Mardi Gras hand in hand with a clown.

"Don't tell me the people out there were scared of him. Old ladies came running out of buildings to grab him and kiss him. They loved him. He was their protector. You could see it in their faces. 'Ah, he's a *good* boy. I don't care *what* he does—he looks after us.' Then they'd catch sight of Huntz and fall apart. I don't remember seeing a face all afternoon that didn't drop open at the sight of those two. It was a holiday. We walked the streets, collecting a crowd, stopped somewhere for coffee and a lemon ice, and wherever we went, the people came running out with open arms and shiny faces. Nobody backed away. I remember thinking to myself, 'You don't get that from being cute, or from being heavy either.' To earn that kind of love, he had to be doing something for them. He was King Joey. We had a glorious afternoon."

Then Jeffie got pregnant, and it made her nervous. She still wasn't sure of herself or of Joey. They were still jockeying for position, and a baby would pin her down. Pregnant herself—"for the first time, and at twenty-nine it seemed like a miracle"—Joyce watched Jeffie turn edgy and difficult. "I hated to see that. They both wanted to be able to give up some part of themselves to the other, but neither would let go. Neither was going to surrender, and even though they had a thing that lit up the room, I knew it was brewing up for a fight —a big one."

Jean saw it coming, too, and was as helpless to prevent it. She had wished them both luck when they set off for Miami to get married but was not in the least surprised when Jeffie flew back a few days later bellowing with fury and outrage. "She went to some rotten, cruel, sadist motherfucker on Eighty-sixth Street who gave her an abortion without anesthesia. At four months. It hurt a lot, apart from the humiliation. It was 'Get on the table and keep your mouth shut. Now get up and get out'—one of those numbers. Terrible. And it cost her a thousand dollars. I remember it was cold and wintry, and it seemed like the end of everything. After that, she said she never wanted to see him again. She made everybody promise not to tell him where she was. Then she went to rest up at Joyce and Al's, which was the first place he would look. Very romantic, I thought."

Joyce and Al, however, were less impressed by the romance of the situation than by its dangers. Jeffie, naturally, had first claim on their loyalties, but Joey, as a friend, had a claim on them, too, and they were far from certain of what he might do if they seemed to be keeping her from him. Wiser than Joyce in the ways of Joey's world, Al knew the line might be crossed unintentionally. He was also worried by the possibility that some of Joey's men might take it into their heads to "solve" the problem for him.

Joey telephoned soon after Jeffie had been put to bed in the study, and asked Joyce if he might speak to her. Joyce told him she was lying down and couldn't come to the phone. "Jeffie had put me in the middle of it, and it was a lousy position to be in. I had to challenge Joey, and I didn't want to. I could understand both sides. I was going to tell *him* he couldn't see his old lady? In a way, I knew he was right. Even though she didn't want to see him, she was still madly in love, and I knew somehow she wasn't going to go through with this. I guess he knew it, too. He couldn't believe that she didn't love him and didn't really want to go home with him. Even if she *said* she didn't want to, that had nothing to do with it. *He* wanted her to. On the other hand, groovy as he was—and I really loved him in a funny sort of way, and he loved me—I thought she was probably better off without him. If she hadn't run away, I don't know that I would ever have told her to—it wasn't my decision. But once she did, then I had to be with her.

"So then he was going to come over. 'I should be able to just *talk* to her,' he said, and when I told him she didn't want to see him, he said he wanted to hear it from her, not me, and that was that. I couldn't stop him. He knew, and I knew, that if he could get to talk to her, he could get her to do what he wanted. Then the doorbell rang, and I had to let him in. Al was out, and I remember standing at the top of the stairs with my big belly watching him come up. He had a look in his eye that made me nervous, a look that said if he wanted to take her out of there, he was going to take her out of there, and I'd better not get in his way. But I wasn't really frightened. I don't think he would ever have hurt me. I was never afraid of him in that way. And although he was in a fury, he didn't bawl me out. Joey had great dignity. He just let me know I was being disrespectful, that I had quite a presumption in trying to stand between them.

"I think he knew what kind of a spot I was in. Anyway, I handled it straight out. I couldn't just smile and be cute. 'Listen, Joey,' I said. 'It's not up to me. I'm in the middle, sure, but that's where I have to be if she feels she really doesn't want to see you. She's got no place else to go. She's lost the baby and she's bleeding. So what do you want me to do? Throw her out on the street? She's lying down and can't be moved.' I was shaking all over, although I was sure he wasn't going to have anyone come and do something bad to me. 'That's all right,' he said. 'I told you—I just want to talk to her.'

"So I backed off. Not out of fear—out of respect. I know Jeffie. I couldn't say, 'You dirty rat, what have you done to my girlfriend?' She's very strong, and she's not going to do anything she doesn't want to do. There are few men capable of making her feel like a woman, but she wants that feeling, and I want it for her. 'Okay,' I said. 'Go ahead. Go talk to her. But just remember the condition she's in. She's got to stay where she is and cool it for a while.' So he went in and she screamed and yelled and he came out again, but he stayed until he made his point. He kept going back until he won.

I remember the look he gave me as he helped her down the stairs, still bleeding. It was a look that said, 'I win. Don't mess with me because I win. This is what I said would happen.' And he was right. He knew her better than she knew herself. No matter how she felt, he knew she really wanted to go with him. She was the farthest thing from what he should have had. Jeffie couldn't cook. She wouldn't put up with the bullshit. She didn't go for the pseudo glamour. She didn't even like the stories they told. But he didn't want it easy. He wanted her. They loved each other and she had no choice. He made up his mind to it."

But it was still too much for Jeffie to swallow. As soon as she was on her feet, she ran away again. And although he could hardly have expected to catch her at Joyce's a second time, Joey called in every day, obviously bent on repairing their friendship as much as finding out where Jeffie was. One snowy night, he found Jean there, and when it was time to leave, offered her a lift home in the car that was coming to collect him. " 'No,' I said. 'I want to go now,' but he insisted. 'It's a blizzard out there,' he said. 'Why don't you wait a few minutes? You'll never get a cab on a night like this.' Al and Joyce backed him up, and he seemed so genuinely concerned about my walking out into the snow on that deserted street late at night, that I said okay and stayed.

"Then the car came and we left. We slipped and slithered down to Bedford Street—it really was a terrible night—and when we stopped outside my house, he said, 'I could use a drink. Why don't we go to the bar on the corner?' Well, now I got leery, because I knew he was looking for Jeffie, and I couldn't figure out what he had in mind. I also wanted to go to bed. But curiosity got the better of me, and I knew I was safe in that bar. The guy who ran it, Guido, had known me for years, and was like Daddy. Didn't matter who I was with, Guido was my protector. So we crossed the street and sat at the bar and got to talking. We talked for hours. About everything —life, music, Jeffie, art, books. Name it. I couldn't believe this guy. He knew everything. He'd read everything. Couldn't get over it. Looked like a gangster, talked like a poet. And I could see he wasn't working up to a pass. He made not the slightest move in my direction. Joey couldn't have cared less about me in that way than if I'd been a pussycat.

"Then he said, 'What time is it?' I didn't know—I didn't have a watch—so he asked Guido, who told him it was around one o'clock. 'One o'clock?' says Joey. 'One o'clock,' says Guido. 'Okay,' says Joey. 'One o'clock.' Then he tells me about some guy who's having an accident on the bridge, some guy Jeffie knows. He's having a terrible accident and he's going to get killed. So I looked at him. And I laughed, because I figured it had to be some kind of a joke. 'You got to be crazy to tell me a thing like that,' I said, sort of going along with this melodrama. Never occurred to me that he might be serious. I really thought he was putting me on, that it was some kind of an act to scare me into telling him where Jeffie was, although we hadn't gotten around to that yet. And I was a bit disappointed we were playing games because I'd been having such a good time talking to him. 'What about your driver?' I said. The snow was building up on the cars outside. 'Don't worry about him,' he said. 'He's used to it.' Then we got into something else and the moment passed. In the end, we finished a whole bottle of brandy and closed the bar.

"When we finally got outside, he said, 'Oh! Look at that. My driver left.' 'Oh,' I said. 'Did he really?' 'Yes,' he said. 'And I've no place to go. Do you mind if I come down to the house?' Well, now I got a little panicky. But I was pretty sure he wasn't going to grab at me or anything and I couldn't very well let him walk back to Brooklyn, so we went home to my apartment. Maybe he wanted to see if Jeffie was there—I don't know. Anyway, I made some coffee, and we're sitting across from each other drinking it, and everything's warm and friendly—I'm really getting to like this guy a lot—and he suddenly says to me, 'Where's Jeffie?' 'Jeffie?' I say, as if the name sounded vaguely familiar. 'I've no idea. Not the slightest.' I mean, what do *I* know about gangsters? It was ten years since I'd met one, and he'd been a heavy, a nasty experience. But this guy was a bright, sensitive, cultivated intellectual, right?

"He pulls a gun on me. He says, 'If you don't tell me where Jeffie is, I'm going to kill you.' Now I've had a fear of firearms all my life, but I looked at him and I looked at the gun and I laughed. I thought it was *funny.* I really believed it was all a joke. 'You're putting me on,' I said, 'With all the other stories, you're putting me on. And I'm not going to tell you. So why don't you just put that thing away and drink your coffee.' Not frightened at all—not for a moment. Not even when he pointed the gun right at me and said, 'Then I'm going to have to kill you.' I thought that was even funnier, like something out of a Laurel and Hardy routine. I guess I must have been drunk. 'Listen,' I said. 'I don't know who you are, but Jeffie is a very dear friend of mine, and I'm not going to tell you where she is—okay? So if you'd like to kill me,' I said, like something out of *East Lynne,* 'go ahead. I have no family. No one's going to miss me except Bianca, my pussycat, and I'll be out of this vale of tears.' Then we both laughed, and he put the gun away.

"Now he said he was tired. So I told him, 'If you want to go to sleep, you may go to sleep on the couch,' and I went into the bedroom and passed out. Two hours later, I got a phone call—it was about four or five in the morning. I picked it up and it was Jeffie. Screaming and raving. Furious. 'You goddamn whore—balling my old man.' 'I *beg* your pardon,' I said. 'Would you mind repeating that?' And she didn't mind at all. In fact, she repeated it a lot. She'd gone crazy. There'd been concern on her part from the very beginning about having me around Joey, even though he couldn't have been less interested. 'Well, he's *there,* isn't he?' she yells at me. 'Yes, he's here,' I said. 'At least, he was. I don't know—' And off she goes again, like she's climbing into the phone to get at me. So now *I* started to get mad, and we had a big screaming fight. 'What's your interpretation of a friend?' I said. 'You're telling me I've never *been* a friend of yours. A friend doesn't ball another friend's old man. Amoral I may be, but I wouldn't *do* that to a friend.' I'm in shock from these accusations. And then I think, 'Why do I have to defend myself? I didn't do anything. Why doesn't she know that?' So I told her, 'If you can accuse me of that, then obviously you know what it is to do it to a friend,' and that sort of calmed her down. I explained what had happened, hung up and went back to sleep."

Jeffie, however, did not, nor did Joey. She had called Jean from Lyn Morgen's apartment on Eighth Street, where she had been hiding out. Lyn knew nothing about her abortion or her stay at Joyce's—only that Jeffie had gone on a trip with Joey to Florida to get married and had come back "a screaming lunatic." A few hours later, the phone rang and Lyn went to answer it, with Jeffie at her heels urging her not to say anything if it was Joey. "Jeffie sat down beside me as I picked it up. The telephone was in the window, a huge picture window. Everybody on the street could see you when you used it.

" 'Hello, Lyn,' he said—I knew him well enough to recognize the voice.

" 'Hello? Who is this?' I said.

" 'It's me.'

" 'And who's me?'

" 'Lyn,' he said, 'it's Joey.'

" 'Oh?' I said. 'Joey who?'

" 'What do you mean, Joey who?' he said, getting mad. 'It's *me*. Joey. Like, Joey Gallo.'

" 'Oh,' I said.

" 'Yeah. Right. Where's Jeffie?'

"Well, Jeffie was sitting right next to me in the window, and we found out later that he was calling from across the street and watching us all the time. But I didn't know that, of course, so I said, 'What do you mean, where is Jeffie? Jeffie was with you. What have you done to Jeffie?' Then he said something about it wasn't what he'd done but what he was going to do that I ought to worry about, and after a bit more back and forth, he hung up. I'd been putting my life on the chopping block without even realizing it.

"Later on, she told me a story about some man who Joey thought had kissed her and whose head was off in an automobile accident. If you were a man, it wasn't healthy to be interested in Jeffie. But as a kind of sister substitute, I guess it was all right. Anyway, she went around to her apartment and he found her there. Next thing I heard, he'd gone with her to California. And then that they were married."

By now, Jeffie had "forgiven" Jean, and after the wedding, she spent more time with them than any of Jeffie's friends, particularly when they moved to Eighth Street. "I was decorating the house, buying curtain materials, and helping Jeffie build a closet where his suits would hang two inches apart. Whenever I saw Joey, he was always very kind, very sweet and gentle. 'Listen, Jean,' he said to me one time, 'would you mind telling Jeffie—you're the only one that can do it—to please pick up her underwear from the bathroom floor?' He was kind to me because he knew how much I loved Gabriel, and Gabriel wasn't in my life any more. In those days, I was very caught up in being alone and not being able to handle it. So he was trying to be the man and the strength in my life because he knew there was no one else to do that for me. He was very sensitive to my loneliness. I'm sure that's why I was around so much—not because Jeffie wanted me there. Jeffie was so in love, and women in love don't want company of any kind, not man, woman or child. It was because of him. It was always Joey who insisted that I be with them, that I go with them to the Luna. He was being kind to me, and that's why I loved him.

"I loved him for other reasons, too. I loved him for his knowledge of music, his knowledge of literature, his sensitivity to painting—for his cultured quality. I loved him for interesting Jeffie in books. Jeffie had never read anything in her entire life until she met him—except maybe for Reich. And now she had to keep up with him. 'What is he talking about? What does he mean? I have to read this and read that.' He was an educated, intellectually curious young man who felt he was Machiavelli. He had quite deliberately based his life on Machiavelli's principles—he told me that. He truly believed that you could only decide if an action was evil or not by knowing what its purpose was and by whether or not it succeeded in its purpose. There were a lot of parallels between his life and Machiavelli's. They even looked alike, except for their coloring.

"Not that I really understood what he was doing. There wasn't much about him in the papers then. The gangster stuff was just melodrama to me—black humor. I'd read Kennedy's book. And when I heard there was an inter-Mafia fight, I said to myself, 'Bravo. He's so bright and the others are so nasty. That takes guts.' I believed the same myth that Jeffie believed, that he was only taking care of a whole group of people, his family—that he didn't really want to be into this but it was a role he had inherited. When my friends started screaming at me, 'How could you get involved with this hood, this dangerous criminal?' I'd say, 'You're wrong, you're wrong. Don't *say* things like that. He's not guilty of any of this'—although I knew he was into *something*. The gun he'd pulled on me was real, and he wasn't going to the office every day. But I didn't care. So far as I was concerned, he was the Don Quixote of the underworld, and I tried to tell them that.

"No good. 'He's a criminal,' they'd say. 'Period. We don't want to hear about his intellectual capacities. He killed this one and that one and this one and that one.' Then I'd say, 'There's no proof. Give me proof, and maybe I'll believe it.' Then they'd say, 'Well, Bobby Kennedy and blah blah blah,' and run down the list of all the so-called authorities who'd accused him of this and that. Finally I'd blow my stack and start screaming at *them*. 'Fuck what Joey did. Prove it. Don't tell me about what they think he did or know he did. Show me the *proof.*' I lost a lot of friends that way. Eleven years later, I can't approve of what he did, but it doesn't matter now. He's gone.

"The only beef I had with him then was, why was he wasting his time with these people, with guys like Ali Baba? I kept thinking, 'How can this lovely, brilliant man that I adore have anything to do with this trash?' The answer was, of course, that he was doing it out of a sense of duty, although he never said so. But that wasn't good enough for me. I was a marvelous nag. 'Why don't you paint? Why don't you write? Why don't you get out? Do what you want to do. Paint. Sing. Dance. Perform. Write. You're an artist. What are you doing?' And he never got angry. He'd always laugh at me and say, 'Jean, Jean,' as if I didn't understand, which I probably didn't. But these people around him were nothing. They weren't rich, with the chauffeurs and Cadillacs. They didn't even have style. But they were his, and I never had a moment of fear in his company. I always felt there wasn't anything in the world he wouldn't do to protect me.

"Easter Sunday that year, he took Jeffie and me to a party in Brooklyn. It was at a club over a Food City or an A & P—a typical Italian affair with crepe-paper bunting, a band, a long bar and bottles on every table. Lots of noise and booze. Everybody's in their Sunday best, and very obsequious with Joey, very polite and respectful. They sat us down at a table, with Jeffie on his right and me on his left—his fat driver was somewhere around—and we had a good time, talking and drinking and watching the dancing. I'd never been to a real Italian party before. So the wine went down and the hours passed, and then suddenly in through the door came three men. With hats. I jokingly said to Joey out of the corner of my mouth, 'Hey, three guys just came in the door. With hats. They're either cops or friends of yours.'

"He sneaks a look and he says, 'They're cops. Now listen—we're getting up and leaving. Quietly. Stick close to me.' So we stick close to him, slide out through a back door and find ourselves on the roof. *Me.* On a *roof* yet—looking around to find a way down. No way down. So we cross the roof and climb over an abutment to the next roof. It's unbelievable. It can't be happening. I've got a big handbag, I'm wearing high heels and we're running across the next roof still looking for a way down. No way down. Only up. Up a sort of ladder on the side of the next building to an even higher roof. And Joey's saying, 'Come on, move. Move, move, move'—sort of shepherding us from behind.

"Well, Jeffie and I are hysterical with laughter by now. I couldn't see anybody chasing us, so I said to Joey, 'Oh, cut it out. You're putting me on. This is a Marx Brothers movie.' I really thought he was doing the whole thing for my benefit, as a lark to give us an amusing evening. But no, he was serious—we had to climb up the side of this building. So I said, 'Well, I can't possibly climb up there carrying my purse. *You'll* have to carry it.' 'I'll be delighted,' he said, and I started up the ladder. 'If I have to go to jail,' I said, 'who's going to take care of Bianca?' Well, they both seemed to think that was very funny, and now all three of us are rolling about on this ladder high above the street with the wind blowing my hair around. It's starting to get light, and I'm looking down at him carrying my purse and saying, 'Oh, they're going to arrest you for being in drag.' I still thought it was all a joke.

"Anyway, we get up to the roof, and there's a door opening onto a stairway that takes us down to the street and his waiting white Cadillac. And he was right. Lo and behold! there *is* a paddy wagon outside the club and the cops are bringing people down and shoving them inside. So bravo, Joey. We'd not only escaped getting busted, but had our biggest lark in years. Jeffie and I were weak as kittens from laughing, and I was ready to go home now. But Joey was just getting started. 'Okay,' he says. 'Now let's go back inside.'

"I mean, how can you refuse a guy like that? He leads us back up the stairs to the club, giggling like idiots, and there are the three guys in hats. 'Oh, hello, Lieutenant,' he says. 'What's going on?' One of them comes over and says, 'Listen, Joey, this is a very serious arrest. They've been selling drinks after hours. What do you know about it?' *'Me?'* he says, all surprise and innocence. 'What would *I* know about it? I just got here, didn't I? I came to meet my brother. But I don't see him here, so hello and good-bye and thank you very much.' We went back down the stairs with a bunch of other people. *They* got into the paddy wagon and *we* got into the Cadillac.

"Now I'd really had enough. Now I had a headache, and all I wanted to do was get into bed and sleep. But then darling Jeffie says, 'Oh! I lost my sweater—my cashmere sweater.' Joey looks at her. 'You *what?*' 'Yes,' she says. 'I must have dropped it climbing around up there. It's a fifty-dollar sweater.' I'm listening to her and groaning to myself, 'What kind of provocation is this? We've just run over the rooftops. We've been back inside out of frivolity and bravado. Now Jeffie's going to do *another* number?' It's bright daylight by this time, forty-three people have been arrested and she wants him to go climbing back over the roofs looking for her *sweater?* He's going to let her have it right between the eyes. But no. He gets out of the car, ducks back into the building we came down from and reappears a few minutes later with the cashmere sweater. Still in a good humor, still laughing and joking. He *adored* her. They were into all these funny numbers before the police got serious with that trumped-up charge."

Joey's charm and intellectual capacity continued to elude Lyn, however, even after he insisted on taking her to dinner at the Luna, along with her husband, Jeffie and about eight others, in honor of her ability to keep her mouth shut. "I was a heroine because I hadn't told him where Jeffie was. He did a whole toast thing. 'Here's to Lyn Morgen,' he said. 'You could torture her and she wouldn't give you any information she didn't want to give. She belongs with us. We could use someone like her.'

"I said, 'Listen, Joey. If somebody tortured me, I would not only tell everything I knew, I would also make things up. So forget it. I am not the girl for you.' Big laugh. Jeffie was talking very romantically that night about how they could go to Europe and start all over again, but I wasn't paying much attention. I was very nervous. He was doing his godfather routine with all these hoods."

Rick Morgen was not very comfortable either. "Jeffie had told me a story about how she needed some maternity clothes, so Joey gave her $250 to go shopping. She was very pregnant then, slow-moving and not thrilled with herself, and she didn't get out for a couple of days. The next night, he comes in and says to her, 'Give me the money. I must have the money.' She says, 'Well, why, baby? I was going out to buy clothes.' So he says, 'Listen, I got to have it. I found the greatest buy in machine guns. I can't pass it up.' So she gave him back the money. 'Had to do it,' she told me. 'Otherwise it would have been like taking candy from a kid.' She told me that. And now I'm sitting down to dinner with this guy, this genius hood who never made it. He was a loser. From all his activities, there was never anything concrete. No money—nothing. They were in debt up to their ears by this time, but the newspapers were turning him into a folk hero. Greatest hood they ever met because he once read a book. They ignored the fact that he had destroyed labor unions, killed people, exploited, extorted, tortured, tormented. Of *course* people liked him. You couldn't afford *not* to like him. Don't say in Bay Ridge, Brooklyn, that you don't like Joey Gallo.

"Though Lyn was the guest of honor that night, he was more concerned about what I thought of him than what she did. It was another part of that whole scene—their underlying contempt for women. This need to display their masculinity all the time; the fact that they use guns to prove their manhood—it's loaded with homosexuality. But I have to say that Joey was a masterpiece in his own way. He was an intelligent man, and he played this role magnificently. All things considered, with his desire to be a leader, and having been born into those circumstances, the only world he knew, he probably had no choice. He had all that energy and drive. Maybe if he had been allowed to develop in other ways, he could have done something interesting. He had it in him. It's unfortunate. Maybe the world lost a great leader—but I don't really think so."

Joyce, however, was convinced of it—or if not a great leader, then a figure of compelling strength. "Joey never fell down. He was always in control—not necessarily of the situation, but of himself. I never saw him for an instant beyond himself, undone by himself, undone by circumstances. Nothing got by him. He never forgot who he was. I have seen the greatest artists of this century fall in their own puke, but never Joey. Never once.

"After my kid was born, we didn't see quite so much of him. The war was on now, and I think he was trying not to involve us, because things were getting rough. He was in the papers almost every day. They were trying to make him the scapegoat, to make it look like they were finally getting the big guy. It got worse and worse, until I knew they meant to do it to him this time, no matter what. Things were going terribly. The night before his trial began, he and Jeffie came over and we went out to dinner at a French restaurant around the corner. They were very happy, the two of them, in spite of what was about to happen. He said he was going to stand mute and offer no defense—his lawyers had told him to. That scared me, but he acted as if it were just some kind of legal maneuver he had to go through. I don't know whether he was trying to reassure Jeffie, who was so pregnant she was popping at the seams, or whether he actually believed it. Sometimes he really felt that he was charmed, I think—immune to cause and effect. The bullets would always miss and the bombs would fall over there. But I wasn't so sure. I wanted them to get out while there was still time.

" 'Listen, Joey,' I said. 'Why do you have to go through with this? They're going to get you, don't you know that? Why don't you just leave? Tonight. You and Jeffie.'

" 'No, Joyce,' he said, and he smiled like I'd asked him to do something dishonorable and didn't know it. 'I can't do that.'

Joyce, Jean and Lyn   143

" 'But why not? Why can't you go to Florida or Mexico? Anywhere. Just get away from it. What if it goes the wrong way?'

" 'Listen,' he said, 'I've no choice. I can't run away. This is what I've got to do.'

" 'But, Joey, what have you got to do that's more important than staying alive and staying together, you two? You've *got* something now. What difference does it make where you are? You've got enough money for a ticket. Go. Do something else.'

" 'Too late,' he said. 'It's done. I've got to go through with it.' He wasn't even thinking about it. His mind was completely made up.

" '*Why?*' I said. 'What's more important than your freedom?'

"But he just smiled."

9

The Trial

Joey's bid for a principality in Brooklyn had more or less coincided with a public declaration of war on organized crime by the new Attorney General, Robert Kennedy, and the timing proved disastrous for the Gallos. They were now required to contend with vastly superior forces on two fronts. With the support of a sympathetic local population, Joey's hit-and-run, urban guerrilla tactics might just have succeeded against Profaci's static defense of fixed interests, but, pinned down by police and FBI surveillance, the gang was comparatively easy meat.

Joey himself was the real prize. For Profaci and the acting heads of the other New York families, his prompt elimination as a symbol of revolt was vital if their authority was to be preserved. For Kennedy and law-enforcement officers at every level of government, his prompt elimination as a symbol of gangsterism would earn their campaign a spectacular early victory. As a racketeer whose notoriety far outran his real power, Joey was a perfect target of opportunity —and not least because the Attorney General had helped make him notorious in the first place through the McClellan Committee hearings. With the personal animosity that was known to exist between them, word soon got around that any excess of zeal in putting Joey out of business was more likely to invite praise than censure.

The problem, however, was finding a charge that would stick. As always, prospective witnesses inevitably suffered near-total amnesia as soon as they learned against whom they were being asked to testify. But pressed by reports that the Gallo-Profaci dispute was wobbling on the edge of a bloodbath, the Police Department very sensibly started to look for a witness who might have even more to fear from *not* testifying, and found one in Theodore Moss, a young New York shylock with a legitimate-business façade.

On April 19, 1961, the body of Morton Rosenberg, part owner of a restaurant in Manhattan's garment district, was found riddled with bullets in the Bath Beach section of Brooklyn. On him were papers that led the police to Moss in what seemed to be shaping up as a typical loan-shark victim homicide. In looking around for his executioners, they pulled in Joey for questioning, as was now customary whenever bodies were found in Brooklyn, and, as usual, no arrest was made as a result. But this chance connection apparently gave both Joey and the Manhattan District Attorney's office an idea.

Joey's was simpler. Crippled for money by the police blockade of President Street, he decided to move in on Moss and become his "partner," counting not only upon the persuasiveness of his reputation but on the natural reluctance of shylocks to call for a cop. He was not to know, however, that his victim had other problems. The exact nature of Moss's deal with the District Attorney's office after the Rosenberg killing remains a mystery, but part of it included his willingness to testify against Joey in return for around-the-clock police protection for himself and his family. Indeed, he went further. Though plainly terrified by the risks he was running, Moss went out of his way to assist the D.A. in an attempt to secure the corroborative evidence necessary to sustain an indictment. On May 12, he made two telephone calls, which the police recorded, to a friend who had turned coat and was working for Joey, and that evening, he led Joey into a police trap at the Luna. As they left the restaurant, Joey was arrested and subsequently accused, with four of his men, of conspiracy to extort and the attempted extortion of a half-interest in Moss's *legitimate* operations—three bars and a check-cashing business.

In Felony Court next morning, Assistant District Attorney Paul Kelly truthfully described the case as being "of an unusual nature with unusual circumstances." Not the least unusual thing about it was the extent to which he showed the prosecution's hand. He put Moss on the stand and made him tell his whole story—no doubt to get his testimony on the record before he had a chance to change his mind. Describing Joey as "a vicious muscle man," Kelly then asked Magistrate Reuben Levy to refuse applications for bail—again, no doubt, with the idea of stiffening the resolve of his star witness. This the magistrate seemed ready to do until Joey protested, whereupon he changed his mind and set the figure at $100,000, which, in Joey's financial circumstances, was just as good as a refusal. He was taken to the Tombs.

Sidney Slater went with him, along with the other codefendants. Later, he explained how Joey's involvement with Moss had come about, but by then, he, too, was under continuous police protection, having turned informer, and could hardly risk contradicting the D.A.'s office while it was keeping him alive. "One night, Hyman Powell came in and said, 'I got a real pigeon for you, Joey—a shylock named Teddy Moss who's got half a million on the street and is having trouble making collections. The guy needs some muscle. He also owns thirteen gin mills, and most of them do all right. He's got a check-cashing business going for him, too.' Joey grinned. 'I guess maybe he needs some partners,' he said. Then he turned to me and said, 'Sidney, tomorrow you get hold of Al Schaeffer and Tony Leone and have a meet with this Teddy Moss. See what he's like. Try to borrow some money off him. Or think of some scheme so we are tied in with him.' "

Slater's account makes no mention of the Rosenberg killing, nor does it square completely with Moss's testimony at the trial, but it does undermine the prosecution's contention throughout that Moss was a respectable businessman and the entirely innocent victim of unscrupulous racketeers. Joey hinted at this darker side when his lawyers finally won a hearing on his plea for a reduction of bail. In fact, he believed at the time that Moss was the prime mover in framing him—not the D.A.—in an attempt to distract attention from the link between Moss and the murdered Rosenberg. This became clear when Joey appeared in court on June 22. The trial had been set for August 7 before Justice Joseph A. Sarafite, and, quite apart from his violent distaste for life in the Tombs, Joey had many pressing matters to attend to on the outside, some of which he proceeded to explain:

"Your Honor," he said, "my mother has a restaurant, and I work with my mother. I have been arrested many times, and at one time, I was out of the state and I heard there was an indictment against me, and I came back on my own. Another time there was another indictment against me, and I came in on my own and surrendered. I have been on bail so many times, Your Honor, and have never skipped. I am a good performer. I have always showed up on the date that I had to come to court.

"I know I am innocent in this, too, Your Honor, and I know I can prove my innocence if I am able to get out into the street and get my witnesses together that are necessary to prove my innocence. There is a lot in this case that is underground, and I think the D.A. is being hoodwinked by a smart operator. Your Honor, in this case there seems to be a homicide involved, and this man here [Moss] is definitely involved in this homicide, and through the squeeze, not knowing me, he put me into this swindle, Your Honor, and I can prove it if I am just given a week's time to get out into the street. But at that high bail, Your Honor, it is almost impossible for me to make bail. All I want is a chance to prove my innocence. I will not skip. I never did. If I have to go to jail, I want a shot to prove my innocence."

Joey spoke calmly and with dignity, creating just the kind of impression that Assistant District Attorney Paul Kelly was most anxious to destroy. Opposing any reduction in bail, Kelly expressed the general desire of law-enforcement officials, from the Justice Department on down, to keep Joey behind bars. "Defendant Gallo," he said, "is a hoodlum and a racketeer who is well known to the FBI and the U.S. Attorney. He once offered to take care of anybody who needed taking care of in New York County, and he is well known to the New York Police Department, the Brooklyn District Attorney's office, the Nassau District Attorney's office and the Manhattan District Attorney's office. He has unlimited resources. He can go out and levy tribute, just as he attempted to levy tribute here, at any time he wishes, and bail can be made. . . . Gallo has had an opportunity to hear the testimony in this case . . . and he has reason to flee. . . . Also, there has been a grave threat of assassination of the People's witness. He is under constant bodyguard by sixteen detectives."

The judge evidently thought this precaution sufficient, for he reduced bail to $35,000 and Joey went free, confident of beating the rap. As Kelly had said, he had indeed heard the testimony. The People's case rested on a star witness, whose character and credibility were both very vulnerable to attack, and upon corroborative evidence of the flimsiest kind from a detective who claimed to have overheard part of a conversation between Moss and himself at the Luna. In Joey's opinion, any competent attorney could pick the People's case to pieces. Dismissing the matter from his mind, he returned home to Jeffie and the cold war with Profaci. But he had reckoned without his lawyer, David Price, who had already secured one postponement of the trial, originally set for June 21, on the grounds that he was busy with another case in Brooklyn. From then on, he proceeded to defend Joey in a way that would have sent him up for a parking offense. Through a series of miscalculations, he contrived, in the end, to send Joey into court, not only without a lawyer at all, but with strict instructions to stand mute and offer no defense. By following this advice, it was thought, he would go free on appeal on the constitutional grounds that he had been denied representation by a lawyer of his choice!

The seeds of this strategy were sown on August 7, when Joey appeared before Judge Sarafite with his codefendants Ali Waffa,

Sidney Slater and Michael Albergo. (The fifth defendant, Tony Leone, was also called but failed to answer.) Although the People were ready for trial, the accused were not. Robert Weiswasser, the newly qualified assistant in the firm of Price & Iovine, rose to inform the court that Price, who was then seventy-three years of age, had been ordered to rest by his doctor after an arduous two-month trial in the Appellate Division. His partner, Joseph Iovine, as Joey's uncle, had, of course, disqualified himself from any active role in the case. Accordingly, he had no choice but to seek a further postponement, a motion in which he was immediately joined by the other defense lawyers, all of whom were having trouble with their clients. Having no choice but to accede to their request, Judge Sarafite thereupon ordered another hearing on August 30 to fix a new date for the trial.

But the situation had hardly clarified by then. Joey was up to his neck in publicity and grand jury subpoenas following the attempt on his brother Larry's life, Price was still missing and so was Tony Leone. "I don't think he is going to show, Your Honor," Joey said helpfully, after his lieutenant's name had been called several times. The excuse offered was that he was in the hospital with conjunctivitis, but the real reason for Leone's absence was rather more substantial. He was then—mistakenly, as it turned out—on the "most wanted" list for killing a Brooklyn cop. Visibly exasperated, Sarafite set the trial for October 23, warning all concerned that he would tolerate no further delay over questions of legal representation.

The first thing he heard on October 23, however, was Ali Waffa's lawyer asking for permission to withdraw from the case because his client refused to cooperate. Bowing reluctantly to his wishes, Sarafite gave Ali a week to find a new one, and then turned to Joe Iovine, appearing for his partner, David Price. As trial counsel, Price needed more time, said Iovine. He was engaged on four other trials and representing thirteen material witnesses, including Joey Gallo, before the Brooklyn grand jury investigating the murder of Joe Magnasco on October 4. "In view of the notoriety and the publicity which this case has received," Iovine went on, referring to the Magnasco killing, "this is not the appropriate time to try *this* case. I sincerely believe a month from now perhaps might be more appropriate. I believe the defendant, Joseph Gallo, deserves the opportunity to make an application before the Supreme Court for a change of venue." Leone's lawyer, new to the case and faced with the problem of an absentee client, at once joined him in asking for a week's delay for a change-of-venue motion, and Sarafite again had very little choice but to comply with their request.

Then followed one of the more bizarre blunders committed by Joey's defense. Having made a motion in the Appellate Division for a change of venue on the grounds of unfavorable publicity, and having learned that November 8 was the earliest date by which it was returnable, his attorneys entirely omitted to ask for a stay of trial until such time as the motion could be heard. When the unfortunate Weiswasser informed the court of this on October 30, he was at once accused by Assistant District Attorney Paul Kelly of resorting to unreasonable, dilatory tactics, and flouting the People's rights. It helped not at all when Weiswasser went on to report that Price was now ill in Florida and could not be present. With mounting impatience, Judge Sarafite adjourned until the afternoon so that Weiswasser could remedy the oversight and go back to the Appellate Division for a stay of trial. And when he was then told that judgment had been reserved on the motion, Sarafite again adjourned, this time until the following day. Mobbed by reporters on leaving the heavily guarded courtroom, Joey seemed full of confidence.

Next morning, Assistant District Attorney Francis X. Clark, jointly prosecuting the case with Paul Kelly, informed the court that Weiswasser's motion for a stay of trial had been denied. He further announced that the People proposed to sever Joey's codefendants from the proceedings so that he could be tried separately. (They had planned to do this anyway, but the reason for doing so now was that Tony Leone's attorney had been far more successful than Joey's; he *had* managed to obtain a stay of trial for his client.) Judge Sarafite then demanded to know if Weiswasser had conferred with Price. On learning that he had so far failed to reach him, both by phone and telegram, Sarafite then adjourned until the afternoon to give him time for a further attempt.

When the court reconvened at 2:30, Weiswasser was able to report that he had finally managed to trace his employer, who had been ordered to Florida for a month's vacation by his doctor. Although his wife was also ill, he planned to be back in New York on December 4, and would at once address himself to Joey's case. On hearing this, Clark immediately objected to the idea of yet another postponement, and asked the court to exercise its power to assign an attorney to represent the defendant so that the trial could proceed without further delay. Invited to comment on this proposal, Weiswasser conferred briefly with Joey and then stated for the record the position that Price & Iovine would take, not only during the trial, but in all the subsequent and equally fruitless appeals.

"Your Honor," he said, "Gallo informs me that he has paid Mr. Price his fee in this matter. He has retained Mr. Price and *he* is the attorney he wants to represent him. He feels that inasmuch as his attorney is sick, it is not his fault, and he feels that this might be a deprivation of his constitutional rights under the New York State Constitution, and the Fourteenth Article, or Amendment, under the Federal Constitution, and also Section 308 of the Code of Criminal Procedure, to appoint another attorney for him at this time." Having thus set out the legal argument for an adjournment, Weiswasser then added that, as a material witness before the Rackets Grand Jury in Kings County, Joey had been subpoenaed to appear every Monday, Wednesday and Friday until further notice. And since he had been held there for some days in default of $25,000 bail, it had been impossible to work on the preparation of his defense because visiting hours in New York Civil Prison ended at 5 P.M. Furthermore, in the absence of his principals, he was not prepared to accept the responsibility for trying the case, since he had been admitted to the bar only ten months before.

Unimpressed by these arguments, Judge Sarafite then gave Weiswasser a humiliating public lesson in court procedure. "When I gave you a week on October 23," he said, "you could have made your motion for a stay immediately. You did not have to wait until Monday and compel the court to take an adjournment until 2:30. And once the court decides—the Appellate Division heard you—that no stay is granted, obviously the legal significance of that is that you go to trial. What else could it mean . . . ? You asked for time; I gave you time. You did not have a stay; I gave you time for a stay. You did not get a stay. The case is marked ready."

Weiswasser stayed on his feet, grappling with the implications of this ruling. "As I understand it, sir," he said humbly, "when you gave me a week to make this motion, you anticipated that we would go to another court for an order requiring Your Honor to stay proceedings until that motion could be decided?"

"Why, of course," said the judge. "That is the most important part of it." He then ordered Joey to find another attorney and be ready for trial on November 6 without fail.

This was the cue for another spectacular blunder. No doubt with the intention of showing that lack of funds precluded the employment of any other attorney but the one he had paid for, Joey was advised to visit the offices of the Legal Aid Society that afternoon and ask the chief of its criminal division for a free lawyer to defend him —a request duly reported next day in the New York *Post.* He was, of course, turned down. The society's rules specified a bail limit of $1,000 before an applicant could qualify for free legal service, and Joey was out on bail totaling $65,000 in three cases. But his apparent willingness even to consider working with another attorney completely destroyed the position he had taken on David Price's instructions. The gesture may have dramatized his financial difficulties, but it had also proved that he did *not* believe Price to be indispensable to his defense. Though no one on Joey's side seemed to realize it, the last obstacle had been removed to an immediate trial with a court-appointed lawyer to represent him.

Judge Sarafite certainly realized it, however. The very next day, November 1, he ordered Joey and Weiswasser to appear and report on their progress in finding a new defense attorney. Joey, however, was not to be found. With his habitual disregard for the convenience of judges, he had taken Jeffie upstate for a few days to celebrate her thirtieth birthday, and it was not until the afternoon of Friday, November 3, that he finally showed up in court. No, he had not engaged another lawyer. "My Uncle Iovine will be in the city tomorrow morning," he said, "and I am waiting until then, and will get them together and we will come up with something for Monday morning."

This was not good enough for the judge, who had meanwhile learned that Weiswasser had reargued the motion for a stay of trial in the Appellate Division and had again been turned down. Overruling his protestations that he had been strictly instructed by Price not to participate in the trial and that, in any case, he had interviewed no witnesses nor made any preparations at all for Joey's defense. Sarafite assigned Weiswasser on the spot as Joey's attorney and undertook to find "an older member of the bar" to work with him. Later, he named Irving Mendelson, a noted trial lawyer, as cocounsel and confirmed that the case would be tried, as ordered, at ten o'clock on Monday morning, November 6.

As it turned out, the proceedings were not to start until the afternoon, owing to a series of motions that took all morning to argue *in camera*. The first was a formal application by Francis Clark to try Joey alone, on the grounds that he was the prime mover and that his codefendants were just aiders and abetters. Broadening his theme in anticipation of further delaying tactics, he added that Teddy Moss had now been in protective custody for six months. "He is extremely nervous," said Clark. "He is in a very bad mental condition. He wants to run. He has been approached by different people in an attempt to get him to repudiate his position. He is in great fear, in spite of the fact that he is in protective custody. The case has been delayed long enough, and we have been subjected here to, in my estimation, a deliberate plan of stalling on the part of defendant Gallo's attorneys."

Replying to this, Weiswasser rejected any idea that Moss might be suffering from the suspense. He had not only continued to attend to his business affairs, but had allowed the police and the District Attorney to use him as an example to reluctant witnesses in other matters. They had confronted these people with Moss, Weiswasser claimed, so that he could say, in effect, "I am ready to testify against Joe Gallo, one of the biggest. What are you afraid of?" Having again repeated his arguments for postponement, he said that David Price would be ready for trial on December 4.

His court-appointed co-counsel, Irving Mendelson, then rose to support his application, although for different reasons. "Mr. Gallo doesn't want me as his lawyer, and won't talk to me as a lawyer," he complained. "I then proposed that Mr. Gallo talk to me through Mr. Weiswasser. That he declined to do. Then Mr. Weiswasser assumed the position, under instructions from Mr. Price, that *he* wouldn't talk to me—that is correct, isn't it?" he added, turning to Weiswasser, and apparently it wasn't, for they began to wrangle in a way that made clear how embarrassed both were by this confused, baffling and wholly unprecedented situation. Cutting Weiswasser short, Mendelson then asked for an adjournment until December 4. He was now getting angry. "If Mr. Weiswasser wants me to assist him because of my thirty-eight years and eleven months of experience—whatever that means—I will be very glad to do it, but I cannot do it now because no one wants to talk to Irving Mendelson. . . . I am not going to put myself in the position of taking orders from Price, from strategic headquarters in Florida, where I would like to be myself."

But Judge Sarafite was not to be moved. Echoing the general criticism of Price, he said that, as a veteran at the bar, he "unquestionably knew as well as anybody that a speedy trial would be necessary. . . . It seems to me that when this case was set for October 23, Mr. Price had an obligation to either appear ready for trial or to have someone else appear ready for trial." As to his illness, he went on, there was "no affidavit or doctor's certificate, which is rather a cavalier way to treat a court." Turning then to what he considered the crucial issue, he felt he had given Joey every latitude. "Now because a defendant is entitled to a lawyer of his choosing, in effect I said to the defendant, 'I am going to give you a week to get another lawyer.' And apparently he hasn't lifted a finger to get another lawyer. . . . You can't defeat the administration of justice by that kind of conduct. I will not tolerate it. . . . The application for adjournment is denied, and the case is marked ready."

The trial began in the Court of General Sessions, County of New York, Part 8, at three o'clock. Weiswasser and Mendelson rose immediately and again asked to be excused from representing Joey on the grounds of his refusal to cooperate, and their request was again denied. "He knew that this case has been pending since May of 1961," said Sarafite. "It has been on the calendar numerous times. He has had adequate and sufficient warning that this case is going to trial, and if his lawyer is not here, that is not the responsibility of the court. No defendant can run the calendar of the court and dictate when his case shall go to trial by means of the choice of a lawyer who cannot represent him at the time that he should be represented. Proceed with the trial."

Despite his inexperience, Weiswasser was still not prepared to yield. "If Your Honor pleases," he said, rising with all the dignity he could muster. "I say this defendant refuses to have me act in his behalf as trial counsel. I do not feel, sir, that I should be made to represent a man who does not want me to represent him. Therefore, if Your Honor insists that the trial proceed, sir, I must respectfully decline to take part in the proceedings and will sit mute."

His Honor stared at him for a moment. "You are assigned, Mr. Weiswasser," he said coldly, "and it is up to you to determine what you deem to be the proper course for you to take as an officer of this court. Proceed with the trial."

Having fired the last of his ammunition, Weiswasser shrugged and sat down to confer with Joey, who might have been sitting among the spectators for all the relevance this seemed to have for him. But then Mendelson, whose own position was no less awkward than Weiswasser's, proposed a compromise. He urged Sarafite to allow one juror to be sworn and then adjourn for two weeks in the hope that Price would appear or that Joey could be persuaded to see the danger he was in. After some discussion, the judge reflected for a moment and finally agreed to go over for *one* week when a juror had been picked. The prospective members of the jury were then admitted to the courtroom, and Francis Clark told Joey to stand. "If you wish to challenge an individual juror," he said, "you must do so when he is called and appears and before he is sworn. Do you waive the further giving of this notice?"

Joey glanced around the court before replying. "I refuse to participate in this proceeding," he said severely, "because I feel my constitutional rights have been violated. Until I have time to speak to counsel of my choosing, I will remain mute."

Clark then explained the nature of the charge to the prospective jurors, estimating that the trial would last five days. That done, Stanley E. Gellers was sworn as first juror and jury foreman, and Judge Sarafite adjourned the trial until Tuesday, November 14, at ten o'clock.

Outside the courtroom, Joey more than made up for the unaccustomed strain of sitting mute. Surrounded by reporters, he cornered Mendelson in the hallway by the elevators. "Mendelson—that's a musical name," he observed pleasantly. "And I'm hip to the tune you're playing. It's my swan song. How can you choose jurors for me when you don't even know what my position is?" The attorney's only answer was to wag a reproving finger. Then, from the safety of the descending elevator, Mendelson told the reporters: "He won't talk to me. The judge demands that I represent him. What can I do?"

In one sense, Mendelson had done too much already. Joey's question about choosing a jury had been very much to the point, for the defense had just made its third major blunder. By allowing a juror to be selected, Mendelson and Weiswasser had eliminated the last possibility of securing a change of venue on the grounds of unfavorable publicity—and at precisely the moment when such an argument stood its best chance of success, for the Gallos were now hitting the headlines every day. Clearly, no motion for a change could be entertained once the trial had actually begun, which it had with the swearing-in of Stanley Gellers. When the court reconvened on November 14, Mendelson at once made a motion for the withdrawal of the juror and the declaration of a mistrial.

Judge Sarafite, who had clearly been expecting something of the sort, then asked Weiswasser if he joined in that motion. Suspecting that to do so might compromise his declared intention of playing no part in the trial, he refused, although he wanted a mistrial more than anyone. "I certainly take the same position that I did the last time," he said, "and that is to respectfully decline to take any part in the proceedings and to remain mute."

With the two repudiated attorneys thus disposed of, the judge now turned to Joey himself. "Mr. Gallo?" Joey raised his eyebrows inquiringly. "Stand up when you are addressed," he said, and Joey did so, bleakly. "Do you join in this motion for a mistrial?"

Sensing the trap that Weiswasser had seen, he took evasive action. "I have a lawyer, Your Honor. David Price."

"He is not here."

"I know that, Your Honor."

"Do you join in this motion for a mistrial?"

"I am not a lawyer. I could not truthfully answer that question."

The judge sighed and tried another tack. "Do you *object* to this motion for a mistrial?"

"I would have to consult with my attorney," said Joey patiently.

"Your attorney is not here, according to you."

"Then I wish Your Honor would consult with my attorney."

"We have already decided that, Mr. Gallo. I cannot consult with your attorney. He is not here."

"Then I cannot answer if he is not here."

"Very well," said the judge, having clearly lost the first round on points.

Assistant District Attorney Francis Clark then opposed the motion for a mistrial, reading from an affidavit by David Price filed with the court on November 6, after the adjournment. Price, he said, who claimed to be under a doctor's care, although no supporting certificate to that effect had been filed, stated that he knew the case had been set for trial on October 23 but did not believe that such a recent case would be preferred over older indictments. He asked for an adjournment to December 4. Dismissing this suggestion as an obvious ruse, Clark went on to report that Joey and Weiswasser had applied to the Legal Aid Society for counsel, which at least suggested they were prepared to consider an alternative, and were therefore engaged on a deliberate course of obstruction. To aid the defense in its preparations, he asked that the minutes of the Felony Court hearing in May be marked as a court exhibit since these would provide a preview of the People's case.

Persuaded by these arguments, Judge Sarafite denied the motion for a mistrial. Mendelson immediately took exception to the ruling and moved for an adjournment until December 4. This, too, was denied, and Mendelson again took exception to it. He then asked Weiswasser, through the court, if he, Mendelson, had any alternative to serving as counsel, since Joey still refused to have anything to do with him. To this, Weiswasser replied with his now standard refusal to take any part in the proceedings. Once again, he, too, asked to be released from his assignment, and was again refused. Whereupon, Mendelson declared that he now would also remain mute. He would make no more motions or take any further exceptions. But he would ask the court to inquire of the defendant Gallo if that was his desire, so that this would show on the record. Acknowledging the propriety of this request, Judge Sarafite then turned to Joey for the start of Round Two.

"Mr. Gallo?" he said, and this time Joey rose without being asked. "*Is* that your desire?"

"Your Honor, I stated my position," he replied. "I refuse to participate in any of these proceedings without my counsel."

"I heard that before—you said it and I heard it. This is a different question. Mr. Mendelson now states that you told him you don't want him to participate in this trial. Now I'm asking you—is that your desire?"

Joey shook his head. "My desire is to have Mr. Price represent me," he said.

"And I take it from that that your desire to have David S. Price means you have no desire to have Mr. Mendelson—is that correct?"

"I refuse to answer any questions pertaining to this part of the case," he replied, suddenly scenting danger in a straight answer. But the judge persisted.

"Do you want Mr. Mendelson to remain mute during these proceedings in the courtroom at the trial?"

"Your Honor, I have made my position clear."

"What do you mean, you made it clear?" asked the judge irritably, dropping his guard, and leaving Joey with a clear opening.

"That I refuse to have any participation in any of these proceedings without counsel of my own choosing," he said, thereby clinching the second round.

After a fruitless appeal to Weiswasser, who employed his now usual evasion for fear of compromising his position, Judge Sarafite gratefully accepted a suggestion from Francis Clark and returned to the attack by asking Joey if he intended to represent himself. Joey replied that he was not a lawyer and would remain mute. The judge then asked if he had instructed his counsel to remain mute also. "Your Honor," he said patiently, "I never instructed them to remain mute or not to talk or anything."

"Oh, you didn't?"

"No, I did not."

"You *want* them to participate?"

"I don't care what they do, Your Honor." Round Three to Gallo.

Nonplused, judge and counsel then engaged in further inconclusive argument until Clark again proposed a possible way out. "Your Honor," he said, "I would conclude that since the defendant Gallo does not wish either of the assigned counsel to represent him, that leaves him in the position of representing himself. Now if I am wrong, I would like to know it."

"Well, I see no other conclusion from the facts," said Sarafite and addressed himself again to Joey. "In the light of everything that has happened, do you want either or both of these lawyers to stay in the courtroom during the trial?"

"Your Honor, I am so confused that I have to stand mute," he replied. It was the first hint of strain.

"What is confusing you?" asked the judge, quick to seize the advantage. "I thought you were very clear in your mind."

"Everything is confusing to me. I am not a lawyer, Your Honor. I have to stand mute."

Conscious of his duty to be impartial, and no doubt aware that every word would be weighed on appeal, Sarafite then took Joey through the whole catechism again, finally suggesting that he might like to have Weiswasser present in case he changed his mind.

"Your Honor," said Joey, "I refuse to participate in any of these proceedings."

"I didn't ask you that. . . . Do you mean by that you refuse to answer my question?"

"I truthfully couldn't answer your question," he replied, skirting, for all he knew, a risk of being held in contempt.

"Why?"

"I am not a lawyer."

"You don't have to be a lawyer to answer the question whether you want a lawyer to sit there in the courtroom," the judge said, backing him into a corner.

"Well, I stand on the Constitution of the United States of America," said Joey, furious at being hounded and with the obvious inadequacy of his reply.

The judge smiled. "Have you any particular section of the Constitution on which you are standing?" he asked mildly, pinning him on the ropes.

"No, sir."

"You mean on the whole document?"

"I stand on the Constitution," he repeated.

"On the whole document. Now do you want Mr. Mendelson to sit there even though he is going to remain mute? Do you want him to sit in the courtroom during the trial?"

"Your Honor," he sighed, "I refuse to participate in any of these proceedings."

"Do you refuse to answer my question?"

"I refuse to participate in these proceedings," he said doggedly.

"Do you mean by refusing to participate in these proceedings that you are refusing to answer my question?"

"I have to remain mute, Your Honor."

His Honor gave up and settled for a draw. "Very well."

He then ruled that Joey was deemed to be representing himself, and proceeded to explain what that meant. "Do you understand what I have just said?" he asked in conclusion.

"Your Honor," said Joey, "I refuse to participate in any of these proceedings." And, indeed, those were the last words he spoke on the record before the verdict two days later.

Though relieved of their assignments, Weiswasser and Mendelson elected to stay in court, and a jury of nine men and three women was then empaneled. There were no challenges. Stanley Gellers, the original juror, having enjoyed his brief rise from obscurity, returned to it by excusing himself on the grounds that he now knew about the case and could no longer be fair and impartial. No doubt this was true, but a possibly more persuasive reason was suggested by Francis Clark when he asked the court not to reveal the home addresses of jurors and witnesses. An appreciative murmur stirred the spectators crowding together on the public benches, their sense of drama already titillated by the search they had undergone at the door and by the armed guards everywhere. The air of expectancy was like that at a bullfight.

But there was little enough to excite them when Clark rose after the lunchtime recess to make his opening address to the jury. With the tangled dispute over Joey's legal representation now temporarily resolved, to the prosecution's satisfaction at least, the proceedings were so lacking in tension and incident without a contribution from the defense that they settled into the flat recital of a story already well known in its essentials from the media's coverage of the earlier Felony Court hearing. In fact, the trial soon took on the air of a rather tedious formality that had to be gone through before Joey could be locked up in the public interest.

This impression was reinforced at the end of the day when Clark concluded his outline of the evidence to be presented and Judge Sarafite adjourned until the following morning. No sooner had the jury left the court than he revoked Joey's $35,000 bail and ordered him to be detained for the duration of the trial. No reason was given for this apparently arbitrary decision, and when Weiswasser rose to protest, saying, "At the request of the defendant—" Joey grabbed his arm, made a gesture of scorn and said, out of earshot of the court reporter, "Don't even bother with it. He's too prejudiced." Weiswasser hesitated, then nodded. "I beg your pardon," he continued. "No remarks will be made as to the remanding."

No reason ever appeared on the record to account for Sarafite's decision. The Assistant District Attorney had not asked for Joey's bail to be revoked, nor had there been any suggestion that he might abscond. As it turned out, a police raid on President Street next day went more smoothly than might have been the case if Joey had been at large, but this still lay ahead when the trial resumed at ten o'clock on Wednesday morning, November 15. Before Clark could call his first witness, Teddy Moss, to the stand, Weiswasser asked for the court's permission to make a statement on behalf of David Price.

"I spoke to Mr. Price on the telephone last evening," he said, "and informed him of the status of the case. He asked me to make a statement in his behalf to Your Honor to the effect that after the hearing in Felony Court, which concerned this defendant and the codefendants who have been severed, and the defendants were held, Mr. Paul Kelly then stated to Mr. Price in effect that he would move this case in front of Judge Sarafite, and the defendant, Joseph Gallo, would then get about seven to fifteen years. In view of this, Mr. Price feels a motion should be made by the firm of Price & Iovine in behalf of the defendant Gallo that Your Honor disqualify himself because of the possibility of prejudice."

To his credit, Weiswasser seemed thoroughly uncomfortable in having to serve as a vehicle for this ill-judged, futile and transparently desperate maneuver to salvage something from the wreck of Joey's defense. Based on nothing more than the unsupported word of an absentee attorney who had so far failed conspicuously to satisfy the court about his honesty of purpose, it never stood the smallest chance of success. If anything, it could only have hardened opinion against Joey, if that were possible, both then and later at the appeal stage. More amused than affronted, Judge Sarafite dealt with this fourth major blunder by the defense with almost contemptuous ease.

"Number one," he said, "this is news to me. Number two, if that statement was made, it was stupid and should never have been made. Number three, your motion to disqualify is denied." Assistant District Attorney Paul Kelly then chipped in with a vigorous and categorical denial that any such conversation with Price had ever taken place, and the judge added the finishing touches. "Any case that appears before me on the calendar," he said, "appears there without any discussion with me at any time. That is my rule, and it was so in this case." Without more ado, he ordered Kelly to proceed, and Teddy Moss was sworn in, seemingly more composed and better rehearsed than the prosecution had earlier led the court to expect.

In the light of subsequent events, it would seem that, although Moss was not quite as upright and law-abiding a businessman as the District Attorney would have had the jury believe, the substance of his story, if not the whole truth, was broadly true as far as it went. It was never tested under cross-examination, for which Clark and Kelly were no doubt suitably grateful to Price & Iovine, but it held up well enough later on to secure the convictions of Tony Leone, who, significantly, pleaded guilty, Hyman Powell and Michael Albergo, all of whom *were* defended by counsel. (Sidney Slater, of course, had turned informer to avoid prosecution, while the case against Ali Waffa was eventually dismissed for lack of evidence.) No witness was ever produced to challenge the essential accuracy of Moss's account of his dealings with Joey, and certainly none of the innumerable appeals staged afterward relied on evidence designed to refute it—they all hinged on Joey's constitutional right to counsel of his choice or on the argument that the unfavorable publicity had denied him a fair trial. What line the defense would have taken had he won a new trial is a matter for conjecture—to judge from Joey's remarks at the bail hearing, he would probably have tried to discredit Moss, probing his relations with the murdered Rosenberg in an effort to show that his testimony was tainted, that the District Attorney had "bought" it in return for clemency in another connection—but on the record, he never denied the details of the case against him. And, for what it is worth, they were later more or less corroborated by Sidney Slater.

Moss told the court that on April 24, five days after the Rosenberg killing, Hyman Powell had brought Slater around to see him at his office in an umbrella store next door to the G & M Check Cashing Service, in which he had a half-interest, at 282 Seventh Avenue in Manhattan. Besides this business, which had a volume of about $5.5 million a year, he also owned Shine's Bar & Grill on University Place, a half-interest in Dunleavy's at 381 Third Avenue, and a quarter-share of Ted's Club on Fulton Street. Slater, he said, told him about his connection with the Gallos and wanted to know if he needed any help with collections or any jukeboxes or pinball machines. On being refused, he left two phone numbers for Moss to call if he changed his mind. Two or three days later, Slater stopped by again, renewing his promise of assistance, and on May 3, showed up once more, this time with Tony Leone and Al Schaeffer, to offer him a truckload of hijacked liquor for $48,000. According to Moss, when he virtuously refused to have any part of such a deal, Slater said, "Well, I'll have to call Joe."

"About ten, fifteen minutes later, I see the door open and four people walk in," Moss continued. "The first person that walked in wasn't there before with the other three, and he comes walking to the back and up the stairs, and he comes up to the balcony and he walks around a few minutes, looking around the place, and then comes up to me and touches me around. Then he sits down next to me in a chair on the side.

"I said to Joe, I said, 'Do you remember me? I was in your place on Church Avenue. You made me a hamburger once.'

"He didn't remember; a lot of people went there. 'What seems to be the trouble here?' he said.

" 'There's no trouble,' I said. 'These people want me to handle something which I am not interested in.'

" 'Come on,' he said. 'You better come downstairs with me. I want to talk to you.' "

Moss said he then followed Joey out into the street and together they walked around the block discussing the situation.

"These are friends of mine," said Joey. "I want you to see what you can do for them. Help them out."

"There's nothing I *can* do for them," Moss protested. "I haven't got that kind of money, and I am not interested in this kind of deal."

Joey was silent for a moment. Then he said, "I hear you were called down to Bath Beach police station in reference to the Rosenberg homicide."

"Yes, I was."

"What did they ask you there?"

"They asked me how I knew him and what business dealings I had with him, and at the end they asked me if I knew a fellow by the name of Joe Gallo, which I told him I didn't, and that was it."

"That's all they asked you?"

"That's all."

"You didn't tell them anything else?"

"There was nothing for me to tell them. I don't know anything about it."

"Do you *want* to know anything about it?"

"No. I am not interested. I don't want to know."

"You are better off that way. You will remain healthier. You see what happens to wise guys?"

"I am not a wise guy," said Moss. "I just want to be left alone."

With that, according to Moss, they headed back toward the umbrella store. "Look," said Joey, as he left him there with the other three, "you do what you can for these fellows. They are friends of mine." But after he had gone, Moss stuck to his guns, persisting in his refusal to consider the liquor deal, and Slater eventually went away with the others to fetch Joey back again.

"Joe came up the stairs first and they all sat down," Moss continued. "Joe sat down next to me and stayed there about a minute. Then he picked up a book and threw it at Sid Slater and started cursing at him. He said, 'Why did you bring me here? I thought you had everything all sewed up.' Then he faced me and says, 'Look, I'm not fooling around. You better go along with this deal.'

" 'Look, I have nothing,' I says. 'Leave me alone.' I went to the desk and I pulled out some loan payment books that I had from the bank. I said, 'If I had any money, I wouldn't have all these payment books. Please leave me alone.'

"He says, 'Who do you think this city is run by—people like you or people like me?'

"I says, 'I don't know who it's run by. I just want to be left alone. I can't handle any of this.'

"He says, 'Look. I've been here long enough. I'm not going to see you again. You'd better do right by my friends.' And he got up and left.

"Tony Leone and Al Schaeffer then left also. After they left, Sid Slater said to me, he says, 'Oh boy, we're in trouble.' He says, 'You see what he did? He just threw that book at me. If I go back without this deal, I'm going to get my head busted.' "

Despite this bid for sympathy, Moss told the court, he continued to resist the proposition, and Slater eventually left, promising to return the following Monday to see if he had managed to raise any money, even $500, to finance some part of the deal. That night, Moss called Mike Albergo, who worked for him at another bar he owned called the Rumpus Room in Queens, to ask for his advice. As a result of that conversation, Albergo met Slater at the umbrella store on the Monday and told him to leave Moss alone because "he's a good kid." Slater asked Albergo his name, shook hands and left.

Next day, May 9, Moss left his office at about 4 P.M. and drove uptown to get a haircut at the Dawn Patrol barbershop on Broadway between Fifty-first and Fifty-second streets. "About five or ten minutes after I was in the chair," he said, "I notice through the glass, in the mirror in front of me, that Joe Gallo and Al Schaeffer walk in. I don't believe they had seen me, and they just walk right to the back. And I was watching them through the mirror and I seen them sit down on two of the chairs opposite me in the rear. When I finished my haircut, I got up and started to leave. Joe Gallo caught my eye and waved me to come back to him. I walked back there and he says, 'Wait around a few minutes. I want to speak to you.'

"I says I was in a hurry. He says, 'Wait around a few minutes. We'll only be five, ten minutes.' So I said okay. I went up and I paid for my haircut and I walked back again where he was having his hair cut and he asked me if I took care of his and his friend's haircut also. I said, 'No, I didn't.' He says, 'You're not a sport.' I waited around a few more minutes and I said, 'I got to go across the street. I'll be back.' So I left the barbershop and I walked across the street and bought a newspaper. My car was parked across the street and I had an envelope on me with some papers and money in it, and I put the envelope in back of the car, in the trunk. As I was closing the trunk, I see Joe Gallo coming out of the barbershop, putting on his coat, and I walked back across the street toward him.

"He says, 'Come on. Let's take a walk.' So we started to walk to the corner of Fifty-second Street. . . . Joe says to me, 'You know, this is a big city, and a lot of strange things can happen to wise guys. As we are walking now, a brick can fall on your head. You can fall down a flight of stairs. Or a car can run you over. A lot of things can happen.'

"I says, 'Well, I'm not a wise guy.' I says, 'What do you want from me?'

"He says, 'Who's this guy Mike you had up in your place Monday?'

"I said, 'He was just a friend of mine. He just happened to be there at that time.'

"He says, 'Well, how come he put his two cents in?'

"I says, 'Well, he was just trying to help me out. He thought he was doing me a good turn.'

" 'Well, does he know who he's getting involved with? Did you tell him?'

" 'No, I didn't tell him.'

"He says, 'If you are a friend of his, why don't you tell him? Maybe he'll mind his own business. He could wind up with his head broken.'

"I says, 'No, I didn't tell him. He didn't mean any harm.'

Joey then asked Moss for Mike's last name, and Moss pretended he didn't know it. They continued walking around the block.

" 'I hear you're a pretty smart kid,' he says. 'That wasn't too smart of you, not going along with my friends after I asked you to help them out.'

" 'Well, I couldn't go along,' I says. 'What do you want me to do? Go out and steal for you?'

"He says, 'Now look, don't lie to me. I got you pretty well checked out. I admire you. You're an ambitious kid. You're only a youngster. I like those kind of kids for partners.'

" 'Well, I don't know who you got your information from or who checked me out,' I says. 'I have nothing. I just want to be left alone.'

" 'Now look,' he says, 'don't start lying and we'll get along fine.'

"And I says, 'I'm not lying to you. I don't know how I can convince you.'

"At that time, he told me to keep quiet for a minute because somebody passed in front of us. And as the fellow passed, he said, 'You see that? You got to watch where you're talking. That's a cop. Now look, we can be friends. I'm in a lot of trouble now. The cops

168 JOEY

have been pulling me and my family out of the house ten times a day. Until the heat blows over, I'm going to be leaving town, and I want to know before I leave who my friends are and who they aren't. I want to remember you as a friend.'

"I says, 'Well, look, I don't know what would make me a friend of yours, but I have nothing and I can't help you out.'

"He then said to me, 'I seen you put an envelope in your car.'

" 'Yes, I did.'

" 'What was it?'

" 'Some personal belongings of mine.'

"So he started to think for a minute, and then he said to me, 'If you were in my place, what would be your next question?'

" 'Well, you'll probably ask me to see the envelope.'

"He said, 'You're right. I want to see that envelope.' "

For reasons he did not explain, Moss then said he would show Al Schaeffer the contents of the envelope but not Joey, and persisted in his refusal even though Joey again threatened him. If anything happened to Moss, he said, no one would ever pin it on him because he would make a point of being in California at the time. But when Moss still protested that he just wanted to be left alone, Joey said, "Okay, pal," took his hand, shook it and let him go.

Moss's testimony to this point establishes the desired tone of injured innocence. There is also a none too subtle suggestion that Joey was claiming responsibility for the Rosenberg killing, and he is made to say that he is in a lot of trouble from police pressure, which is not only an unlikely confession from someone playing a heavy, but completely out of character for Joey in any of his roles. It also seems that, at this stage, he was relying exclusively on his reputation to cow Moss—there had been no displays of muscle—and, if his would-be victim was really as innocent as he pretended to be, this, too, strikes a false note. In May, 1961, Joey was not the public figure he became six months later. He could trade on his reputation only among those who knew of it, whose business took them into *his* world. The oblique, almost casual approach that Moss described, therefore, as well as his failure to go to the police, strongly suggest that Joey was, in fact, seeking to move in on Moss's loan-shark business, and that the bars and grills were just incidental. Seen in this light, the behavior of both makes better sense. Otherwise, most of the circumstantial detail and the generally furtive air of cheap menace in Moss's story rings true.

The following night, May 10, Moss went on, he received a phone call at home from Mike Albergo, who said that "they" wanted to see him downtown. Knowing who "they" were without having to ask, Moss told him to call next morning and tell him what happened. A few hours later, at 3 A.M., Albergo phoned again to report that he had spoken to "them," that everything was all right, and that they wanted Moss to join them right away at the Luna. Taken by surprise, Moss at first agreed, then changed his mind and called back five minutes later with the excuse that his wife Goldie was hysterical and wouldn't let him go. After a muffled colloquy at the other end, Albergo said okay. He would call him at his office in the morning.

That was the night Albergo changed sides. How it happened was never described in court, although the District Attorney knew all about it from Sidney Slater, who was there at the Luna with Joey, Sonny Cammerone, Tony Leone and Joe Jelly. "Mike Albergo came in, saw the setup and almost dropped dead," Slater said. "He knew everyone at Joey's table carried a gun. He said very politely, 'How are you, Mr. Gallo?' and Joey knew the deal was set. He told Mike the liquor was just an angle to start moving in on Moss, that he was taking over Teddy's loan business. 'I'm going to take that over with or without your help,' he said. 'If you want to help us out, you can have the Rumpus Room. And I mean as owner, not just a front man like you were for Moss. If you don't want to help us out, we'll fit you for a wooden kimono, and I mean tonight.'

" 'Okay,' Mike said, sweating a little. 'What do you want me to do?' "

What he did, according to Moss's testimony, was to call, as arranged, on Thursday morning, May 11, and tell his former employer to be on the corner of Mulberry Street and Canal Street at 1 P.M. Moss did as he was told and was met there by Albergo and Tony Leone, who took him to a storefront club on Park Street.

"Tony and Mike and me sat down in the back," he told the jury.

"About five minutes later, Joe Gallo walks in with another man, Ali Waffa. Joe walked up to me and looked at me and then smacked me across the face. He says, 'You know, you're a wise guy. Now ask me —"Why am I a wise guy?" ' And he smacked me again. And as he smacked me, I picked up my hands, and he hit me again. 'You're tough?' he says. 'You want to fight here?'

" 'No,' I says.

"He says, 'Now ask me the right way—"Why am I a wise guy?" '

"So I asked him, 'Why am I a wise guy?'

"He says, 'Because you got this innocent person'—and he pointed to Mike Albergo—'into the middle of something that he had no business knowing about.'

" 'I didn't get Mike into anything. You can ask Mike about it.'

" 'Don't lie to me,' he says, and he smacked me again.

"I says, 'Well, ask Mike. Mike will tell you that I told him I didn't want him to be there Monday. It was just an accident that he happened to be there.'

" 'Don't lie,' he says. 'You knew that Slater stopped by your check-cashing place at ten o'clock that morning and left a message that he would be back at four.'

" 'Nobody ever gave me the message,' I says. 'I didn't know anything about it.'

Following a well-worn formula, Joey then went out with Mike and left Moss alone with Tony Leone and Ali Waffa. The three sat in silence for several minutes, and then Leone asked suddenly, "How old are you, kid?"

"I'm twenty-eight," said Moss.

Leone shook his head. "You're just a young kid," he said sorrowfully. "Too bad."

Silence. After several more minutes, it was Ali Baba's turn. "You know, they're mad that you didn't show up last night," he said.

"Well, I called them back," Moss protested. "I told them I couldn't make it."

Ali Baba shook his head. "They're not fooling around," he said. "You better go along with them. They're awful mad."

More silence. A few minutes later, Joey relieved Leone and Ali

Baba and replaced them with Albergo, who leaned forward confidentially and told Moss in an undertone, "I don't know how we got into this thing, but they're big and they're not fooling around. I spoke for you, and the best thing is to go along with whatever they want."

"Is there anybody we can see?" asked Moss, betraying a more intimate knowledge of the underworld than was altogether fitting in an honest businessman. "Anything we can do to get these people off me?"

"No," said Albergo. "They're the biggest. The best thing is to go along with them. You know, last night when I called you, they had somebody out by your house and they were out to get you."

Right on cue, the smiling master of ceremonies then led the rest of his cast back into the room. "Joe Gallo walked up to me," Moss told the court, "and put his hand on my shoulder and says, 'Sorry you had to do things this way, but some people only understand one language. But I spoke to Mike and I know that everything is going to be all right. You're going to go along with everything we want. You just tell me the truth—tell us everything—and we'll have no problem.'"

Albergo then excused himself, and Joey sat down beside Moss with the obvious intention of getting their partnership under way in a spirit of goodwill. "You're a young fellow," he said. "You're ambitious, and that's the kind of people I like to be partners with. You're going to be better off in the long run. You'll still run everything the same that you have been, except that we'll take a lot of the headaches off you. We'll take care of a lot of things for you, and you'll even do better than you were doing before. You'll even make more money. I'll come up with a lot of things. You'll be my partner."

"But I'm not interested in those things," Moss said feebly.

"Well, you'll be interested now."

"Why? Of all the people in this whole world, why did you have to pick on me?"

"Well, if it wasn't me, it would probably be someone else," said Joey reasonably. "I got a lot of people to feed. At one time, there were a lot of ways for us to make a buck. There was dope and there was gambling and there was numbers and there was moneylending.

But now they clamped down on all that stuff, we got to find other ways. But you're not going to be sorry. Mike put in a good word for you, and I know what kind of a guy you are. You just level with us, and that will be all right. We better get out of here. Let's go get some coffee." As they went through the door, Joey clapped him on the back, "Don't look so sad, partner. Everything's going to be all right."

In his recollection of this last speech, Moss again undermined the plausibility of his own testimony by making a major racketeer like Joey appear to compliment the Police Department on its success in cutting off his sources of criminal revenue. At no time in his career had there been any suggestion that Joey was involved with drugs—except hashish, and then only for his own use—and if gambling and moneylending had been suppressed, it was certainly news to most New Yorkers, including Moss.

He went on to describe how he sat in the Columbus Restaurant with a cup of coffee while Joey figured out with pen and paper what they were going to do with his bars. The Rumpus Room was going to Albergo. The others would be sold if they didn't pay. At the end of each week, Moss would tell him what each had made—"I trust my partners"—and they would split the profits. He wanted to see the books, and Moss gave him the name of his accountant. He also insisted on another meeting when Moss said he had to go because his wife was waiting for him.

"When do you want to make it?" Joey asked.

"Leave it go for a week or so," said Moss. "Everybody's nervous and excited. I have to talk to them."

"We can't let it go for a week. We'll make it tonight."

"I can't *make* it tonight. My wife is hysterical and everything. I have to be with *her* tonight."

Joey stopped smiling. "Who is the boss in your family—you or your wife?"

"*I* am."

"Then if *you* can't talk to her, *I* will talk to her."

Tony Leone didn't like the sound of that. "Don't worry, Joey," he said, in a soothing tone. "He can handle her."

"*Can* you handle her?" Joey demanded.

"I will talk to her," said Moss. "But I still don't want to make it tonight."

"Well, how about tomorrow?"

"If it has to be tomorrow, it will be tomorrow."

"Okay. When you go back, don't talk to anybody or tell them anything. All right?"

With that, Moss hailed a cab and left, having agreed to meet again with Joey at the Luna at 7 P.M. next day.

"Now that afternoon, I spoke to a man from the District Attorney's office," he told the court, without going into details or stating who had, in fact, approached whom—a circumstance that the defense, had there been one, would no doubt have been anxious to explore. All Moss was prepared to say about it was that, on the following morning, May 12, he went with his father to the Prince George Hotel on East Twenty-eighth Street in Manhattan, where he met Assistant District Attorney Paul Kelly and several police officers. On their instructions, he then made two tape-recorded telephone calls to Mike Albergo, presumably to provide the District Attorney's office with evidence corroborating the allegations Moss was to make against Joey.

The logic of this was obscure. Although Moss may well have concluded by now that Albergo had defected to the enemy, he was still obviously pretending to be Moss's friend—his usefulness to Joey depended on it—so that Kelly could hardly have expected Albergo to incriminate himself, or Joey, by admitting he was Joey's agent. The most he could have hoped for was to hear Albergo urge Moss, as a friend, to go along with Joey for fear of what might happen if he didn't—advice which might have been bad but would not have been criminal. If this *was* the intention, it was completely vitiated in the event, since Moss and Albergo never once referred to Joey by name in either of their two recorded conversations; it was always "they" and "them." And even if they *had* done so, the tapes would almost certainly have been ruled inadmissible as evidence, as indeed they were, by Judge Sarafite, when the case for the People rested. It is, therefore, hard to see what Kelly hoped to gain, either from recording the calls or from presenting the somewhat garbled transcripts in court, particularly as they tended to throw more doubt than light on the story Moss had to tell.

At one point in their taped conversation, for instance, Moss said: "I don't owe them anything. I never did business with them. I don't owe anything. How far do they go with something like this? Would they kill a guy over—"

Albergo: "No, honest. Honest, Teddy. How can they do it? How can they hurt anybody? How can they hurt anybody? You're a legitimate guy in the first place, right? You're legitimate. You've got a clean business, your check-cashing business. You've got an interest in a bar or something—it's a legitimate business. And you're shy-locking. You're a kind of shylock. I don't know what you done with this guy [inaudible]. That was your biggest mistake you made."

This passage, and others like it, hardly support the idea that Albergo was trying on Joey's behalf to frighten Moss with threats of violence, or that Moss's check-cashing business and bars were much more than a "legitimate" front for his shylocking. The "guy" associated with Moss's "biggest mistake" is not identified in what now becomes a confused and scrambled account of what was said, although a moment later, Moss asks, "You mean, they knew Morty?" —referring presumably to the murdered Rosenberg—and Albergo replies, "I assume they did. They must have known him."

There were further puzzling references, never explained in court, to a payment of $35,000 or $38,000 that Moss had made to some-body, and to $4,000 or $5,000 in cash that Albergo was keeping for Moss in the office of the Rumpus Room—a bar that, curiously enough, Moss never admitted to owning in his testimony. "They've seen it," said Albergo. "They were down there last night—I told you that." He also insisted that he didn't want it. "That is your money," he said. "I don't want your money. I don't want nothing that belongs to you. I just want to work for my money, and I don't think it's fair. It's yours, and you're entitled to it." And again, later on: "I don't want nothing. This is all yours. For the minute, I didn't say nothing, but tonight I am going to tell them. As long as you are there, I can talk a little bit for you. I can. I will talk. Both ways. Not for myself. For you. They're interested in one thing."

Unfortunately, Albergo never specified what that one thing was, but these were practically the only references made to any of Moss's legitimate business in the course of their conversation, so that the indications are that "they" were interested in something more important. At any rate, Moss kept his rendezvous at the Luna that night, and was reassured to see a detective and two policewomen, whom he had previously met in the District Attorney's office, already seated at a table in the rear of the restaurant. But then Albergo gave him a nervous moment. When he arrived, he announced that the meeting place had been changed to another restaurant across the street.

"No," said Moss, panicked by the thought of losing his police protection. "They told me to meet them here. I will stay here."

Albergo then went off to report this fresh defiance and returned some minutes later with Joey, who took them both to the rear of the restaurant and sat down next to the detective and policewomen at an adjoining table. Having ordered some wine, Moss said, Joey then left him alone for a couple of minutes with Albergo, who told him to cheer up, and came back followed by two other men.

"Joey introduced me to both of them—I don't recall their names, and he says, 'He's all right. He's going along with us. Where is everybody?' They were across the street. He said, 'Do you want to join us for dinner?' They said, 'No.' He told them to go back across the street and wait for him, and they left. Then Joe says, 'Before we discuss business, let's get something in our stomachs,' and he asked me what I wanted to eat. I told him I wasn't hungry. He said, 'Go ahead—have something. They have good steak here.' And I said, 'No, I don't want anything.' He said, 'Have something,' so I ordered a shrimp cocktail. And he suggested something to Mike that was supposed to be a specialty of the place, and he and Mike ordered it. Then the owner of the place, an elderly woman, came up and was talking to Joe at the table, and there was just some general conversation between them. . . .

"Joey says, 'It's nice to eat steak. It's nice knowing everybody has a buck in their pocket so that they can afford to buy good food.' And he looked at me and he said, 'Don't you agree?' And I says, 'Yes, it's nice. It's nice for everybody to eat well.' "

When they had finished eating, Moss went on, Joey said okay, it was time to get down to business. "And then I said to him, I said, 'Look, Joe. I told you before I didn't have anything. I don't want any part of this. Just leave me out of it.'

"He says, 'Didn't you learn from yesterday's meeting that we're not fooling around? What are you—stupid or something?' And he got up from the table and he told Mike, he said, 'You'd better speak to this stupid kid.' And he said something to him in Italian and walked out of the restaurant.

"Mike says to me, 'You got them mad.' He says, 'You got them mad,' and that I should go along with them.

"I said, 'Mike, I told you—I've nothing. And I want out of this thing.'

"He says, 'Well, I will tell you what. When he comes back in, I will speak to him and I will tell him what I told you this afternoon about putting somebody in with you just to prove that you have nothing. I don't know how we got in this mess, but we got to try to get out of it. They're not fooling around. You know what he said to me in Italian?'

"So I said, 'What?'

"He said, 'Well, if he needs some time to think it over, we'll put him in the hospital for four to five months, and that'll give him time.'

"Then Joe came back to the table and he said, 'What's it going to be? Does he need time to think this over in the hospital or is he coming along with us?'

"Mike got up with him and they walked to the back, to the kitchen entrance. They're gone a few minutes and then they both came back to the table. Joe was about to sit down—Mike had already sat down —when some fellow came in the front door and called Joe to the rear of the restaurant. They weren't too far away from me, and I overheard them say, this one fellow say to the other, 'The place is crawling with cops.'

"Joe came back to the table and he says, 'Your wife didn't call the cops or anything?'

"I says, 'No. I wouldn't be here if she did.'

"He said, 'Well, I can't understand why all the cops are around.

There's no more policy around here or bookmaking. Let's get out of here.'

"And they all got up and we started to walk out of the restaurant. We did leave the restaurant and Joe and Mike turned to the right, starting to walk up Mulberry Street, and I stood there. Mike called to me, he said, 'Come on. Let's go.' I said that I wasn't going to go there. Joe said, 'If he don't want to go, just leave him.' And then the policemen came on the scene."

That concluded Moss's testimony. While he was telling his story, Joey had seemed hardly to be listening. He had gazed at the ceiling, stared absently at the spectators and doodled on a scratch pad with studied concentration. There had been no surprises. Very little had been added to the evidence which he had already heard in Felony Court, apart from the tape transcripts, and even without a defense attorney to probe the weaknesses in Moss's story, he had little enough to worry about at this stage. He knew the jury would never convict him on Moss's word alone. He was also confident, from his own knowledge of what had been said at the Luna that night, that the District Attorney had no real corroborative evidence to back up the allegations of their star witness. He twisted around in his chair and smiled reassuringly at Jeffie as Detective Alfred Halikias was sworn in.

Halikias testified that he had arrived at the Luna with Police-women Louise Ingrisini and Joanne Vitaglia at about 6:30 that evening and taken a table in the back of the restaurant. Moss had arrived at 7:02, followed by Albergo and Joe Gallo at 7:15. He had then heard Joey say, "Well, I don't want to talk no business until we've had a feast. Let's go to the rear, where we'll have more room." They sat down at the adjoining table and Joey ordered dinner. At about 7:50, they were joined by two men, later identified as Anthony Cammerone and Nicholas Bianco. "Mr. Gallo asked them if they wanted anything to eat," said Halikias. "They declined. Then Mr. Gallo said, 'This fellow is all right. He's going to come in on the deal with us.' "

At 8:01, Cammerone and Bianco left. "Gallo was heard to say, 'Listen, you fuck, don't talk like a little girl. I want straight answers.'

Mr. Moss replied, but I wasn't able to hear what he said." At about 8:07, Gallo and Albergo went to confer by the kitchen door and remained in conversation for about eleven minutes before returning to the table. "Gallo was then heard to say," Halikias went on, " 'Now listen. You got to come in with us on this deal because I'll put you in the hospital for a couple of months, and you'll have something to think about when you're stretched out in the hospital.' "

A few minutes later, a man subsequently identified as John Manna entered the restaurant and took Joey to the rear for a whispered conversation. While this was going on, "Albergo was overheard to say to Moss, 'Listen, Teddy, I spent nine hours with these guys last night. You heard what they said. They're not kidding. They'll put you in the hospital.'

"Gallo returned to the table and says to Moss, 'Did your wife know you were coming down here? There's cops all over the place.' 'No, she wouldn't do a thing like that,' says Moss. 'Well, I don't know what they would be doing down here. There's no more policy down here.' " Joey then called for the check, paid, and the three of them left at approximately 8:31.

With that, Paul Kelly ended his examination of the witness and rested the People's case. Joey meanwhile, in marked contrast to the ostentatious boredom with which he had listened to Moss, had attended to Halikias' testimony with mounting irritation. As the detective stepped down and walked past the defense table, Joey suddenly erupted to his feet and called him a motherfucking son of a bitch. Halikias stopped in his tracks, and a court attendant hastily pushed between them. But once launched, Joey was not easily silenced. Broadening his criticism of the prosecution's tactics, he called Kelly a dirty rat and went on cursing and shouting for some time before Judge Sarafite, hammering away with his gavel, finally managed to restore order.

A good defense attorney would certainly have been more temperate in his comments, but hardly less vigorous in his attack on the People's evidence. To convict Joey, Kelly needed Halikias, as a reliable independent witness, to corroborate what Moss had said about his meeting with Joey at the Luna. Everything hinged on that, for otherwise it was just one man's word against another's. To prove the crime of attempted extortion, he needed Halikias to prove that Joey had threatened Moss, since extortion is defined by statute as the obtaining of property from another with his consent induced by a wrongful use of force or fear.

But there were very obvious discrepancies between the account given by Moss and the story told by Halikias, whose testimony was even inconsistent with the outline of the case provided for the jury in Francis Clark's opening address. Where Moss and Clark both agreed, for instance, that the threat to put Moss in the hospital came *before* Joey went into a huddle with Albergo by the kitchen door, Halikias said it came *after*. Similarly, Moss and Clark also agreed that Joey left the restaurant after making the threat, whereupon Albergo made his final attempt to talk Moss around. Halikias, on the other hand, makes no mention of Joey leaving the restaurant at all, and says that Albergo talked to Moss when John Manna came in to warn Joey that the place was crawling with cops.

There are other problems, too, in reconciling the testimony of the People's witnesses. Unlike Moss, Halikias does not seem to have heard Joey utter the threat in Italian—nor does he say whether he would have understood it if he *had* done so—and all three versions of the story conflict as to the exact wording of the threat in either Italian *or* English. According to Clark, Albergo said to Moss, "He told me in Italian, if you need some time to think this thing over, he will put you in the hospital for three months, and that will give you time to come around to his way of thinking." Moss himself put it differently: "He said, 'Well, if he needs some time to think it over, we'll put him in the hospital for four or five months, and that'll give him time.'" Halikias testified to yet a third variation, with Joey speaking apparently in English: "Now listen. You got to come in with us on this deal because I'll put you in the hospital for a couple of months, and you'll have something to think about when you're stretched out in the hospital."

Somebody evidently hadn't learned his lines properly. And since Moss's testimony tallied closely with Clark's opening address in all but a few details, that somebody seemed to be Detective Halikias—

the reliable, independent witness upon whose unimpeachable testimony the People's entire case depended. Had not the elderly Price been absent in Florida, or had he not instructed the youthful Weiswasser to take no part in the trial, or had he not made it impossible for Irving Mendelson to do so, the indictment must surely have been thrown out on defense counsel's cross-examination of Moss and Halikias. As it was, when Judge Sarafite at last silenced Joey's outburst, he deemed a motion to have been made to dismiss the indictment on the ground that the People had failed to establish a prima facie case, and then denied it. After further discussion, he then also deemed a motion to have been made on behalf of the defendant to dismiss the indictment on the ground that the People had failed to establish the guilt of the defendant beyond a reasonable doubt, and this, too, was denied. He then adjourned until the following morning, Thursday, November 16.

It was a black day for the Gallos. While Joey was being tried without counsel in the Court of General Sessions, his father had undergone a trial of another sort at a hearing in the offices of the Immigration and Naturalization Service, which was seeking to deport him as an illegal immigrant. And there was more to come. At six o'clock that evening, acting on another tip from Sidney Slater, the police again raided President Street, a well-planned operation that may not have been entirely unconnected with Judge Sarafite's unexplained, and otherwise inexplicable, decision to revoke Joey's bail twenty-four hours earlier. They were looking for arms, but, according to Slater, in the wrong place.

"The Gallos were quietly collecting an arsenal at 51 President Street," he wrote in the *Saturday Evening Post.* "They had hand grenades, rifles with silencers, shotguns and plenty of revolvers. When I told this to Inspector Martin, he looked worried. It could be that the Gallos were getting ready for an all-out attack on the Profacis, so Inspector Martin decided to raid Gallo headquarters. I told him the guns and grenades and bombs were all in one room on the second floor where Lefty Big Ears Castiglione slept. The next afternoon, Martin's men raided the place. They found four guns in the cellar, but somehow missed the locked room that held the real arsenal. The next day, the Gallos moved the weapons, and I never could find out where they had hidden them." Fourteen arrests were made, and on the following morning, November 16, Joey's father and his brother Al also appeared in court, on the usual harassment charge of consorting. But while they were both released in their own recognizance, Joey was now up to his neck in a legal quagmire and about to be swallowed whole.

On resuming the trial, Judge Sarafite ruled that all evidence of conversations between Moss and Albergo, except those in Joey's presence, was to be struck out, including the transcript of their phone ·calls. He had entertained some doubts about its admissibility, he said, and was resolving them in favor of the defendant. The jury was instructed to disregard it in considering a verdict.

"Thank you, Your Honor," said Joey ironically, making his first contribution for the record in almost two days.

This ruling, of course, pretty well disposed of the People's case against Joey on the conspiracy charge, but it hardly mattered at this stage. The jury had been given every opportunity to draw conclusions that were never challenged by the defense and which, as a result, were not likely to change now as a result of what seemed a mere technicality. Had the judge been forced to rule on the admissibility of Moss's testimony at the time it was given, however, half the indictment might well have been dismissed for lack of evidence. As it was, Francis Clark was given a few minutes to revise his summation notes and he then restated the People's case in a calm, dispassionate monotone, having no need of histrionics. In the absence of any defense, the jurors had little enough choice in arriving at a verdict. Judge Sarafite charged them for nearly an hour, explaining the law on conspiracy and extortion but evidently feeling it no part of his duty to stress the discrepancies in the evidence of the People's witnesses, and the jury retired just before noon. Surprisingly, it deliberated for an hour before lunch without reaching a verdict, and returned to the courtroom at 2:45 to hear the testimony of Detective Halikias read back to them. One juror at least was clearly not convinced by the corroborative evidence, which again pointed up the underlying weakness of the People's case and the disastrous mishandling of Joey's defense. But in the event, a second hearing was sufficient to resolve the doubt. After retiring again for five minutes, the jury came back at 3 o'clock with a verdict of guilty on both counts.

Joey nodded impassively, having expected nothing else, and refused to be sworn. When the clerk asked, "What is your true name?" he replied, "I respectfully decline to answer any questions in this inquest, Your Honor."

"Are you going to give the same answer to every question that will be put to you by the captain?" asked Judge Sarafite. "Just yes or no, please."

"Yes," said Joey.

He was remanded to City Prison for sentencing on December 21. Catching Jeffie's eye, he mouthed the words "Don't worry" as they led him from the court, and she was almost reassured by his still unshaken faith that he would beat the conviction on appeal.

Five weeks later, with their child due at any time, her confidence had faded, but again he nearly persuaded her to disbelieve in the inevitable. Impeccably turned out in his best gray suit, a white shirt and blue tie, he strode jauntily into court as though expecting to be exonerated rather than sentenced, smiling and waving to people he knew among the spectators. His self-assurance was such that, for a moment, he almost convinced them, as he had convinced so many in his life, that Joey Gallo belonged to another order of creation, with powers to suspend the ordinary workings of cause and effect. But only for a moment. When Paul Kelly rose to recite his record and ask for the maximum penalty, he left no one in any doubt about the real reason for prosecuting Joey, or with any real hope for success on appeal.

"In the current war taking place between the Gallo gang and established interests," he said, "there have been killings, shootings, stranglings, kidnapings and disappearances, all directly involving the Gallos. Interestingly enough, since the defendant's being remanded on November 14 in this case, there have been no known offensive actions taken by the Gallos in this dispute. This would give some credence to the belief that Joe Gallo is, in reality, the sparkplug and enforcer in the mob, and his absence from the immediate scene has accounted for the lack of sustained violence on the part of his associates."

Robert Kennedy could hardly have expressed it better. Readily concurring that Joey was "a menace to the community," Judge Sarafite chalked up the first victory in the Attorney General's assault on organized crime by handing down the maximum sentence of seven and one-quarter to fourteen and one-half years' imprisonment. Though roughly done, the prosecution had served its purpose: Joey Gallo was off the streets. With the war against Profaci scarcely begun, they had pulled the teeth of the Gallo gang. But although standing mute, Joey still managed characteristically to have the last word. As he retired from the limelight for the next nine years, he issued a handwritten statement to the press through his Uncle Joe Iovine:

> In his zeal to detect and apprehend criminals, in his striving to maximize police efficiency, District Attorney Kelly, as do many law enforcement officials, seems to have forgotten that there are other Values in our Society which must be balanced against every American Citizen. . . .
>
> I believe the pressure to do something about the rising crime wave is causing too many law enforcement officials to forget that . . . 'A civilized system of law is as much concerned with the *means* employed as it is with the ends themselves' (Justice William Douglas) . . . that 'it is a fair summary of History to say that the safeguards of Liberty have frequently been forged in controversies involving not very nice people' (Justice Felix Frankfurter).

Joey had a point. Though no one can say he was not guilty, there is a reasonable doubt that he was guilty as charged.

Three weeks later, on January 11, 1962, Joie Marie Gallo was born in New York Hospital. Lyn Morgen had taken Jeffie there that morning.

"She called me at about nine o'clock and said she had pains. So I said, 'Ooh! Ooh! Pack your bag. I'll be right over.' I was out of bed and dressed in five minutes and at her house. She was doing all the Reichian things with the natural childbirth and breathing—had it been me, I would have run to the hospital and gotten an anesthetic and that would have been that, but Jeffie wanted to feel it all. So I took her to the hospital and I waited. I did the whole pacing scene. When she checked in, they said, 'What's your husband's name?' She said, 'Joseph Gallo.' 'And what's his occupation?' 'He's a freelance writer,' she said, 'and he's on an assignment.' "

10

Attica

To be locked up was the worst thing that could have happened to Joey, but he was well equipped to deal with it. Though free of most conventional inhibitions, he had nevertheless lived within iron constraints all his life. Of these, by far the most crippling was his concept of masculinity. Joey could never permit himself to respond to any situation in a way that might seem to compromise his manhood. In dealing with any given set of circumstances, the final criterion was not "What does logic or self-interest dictate?" but "How should a *man* behave?"

To Joey, the idea of being a man had an almost mystical significance—it was a priesthood. A man never yielded his true self to anyone. A man could be defeated, but never subdued. A man always rose to a challenge, and stood by the consequences without whining. A man was the prime mover in his own life, and the measure of his quality was the respect he inspired in others. It was not enough to *be* a man; it was necessary to be seen as one in other men's eyes. A man was required to be strong, decisive, proud and brave—to a degree dependent upon the company he kept. In Joey's case, this often meant he had to be hard, willful, arrogant and reckless, but it did mean also that, in some ways, he found it easier to honor his code within the harsh and narrow limits of an all-male prison than he did in the softly treacherous world outside. The challenges were clearer cut, the values less equivocal. To survive, on his own terms, would be a feat that all could respect.

Survival was the one, all-encompassing problem Joey faced in prison. Profaci and his fellow Dons wanted him dead, and every man inside who depended upon mob goodwill to support his family or pay for his lawyers had to be regarded as an enemy. He could never really trust a white inmate, nor could he trust the guards. Bribery was not unknown, and, in any case, he had no reason to suppose that the authorities were especially anxious to keep him alive. In prison, he had no followers. He could buy no favors, inside or out, for money was short and his brothers were penned up on President Street. He was locked in with his enemies, with nowhere to hide.

The first move against his life was made within a day or two of his being sentenced, while he was still lodged in the Tombs. As columnist Victor Riesel later described it,

Word came to the authorities that the Dons, against whom he had rebelled and whom he had bloodied, were going to poison him through his food. Since prisoners are not served individually à la Club 21, this meant poisoning the whole steam table, and killing some 23 other inmates. But this didn't trouble the Dons. They wanted to get Joey. But the prison cook tipped off the chaplain who told the authorities and Joey was handcuffed and shackled and whisked off to Sing Sing.

For a time, he was buoyed up by hopes of an early appeal and a quick release. After spending Christmas in Sing Sing, he was transferred to the bleak Gothic fortress of Attica State Prison on January 11, 1962, the day his daughter was born. But a month later he was back in Brooklyn before Judge Samuel S. Leibowitz in Kings County

Court. On January 15, the Appellate Division and the Court of Appeals had finally confirmed Joey's conviction of September 9, 1960, on the coercion charge. (Sentenced at that time to an indefinite term of up to three years' imprisonment, he had been bailed out on a certificate of reasonable doubt after serving two months in the penitentiary on Rikers Island.) On January 24, 1962, the Kings County District Attorney, Edward S. Silver, had moved to make this conviction the final judgment of the court, and Leibowitz had ordered Joey to be brought down from Attica "for the purpose of having him dealt with according to law."

When he appeared before him, on February 14, Leibowitz said he had heard that David Price was trying to free Joey pending appeal of the Manhattan extortion conviction. To prevent this, he was going to send him back to Rikers Island to complete his interrupted sentence. "I'm going to put him in the pen, where I know I've got him, so he can't be sprung on a writ and go back to President Street, take up his position as boss of a murder gang and start another bloodbath."

Joey, having sampled the joys of Attica, had no objection to this at all. Apart from anything else, it would mean just a cab ride for his visitors instead of a thirteen-hour round trip. "Judge, may I say something?" he said, rising to express his gratitude.

"No," said Leibowitz. "Sit down."

Joey obeyed, with a cheerful nod, and his mother, who was sitting behind him in court, kissed his manacled hands. As he was led away to Rikers Island, he raised them in salute to the bench and called out, "Thank you, Your Honor."

His thanks were premature. New York's Attorney General Louis J. Lefkowitz immediately sued in the Appellate Division for an order directing Joey to be returned to Attica on the grounds that his sentence for extortion had been unlawfully interrupted. This order was granted on March 26, and he was sent back upstate, out of the public eye, to renew his solitary struggle for survival and brood on a growing suspicion that all his appeals were doomed to failure. This suspicion became a certainty when Tony Leone pleaded guilty to the extortion charge a few months later in order to cop a shorter sentence. The last possibility of Joey's release on a certificate of reasonable doubt pending appeal at once disappeared. From then on, the only room left for maneuver was not on the facts of the case, but on the constitutional issue of Joey's choice of counsel, on alleged faults in applying the law, and on pleas for a new trial based on the allegedly prejudicial effects of the publicity surrounding the Gallos at the time of his conviction.

None of this worked. For the next nine years, Joey was to employ lawyer after lawyer and argument after argument without success—indeed, the matter was still before the courts upon his release in March, 1971—but his unremitting campaign gave him a sense of purpose that got him through those years and probably saved him from being certified as criminally insane and confined, perhaps for life, in Matteawan. Even so, his adjustment to the danger and privations of prison life was slow and painful. He refused to see Jeffie and the baby for almost a year. After that, she visited him occasionally, but still had to rely mainly on his letters.

Jeffie,

The other night, I was too tense to eat or perform my regular program. A few laps around Central Park, at a brisk pace, and I was sweating cool, the "thing" of me was moving gracefully and I was connected with the pulse of life in experiences that had no significance —until REICH. Time, space and human animal converge, crash and become indistinguishable—repetitious and boring—the "Big Change" drives the human animal ahead at a frantic chase, till Death deftly cuts the strings, the puppet folds—his show is over.

Lucky unlucky ones applaud while chained to kids buried in an earthen DAM! I breathe true, dig deep and believe in what we have so much that I welcome this interlude of un-naturalness. I form patterns of reasoning that are organized and intelligent with beautiful designs of natural life.

Anyhow, I couldn't sleep, caught a complete cold reading by light from the gallery. What I read that night I shall pass on to you. FIRST! Frances sent me a disturbing letter—last night, it arrived with yours. I was soggy from the cold—today I had some medication and feel better—so I'm sure I don't know what's taken place out there—and wish that it could have been ironed out without airing "dirty linen" in view of my enemies. Frances surprised me—up until now she was TOPS. I sure don't understand her revealing that material to these people. Make sure she gets paid *what* she is due—and *stop* all action against these people until we show some sanity and *unity.*

Today, the books arrived—I kiss you! I write small in order to give more of myself—it's not my nature! If Princess becomes a New Yorker, I will be so happy. Even Juan and Ilma would be a groove—but I guess that's out. Perhaps it's better this way—I need only us to plan and hope about. I really need you to translate me to PEOPLE.

They said don't go, they love and feed us—little poison.
We owe them respect, not to move—when the weights they pile
     upon our hunger make needles stab our eyes.
It's so distant, your Island, how can we reach you?—when you
     bleed so red for us.
Ageless jealousy smiles with razor edged lips and eyes that slept
     with Death,
Come hide under my frosty wing, that the orgone that fires your
     insides will harden love.
You have everything I want!

Hurry! it's getting close to never, why must you linger?
But there are so many before us—
No! No! that's a different line, can't you see it has no beginning?
Hail Pluto! arch-abductor, return to us the strange little creature
     that we may bind and ARMOR it for the life in Death.
We have searched the entire TOMB and there are no signs, symbols
     or ashes.
The Ram, pierced eyes, for battering ICE mountains.
The Scorpion, jaded eyes, reverse sting.
The strange little creature—The Goat, a beard on its forehead,
     opens its eyes.
Yes, they are there beside the undulate dark mass, how could you
     miss them?
Open your ears, feel the sighs of desperation emanating from bound
     protoplasm.

We have felt there, our hands melt!
Black Christ is laughing, the unholy three have risen!

goodnight, tell Joie I'm truly sorry.
Joey Gallo #18140

Although a detailed exegesis of this remarkable letter is neither possible nor called for probably—the allusions are personal, fugitive and open to varying interpretations at this remove—the general thrust of its imagery is clear enough: Joey, Jeffie and Joie—Ram, Scorpion and Goat, "the unholy three," though weighed down by responsibility for others, threatened by his jealous anxiety about her and denied any clear sign for the future, "have risen" and need nothing but one another. And not the least astonishing thing about it is that it was written in one of the brief intervals between almost continuous spells of solitary confinement.

The "Frances" referred to was Frances Kahn, a Bronx attorney who achieved some prominence as a specialist in civil rights cases during the sixties. Joey had engaged her to act for him when the cumulative effect of his experiences at Attica was seriously threatening his self-control. Partly as a stratagem to keep out of the way of his fellow prisoners and partly because he refused to submit to the indignities of prison life, Joey courted punishment so assiduously that he spent most of the first three years of his sentence in isolation. In this way, he substantially reduced the risk of assassination by an inmate, and minimized the danger of the guards' conniving at an "accident," since their responsibility for his safety while segregated from the other prisoners was clear, absolute and undivided. But the strain was appalling. He was being buried alive. In 1963, after his appeal against conviction had finally been rejected in the Appellate Division in June, he began to frame a petition to the courts seeking redress from "the cruel and unusual punishment" to which he was being subjected.

Though, in a sense, it had been self-inflicted for his own purposes, he could not now moderate his behavior without seeming to have caved in under pressure, and he was not about to give the prison authorities that satisfaction. The underlying aim of the petition, therefore, was to draw public attention to his plight as a necessary preliminary to obtaining a transfer to another prison, where he might start again on a different footing. As Profaci and his brother-in-law Joe Magliocco, who had briefly succeeded him, were now both dead from cancer, the war had petered out in an uncertain truce, and he had less reason to fear mixing with the prison population. Accordingly, he drafted a preamble for the guidance of his lawyers—in suitably legal language:

Contentions

Petitioner alleges and contends that he has and still is being persecuted by officers and officials of Attica State Prison in total disregard to his constitutional right as to Article VIII, "cruel and unusual punishments inflicted."

That since his arrival to the above-named institution, petitioner has and still is subjected to cruel and unusual punishment through intimidation and fraud by officers and officials conspiring by so-called "setting up" petitioner through the use of their lackeys, in order that petitioner can be punished.

That petitioner is now confined to a segregated part of the institution for no just reason except to add to his confinement more punishment.

That there are no rules posted for inmates to govern by, for rules are made by officers and officials according to their feelings, and no two inmates are given the same punishment for the same violation. An inmate has no way of defending himself, for the hearing he receives is a one-sided court, with an official sitting as judge and prosecutor.

That petitioner is confined at times for weeks in a 6 × 11 cell without any exercise, and therefore endangering his health physically as well as mentally. (Proceed on these lines. I want as much as can be found in the statutes on this particular situation to be entered in this writ.)

But another year of this subhuman existence, of daily harassment, abuse, beatings and incessant psychological pressure had to be endured before Joey's case was ready for court. In Frances Kahn, he had found an attorney whose pugnacity in response to bureaucratic indifference and the arbitrary use of authority matched his own. Spoiling for a fight with the New York penal system, she urged Joey on to work the petition up in much greater detail, so that when the final version was brought to judgment in the State Supreme Court at Albany in September, 1964, it provided a fairly full account of his ordeal in Attica. It was a story that lost very little of its horror or of the pervading atmosphere of brutality through being told in the flat understatement of a legal document.

After setting out the grounds for his application to the court, the petition went on to describe how, in April, 1962, Joey had been assigned to work in Cell Block B, 19 Company, and to sleep in Cell 4. By chance, in Cell 6 was a black man named Nelson whom he had known on the outside, and, as the two were working in the same machine shop, they became "very friendly." Observing this,

a Mr. Herman, who is the civilian foreman in charge of the workshop, called petitioner aside for a confidential chat. Mr. Herman informed your petitioner that this prison had an unwritten code segregating the white and the Negro inmate population ever since the prison was built. Mr. Herman further informed petitioner that unless he immediately refrained from fraternizing or socializing with any of the Negro inmates, he would be subjected to personal indignities and be discriminated against by the officer personnel of the institution. Mr. Herman added that his words of advice to petitioner were for petitioner's own benefit since he had many more years to serve in prison.

Thereafter, one Sergeant Henry, an officer who was in charge of the recreation yard whereat petitioner spent his leisure time, summoned petitioner and stated to him as follows: "See here, Gallo, this prison hasn't tolerated mixing black and white for the last 30 years, and don't you try to change things or you'll regret it." Your petitioner protested he was resigned to his fate of penal servitude and would not discriminate against any of the Negroes in the prison population notwithstanding the fact that he could suffer dire consequences at the hands of the prison officials and the inmates. . . .

In or about April, 1963, an inmate named Joseph Wojack, Attica Prison Number 17517, informed the key inmates of B Block that he was now the new leader of the block Ku Klux Klan. Immediately thereafter, inmate Wojack circulated an order to the white prison population of B Block not to permit any Negro barbers to cut the hair of white inmates. Petitioner was taken to the prison barber shop with the other members of his workshop in due course. Petitioner noticed that all the white barbers' chairs were occupied by white prisoners while the colored barbers' chairs were either occupied by Negroes or empty. Your petitioner proceeded to have his hair cut by a Negro barber in compliance with prison rules and regulations. Other white inmates occupied the vacant barber chairs of the colored barbers after they saw petitioner allow the Negro barber to cut his hair.

The next workday, an inmate named Barrett, who was the clerk for Mr. Herman, accosted petitioner and advised him that the Ku Klux Klan was angry with him for setting a bad example in the barber shop. Petitioner and inmate Barrett were then involved in a heated verbal argument. . . . Correction Officer Hollenbach and civilian employee Herman forthwith reassigned petitioner from one part of the Metal Shop to the most remote end of the shop, away from inmate Barrett. Shortly afterwards, Barrett, who weighs 200 pounds and stands 6 feet 3 inches, engaged petitioner in a fist fight. . . .

As a result of this incident, the petition went on, Joey was reassigned to Block A, Cell 36. The four cell blocks in Attica were, at that time, virtually four separate prisons in one—each with its own yard. Inmates were permitted to circulate from one block to another only on July 4—a nicely symbolic touch—and then only with the permission of the officers in charge. Block A was commonly known as the punishment detail, and, though Joey was not aware of it then, Wojack had preceded him there a few days earlier as a result of beating up a black prisoner named Danny who had also occupied a cell in Block B.

Undeterred by his transfer, Wojack assaulted another prisoner, named Presti, in Block A.

Wojack and Presti were both ordered to be confined to their respective cells as "Keeplocked" for several days. At the expiration of said period, they were released to rejoin the inmate population. Immediately thereafter, Wojack entered Presti's cell and struck Presti on the head with an iron bar. Wojack and Presti were both directed to be "Keeplocked" for a 15-day period. During Wojack's confinement in his cell, he continually taunted your petitioner with this remark, "I'll get you, Gallo."

Prior to the expiration of the 15-days punishment imposed upon inmate Wojack, and while there were a few more days for Wojack to be "Keeplocked," on Saturday, May 4, 1963, the cells were opened to allow the men to march to the messhall for lunch. In view of the fact that Wojack and Presti were "Keeplocked," they were supposed to be fed in their cells by the inmate in charge of the Block food rations. The officer in charge opened every cell door with the exception of your petitioner's cell and Presti's door. Petitioner didn't have any inkling that Wojack's door had been opened by the officer and that Wojack was stalking petitioner as his prey by waiting inside his open cell for petitioner to amble by and to ambush him.

Joey's cell was at the far end of the gallery, so that he had to pass Wojack's cell every time he went to and from his own. On this particular occasion, when the officer finally opened his door, he found himself alone, the other prisoners having gone on ahead.

When petitioner was about to pass Wojack's cell to catch up with his fellow inmates and the officer in charge in the messhall, petitioner was attacked by Wojack with a homemade knife.

It must be borne in mind that when an inmate is "Keeplocked," there hangs a bright red metal tag upon the lever which is manually controlled by the correction officer, thereby warning the officer not to open that particular cell. In this instance, the officer was negligent in his duties, whether through inadvertence or design, and this error on the officer's part has resulted in serious consequences to petitioner, as will be hereinafter shown.

Petitioner was interviewed by Colonel Myers, the assistant principal keeper, who stated to him as follows: "You nigger-loving bastard, you'll never live to get the Warden into court."

By an extraordinary coincidence, Wojack's attorney at the time of this attack was none other than Frances Kahn. She had been trying to get him transferred to Green Haven Prison so as to make it easier for his family to visit him, and only five days earlier, she had received a reply from Deputy Commissioner William E. Leonard of the Department of Correction turning her client down for the reason that Green Haven was "presently operating at full inmate capacity, which condition is expected to continue indefinitely." In the event, Wojack was transferred there about four days after his attempt on Joey's life, which was rather like punishing a cat with a bowl of cream.

After drawing the court's attention to this significant, though rather free, nine-day definition of "indefinitely," the petition went on to contend that

the glaring error of the officer in charge by opening Wojack's cell door on May 4, 1963, and by locking petitioner's cell door simultaneously, notwithstanding there wasn't a "Keeplocked" sign on petitioner's manual lever at the foot of the gallery of cells, was a deliberate and concerted plan and conspiracy to obstruct, coerce, hinder and discourage petitioner from exercising his inalienable right to select his acquaintances, whether they be white or colored; that the officials' intended purpose and effect are therefore violative of petitioner's constitutional rights as embodied in the "due process" and "cruel and unusual punishment clauses. . . ."

As further evidence of this, Joey also reported that "a burning cross was thrown into petitioner's cell with a Ku Klux Klan warning," and

that although petitioner is currently segregated from the rest of the population through no fault of his own, and even though he is allegedly imprisoned in Reception B "for observation," he hasn't been interviewed by any psychiatrist for the purpose of observation.

Petitioner is treated like an animal instead of as a human being in that he is forced to eat on the floor. His urine and/or excretion bucket is simultaneously washed with his tin plate. He has found human excrement clinging to his tin plate when served food. He is locked in 22 hours a day. He was locked in for five months without being afforded a walk as physical exercise. He has seen many incidents of guard brutality, gas-gun attacks upon Muslims, etc. . . .

WHEREFORE, petitioner respectfully prays that an order issue out of this court directed to respondents, compelling them to forthwith cease and desist from inflicting cruel and unusual punishment upon petitioner's mind and body, and for a further order commanding respondents to appear before the court for examination as to the functions, powers and duties of prison management in the case at bar, and for such other, further and different relief as to this court may seem just and proper in the premises.

The petition was verified on August 24 and filed with the New York Supreme Court on August 26 with a notice of motion for the orders specified. But long before the actual hearing on September 11, the suit was argued out by both sides in the press, starting on August 24 with a story in the New York *Post* under a three-column headline:

JOEY GALLO IN TROUBLE AGAIN:
NOW HE'S SUING THE WARDEN

Joey Gallo just can't seem to find his niche in life [wrote Paul Hoffman, more truly than he knew]. He certainly never found it in Brooklyn, though he tried hard enough to chisel a place for himself there.

Critics of the Profaci school—or mob—found his work too avant garde. Police critics, less subtle, said that as a visionary —Gallo had imperial ambitions—and in his art, he was extortionate.

Picking out the bones of Joey's case, Hoffman invited comment on the allegations of mistreatment from Deputy State Correction Commissioner Leonard, who, having been named in the petition, not surprisingly rejected it as another provocative act by "an aggressive, belligerent individual who . . . will leave no stone unturned in his efforts to disrupt the prison administration."

What form those efforts had previously taken was not specified, but, according to Leonard, they had certainly not been in connection with desegregating the prison population. "The barbershop in the institution is integrated, with both colored and white barbers in attendance, and every inmate is serviced in their order of arrival," he said. Nor was there any truth in Joey's story about the attempt on his life. "The allegation that Joseph Gallo was attacked with a knife in his cell by another inmate is false," continued Leonard, who clearly had not read the petition very carefully, or else he would have known the attack had taken place on the gallery. "The facts are that while Joseph Gallo was returning from a shower escorted by an officer, he made a derogatory remark to another prisoner. The prisoner attempted to strike Gallo, who grabbed his arm as the officer intervened. No blows were struck." He did, however, admit that Joey had been involved "in three fights with other inmates . . . in each one of which, Gallo was the instigator."

On the question of what punishments had actually been meted out as a result of these and other infractions, Leonard declined to comment. Tending to confirm Joey's original contention that prison officers ran their own kangaroo court for trying prisoners accused of breaking the rules, he merely said that "Gallo will continue to receive the kind of treatment to which his conduct entitles him. Just as soon as the inmate relinquishes his present attitude and is willing to conform to institutional rules and regulations in the same manner as all other inmates, he should not find it difficult to serve the term of sentence imposed by the court."

When arguments were heard, in Joey's absence, before Supreme Court Justice Roscoe V. Ellsworth on September 11, it became clear that the court was inclined to the same view, although judgment was reserved, both on the petition and on Attorney General Lefkowitz's motion for dismissal. While Mrs. Kahn asked that her client be transferred to another prison because of the "cruel and unusual punishments" he was undergoing, the state chose to challenge Joey's suit, not on the facts of the case, but on his right as a prisoner to bring such an action. Second, even if he had that right, Lefkowitz contended, it should have been brought against Warden Walter H. Wilkins of Attica Prison, not Commissioner of Corrections Paul D. McGinnis. And finally, Joey's solitary confinement had been caused by "his own recalcitrance and resistance to discipline."

The state's obvious desire to have the petition dismissed on technical grounds rather than on an examination of the charges seemed a telling point in Joey's favor. Mrs. Kahn was certainly confident enough in tone when she wrote to him on September 17:

> Thus far, I have not received the Attorney General's brief, and they only have until tomorrow to mail it out to me. I will submit a reply brief upon receipt thereof and will mail you a copy at that time. Your family has advised me they will visit you tomorrow. Good luck.
>
> Sincerely yours,
> FRANCES KAHN
>
> P.S. Do you know the name and number of the inmate locking next to you who shouts profanities at your family and I? I wish to report him to the officials, the Attorney General and the Commissioner. He

should be mentally examined and committed to Dannemora State Hospital.

In fact, the state asked for, and received, more time to file its reply memorandum on behalf of Commissioner McGinnis, which it did on September 30. The preamble began:

Petitioner herein commenced an Article 78 proceeding. Respondent filed objections in point of law and, on the oral argument, moved to dismiss. In so doing, respondent admitted the allegations in the petition *for purposes of the motion only.* Respondent has at no time and in no way made any general concessions as to the truth of said allegations or any part of same.

That was all the Attorney General was prepared to say about the facts of the case. The remainder of the memorandum was an elaboration of his oral argument based on the legal technicalities. Joey's proper course, he said, would have been to apply for a writ of habeas corpus directed to Warden Wilkins, who was a necessary party to the action.

Forwarding a copy of the memorandum to Jocy, Mrs. Kahn wrote: "We must now sweat out the decision and as soon as one is rendered you will probably read it in the papers or I shall apprise you thereof." But she was back in action sooner than she thought, this time with a broadside on October 10 against Warden Wilkins for Mary Gallo, who had written to ask his permission to see Joey—the normal visiting arrangements having been completely disrupted by the withdrawal of privileges and other disciplinary measures taken against him:

DEAR WARDEN WILKINS,

Enclosed herewith please find a copy of a letter which you wrote to Mrs. Mary Gallo wherein you advised her that she may visit her son Joseph "for one hour."

The mother of the above-named inmate ought not to be discriminated against by compelling her to make more than a 600-mile round trip to see her son while you permit other families to visit their relatives for days at a time.

Please inform me whether you wrote the words "for one hour" at the conclusion of your letter. If so, I will take it up with the proper authorities in order to support my contention that you are deliberately discriminating against the above-named inmate and his family.

I could appreciate the fact that you would like to run your prison at your discretion but you must remember that you are not above the law and you should not be biased. You are forgetting that it was the error of the officer in opening inmate Joseph Wojack's cell door and closing Joseph Gallo's cell door which led to Gallo's confinement in segregated quarters. Why blame Gallo for the officer's error?

The warden was not to be drawn on the subject of Wojack, however, nor was he prepared to admit to any discrimination against the Gallos. "Your assertion that I would like to run Attica Prison at my discretion and that I am not above the law and should not be biased is absolutely ridiculous," he wrote back, indignation undermining his syntax. "The rules and regulations governing visits to inmates are approved by the Commissioner of Correction and I certainly would be the last one to ignore a rule established by the Commissioner."

This referral of final responsibility for the administration of Attica to the Commissioner would seem to have justified Mrs. Kahn's choice of respondent, but on December 5, judgment was entered against her. Joey's petition was dismissed. In a memorandum, dated November 16, accompanying the decision, Justice Ellsworth stated that "no authority exists in law for ordering the Commissioner's personal appearance and examination and therefore that portion of the application must be and is denied summarily." As for the petition itself, it was "inartificially drawn and contains a somewhat confused mixture of charges and allegations, some made on hearsay and all without support beyond petitioner's averments." The respondent had moved for dismissal on the ground, among others, that the petition did not state facts sufficient to warrant relief under Article 78 and "the court is constrained to the view that such objection is well taken."

> The amenities of a country club cannot be had in prison life [the judge went on, pressing legal understatement to its limit]. Salty talk, threats, feuds and fights are an incident of such life. Realistically, no

court can control all interchanges between convicts themselves or between convicts and their keepers and it would be futile to attempt to do so under an article 78 proceeding or otherwise. While the courts have the duty of protecting an inmate against the violation of his statutory and constitutional rights, their function is not that of running and supervising the internal affairs of the State's prisons.

Pointing out that the Commissioner had broad, statutory powers of control and investigation, he threw in a little advice for good measure: "If the petitioner feels his grievances well founded and meriting investigation, he should in the first instance at least, pursue his remedy of making application for an inquiry to the Commissioner." Rather more constructively, he then added that "it may well be that the remedy of habeas corpus is also available to the petitioner."

Frances Kahn immediately filed notice of appeal to the Appellate Division of the Supreme Court, but more as a gesture of defiance than from any real intention of carrying the matter further. The Gallos were broke. Leave to appeal Joey's conviction to the Court of Appeals had been refused on November 4, and what resources remained had now to be employed in seeking to raise the constitutional issue of his free choice of counsel before the United States Supreme Court in Washington (an application that was also refused —on March 23, 1964).

All in all, it was the blackest of times for Joey, who, after all this effort and expense, was still exactly where he had started—in Attica, in solitary and in greater danger than ever, for now his guards were more or less licensed to do as they pleased.

An odd sequel to Joey's suit against the State Commissioner of Correction came to light nine years later with an application to the clerk of the Supreme Court in Albany to examine the papers in the case. All of them were found, properly filed and indexed in the archives, except the crucial one—Joey's "inartificially drawn" petition, with its accompanying notice of motion, describing the ill treatment to which he had been subjected.

After checking and rechecking what had hitherto been regarded as a foolproof record system in order to eliminate the possibility of a filing error, employees in the clerk's office expressed their bewilderment that the very document on which the case had hung should now be missing, and referred the application to the Attorney General's office, where records were also kept of all actions in which the state entered an appearance.

When this helpful suggestion was followed up, it was again discovered, to everyone's amazement, that all the relevant papers were there but one—the petition. The vital document in the case was missing not only from the archives of the highest court of the State of New York but also from the files of the state's highest law officer.

Coincidence? Or could it be that after events at Attica in 1971 the administration was at pains to remove any evidence from the record which might suggest that the racial discrimination and cruelty that provoked the insurrection had been drawn to official attention seven years earlier and apparently condoned?

If so, those responsible had little enough to fear from Frances Kahn, who seemed likely to be the only other person who might have retained a copy. In the first place, there was no possible reason why she should ever have found out that the petition was missing from the public archives. And in the second place, she was no longer practicing law and her files had been destroyed. She had been disbarred on August 11, 1969, for employing an ex-convict as a law clerk. When this was upheld by the Appellate Division of the New York Supreme Court on February 14, 1972, she abandoned her career and retired into private life.

But they had apparently forgotten about Joey, whose legal papers were almost all he had to show for nine tortured years of imprisonment.

11

Jeffie

Larry Gallo gave Sidney Slater the money to pay Jeffie's medical bills, but half of it disappeared, and she left New York Hospital, after having the baby, still owing about $600. On balance, however, she felt that the hospital probably owed *her* something, for she had been stitched up with a blood clot inside and an operation had been necessary to remove it. "I couldn't sit down for a month, except on a rubber tube, and I couldn't think of a name for the kid because my ass hurt."

Her friends rallied daily at Eighth Street to ease the first problem, and Jean Lerner solved the second by suggesting Joie, which, besides meaning "joy," was a more or less phonetic spelling of Joey. As yet, Jeffie was not unduly anxious about her absent husband because David Price told her whenever she asked that the conviction meant nothing, that Joey would soon be out on appeal. More than willing to be reassured, she took his word for it uncritically, and concentrated on looking after Joie, who worried her a little because she seemed to have no neck. But with the novelty wearing off the mother-and-daughter routine, the hard facts soon began to show through Price's complacency. Not only was Joey still inside, but back in Attica, farther away than ever. Ali Baba stopped by occasionally to take care of the rent and her living expenses, but otherwise she might have been on her own again for all the attention she was getting from his family. Everyone was busy with the war. She felt put upon and neglected.

Norman Granz didn't help much either. Not a word had passed between him and Jeffie in years, but now he looked her up on his way to Europe and took her out to dinner at the Colony. "He ordered for me, and I thought, 'Gee! How nice'—because Joey always used to do that—and we were going on to Ella Fitzgerald's opening at Basin Street afterward. But during dinner, he started in on me about marrying Joey. Got furious. Harangued me through a couple of courses about my moral values, and how could I get involved with these gangsters and parasites? And the more I flumpfered, trying to defend myself, the more insistent he got, venting all his indignation on this rather pathetic little figure, *I* thought, who had a husband in jail, a new baby at home and who had loved him very, very deeply. I was so crushed. When we left and got in a cab, he said, 'Basin Street.' Then he said, 'No. I can't, I can't. I can't take you.' So I struggled out again, said good night with as much dignity as I had left, and that was the last I ever saw of him. When I got home, I sobbed and sobbed."

The other great love of her life was hardly more consoling. With Joie in her arms, Jeffie went up to Attica with Joey's mother to visit him for the first time and show him the baby. After an exhausting seven-hour journey, Joey refused to see them. "Later on, he wrote a letter saying he understood how we felt and he was sorry. He would let us know when it was time for us to come. I realize now he was in a situation he had to adjust to. He had fallen short of his own expectations, and had to get himself together. He wasn't able to reassure us. He was ashamed. But I was very hurt and resentful about it at the time because I didn't understand."

Indeed, all concerned were so preoccupied with their own problems at this point that no one understood much about anybody. The next person to fail the test in Jeffie's eyes was Olga. "My mother decided to come in from the coast and help me—Joie was now a few months old. So she arrived with her trunks and her hats and her usual impossible attitudes. I think she meant to be helpful, but she never knew how, not where I was concerned. She used to sit across from me on the couch, crying, as I nursed Joie, that I loved my baby more than I loved her. I knew she wouldn't stay long, so I tried to be cool, but then she started getting ill, gasping for breath and not being able to walk because I wasn't responding properly—she wasn't well anyway—and in the end I'd had as much of that as I could stand. After about three weeks, I went crazy. I grabbed up a carving knife, put it to her throat and told her I'd kill her if she didn't get the fuck out of there the next morning. So she left."

Meanwhile, back on President Street, the war grumbled on like a corked volcano, popping off briefly now and again as one side or the other eluded police surveillance, then subsiding as the cordon drew tighter. A week before Joie was born, Sidney Slater had carelessly dispensed with a bodyguard and taken his girlfriend to Sammy Davis, Jr.'s opening at the Copa. As they were finishing their drinks after the last show, Jiggs Forlano, the former Gallo ally who had now returned to the Profaci camp, came up to them and pressured Slater into a private talk at another table, where they were joined by Carmine Persico and Donny Shack Montemorano, who showed Slater his gun and warned him to sit still. The three Profaci hoods had heard rumors that Joey was out of jail on a writ, and were anxious to know where he was.

When Slater told them they had it wrong, that Joey was still in Sing Sing, Forlano leaned across the table and tried to rip out his eye with a newspaper hook, the small, hooked blade attached to a finger ring that newssellers use for opening bundles. Rearing back instinctively, Slater saved his eye, but the hook slashed a three-inch cut just below it. As he pressed a napkin against it to staunch the blood, Persico caught hold of his tie and started to throttle him with it, but then a waiter intervened. He asked, somewhat diffidently, if they wanted a drink before the place closed, and Slater groggily made his escape.

When he reported the attack, the District Attorney's office decided that the chance of putting Profaci's top three enforcers away for a couple of years on a charge of felonious assault was too good to miss —even if it meant blowing Slater's cover as an informer against the Gallos. The gamble failed dismally. In striking contrast with Joey's defense, the Profaci mob's lawyers kept the case dangling *for six years.* In 1968, their clients copped a plea of simple assault and went free.

Three days after the Copa incident, Donny Shack and Carmine Persico were spotted in a black Cadillac taking an early-morning cruise around President Street. Rewarded by the sight of someone leaving Gallo headquarters, they pulled in alongside him and jumped out, evidently with kidnaping in mind. But the Pizza Squad was watching. Two detectives ran toward them with drawn guns, and the struggling trio split up. Persico and his intended victim ran away in opposite directions, and Donny Shack dived back into the Cadillac, which took off with a squeal. The detectives hesitated, cursing, then raced back to their own car to take up the chase. Careering through the streets of Red Hook at speeds ranging up to seventy miles per hour, they managed at last to force the Cadillac into the curb and closed in on foot from both sides. When he saw who they were, Donny Shack slumped back in his seat with relief. "Jesus," he said. "I thought you guys were the Gallos." As he was carrying a .38 in his waistband, he was booked for violating the Sullivan Law.

The pace was picking up. Next day, when Mike Albergo left his home on Troutman Street, Queens, he found his car had a flat tire. His brother Philip was helping him change it when another Cadillac —this time, a green one—swooped silently down on them. Four shots were fired as it passed, three of them scoring hits. Mike Albergo was wounded in the left arm and right shoulder and his brother in the chest. Though none of their injuries was sufficiently serious to keep them in the hospital, the Gallos were incensed. A few nights later, they staged a wild shootout with Jiggs Forlano outside his house in Astoria, Queens, but everybody missed and went home frustrated.

Then suddenly they were heroes. As Larry Gallo and two of the boys stepped out of the Longshoremen's Rest at 77 President Street one cold February morning, they smelt something burning. An oily black waterfall of smoke was curling over the sill of a third-story window two doors down. Calling out reinforcements, Larry led his brother Blast, Tony Shots, Punchy Illiano and three others in a charge up the stairs and into an apartment full of choking smoke and screaming children. "We start grabbing kids and doing everything at once," Punchy told *Life* magazine afterward. "The girl's hair is on fire and I put it out with a couple of whacks with my hand, and the baby's got no clothes on, so I put my jacket over him. Then we start passing the kids out the door and down the stairs and carry the little ones down. The mattress and bed are burning. We throw them out the window. We break the window and everything. We throw the dresser and everything out the window."

When the firemen arrived, they found nothing to do. Six children, aged from ten months to six years, were being looked after by the owner of the luncheonette downstairs, and Larry and Tony Shots were being treated for doses of smoke poisoning that put them out of action for a week. "God bless them," sobbed Mrs. Sista Biaz, when she returned from the grocery store and heard what had happened. "They save my children. They are wonderful boys."

The public thought so, too, when they read the nationwide, front-page coverage of the Gallos' exploit and watched their modest disclaimers of heroism on television. "We only done what any red-blooded American boys would do," said Blast in one interview. "Do you see any horns? I got no horns. We're not animals. We're just human beings trying to get along." Mail, money and congratulations poured into President Street from all over the country, but Blast confessed to a certain skepticism. "With our crummy luck," he said, "we'll probably get a ticket for fighting the fire without a license." After giving Mrs. Biaz all the money the rescuers had on them, some

$50, he was reported as saying, "We were going to go out soliciting some more for them, but then we would have got pinched for extortion."

His caution was probably justified. The only lasting effect of their bravery, apart from transforming local goodwill into near-idolatry, was to give Jimmy Breslin an idea. He spent several weeks on the block collecting material for *The Gang That Couldn't Shoot Straight,* a work that baffled more than it pleased the Gallos, and which, ten years later, set in train the last few demoralizing weeks of Joey's life. But after the fire, it was business as usual once the fuss had died down, and business was very bad. On April 8, they lost their last ally when Anthony (Tony Bender) Strollo drove away from his home in Fort Lee, New Jersey, to buy a pack of cigarettes and was never seen again.

On June 7, however, the balance tilted unexpectedly in their favor when Joseph Profaci died of cancer in the South Side Hospital, Long Island. Just how far he had fallen out of favor with his fellow Dons through his inability to put down the Gallo revolt became clear when none of them showed up for his funeral. They were also disinclined to back Joe Magliocco, his brother-in-law and underboss, as the new head of the family, particularly when the Gallos rejected him out of hand. As far as President Street was concerned, such a change would have meant no change. With their enemies preoccupied with this problem of succession, therefore, the war bogged down for the rest of the year, the only reported casualties being two minor Gallo associates who disappeared in mid-October after refusing a request from Carmine Persico to set up Larry for a hit.

It was around this time that Joey at last sent word to Jeffie that he wanted to see her. They had been writing to one another quite regularly, but neither had so much as acknowledged the brutal possibility of a fourteen-year separation. Though it was present in both their minds, neither had wished to wound the other by betraying any doubt at all about the final success of his appeal. Excited, therefore, at the prospect of seeing him, and yet apprehensive of the changes she might find, Jeffie again set out with Joie on the six-hundred-mile round trip to Attica, telling herself not to expect too much, to be ready to make allowances.

Though thinner and pale from confinement, Joey greeted her as though they were meeting in the lobby of the Plaza Hotel after a few days' absence on business. Having mastered his humiliation, he was again in complete control of himself. The baby, he thought, was cute, but the real object of the visit, as far as he was concerned, was to set Jeffie free. "He said he wasn't sure what was going to happen, but however it turned out, he wanted me to live my own life and not allow anything to stand in the way. 'Go out and have a good time,' he said. 'Don't deny yourself.' Of course, it never occurred to him for an instant that I wasn't already out fucking everything that moved, but I think he meant it. Either he sincerely wanted to free me so he'd be free of responsibility for me, or else it was a subtle way of keeping me. But he did tell his family I was to be a free agent, my own person. I didn't have to go and join the group of wives or get involved in their tight-knit existence. I was to be taken care of, but there would be no rules other than those that he and I decided. I don't really know what his motives were, but I thanked him. Even though he was in prison, he still gave me a sense of security. He kind of got me through all those years just by being the man he was. He was always able to give, and never allowed an inch of his problem to become yours. He never asked anything of me except to be myself and be okay."

But things weren't okay for long. On April 2, 1963, acting on information supplied by Sidney Slater, the police closed down the Gallos' last substantial source of revenue—a Brooklyn policy bank with a play of $15 million a year—and with it went Jeffie's income of $250 a week. Making his first public appearance since the D.A. had blown his cover, Slater told reporters that Joey had taken about $8,000 a week out of the operation as his "fee" for providing protection. "I used to meet a guy every Friday night on Atlantic Avenue," he said. "He would turn over our cut and I'd bring it back to President Street."

Worse was to follow. With Gallo morale at its lowest ebb, Larry gambled on winning the war of attrition with one bold strike at the enemy's general. On May 19, Carmine Persico was superficially wounded in three places by rifle fire, and Larry lost his bet. Seventeen members of the Gallo gang, including both brothers, were charged with illegal possession of weapons, and although they managed to make bail—just—they might have been safer inside, for the penalty for poor marksmanship was a new counteroffensive. Two of their men were killed in June, and on July 24, Ali Baba was shot three times in the stomach with a .45 caliber pistol.

When Joey went to prison, Ali had lost heart. For over a year, he moped around President Street, waiting for a miracle, but then, when even he began to accept that Joey was inside to stay, he decided to go back to sea. Signing on as a cook with the cruise ship *Exeter*, he sailed for the Mediterranean and returned forty-two days later with $600 in his jeans. As he left the American Export Line pier in Hoboken and started to walk along River Street, two men in a stolen gray Chevrolet with New York license plates drove up from behind and shot him down. Jeffie took Joey's mother and sister Carmella to see him in St. Mary's Hospital, Hoboken, before he died, and gave him a good funeral, for "he was part of Joey and me."

Ali's death was particularly hard on Joey, who was already beset not only by his own struggle to survive but by the black news from Brooklyn. With no money coming in, Jeffie now felt she had little choice but to return to California. Out there, she could work at night in the clubs and look after Joie by day, but she did not look forward to telling Joey of her decision, thinking he might construe it as desertion. But instead, he seemed relieved.

"I didn't tell him there was a money problem. I probably didn't have to. I just told him I would be happier with my family and he thought it was a good idea—even though it meant I wouldn't be able to visit him as often. We enjoyed the visits, but they were sad. All we ever talked about was Joie and my friends—all the gossip from my world. There was never a word about his life in prison. And I thought that if I was able to show him that we could manage on our own, it would take some of the burden off him. How can you complain about money to someone who's sitting in jail? I felt that keeping me in the style I was used to was becoming an imposition, so I either had to join them out in Brooklyn or make it by myself. We didn't discuss it in those terms, but he knew. So I went back to Los Angeles and got a job as a cocktail waitress at P.J.'s, a big discothèque, where I worked my ass off from six in the evening until four in the morning and made around four hundred dollars a week. The more liquor you sold, the better station you got, so eventually I didn't have to get in before nine. And after about a year, I was working ringside, which meant you didn't have to get in before ten or serve breakfast, but you still made the same money as you did when you were killing yourself."

She got Joyce a job there, too. In a scene of New Testament quality, Joyce and Al had loaded their worldly goods into a $200 jalopy on Christmas Eve, 1961, and set out in the snow with their infant son for California. But the car broke down two blocks away at Thirty-second Street and Fifth Avenue and had to be pushed back through the blizzard to the corner of Thirtieth Street and unloaded again. Another week passed, in an empty apartment, before they finally got away from New York, but their troubles went with them. Six months later, the marriage broke up and Joyce went to pieces. It was not until Jeffie arrived back in Los Angeles with Joie that she managed to get going again. They rented a house together, hired a maid to look after the children and went to work at P.J.'s.

"Jeffie was horrible—atrociously horrible. Everybody had to suffer the way she was suffering, and she really punished herself. Right off, she insisted that I take the big bedroom and the children the next biggest so that she could sleep in a room the size of a cell. She found fault with everyone, especially me. When Jeffie isn't happy, she isn't going to be happy with night or day, rain or shine, friend or foe. When Jeffie is unhappy, she is *comprehensively* unhappy. She was living on Joey's letters, which were beautiful. They would get her gaga-eyed—then she would boil with rage. She went back to therapy, and was very, very miserable.

"Of course, I was none too happy myself at that time. After being good for so long, I now went completely wild. I tried to tell her that it might be better for her to go out and go crazy as well, but she couldn't do it. She didn't approve. In fact, she was really abominable to me, and it was all on account of Joey. I mean, Jeffie *fought*. If there was anything to be done that might help to get him out of there, then it had to *be* done—she's the most persistent person in the world. She tried every way possible, and screamed at more people, trying to get through to them. . . . If she could have gotten him out by climbing barefoot to the top of Mount Everest, she would have done it. But she was hell to live with, and in the end, it got so bad I couldn't take it any more. Besides, she wanted to go back to New York and put Joie in nursery school."

Jeffie's latest spell in what Joey called "the green death" of California had lasted about a year. She returned just as he was petitioning the courts for relief from the state's "cruel and unusual punishment," and stayed for a while with his sister Jacqueline in Canarsie. Then Georgia Brown flew in from London to star in the Broadway production of *Oliver!* and they jointly rented an apartment on West Fourteenth Street, not far from Joie's nursery school in the village. This done, Jeffie found a part-time job as a telephonist and resumed her checkered relationship with Joey's family.

The pressure was now off. Peace had been declared in Brooklyn after the death of Joe Magliocco, from natural causes, at the end of 1963. In a successful bid for the leadership, Joe Colombo, the youngest caporegime in the Profaci mob, had first won Larry's approval by promising to "spread the bread around," and then the endorsement of the other New York bosses by giving up Profaci's seat on the High Commission and allowing Carlo Gambino to represent him. Though former combatants on both sides were still in and out of the courts on charges left over from the war, life on President Street had returned to normal, and its garrison to their homes. One Sunday, Larry Gallo asked Jeffie to bring Joie to his house for dinner, and, barely hesitating, she accepted. Although she had never approved of the way Italians treated children, the family was obviously anxious to see more of Joey's daughter, and, as Joie was now going on four, what harm could it do?

"Larry was definitely Italian. You couldn't even discuss with him that you don't pinch kids. How else could you show love? And he dug Joie. She walked early and she was always sparkling and fearless. So they got in a fight, this little girl and this big man. He tapped her. Not hard—just affectionately. She hit him back. He tapped her again; she hit him back. He taps her harder; she does the same. So now he wants to see how far she will go. He taps her; she hits him back. And on and on they go, with the entire roomful of people sitting around watching this little kid. And now she's getting mad. She's hitting him harder and harder after every tap, and he loves it. She had such *balls*. 'Do you want to stop?' he keeps asking her, and she won't. She knows she can't win, but she won't. 'Okay,' he says. 'Let's stop.' '*No!*' she says—whack! So then he taps *her* harder. 'You want to stop?' 'No.' This goes on literally for half an hour, and she's *dying*. Several times I was tempted to go in and stop it, but I figured it was not my business. Young as she was, if she went that far with it, I wanted her to learn something.

"Finally, she gave in and started to sob out of sheer frustration. When we left, she said, 'Mommy, how could you let him *do* that? I'm only a little girl.' 'Then don't play big guys' games,' I said. 'If you're going to play with the big guys, you got to know *how* to play. When Uncle Larry asked you if you wanted to stop, you should have said, "Yes—I'm only a little girl." But you wouldn't do it, so don't be mad with me. You had every chance to stop.' Then I took her in my arms and said, 'I'm sorry. But think about what happened. There was something you can learn from that.' And I think she did. She had to know about those things. She had to learn about the streets, too, if I was going to be at work all day. By the time she was seven, if she saw a guy lying in a doorway, she could tell a junkie from a drunk.

"Larry never forgot how long she stood up to him—the tenacity she showed. He told everybody. Joey, of course, heard about it from all the family and thought it was terrific of her. He and I had the same basic philosophy of life, and we wanted her to have it, too. Anything you want to do, if you understand the pros and cons, that's your decision and your right—but stand behind your shit. If you do that, you'll fulfill your responsibilities to everybody. Just stand behind your shit."

Joie learned this lesson so well that her father was one of its earliest victims. Jeffie was now taking her up to Attica once a month so that they could get to know each other better, but Joie's independence and Joey's impossibly restricted circumstances made it hard for them to rise above a stilted exchange of question and answer. As soon as she could, Joie would escape to play in a corner. On one visit, in an effort to break through and produce a more positive response, Joey teased her a little, comparing her unfavorably with one of his nieces. He was going to take down the picture of her in his cell, he said. From now on, his niece would be his pin-up—she was prettier anyway. This hurt Joie's feelings. She wouldn't talk to him after that. A month later, when the car called to pick them up for their next visit, Joie, aged three, informed Jeffie that she wasn't going. There would be no more visits until Joey wrote her a letter of apology. There weren't. And he did.

"Joey loved it. She was a full Gallo in his eyes, right down the line. They understood each other. Everything was fine so long as he didn't treat her like his personal property. One time, she told her father a boy was teasing her in nursery school, and she never liked to be teased. He'd hit her or something. So Joey said, 'Okay, Joie, this is what you do. Next time you see him, you go up to him and say, "C'mere—I got something to tell you." You lead him into the corner, and when he leans over to hear what you got to say, you go—bop! You give him one crack, and he won't bother you any more.' And I thought, 'Oh God! That's terrific! Just exactly opposite to what I'm telling her.' But she thought that was cute. Liked it a lot."

By the end of his third year in Attica, Joey was in bad shape. His petition had failed, his appeals had miscarried, and, he told Jeffie, the prison authorities were threatening to put him in Matteawan. "They had him in solitary and were really trying to do him in. It showed. He'd lost a lot of weight. He had lawyers working, but nobody was doing anything right and he was very agitated, very out of it and very much the prisoner. I felt completely helpless. There was nothing I could do. The family was looking after him—that was their shtick. I wasn't involved with lawyers or food or socks or cigarettes. We just had our personal thing. But it got so that I began to feel more like a hindrance than a help, and I think *he* felt that, too. 'Here she comes again with that goddamn kid when I'm fighting for my life.' It was bad times. I think Joey had at last begun to realize that he could appeal until he was purple, but he was still going to wind up sitting in jail."

Even so, he was still able to mine a little comfort for those who needed it. At about this time, Jeffie learned that her mother was dying. She had been ill, on and off, for some years. When Joey heard about it, he wrote to her through Jeffie:

> Baby, I can't write to Olga without a special okay from the warden, and you know where that's at.
>
> The main reason I TOOK you for a wife was because the Princess was included in the package. Olga knew I meant business. She gave me Ralphie's bed with her blessing, and turned on the gas heater when she thought it would be a cold night, let me put my feet on the Ziegfeld couch, discovered two hearts entwined in a wall in the bathroom, and was *certain* that it was a sign of her and Ralphie's love—such a true faith in matters of the heart.
>
> "Well, Joey said we are three partners"—remember? She told you that when you remarked about her hitting the "petty cash." She broke us up with that. I shall never forget the happiest period in my life — it was a time of my life, that I felt the joy in life. I was a KING. She made us young (somehow before, I always was an old man) and showed us the beauty of courage. "Joey, dear, did you put some bread crumbs for the birds? The poor darlings miss Ralphie too."
>
> We were sitting on the rug and her eyes welled with tears. From the recording machine, her beautiful voice spoke of love, in a haunting Spanish poem. It affected us the same way, as if a current ran through us, connecting us, welding us to each other. That night in the Villa Capri, how she teased Leo Carrillo. I was so proud, and so were my friends. Leo just loved her! What a show-off! She played with him in Spanish, then French, and buried him in the King's English! Oh yes, she then topped it off with a mutual friend, a newspaper editor in Alexandria, Egypt. "Cisco" was young again (Olga's magic). Everyone was aware of how she stimulated him. FOOL! If he had made the right move on the spot, he would be alive today. He died of blandness and boredom.

Jeffie, there are so many wonderful feelings in me, and Olga and Ali bring the memory, warmth and humor of each treasured moment, renewed, so vivid. Each recurrence brings times gone swiftly ever so slowly, so that I savor each tender bruise and curse me for taking me away from god. Tears ease the beating. As they form, they disappear and suddenly a warm glow and quiet joy replace the previous torment. Surely our beautiful ones give these precious parts of their lovely beings to us because our empty old youth would wither and die without the eternal warmth they possess.

What I mean is that they open, they bare their souls so that we may bathe our searching and longing in the simple wisdom that they both possess. The charm found in children like Joie—that's exactly the feeling I miss when in contact with the grabbing, clutching, hungry, shrill, insatiable people—who are lost—groping, hanging on till a YELL that freezes spirits comes from the depth of me—STUNS! and releases me from their BONEY death—to fly away on a magic carpet with Aladdin's lamp, never to return. Wait—gate that roll—sometimes it hurts and comes out swinging wildly. With every cruel blow that sends me tumbling, I return with chin thrust forward and defiance emanating from the entire me. FATE, I challenge you! I fight— we fight or quit and be crushed by the sick, crying, howling hordes of humanity searching for a way out of the TRAP! We bounce back ALWAYS! Because love is no mystery, because life must end, because we do not fear death. We understand the entire transition from Joie to Olga, and we are grateful that it is a part of us. This expression is crude but honest. My love is *understanding*. If you tire, rest. As you once said, "It's a long road," and I got the rhythm and strength for both of us.

Joey Gallo #18140

But to Jeffie, it looked as though his strength was giving out. After a visit in February, 1965, she returned to New York convinced that something had to be done in a hurry to preserve his sanity. "I went to see Larry as soon as I got back and told him that Joey was like a crazy man. He looked terrible—gaunt and drawn. His eyes were revolving in his head. They were going to judge him insane if he didn't cool it, and he wasn't cooling it. 'Listen, Larry,' I said, 'he's losing control. He's really going this time. We got to get him a psychiatrist.' And Larry said, 'Okay. If you know somebody and want to send him up, go ahead—I'll take care of it. But remember —Joey never did a thing in his life he didn't plan well in advance, so take it easy.'

"I guess Larry knew Joey better than anyone, except me. But he hadn't seen him in quite a while. So I called Commissioner McGinnis on the phone in Albany, and I said, 'Look, we both have a problem. You've got a prisoner you can't cope with and I have a husband I want to help. So please can I bring my shrink?' He was very nice. After a bit of discussion, he said yes."

12

Dr. Bruce

When Jeffie's psychiatrist, Dr. Albert, moved from New York to California in 1960, he referred his patients to a brilliant young colleague, Dr. Bruce. Jeffie didn't like him at first. She thought he was "a snotty kid," despite his M.D., his Freudian training, his subsequent studies of Reich, his work on the faculty of an eminent East Coast medical school, and his extensive private practice. But he soon gave her cause to revise that opinion.

When did Jeffie first become a patient of yours?

November 3, 1960. She presented me with problems that certainly antedated her ever knowing Joey Gallo, but which were just as certainly being exacerbated by the fact that she was in love with him. He was already in terrible trouble. So we made a therapeutic contract for her to come and see me regularly once a week. That lasted three months. Then she called and left a message with my answering service. "I am getting married," she said, "and going South."

At that point, did she have any particular complaint about Joey and his treatment of her? Did he constitute a problem over and above those she already had?

From the start, Jeffie described Joe to me as the most incredible human being she had ever met—and she'd met a hell of a lot of people, and a lot of them unusual. The most difficult thing about him was that he could be the most exquisitely receptive, soft and sensitive guy in the world, but on the other hand, he could act as if he were totally *in*sensitive, *un*feeling and *un*aware of other people's needs. I'm oversimplifying, of course—but after I met him, I knew exactly what Jeffie meant. Joey was not somebody who lent himself to simple descriptions. He was enormously complex.

But that was the division, was it? He was sensitive and tender with her, but apparently unfeeling and tough as a racketeer?

It wasn't just that he was tender and sensitive on a personal level —he seemed to be one of those people who dared to be vulnerable sometimes. It has to do with the capacity to open yourself up and be naked and take the chance of getting hurt. From what Jeffie told me, and from what I saw for myself later on, it seemed that here was a guy who could let go and let down enough to feel all the shit in the world, all the enormous amount of hate and destructiveness in the human animal. He had the capacity to do that. And he *dared* to do it—although I don't know whether, in fact, he had any choice. I rather suspect he didn't, and that may be the crucial point. I think it was that that wanted to be killed.

There's a technical diagnosis which is not generally used in psychiatry—only by a few people in child and adolescent psychiatry—and that is, pseudo-psychopathic schizophrenia. It is applied to somebody whose basic difficulty in dealing with the world is some kind of schizophrenic disturbance, and whose major defense against the enormous anxiety of being as naked and open as a schizophrenic is to act as if they were a psychopath, which is just the opposite— a cold, hard, calculating person who can feel no guilt and no anxiety and manipulates people like crazy.

Dr. Bruce **219**

It has been suggested that Joey deliberately cultivated a reputation for insanity and used it as other gangsters used a gun; that he encouraged people to believe he was unpredictable and reckless, by behaving in a way normally associated with an unbalanced personality, because it helped intimidate his opponents. Is that at all like saying the same thing?

No, it isn't. My feeling is that he was genuinely schizophrenic—and I think one has to be careful here because that's a label which people often use to close a discussion, as if it said everything you really needed to know about a person. What I mean is that because of Joey's sensitivity and his lack of the defenses that most of us have, the world drove him crazy. There were times when he really had trouble distinguishing between fantasy and reality—so that by that definition, he could be called schizophrenic—and he had real paranoid alienation, a real conviction sometimes that people were out to get him when in fact they weren't.

But he used these things, too, as you say. He was *driven* to use them. He *had* to use them—he really didn't have any choice about this. He was just enough in control so that he *could* use them to intimidate people or manipulate them, but to me there's a red thread through the fabric of all his behavior. However much Joey Gallo used people, it was nothing compared to the way his basic psychological makeup used him. He was far more a suffering pain slave to what drove *him* than he ever made anybody else a slave by driving *them*.

This, of course, is an elaboration based on later knowledge. Presumably, all you had to go on to start with was Jeffie's account of the man she was in love with.

I went through quite an agonizing period before I went to see Joey. First of all, there was some risk involved. I really had to ask myself if I should do a consultation on a mobster with a gang war going on in New York. If word leaked out that Joey Gallo saw a shrink, his enemies might ask themselves, "Well, what the hell did he tell the guy? Maybe that guy shouldn't be allowed to run around loose." When I saw Joey, my family didn't even know about it. On the other hand, corny as it may sound, when you take the Hippocratic Oath, you do feel, well, responsible. You should try to respond when somebody's hurting because who the hell else is going to do it?

Having decided to do the consultation, then, I now had to ask myself how many a priori assumptions I had formed about the guy I was going to see that might get in the way. The answer I gave myself was that, on the basis of Jeffie's pathology, there was a tendency on my part to assume that she was acting out her whore fantasy again, that she had picked a psychopathic mobster as all she deserved. I was tending to assume that she was rationalizing her staying with this guy and being in love with him by fantasizing that he had this other, gentler face. I found myself taking with a big dose of salt, not just a grain, everything she said about this whole other side of Joey—which, as it turned out, she had described very accurately. And when I recognized this, I saw it as a danger, because if I thought I was going to see a routine psychopath, that was not only not fair, but would also produce bad medicine. So what I tried to do was say, "Hold it! You've never seen this guy." I made a conscious effort to approach the consultation as openly as I could. I was going to let Joey Gallo present Joey Gallo. As I soon found out, you only had to give him half a chance and he'd do it!

Wasn't this a very unusual situation for a psychotherapist to find himself in—being invited to make a snap diagnosis?

Let's put it another way. What had happened was that Jeffie had become convinced from what Joey had told her that he was going to be killed in Attica, that he certainly *would* be killed if he were to go "in population," as they call it. And while she wasn't sure to what extent he was caught up in some really paranoid delusional thinking about the plot afoot to get him, which, according to him, involved the prison officials as well as the prisoners, she was quite certain that, whether the plot involved everybody or just a couple of people, unless Joey got help, and quickly, he would be a dead duck. As far as she could see, the one real hope of saving him was to get him transferred from Attica to some other prison.

The problem about that, however, was that, because of his notoriety and his image as a manipulative mobster, especially with correction officials, it was damned unlikely that even the best criminal lawyer could pull it off. It seemed to Jeffie—and I agreed with her —that the only chance he had was if somebody with an unimpeachable reputation and no ax to grind was brought in, in a strictly professional way, to try to assess what Joey's real situation was at Attica. So that was my role. It was not to make a diagnosis of Joey in a psychiatric way, but rather to try to evaluate realistically the chances of this man surviving—and not just "in population"—in this maximum-security state prison.

So Jeffie then got Commissioner McGinnis to agree to this. Did you, as an outside psychiatrist nominated by the prisoner's family, sense any reluctance on the Commissioner's part, or encounter any obstructiveness at the prison?

McGinnis was completely cooperative. Whatever he said to the officials at Attica—to Warden Wilkins and his crew—was enough to ensure that I got the red-carpet treatment. Everybody was extremely helpful. It was the first time I had ever gone into a state prison, and Joey was undoubtedly the most notorious patient I had ever been asked to see, so that I was excited about it and nervous, too. I felt it was terribly important to be very professional about the whole thing.

I flew up on March 6, 1965. Arrangements had been made so that I could spend as much of an eight-hour day with Joey as I thought necessary, and so I got there about midmorning. Driving out from Buffalo to Attica across that flat, farm country, you suddenly see what looks like a medieval castle on the horizon. You get closer and closer, and there's this great gray fortress, coming out of nowhere in the middle of nowhere on top of a hill. It's an eerie sight. I walked up to the door, and I remember wondering how the mailman made his deliveries because the place seemed sealed up. But there was a bell, and I pushed it, and a little window opened in the door—it was like a speakeasy. I announced myself to the guard, who was obviously expecting me, and I was let in right away.

Then I was searched. I had to go through the same sort of device as the airlines use, a metal detector. They took off my tie clip and pen, and because my briefcase also triggered off the thing, they went through my medical equipment—the stethoscope, ophthalmoscope and so on that I had brought with me to do a physical examination. Finally, after I took off my belt, which had a buckle, I was denuded enough to be taken to the warden's office. We went through another door into a courtyard, and I had two guards in front and two behind. Nobody walked *with* me. I got the very distinct impression that they were afraid of me. I'm sure that everybody in the place knew that a shrink had come to see Joey Gallo. They must have really felt that this was a dangerous guy and, you know, you'd better not talk to him because who knows what he'll do with what you say. It was as if a jar of nitroglycerine had just been passed into the prison, and these poor bastards were assigned to carry it from place to place. It was all very Army-style, saluting officers as they came by and a lot of mumbo-jumbo every time we had to go through one of the gates.

When we finally reached Warden Wilkins' office, he had his deputy there, a Colonel Myers. It was one of those official, pro forma interviews to assure me of their fullest cooperation and so forth. Wilkins, who was about to retire, struck me as an old-line bureaucrat, but there was a human quality about him, too—he was approachable. Myers was different. To me, he came across as the upward-striving type, looking to make a mark. He didn't think much of Joey, that was obvious. He made some gratuitous comment about Joey being an agitator. "You know, Doc," he said, "we want to cooperate, but you know how it is with guys like this. They're always looking for the slightest little opening to manipulate you." But then Wilkins gave him a look that said, "You're out of line," and the guy abruptly shut up.

Was Joey brought to you there or were you taken to his cell? And did you see him privately or was a guard present?

I was taken to a small room about ten feet square in the depths of the prison. It was totally bare except for a small table and two chairs. There was one window looking out on a courtyard and another, about a foot square, in the door—both heavily barred. And suspended from the high ceiling, in such a way that it couldn't be reached even by standing on the table, was a single bare bulb with a conical shade. The whole effect was totally institutional and yet somehow contrived, like a stage set. It had a theatrical quality, and so did Joey's entrance.

I was standing outside this room, waiting for him, and in the distance, I could hear these clangs and clunks of doors being un-locked and locked, getting closer and closer, like something out of Kafka. Then at last, there he was, on the other side of the last gate of bars—a prisoner and four guards. Four! Not one or two, but four. And another four on my side. Again I sensed they were scared by this whole business because the guy with the keys couldn't get the gate open. No way. He kept fumbling with one key after another. It was such a wild scene—after all this, they can't get him through the last gate to see me. But finally he made it, and he brought Joey into this room. "Doc, this is Joey Gallo," he said. "I'm going to lock you in here with him, but if you want anything, just come to the door and call. There'll be a guard outside at all times." Then he left us alone together.

What were your first impressions of Joey?

I remember being struck immediately by his eyes. I hate to sound like a Victorian novelist, but they really were like a couple of burning coals, set deep in his prison pallor. He was also terribly thin. Here was a guy who had clearly undergone a fairly recent, fairly significant weight loss—you could see that from the way his prison clothes hung on him. He was terribly pasty and looked anemic, but his eyes were simply on fire. If you've seen a lot of crazy people, people who are paranoid or schizophrenic, and acutely so, you get to recognize what they look like, what their eyes look like—and I'm not describing that. I'm not talking about the burning eyes that novelists associate with madmen. What I'm talking about are the eyes of a guy who was totally focused and concentrated on me, trying to assess what he had to deal with.

As soon as they locked us in, he took over. It was as if he were in his living room and I had just been brought in by the servant. I don't mean that he was being grand or anything, but, in a very natural kind of way, he said, "Have a seat, Doc"—indicating one of the two chairs—and then sat down in the other one. And I started in at once, because obviously he didn't know what the hell was going on. I remember my opening line. It was "Jeffie sent me."

Had he not been prepared for your visit? Didn't he know who you were?

Well, he had some idea. As soon as I started to explain, he said, "Yes, well, Jeffie mentioned you." He had had a feeling that she might do this, but he hadn't been expecting me on that particular day, and the warden hadn't set him up for it. Joey had simply been told that he had a visitor. So I told him who I was and started to explain how this was a new experience for me. In fact, I wanted to share my conflict with him. I felt it was vitally important to be as open with him as possible or I would get nowhere, because, like any inmate of a penal institution, Joey was in a paranoid situation. As soon as I started to talk, he took my pad and pencil and wrote: "The room is bugged"—which may, indeed, have been the case; I'm not saying that's paranoid—"and the guy is watching us through the window. Don't say anything unless it's okay for them to hear and know about it." Then he pushed the pad back and said, "Okay, Doc —go ahead."

That settled it. I wasn't going to play "the big consultant who's come here to evaluate you"—I was just going to be me. First of all, I had nothing they might overhear that could possibly be used against him—I had no knowledge of his criminal activities. Second, I wasn't going to talk about Jeffie, so I wouldn't be revealing her private business. And third, as long as I took care not to come across with any obvious antiestablishment, antiprison bias, anything I said could only be helpful, even in the eyes of the prison authorities. And there was no doubt that he believed what he had written on the pad. His eyes kept flicking to the side, toward the window in the door, and then around the room, as if to find the planted microphone. It was clear to me that here was a guy not only in a paranoid position by definition, but whose *gestalt* at that point in his life was "My whole world is out to get me."

So how did you set about winning his confidence?

By being absolutely straight. I began with quite a lengthy opening statement about my conflict over coming, why I decided in the end to come, how concerned Jeffie was about him and how aware I was that anyone in his position must have concerns of his own about his physical welfare and emotional well-being. That seemed to strike the right note, because Joey's immediate response was "Doc, you know, I'm glad you brought your instruments with you because I really need a check-up and I don't trust these prison doctors. They don't give a shit about you, and they have thousands of prisoners to see, and, you know, they give you a once-over-lightly. So I really want you to give me a good check-up."

"Fine," I said. "Why don't we start there? We can chat while I'm doing my thing." So I started in on the physical examination, and I said, "Look, the most important thing we have to talk about is what's going on here and why you think you ought to be moved to another prison. I mean, that's what I'm here for—to see if there's anything I can do to help that happen. But first of all, I think I should get to know you a little bit. It will make what I say more meaningful. So while I'm tapping and listening and all that, give me a capsule autobiography. Who you are, where you came from, how many brothers and sisters—you know, that kind of stuff."

Which he proceeded to do, and I got about what you'd expect— the familiar stereotype of the tough Italian-American kid growing up in the streets of Brooklyn. A guy in his position was not about to go into any great detail when he might endanger himself and his family by doing so. It was not particularly helpful in terms of hard information, but it got things going.

So when did you first feel that the barriers were coming down?

I didn't ever feel they were up. Joey was very direct, and I tried to be, too. We were simply laying foundations. But I guess you could say that that phase ended in the latter part of the physical examination.

I should explain that three months before the visit, my wife and I had signed an option to buy a beautiful but dilapidated, five-story brownstone. The house was boarded up—it had to be completely renovated—but we were madly in love with it, and kept going over there to plan how we would fix it up. But every time we unpadlocked the door and went inside, we would find that it had been vandalized just a little bit more. The kids in the neighborhood had broken in through the roof and were systematically ripping out the plumbing —the pipes were all copper and worth a lot of money—the wiring, the hand-painted tiles around the fireplaces. . . . My wife and I were bleeding from every pore. Our beautiful house was being destroyed before our eyes.

Okay—after three months of rage and anguish, I go to see Joey. And while I'm doing my nice, careful, routine physical exam, he's telling me about his childhood in Brooklyn. "I tell you, Doc," he says, "that's when I first got involved with a gang. Now don't get me wrong—they had nothing to do with the Mafia or any of that shit. It was a gang—you know, a street gang. Everybody had a gang. So we had a gang, and, you know, one of the greatest things we ever got into was ripping off brownstones."

He then proceeded, in great and lurid detail, to describe how they would tear a brownstone apart, even when it was just temporarily vacant between tenants. In those days, he would have been about the same age as the gang of kids now ripping off *our* house. He told me how they would break in through the skylight, what the copper tubing was worth per running foot, how you could get a better price from the fences if you sold it by weight—and meanwhile, I'm being very objective and professional, trying to resist the impulse to jam my throat stick right down his gullet and shout out, "I'll get *one* of you bastards! Back into solitary!" It was really very funny. He could see from my face that something was bothering me, and when I told him the whole story, we both cracked up. From then on, the talk was very easy and relaxed.

Did your physical examination show anything other than just general debility? Were there any marks or signs of ill treatment?

No. I can't say what laboratory tests might have showed, of course, but physically he was a tough guy who had withstood whatever it was he had had to take through all those months of solitary. His blood pressure and pulse were within normal limits and there were no recent scars or bruises. But as I was looking for possible signs of the beatings that Jeffie had told me about, he gave me a wry grin and said, "Doc, you're not going to find any black and blue marks." Then he leaned his head close and whispered, "They do it with pillows." "*Pillows?*" I said. Then he explained that if you put a pillow against a man's body and beat him, you could inflict a lot of pain without leaving marks. He explained this without bitterness, which impressed me. In fact, all through that day, I never for a moment got a sense of personal bitterness. He was sarcastic, yes. Cynical, yes. But it was *Weltschmerz*—he was caught up in the world's pain.

Joey had kept his dignity. When I told him about my doubts over getting involved with a Mafia figure, for instance, he just listened, whereas somebody full of psychopathic grandiosity might well have said, "Don't worry, Doc. I got plenty of connections outside. You're safe." And he didn't feel it necessary to threaten me or warn me in any way—you know: "Well, I'm sure, Doc, you're going to keep your head straight about this." Nor was there any fake humility— "Oh, I'm so grateful to you, Doc, for risking your life on my account"—or any of that kind of crap. What made Joey unusual was that he showed a genuine ability to understand another human being in a way that was truly empathetic, nonjudgmental and noninterfering. This is rare enough anyway, and far more than you have any right to expect from a guy who has been depersonalized, humiliated and sort of dehumanized by the experiences that everybody undergoes in a big prison.

Having finished the physical examination, did you then get on to a discussion of those experiences?

Well, by now it was close to noon, which was lunchtime in the prison, and there was an understanding we would break then. So I said, "Look, we both know the main reason I'm here is to try to get some sense of not just how rough it's already been, because that's obvious, but whether there's really any chance of things getting any better for you, or whether it's just impossible and what's really needed is to get you moved to another prison." And he nodded. "So whatever the difficulties are of discussing the problem under these circumstances," I said, "you've really got to talk about it, and that's what we'll do this afternoon—okay?" We agreed, and I rapped on the door for the guards. I told them we were breaking for lunch, and that I would like to see Joey again in an hour. They said, sure, they'd arrange that, and marched him off in one direction and me in another. There was a diner, they said, across the road from the prison.

Then a funny thing happened. As they took him away, I got my first real sense of what it must be like to be a prisoner. I suddenly became acutely anxious. Getting into the prison that morning, through all the doors and so on, I had been kind of excited. It had been an adventure of sorts. But now, as they escorted me out again, it seemed to take forever. Some gates had to be opened with keys, others had a wheel to turn because they were too heavy to be opened by hand, and with all this clanging and banging, it was like going from one airlock to another. Interminably. Then you began to see light at the end, and it was, you know, "Hurry up and decompress me. I want to be out in the fresh air." It was like being buried alive and clawing up to the surface. I felt really bugged. Crawly. It feels dead inside a prison. The air is dead. It's immobile and dreamlike. The guards move slowly. The prisoners move slowly. Everything is slowed down in that bleak, ghastly place.

Then I was out, and it didn't help much. There was just this huge, forbidding fortress in the middle of nowhere, a typical greasy-spoon diner across the road, and then nothing but potatoes in the fields for what seemed like a thousand miles. Even outside, the sense of desolation, of being shut away from warmth and human life was quite unnerving. I couldn't shake it. While the woman cooked up a burger for me, I sat there, saying to myself, "Well, Jesus, you ought to be feeling better now. What the hell's the matter?" I mean, I was really trying to figure it out intellectually—in just the way you'd expect from the sort of compulsive personality it takes to get through medical school and all the rest. Couldn't understand it. And now I was anxious to get back inside and get the whole damn thing over with, but I knew I had to wait until one o'clock, so I walked up and down in the road until it was time. Then I dragged myself back and buried myself in there again.

Did this insight into the nature of prison life, its bleakness and isolation, its stifling quality, help or hinder you in evaluating Joey's situation? Might not the sympathy it aroused—sympathy you would have felt for anyone confined in such circumstances—have colored your judgment?

I think it probably helped, although the first thing I said to him when we resumed was "Look, we don't have to finish this up today —I could come back again. But I feel a real sense of urgency about you getting out of here, so I'm going to push as hard as I can to get as much as I can." And he said, "Okay. Fine." I then told him that Jeffie had given me an idea of what had been going on but that I now wanted to hear it directly from him.

So he started to tell me, and, leaving aside for the moment all speculation about his motivations, what it amounted to was that Joey had found himself thrown into a racist situation at Attica, where all the guards were white, and his behavior in response—in a state prison from 1962 onward—had been that of a moderately radicalized student on a college campus five years later. He'd raised holy hell because white prison barbers wouldn't cut the hair of black prisoners. He'd raised hell because black and white were segregated in the mess halls. He'd raised hell because many of the guards were brutal with black prisoners.

When I say he raised hell, I mean he opened his mouth, that's all. How much can a guy do when he's an inmate in a maximum-security state prison? He can't make posters and picket the warden's office. He can't write inflammatory literature, mimeograph and distribute it. All he could do was talk—and Joey was a hell of a charismatic talker. And whenever he got the chance, he also demonstrated to the prisoners what we call in my trade "modeling behavior." He modeled nonracist behavior—this Italian-American Catholic who, as a group, are supposed to be violently antiblack. He modeled nonracist behavior by talking to black prisoners, trying to eat at the same table with them and having his hair cut by them. This was simultaneously to demonstrate to the white prisoners their own racism and to the black prisoners the need for them to make some demands about the terrible position they were in. It only occurred to me recently, when it hit me like a ton of bricks, that Joey was up to his neck—six years ahead of his time—in a race situation in Attica that damn nearly destroyed the place when it finally came to a head.

Did he describe how the guards and prison officials reacted to this? Their main complaint seems to have been that he was "an agitator" and "belligerent."

Well, it appears that his agitation against racism enraged the guards, and one in particular, whom he always referred to as "the Nazi." And there is no doubt that he did it in a way that was extremely anxiety-provoking, if not threatening, to the people in charge there, so that they felt he had to be isolated. But I have no way of knowing to what extent, if at all, there was any collusion between the authorities and certain prisoners, who, either because of their Mafia connections or race prejudice, wanted to bump him off. All I know is that Joey himself felt very, very strongly that the Nazi had set him up as the victim for attack by a big, psychotic prisoner with a knife, and that the only way he could protect himself was by staying in solitary. He was quite certain he would be killed if he was out "in population." It was relatively easy to stay in solitary, because all he had to do whenever they let him out was make another verbal assault on the racist scene and they would slap him back again.

You have to remember that he was being extremely cautious in talking to me in case we were overheard. When I asked him for details, he would write on my pad something like "The captain has his friends. He's got a whole group of followers, and when he tells them to lean on you, they all lean on you. I've had to deal with all of them." It must have been almost instinctive with Joey never to mention names. You must also remember that his behavior was conditioned by the feeling that he should not have been in prison at all. He told me that he'd done a lot of things they *could* have got him for, but that this wasn't one of them. He was in on a bum rap, a phony deal. There was a hell of a lot of legal machinery to be dealt with, he said, if anything was to be done about that, but meantime he wasn't about to sit there and rot. He was going to do something meaningful.

He really felt that his actions had been meaningful—in that sense? We're getting into the question of motivation here, but did you think he was sincere? Was racism genuinely repugnant to him?

I believe he truly felt the horror in the world. Joey knew I had studied the work of Wilhelm Reich and had been trying to do that kind of therapy as well as the more classical kind. He had read a great deal of Reich, including *The Mass Psychology of Fascism* and *Listen, Little Man,* and he wanted to discuss it with me. He saw prison as a practical example of what Reich had written about in terms of people being destructive and hateful and horrible toward one another. Now these are difficult books. Apart from Reich's heavy style, his conceptualization is intricate and complicated. And I suppose it was partly from prejudice on my part, but I was astounded that an uneducated Italian-American gangster from Brooklyn should, first of all, spend so much time reading and thinking about such matters, and second, that he should display such a grasp of basic human psychopathology, of the difficulties we human animals have had in making our way on this planet.

It was really astounding to me that this guy, in this room, in this prison, had become involved in the kind of sophisticated theorization that's necessary in attempting to deal in a speculative way with human character structure and human functioning on a global basis. He showed an astonishing grasp of Reich's work. He also had it in context historically. He was quite painfully aware of the conflicts built into the sociopolitical structure of America. He spoke of the violence woven into the fabric of American history, and the treatment of the American Indian as an example of amoral behavior juxtaposed with the Protestant work ethic on which the country was founded. Now, this is the kind of thing you might expect to hear bandied around as cocktail conversation in university circles but not from a gangster in Attica State Prison.

I was about to say it was altogether an impressive performance, but I don't think that's fair. I don't think he was performing at all. He was incensed about these things, as wrongs that had to be righted, and he thought everybody had to take some responsibility for righting them. We couldn't wait for the President or the politicians to do it for us. People had to assume the responsibility for their own behavior. They couldn't look to some authority figure to take over the responsibility for righting the wrongs and injustices which they themselves were guilty of. His concern was real. But to what extent he was putting his money where his mouth was and trying to practice what he preached right there in the prison, I don't know. To what extent he had identified himself with these downtrodden people, as an Italian-American Catholic from Brooklyn who was treated with contempt by many areas of society, so that it was a matter of "Save the black, save me"—on a totally unconscious level—I really couldn't say. I wouldn't even attempt to speculate. While I saw him as having a core personality structure that was paranoid schizophrenic, this was an individual who was quite reality-bound in terms of what he observed going on around him.

Now whether he correctly perceived any malice aforethought on the part of the prison authorities or any organized plot to kill him or get him out of the way as an *agent provocateur,* again I can't say. I don't know to what extent his perceptions had been distorted by the nature of that damn place. I already had an inkling of the anxieties it could generate after only half a day there—and as a visitor, not an inmate. All I know is, his presentation was relevant, coherent and logical. It was strikingly impressive. He was not giving me a prepared speech but spontaneously unloading to somebody who'd come unannounced and said, "Hey, go ahead and unload."

And you found what he said entirely convincing?

Well, you know, I'm painfully aware of a lot of the crap that goes on in my profession, and it's very upsetting to me. One of the things I feel most strongly about when working as a psychiatrist is the need to use myself, as the only instrument I really have, in trying to understand what's hurting somebody and to help them do something about it. So that while listening to Joey, I was responding on a gut level—not as a conscious effort, because I'd practiced this long enough by then to do it sort of instinctively—and at the same time, keeping a small part of myself set aside, so to speak, to evaluate what I heard, to judge what the hell this was all about and what some of the nuances were all about, so that in the end I could try to put the two together. That's how I work. So while Joey was giving me this complex presentation, which I found most impressive on a gut level, the psychiatrist part of me was able to recognize moments where things got disorganized, where associations got loose in a way that's symptomatic of schizophrenia.

But I don't think that's the point. In my judgment, here was a man who quite correctly perceived the hate in people, a hate that is mostly kept in check but which, in the prison environment, is kept in check in a particularly terrifying way. And he hadn't tried to hide from it. He had confronted it head-on. Whether he was trying to save the blacks in Attica in order to save Joey, because he identified with them, or whether he saw injustice and felt he had to assume a responsibility for doing something about it—whatever the reasons were, he had let himself become involved. He had *forced* himself to become involved.

Okay. Now somebody else might say, "Bullshit! A psychopath is a psychopath is a psychopath. He likes to manipulate people. He was having a ball. He was manipulating these blacks in the name of humanity just so he could get at his keepers, to instigate rebellion. His real purpose was to screw the screws." All right. If somebody wants to interpret it that way, they will. I can only give you my interpretation and my opinion, which is that it ain't so. Jeffie says I came out of there cross-eyed. Well, if I did, it wasn't because I'd just seen the world's most magnificent psychopath. I'd seen a lot of those at City Hospital, where I was working with adolescent psychopaths who were virtually untreatable at fourteen. What I'd just been exposed to was a guy with an astounding, three-dimensional conception of and feeling for the human condition.

Well, let's come back to that later when we've got the whole conversation in perspective. If, as you say, he had "a core personality struc-

ture that was paranoid schizophrenic," wasn't it rather remarkable that he had survived as well as he had in this utterly hostile environment for three long years? Did he tell you how he had managed it?

That was the next thing we talked about. It was getting late, and he'd been talking, without much of a contribution from me, for a long time. Then he said, "You know, Doc, I think I can trust you. I'm not going to let them kill me. I'm gonna keep myself alive. I read Reich, and I'm trying to do therapy on myself. Maybe you can help me." He then began to describe, very technically and specifically, some of the things he'd been doing to keep himself alive. His great fear was that, under the provocation he'd been getting, he might flip out and attack a guard, which would provide them with the perfect pretext for killing him. Because even if somebody could later prove it was a setup, which wasn't likely, it wouldn't help him very much as he'd be dead. His will to survive was something incredible. Anyway, he had recognized that a part of Reich's approach to therapy was to help a patient directly express some of the held-back feelings that his life circumstances engendered. I don't mean kicking people in the shins or acting out all over the place, but literally getting rid of the feeling, attempting to express it in order to deal with it better.

So what Joey had been doing, whether in solitary or not, was to lie down on his stomach on his cot, bury his head in his pillow or blanket and scream silently. He would scream in every way short of letting any sound come out. He would do this quite deliberately and in an organized way, thinking about the Nazi and everybody else whom he saw as an adversary, trying to work out his rage so that he wouldn't be provoked into losing his temper. He would also take his blanket and twist it and choke it—again silently, because he felt he was under observation a lot of the time, particularly in solitary. He never knew when somebody might be looking through the peephole, and he thought it was imperative to do everything silently in case they caught him at it and shipped him out to Matteawan, figuring he was cuckoo. He was really afraid of what they might do if they had an excuse to give him a shot and knock him out.

So now he wanted to know if there was anything else he could do as well that might help to ease the pressure of the enormous rage that kept building up through his being incarcerated, especially on a bum rap, and through being provoked all the time by his environment. And I suggested that, as he had a pillow—which he did except while in solitary—he should bury his face in it and *really* scream. Since the door was solid, with just a small window, the guards would never hear it unless they happened to be standing right outside. He could do better with a *real* scream. I also showed him how he might go around biting at the air, as this would help get out some of the biting rage. And kicking. He could lie on his bunk and kick into a pillow or rolled-up blanket. Provided the guards weren't glued to the door, he could probably get away with that. These were just some of the suggestions I thought might enhance the benefit of his self-therapy, and he seemed to think they had merit.

"Doc," he said, "you don't know how bad it can get here sometimes. I'm not sure how much of that I'm going to be able to use, but I'm glad you told me, and if I can use it, I will." It had already occurred to me, of course, that I was probably more useful to him in another way, just by being there. If the room *was* bugged, if prison officials had overheard this conversation, they would now have to be doubly careful about his safety, knowing there was an independent witness to whom Joey had described his fears. And that was about all we had time for.

Okay. Now let's get back to Joey's earlier discourse on Reich. Could you talk to him as an equal, or did you have to make concessions for him, as a layman?

No concessions. The thing that fascinated me was the immediacy with which Joey related to Reich's ideas. It was very different from any discussion I might have had with a fellow professional. Joey related to Reich in a very vulnerable, very personal way. "This is why the world is fucked up, and this is why *I* am fucked up. This is why I grew up the way I did, and this is why my old man treated my old lady that way." There was no distance between him and the idea. There was none of that intellectual detachment that is often so irritating. You know—"Isn't it fascinating how the world has evolved?" He responded as an involved, concerned, three-dimensional human being.

When he talked about political and economic systems—and he had obviously read widely in Marxist literature—it was again in vivid, real and immediate terms. People were economically enslaved. Businessmen could bullshit them to death, but the truth was they were simply another kind of gangster. Now that may sound like a rather predictable exercise in self-justification, but it wasn't meant like that. He was trying to show how it all fits together, how the sociopolitical, the economic and the psychological states of man were all interwoven in a horrible, hateful pattern. Again, some other psychiatrist might say, "Oh, very interesting. One of those global delusional systems," and I would have to say, "Horseshit!" It didn't have that ring at all.

As I said before, I think Joey Gallo saw the world so clearly and honestly that it drove him crazy, and that his craziness took the form of what is sometimes called pseudo-psychopathic schizophrenia—that his defense was psychopathic, criminal behavior.

Did you get around to discussing his "criminality"? I mean, having arrived at a logically tenable view of a world he found hateful and horrible, had Joey consciously decided to make war on it as a matter of principle? Or was the whole thing a gigantic rationalization of his criminal activities, a justification for the antisocial attitudes he had to start with?

We didn't get into that. I intentionally avoided it. My feeling was that, for better or worse, this was Joey's major defense against a total breakdown. I wasn't in a position to be his therapist, and so I was hardly in a position to endanger what he was using for survival. But if Joey *had* ever become a patient of mine, that would, of course, have been the whole challenge—could I have helped him give up his antisocial, or dissocial, behavior pattern and find some other way to handle the anxiety that the world was causing him?

Yes, but you had just heard his exposition of an attitude toward society that one might have expected to hear from a social reformer.

Wasn't that entirely incompatible with the nature of the life he'd led up to that point? If he saw himself as an enemy of society for intellectually respectable reasons, why did he resort to crime? Why did he choose to attack society from the outside rather than work to reform it from the inside? Did he give you any clues as to that?

Joey's pattern of behavior was entirely consistent. Before prison, he was a rebel against the establishment in his own Mafia subculture, challenging what he considered to be the injustices of that system. *In* prison, he expressed the same attitudes in a different way, the differences being determined by the differences in his environment.

If I were to toss all professional caution to the winds, my guess would be that Joey chose to do what he did because the behavior had been modeled for him. It was one of the few ways in which an Italian-American kid from a disadvantaged background could make something of himself. I don't have enough family history on him to know precisely why he became a gangster or why he became the kind of gangster he did. The dynamics are enormously variable and complicated. But I'm sure it would make sense if you could piece together enough data.

I am also quite certain that his world view had not been worked out in prison in order to rationalize his behavior there. I remember hearing through Jeffie of Joey's concerns, rages, speculations, passions and pain long before he ever went to Attica.

I know that's true, but there were many inconsistencies between what Joey said and what Joey did. On race, for instance. Joey didn't like blacks. He often said so. Now was that just the protective coloration, so to speak, of an Italian living among Italians, or was it truly felt? And either way, how does it square with his denunciation of the world's injustice? It's hard to reconcile what he said about blacks with what he seems to have tried to do for them in prison.

Well, Joey was a terrifically prejudiced guy, and he could hardly have been otherwise, given his background and the subculture in which he grew up. But while on a strictly, and deeply, personal level, he was a knee-jerk nigger-hater, he was also a white equivalent of Malcolm X. He was rising above his own prejudices, above his own racism—just as Malcolm X rose above hating white men. I don't think it's just a coincidence that each was killed by his own people as each arrived at that point.

I don't think Joey ever had a chance to make it all the way, but I think he had come to recognize prejudice for what it was, as another manifestation of man's basic neurosis or sickness or whatever you want to call it. He could recognize it and try to deal with it that way, but he had probably not yet reached a stage in his own personal growth and development where he could stop being a nigger-hater—in the general sense. I imagine that he was quite capable, however, of dealing with individual blacks on a friendly basis.

There is another, and more self-serving, explanation, of course— that he threw in with the blacks because he had no choice. Some of the white prisoners were out to get him, he said so himself. He also said that nobody could survive in prison on his own, at least not "in population." You need a constituency. Is it possible then that he agitated on behalf of the blacks in order to ingratiate himself with them, and thus gain some protection from his identification with that group?

I think I've probably already answered that. I mean, I can fully understand why somebody might see it that way, and I think ordinarily that would be the explanation which made sense—if you were dealing with an ordinary psychopath who would manipulate his environment for his own ends as necessary, regardless. But I don't think it's the *right* explanation. Unless I was conned by one of the greatest con artists of all times—which is entirely possible, I suppose—what he said had the ring of truth to me. That's a clinical impression, which is something less than absolute proof, of course.

For what it's worth, you should also remember that the most Joey could expect to get out of me was the expression of a positive opinion that he was not safe "in population" at Attica and should be transferred to another prison. That was the most I could possibly do for him, and I don't think he had any great hopes of its working anyway. So, bearing that in mind, I don't quite see why he would want to throw in all this other stuff gratuitously, particularly if it wasn't true.

Dr. Bruce 239

Perhaps it represented a more subtle challenge. After all, he didn't have too many opportunities of trying conclusions with someone who knew what he was talking about and could reply in the same vein.

Well, perhaps. But at no time did I sense that Joey was simply trying to impress me or that he was striving for any particular effect. He was an enormously exciting and stimulating individual just to be with. I haven't looked at *Reader's Digest* in twenty years, but they used to have a feature every month called "The Most Unforgettable Character I've Ever Met," or something like that. If they're still running it, Joey Gallo has my nomination. Coming to the view he had, from where he had come to it, and then holding on to it through everything—there had to be an extraordinary quality in that human being for it somehow to have supervened. When *I* talk about social injustices, coming from a nice, middle-class, freethinking, liberal background, what the hell else do you expect? But when a guy like Joey comes to it, picking it out from his guts, learning about it, not in spite of his environment, but *from* his environment, and holding to it instead of retreating into the usual cynicism and bitterness— that's astounding. It really is *astounding*. I don't know that you can do it *without* becoming schizophrenic. You have to be so naked, so open and aware to sense the *Weltschmerz* in all that pathology around you and not just some local plot against you. He deserves every credit for that.

You also have to give him credit for trying to test and refine his conclusions by reading and by the kind of conversation he had with me that afternoon. When we talked about Reich, for instance, it was amazing to me that he had not only understood what he had read but had integrated it into his own systems of thought. I mean, in terms of its applicability to current social and political situations, Reich's work was still relevant, but it was dated in the sense that it had been written many, many years previously. Joey had understood Reich's analysis of the failure of the Russian Revolution, for example —which is what *The Mass Psychology of Fascism* is all about—and gone on to consider modern Russia in the light of Reich's conclusions. Applying the same principles, he had gone on still further to speculate about whether the same psychodynamic elements in people that had allowed a Hitler or a Stalin to come to power and remain there could operate in the United States. What he found useful in Reich had been integrated with ideas and conclusions he had derived from other sources, including his own observations.

As I said before, this wasn't a fascinating, intact, encapsulated delusional system of a schizophrenic patient—this was a coherent, immediately relevant, totally appropriate and extremely perceptive approach to the real world. He even put his finger on what had been bugging me about the prison. It was that I couldn't have distinguished the inmates from the guards without their different uniforms. I found that very upsetting, and it made it even more shocking and ludicrous that the one bit of life I saw in the whole place should be a prisoner, this ball of fire with his eyes blazing and his mind boiling with curiosity. No wonder he disturbed the rhythm of everybody else. No wonder they tried to bury him in solitary.

Okay. Now before moving on to what you did to get him out, can we look ahead a bit and see how his subsequent behavior fits with the tentative conclusions you reached on the visit, whether it remained consistent? As you say, his will to survive was strong. Nine years of imprisonment failed to break it. And yet, within a year of his release, which is what he most wanted, he seems to have given up. It was almost as though he chose to commit suicide. Is that a reasonable reading of his behavior?

I think so. It's guesswork, of course, but I can't help wondering if two factors may not have played a part. The first was the enormous expenditure of, if you like, survival energy over nine years. How much did he have left? And second, perhaps the crystallization of ideas that undoubtedly took place in prison sealed his fate. I mean, what if he now saw the futility of the life he had led before going to prison and then found upon his release that he had no choice—from his point of view—except to go back to it and repeat the pattern? That might well have prepared the ground for suicide.

Once he knew he was getting out, he must also have known he was trapped. He was going to have to go back to his family and followers, whose outlook hadn't changed. Even if he could have beaten the parole restrictions somehow and gone to live in another state, or even another country, his name was so infamous that he would have had to take on a totally new identity before being accepted in another role. In any case, Joey's narcissism would never have allowed him to work out a new life as some nondescript fellow in another town with a run-of-the-mill job.

No, I think it was all over before Joey even got out of prison, and I think he knew it—somewhere in his gut he knew it. Getting out was almost an end in itself, a necessary step before making the final gesture of determining his own destiny. Suicide—albeit in a most indirect kind of a way, and perhaps even without planning it on a conscious level. It's pure speculation, I know, but, as a psychiatrist, I'm prepared to stick my neck out and say there was a distinctively suicidal pattern to Joey's behavior in the closing weeks of his life.

But wasn't the transition from his determination to survive at all costs to this pattern of self-destruction a bit abrupt? I mean, after making every effort to take everything they could dish out for nine years, to face it, absorb it, come to terms with it and survive—you don't consider that incompatible with what followed?

Not at all. The recognition that it had all gone for nothing could have come very quickly. There's a psychological isolation as well as a physical isolation in prison. Your whole psychological set is cut off in a pretty arbitrary way while you're inside the four walls, right up to the last moment. And it's usually reinforced by the fact that damn few prisoners come out with very much more to look forward to than more of what got them behind bars in the first place, and Joey was no exception in that sense. In fact, in his case, here was a guy whose whole scope, whose capacity to feel and think was so much broader than most people's, that the crash, when it came, just had to be that much more brutal. I think it's entirely consistent with his previous behavior that a man as quixotic as Joey should not lay himself open to misinterpretation by committing suicide in an orthodox way but should instead, consciously or not, allow himself to be rubbed out.

All right. Now, after your visit, which ended in a discussion of various things Joey could do to improve his self-therapy, what happened next? I presume you reported your findings to the Commissioner of Correction.

Yes. Two days later, on March 8, 1965, I wrote him a very cautious, very formal letter:

> DEAR COMMISSIONER MCGINNIS,
>
> I had a four-hour consultation with Mr. Gallo on March 6th, and would like to share some of my impressions with you.
>
> Penological considerations are not in my province, of course, but I came away from my meeting with Mr. Gallo with a very strong conviction that, from the psychological standpoint, he will never be able to "make it in population" at Attica Prison. It was also my impression that, following Warden Wilkins' retirement in July, the situation will become even more untenable for both the prisoner and the prison authorities.
>
> Mr. Gallo has asked me to communicate to you that he is most anxious to be transferred to "any other" prison. Again from the psychological viewpoint, there is no question in my mind that, after the developments of the past three years at Attica, the chances of a more successful accommodation, from both the prisoner's and the authorities' point of view, would be considerably greater at any of the other state prisons than they are at Attica.
>
> I made a number of suggestions to Mr. Gallo which were designed to help him, in a practical way, to make a less pressured adjustment to prison life. He was most interested in these suggestions, and indicated his desire to be in touch with me periodically.

I then thanked him and the staff at Attica for their courtesy and cooperation, and sent copies of the letter to Joey, Jeffie and the warden.

On March 11, I got a letter back from the Commissioner, which meant essentially by return mail between New York City and Albany. After the usual preliminaries, it said:

I would like to thank you for your prompt response to me concerning your visit with the inmate. For a long period of time, we and the authorities at Attica have had a difficult time with the inmate, and I concur with your feeling that the inmate will never "make it in population" in Attica prison.

Some time, if possible, in the interest of the institution and for the welfare of the inmate, I would like to discuss with you further some of these problems. I would have no great objection to the transfer of this inmate to another institution at the right time and under such conditions that would not give him and others the idea that he could bulldoze or, let us say, "write his own ticket" while confined in institutions of the State Department of Correction. I am only interested in his serving out his sentence as imposed by the Courts in accordance with the rules and regulations of the Department, which is required of all inmates. If we could get together, I do believe it would be helpful to all concerned.

Now, my interpretation of that was that he really wanted to cooperate but had to take a hard line for the record. So I got off a letter to Joey a week later, on March 19, telling him of this encouraging response, and asking for his permission to pursue the matter with the Commissioner. This was necessary, of course, because he was protected by rules of privilege in his dealings with me. He replied on March 23, which was again by return mail:

I authorize you to engage in further discussions with Commissioner McGinnis in my behalf. My family and attorneys will supply you with any pertinent data you deem necessary for your discussion. I am touched by your sincere interest in my situation—I feel safe in your hands. Stay loose, my friend. Joey Gallo.

The phrase he used to sign off with was interesting. When we'd talked about how he could avoid being provoked into attacking a guard or an inmate, I had said to him at one point, "Christ, you know, I can imagine what it must be like. I can't even sit here and talk about it without getting uptight." And he had immediately become very paternal and concerned about my welfare. He didn't say, "Stay loose," then, but he did say, "Oh, come on, Doc. I'm sure you have enough troubles. I'm the one that's living here." He had obviously remembered that.

Anyway, the next thing that happened was that Commissioner McGinnis called me from Albany. He wanted to know if I'd heard from Joey, and when I told him I had, he said he was going to be in the city and could he stop by to see me? So we made an appointment for April 14, and he showed up in his big black limousine with the New York State Commissioner of Correction license plate, and the elevator man brought him up to my office. Every tenant in the building soon knew he was there, of course, and began to wonder what I'd been up to. I'd had a bit of trouble because my patients screamed a lot, and now it seemed obvious to them that I must have been running an abortion mill up there. I rather enjoyed that. And I was really impressed with McGinnis.

He said he had wanted to meet me in person so we could talk about the situation, and he proceeded to enlarge on what he'd told me in the letter. "Doc, it's a wide-open grapevine," I remember him saying. "If the word gets out that inmates are manipulating the Department and getting themselves transferred and this is the way to do it, we'll have more goddamn psychiatrists knocking at the doors of our institutions than you'll be able to count. I want to be fair if the guy's getting a bum shake, but there's simply no way I can cope with a sudden flood of shrinks wanting their patients transferred back and forth."

He was absolutely right, of course, and on the same day, I wrote to Joey again:

> You will probably have spoken to your wife before you receive this letter, but I want to tell you directly about my meeting with Commissioner McGinnis today.
>
> The Commissioner came to my office and we spent about 45 minutes together. In essence, the Commissioner's position—and he was very willing for me to communicate this to you in this letter—is that as soon as he feels that you've made a "sincere effort" to live according to ordinary prison regulations (and he pointed out that he doesn't mean that he expects you to be a "model prisoner" or a stool pigeon), he will be willing to make every effort to provide you with the opportunity to have a "fresh start" in another prison. He made it quite clear that at this time he can't say when he would recommend a transfer

—that is, in so many weeks or months—but that he will make such a move as soon as he is convinced of your sincerity in wanting to function within "normal" prison routine.

Let me say that I've never been so impressed with any public official —and I'm not writing this in order to palaver the Commissioner. He's straight, honest and tough—and fair. He knows his job and his responsibilities, and my feeling is that he's the kind of man who'll do his job and fulfill his responsibilities, come hell or high water. A good man to have on your side!

I hope that all goes well with you and that you're not letting anything or anyone "get" to you. As you wrote to me in your last letter: "Stay loose, my friend!"

A week later, I received Joey's reply:

I spoke to Jeffie and read your letter. I am happy that the Commissioner is the man that you describe so forcefully. If anyone else made those remarks, I'd be skeptical. There is much I could say but I will wait—I trust you. The conditions here have not changed in the slightest for me. There are those few that derive a pleasure in jooging at me that no RACIST can "get" to me. To have you in my corner has not endeared me to the NAZI. I can feel the vibrations. I will be KOOL for my sake and can assure Commissioner McGinnis of my sincerity. I have the feeling I shall be visiting *you* in the very near future. Loosely, Joey Gallo.

Joey's letter was dated April 22. On June 1, 1965, he was transferred to Clinton Prison, Dannemora, New York.

13

Prison Lawyer

Toward the end of his first year in Attica, Joey began to keep a notebook, a spiral-bound Nifty Steno Memo Book marked down from twenty-five to fifteen cents. It contains little of a personal nature and nothing at all about his prison life as there was no way he could protect it from the guards; he used it mainly to keep track of his reading. Six months later, it was jammed from cover to cover with quotations, often unattributed, citations, lists of book titles and authors, stray thoughts, disconnected passages he wished to polish before including them in letters—and all in a dashing, untidy pencil scrawl interspersed with gloomy Gothic doodles, dense, angular and forbidding.

But if it offers no direct account of his feelings, the notebook provides plenty of indirect evidence. The quotations Joey chose to write down, finding them especially illuminating, memorable or relevant to his situation, are a chain of clues to the way his mind was working—and testify also to his voracious eclecticism and seriousness of purpose. They show that, within a matter of months, he had read works by or about Freud, Reich, Nietzsche, Plato, Spinoza, Hume, Kant, Schopenhauer, John Dewey, Bergson, Santayana, Herbert Spencer, William James, Voltaire, Diderot, Pascal, Locke, Spengler, Wilde, Keats, Shakespeare, Goethe, Theodor Adorno, Will Durant, Coventry Patmore, Oliver Cromwell, Napoleon, Adenauer, de Gaulle, Lenin, Mao Tse-tung, Sun Tzu, Clarence Darrow and Louis Nizer, among others.

The first few pages of Joey's prison notebook clearly illustrate its quality:

Nothing is new to me, I have foreseen and am prepared for it all. What will be, will be? No, my love. It is virtue alone which can beat fortune. No virtue? You're dead. Fortune spins you in her wheel and where you land no one can say, but her power is based on our weakness. There is nothing a firm and elevated mind can't do. Join that with a desire of the soul, then we can't lose!

Hello. Cupie didn't mention anything about the 4 ($). Just like him. I am brought down about money but confident of the outcome. How's Lefty? All the boys are pulling for her. Hy is right. Kelly's making a fool of himself!!! Cupie was to let me know how he made out in Albany? I didn't receive my money from the Police Property Clerk! Boy! Am I *mad!* Tell the lawyers to institute an action immediately.

Come, come—lean on me. What beautiful words, and yet so lonely, it's so anti-nature, so wrong but not unbearable. No, it's you—you're the reason. Why did you happen to me? Clear, all so clear and so close. I shut my eyes and relive the moments that now seem so wasted. Oh, how I would do those scenes again, but so right, so much more had I only known—

The passion of the intellect, which can be as carnal and ecstatic as the rapture of the flesh.

Women are the only private property that has complete control over its owner.

Hobbes: Force and fraud are—in war—the two cardinal virtues.

Aquinas: Things are rather in the mind than in themselves.

Nietzsche: Tradition and convention—the baits of fools who prefer the company of the unprotesting dead and dare not live dangerously in the perilous future! Contempt of pleasure is the truest pleasure of all.

Virtue comes by training and does not insinuate itself into the soul automatically as vice does.

One must repay good and ill, but why just to the person who did us good or ill?

One does not hate as long as one disesteems, but only when one esteems equal or superior.

Nietzsche: "I have done that, says my memory. I could not have done that, says my pride, and remains inexorable. Finally, my memory yields."

He had to be a lively hood for a livelihood.

To prejudice the laughter in one's favor (important!)

Spinoza: He who repents is twice unhappy and doubly weak.

"One who despises himself is the nearest to a proud man" (putting in a sentence a pet theory of the psychoanalysts that every conscious virtue is an effort to conceal or correct a secret vice).

"A free man thinks of nothing less than death; and his wisdom is a meditation not on death but on life" (it may lead to resignation and an Orientally supine passivity; but it is also the indispensable basis of all wisdom and all strength).

Nietzsche: "Laughing lions must come."

Men will never be free till the last king is strangled with the entrails of the last priest.

John Dewey: Complete adaptation to environment means death. The essential point in all response is the desire to control the environment.

Mao: If we have a correct theory but merely prate about it, pigeon-hole it and do not put it into practice, then that theory, however good, has no significance.

Lenin: Without a revolutionary theory, there can be no revolutionary movement.

Mao: Knowledge starts with practice, reaches the theoretical plane via practice, and then has to return to practice.

Joey: Theory becomes aimless if it is not connected with revolutionary practice, just as practice gropes in the dark if its path is not illumined by revolutionary theory.

LU HSUN—the greatest!!

The consecutive quotations from Mao and Lenin suggested to Joey the interesting idea of culling from their collected works a whole series of maxims about the theory and practice of revolution and then arranging them in the form of a Platonic dialogue between the two, with occasional interventions from Stalin and Lu Hsun. This he did in a separate notebook, neatly writing out his selections in ink and broadening the scope of the "discussion" to take in the principles of war. After nine pages, however, he abandoned this revolutionary collage, and the only other entries in the second notebook are a table of Spanish verb endings, tense by tense, and an inventory of his prison wardrobe. By the spring of 1964, he had become increasingly occupied with legal rather than literary matters.

The obvious avenues of appeal had led nowhere. His only hope now of getting the case reopened rested in the resourcefulness of his lawyers and the ingenuity of their arguments, both of which had so far been in short supply. With Price & Iovine holding a watching brief, he proceeded to engage a succession of attorneys whose strategy seemed to have merit, starting with Frances Kahn, and the less headway they made, the more briskly he bombarded them with suggestions, new lines of argument, citations from case law and clippings from legal journals.

His general reading inevitably suffered, but Joey still remained one of the Eighth Street Bookshop's favorite customers. Concentrating more now on twentieth-century writers, and looking increasingly to fiction for verification of the social malaise he was to diagnose for Dr. Bruce when they met, he worked his way through Kafka, Sartre and Camus to Céline, whose squalid nihilism he found particularly congenial. He also ventured into R. D. Laing, pop sociology and current affairs, and began to take an interest even in crime! Here, however, he ran into trouble. When it came to ordering books, he was permitted to send only for those which the prison authorities approved in advance, and then only on the understanding that they might be withheld if, on examination, they were judged "unsuitable" (the criterion of "suitability" being the taste and literary judgment, apparently, of whichever prison officer happened to see them on arrival).

Nor was he allowed to read anything which, from its title, might have seemed likely to inflame the lusts of the flesh. Prompted by another literary sin, Warden Wilkins sent Joey a note on June 4, 1964:

> It has been brought to my attention that the books you are sending home have been marked on the margin of several pages with various symbols.
>
> You will no longer be permitted to receive any books from the publisher and then send them home if they are marked in any manner whatsoever.
>
> The following four books are being placed in your personal property file until you are released or transferred from Attica Prison:
> *The Sexual Revolution*
> *The Discovery of the Orgone*
> *Character Analysis*
> *The Naked Society*
> The other book, *The Honored Society,* was taken out by your wife on her visit on June 3, 1964.
>
> W. H. WILKINS
> Warden

At the time, Joey had more to exercise him, however, than petty censorship. He was working closely with Frances Kahn on the suit they were to bring that September, airing his more serious grievances against the Department of Correction. The last real hope of winning a new trial having died in March, when the United States Supreme Court refused to consider his case, he had turned to the prison library's lawbooks for other possible remedies—a search that took on an edge of desperation after his suit failed. But it was only when Jeffie took a hand, and Dr. Bruce broke the deadlock at Attica by engineering Joey's transfer to Dannemora, that anything useful came of his researches.

So far, two main avenues of attack had been followed in seeking to overturn his conviction—the denial of counsel of his choice and the prejudicial effect on the jurors of massive newspaper and television publicity before and during the trial. Now two additional lines of approach came up for exploration: first, the question of Joey's sanity at the time of his trial; and, second, the purely legal argument that the two crimes of which he had been convicted—conspiracy to extort and extortion—were, in fact, one, and that he had therefore been punished twice for the same offense.

The sanity question, of course, was related to the "no counsel" issue—was he mentally competent when he waived the right to defend himself in court?—while the "double jeopardy" argument was a reserve measure to be employed if all else failed. The most to be expected of it was that the two terms of imprisonment to which he had been sentenced, one on each count, would be made concurrent instead of consecutive, so that the maximum time he would have to serve would be seven years and three months, not fourteen years and six months.

Before exploring the first of these possible new approaches, his lawyers had the unenviable job of getting Joey to agree to let them argue in public that when he stood trial, he had been "in such a state of idiocy, imbecility and insanity as to render him incapable of understanding the nature and consequences of the proceedings, or to properly and intelligently assist or partake of his defense, all of which led to a serious deprivation of due process." Knowing his past sensitivity to any such suggestion, they broached the idea of applying for a writ of error, coram nobis, on these grounds with a certain diffidence, but they need not have worried. By now, Joey was prepared to consider anything that offered even the faintest chance of a new trial, although his endorsement of the proposal was less than enthusiastic. It was not so much that his pride was touched, but that in order to win on these grounds, his attorneys would have to show that his vehemence in rejecting any suggestion of mental incompetence during the trial was, in itself, evidence of his unbalanced state at the time. Any sane man, in other words, would have pleaded insanity. This argument seemed as thin to him as it eventually did to the New York State Supreme Court, but, failing a better idea, he set to work on researching the application with all his customary zeal.

The final draft was prepared in December, 1966. After listing the times Joey had been sent to Kings County Hospital for psychiatric examination, it went on to assert that when Judge Sarafite appointed Irving Mendelson to represent Joey in place of the absent David Price, and Joey learned that Mendelson was a former assistant district attorney, he became firmly convinced that he was about to be "railroaded." There then followed a long extract from the trial record of what Mendelson had told Sarafite about his "client's" refusal to cooperate in his own defense, a statement which referred several times to an unspecified motion Mendelson would have made if Joey had not specifically forbidden him to do so.

"The motion to which Mr. Mendelson referred," the application went on, "was, of course, a motion to have petitioner committed for mental observation because of petitioner's irrational attitude and conduct."

If that casual "of course" was a shade disingenuous—the court had had no possible way of divining what was on Mendelson's mind —the "evidence" adduced to support the contention that Joey's conduct should have alerted Sarafite to his mental incapacity was positive humbug. His refusal to join in Mendelson's motion for a mistrial, for instance, was said to have shown "that petitioner was not acting in his own best interest"—a circumstance that "warranted further inquiry" by the court. Further, Joey had told Sarafite that "everything is confusing to me," and when he had claimed the protection of the Constitution, "the court, instead of realizing the state of mind the petitioner was in, proceeded to make light of the matter by inquiring if petitioner stood on 'the whole document' or some particular section."

That was all they could find in the trial record to suggest he was insane, and, obviously, it wasn't enough. Affidavits were therefore drafted in which Mendelson and Weiswasser, the court-assigned attorneys, would be asked to swear to Joey's "irrational conduct" behind the scenes. Weiswasser's draft stated that when he introduced Mendelson to Joey, at Mendelson's insistence, Joey "immediately and without provocation proceeded to vilify Mr. Mendelson and accused him of assisting the trial prosecutor in framing him." When Weiswasser had tried to pacify him, Joey had given him an earful as well and refused to talk for two weeks. Subsequently, Mendelson had told Weiswasser that, in his considered opinion, Joey was mentally unbalanced, and that he was going to move to have him committed for psychiatric examination.

Following this conversation . . . I informed Mr. Gallo that Mr. Mendelson had a motion in mind which would guarantee a postponement of the trial until Mr. Price returned from Florida. Mr. Gallo made no comment until I stated to him that the motion was to have him committed for mental observation. When I informed him of the nature of the motion that Mr. Mendelson was considering, Mr. Gallo literally exploded and began to vilify me and Mr. Mendelson and stated he was going upstairs to "throw that bastard Mendelson out the window, and you're going right behind him." The conduct and language of Mr. Gallo sincerely caused me to believe that he was mentally deranged and would actually carry out his threats. And I state here now without any hesitancy that for the only time in my adult life I was actually frightened and in fear of my life.

That at least had the ring of truth. But had he known, said Weiswasser's draft affidavit, of Joey's previous mental history, he would have joined Mendelson in making the motion, with or without the petitioner's consent.

With this "evidence" of Joey's "idiocy, imbecility and insanity" and copious citations from more or less relevant case law, the application for a new trial concluded by arguing that Mendelson had been derelict in not pressing his motion since this "effectively deprived petitioner of the protection of his rights"; that Judge Sarafite had been ignorant of Joey's psychiatric background when he insisted on starting the trial; and that the question of Joey's mental competence bore not only on the constitutional propriety of the trial itself but on the validity of his waiving of counsel (if, in fact, he had done so).

This draft petition was designed to fit into what had now become a very involved and intricate strategy to raise Joey's case in the Federal courts. Among his prison papers is the handwritten copy of a letter he received on January 5, 1967, from yet another attorney, listing the steps proposed:

> 1. Submit coram nobis on insanity and await the position of the District Attorney. If an affidavit is submitted opposing the granting of a hearing, then;
>
> 2. Submit Federal habeas corpus on counsel issue and await reply of Attorney General on this, and if they argue we failed to exhaust state remedy, then;
>
> 3. We argue that counsel issue was fully briefed and argued on direct appeal in New York and on petition for certiorari; argued before Northern District Court, who denied the writ without prejudice subject to a petition for coram nobis; point out that coram nobis was sought with an affidavit from Dave Price, Esq., and still the motion was denied without a hearing; that our coram nobis on insanity, which would, of course, have a bearing on the claimed "waiver" of counsel, was recently submitted, accompanied by overwhelming support that relator was incompetent at time of trial and sentence, and again New York has opposed the granting of a hearing. Point out that relator has yet to have his "day in court" represented by counsel. At the trial, not one single word was spoken on behalf of relator. Why is it that he is repeatedly denied the basic right to a hearing with counsel to establish that he never "competently and intelligently waived his right to counsel"? It appears that New York is determined to keep relator imprisoned as long as possible with exaggerated procedural arguments, while at the same time denying relator a hearing in court which, under the circumstances of this case, would have been granted long ago if relator was not Joey Gallo. It

completely defies logic and established law to deny relator the right to a hearing in the face of his overwhelming proof that he did not, because he was incompetent to, waive counsel.

The attorney then went on to advise against appealing Judge Sarafite's dismissal of the earlier coram nobis petition to which he had already referred. Based on an affidavit by Price describing his incapacity at the time of the trial, this had sought to show that Sarafite "had improvidently exercised his discretion in denying a delay." Instead, the letter urged that

> we should direct our efforts towards establishing the fact that we never competently waived counsel. This we are in a good position to prove, and if we do prove it, we have a winner. Whereas, even if we prove, which we can't, that Sarafite may have been a little hasty in not waiting for Price before starting the trial, the People can establish justification for Sarafite's conduct by attributing it to Mr. Price's negligence. . . .
>
> In summary, then, my suggestion is to:
>
> (a) submit insanity coram nobis and disqualify Sarafite immediately by service of subpoena if necessary;
>
> (b) await position of Hogan's office on this, and if he opposes a hearing,
>
> (c) submit Federal habeas corpus on counsel.
>
> (d) if we are denied a hearing by Federal court, appeal to Circuit Court of Appeals.
>
> (e) if Sarafite denies hearing (I mean Sarafite's replacement), appeal insanity coram nobis to Appellate Division.
>
> In closing, should it be deemed appropriate to press the issue of publicity, I would suggest raising this issue via a state habeas corpus, since we have no other available state remedy.

So far, so complicated. Most litigants in Joey's position might have assumed from this that their cause was in good hands and bowed to the superior wisdom of counsel. But after five years in prison, *Joey* was now the final authority on his own case and the law relating to it, as he showed in his reply:

Concerning your opinions on the "no counsel" issue as opposed to the "insanity," I must say I agree with you 100 per cent. The method of attack so far employed certainly did not impress me, and I have expressed my opinion. Unless the sanity issue is coupled with the counsel issue in Federal court, I'd say our chances of success are very slim indeed. I have read the appellate brief, coram nobis and habeas corpus and expressed my opinion that the method of attack on counsel deprivation was very weak. I also feel that the counsel argument in the Appellate Division brief was poorly done.

The only point with which I disagree with you is the trial record failing to reveal a strong case on denial of counsel. But, my position is that the record fails to show a "competent and intelligent" waiver of counsel (cf. Day-v-United States, 357 F.2d 907, 7th Circuit, and cases cited). I agree that we would be hard put to prove that there was an improvident exercise of discretion because the trial court refused to wait for retained counsel. However, proving that the court failed in its duty to see that the alleged waiver and "decision" to defend pro se was competently made is a much simpler matter.

I specifically direct your attention to the colloquy in chamber immediately prior to the commencement of the trial. It was the *court* who decided to relieve assigned counsel and stated that the trial representation would be pro se. Had the court assigned an attorney to conduct the trial, especially since there was no specific objection (other than the stated repeated preference for retained counsel), then I believe we would have a hard row to hoe. However, since it was the *court* who decided to relieve assigned counsel and, for all practical purposes, directed pro se representation by a defendant who stated he was "confused" and "no lawyer," I can't honestly see how the People can square their conduct with constitutional requirements, particularly when the sanity issue is injected into the proceeding. The court may say it was unaware of the mental history at time of trial, but why didn't it take some action after receiving the probation report at time of judgment?

The tone was closer to that of senior counsel discussing trial tactics with his junior than that of a convicted extortionist striving to beat the rap. Joey had become absorbed in another problem-solving exercise. If, to regain his freedom, he had first to become a prison lawyer, then so be it; he applied himself to this requirement as systematically as he had previously tackled the job of taking over South Brooklyn. Define the problem, isolate the best approach without regard to moral scruple or the trouble and risk entailed, then press home the answer by all available means—that was Joey's essential response to every situation. But while admirable in theory, in practice his battle strategy in the courts achieved as little in the end as it had in the streets.

Unimpressed as he was, quite properly, with the insanity coram nobis petition, Joey eventually instructed his attorneys to drop it and couple the "no counsel" issue with the old prejudicial publicity argument in his application for a Federal writ of habeas corpus. This was, in fact, his second such application on these grounds, the first having failed before U.S. District Judge Edmund Port in the Northern District Court earlier in 1966. Judge Port had denied the writ because Joey's claim of an unfair trial, being broader than the right to a change of venue on account of unfavorable publicity, had not been litigated in the New York courts. The second application failed for the opposite reason. U.S. District Judge Edward Weinfeld ruled on July 6, 1967, in the Southern District Court that before the Federal courts could consider the case, Joey would first have to test his claim of prejudicial publicity in the state courts. He had missed with both barrels. When an application for a certificate of probable cause was also denied in the Southern District Court—the certificate being necessary before he could appeal that part of the decision relating to the claim that his constitutional right to counsel had been violated—Joey's last hope of a breakthrough at the Federal level collapsed. After six expensive years of litigation, he had yet to reach first base.

Not that he had the slightest intention of giving up, of course. The issues had still to be tested in the state courts, in accordance with Federal court rulings, and there was still the final resort of a plea for resentencing on a concurrent instead of a consecutive basis, but his legal expenses were draining the family dry. Gallo revenues had improved since Joe Colombo's promise to "spread the bread around," but not sufficiently to please Joey, who had angrily rejected the peace terms his brothers had settled for. Being dependent upon them for everything, however, including his monthly food parcels, it was not until the end of 1969 that he felt free to return once more to the courts. By then, his brother Larry had died and Joey was head of the family. His younger brother Kid Blast, though capable and well liked, could not command the same confidence as Larry had inspired in their followers, and many of them were now longing for Joey's return as for the second coming.

It fell to Paul Vladimir, a Queens attorney, to reopen Joey's case in the New York courts. On December 11, 1969, ten days before the eighth anniversary of the original sentence, Vladimir filed for a writ of error coram nobis, in conformity with the Federal rulings of 1966 and 1967, on the ground that Joey was "denied a fair and impartial trial by reason of massive and hostile publicity concerning him, his family and the case." As evidence of this, "a random sampling" of clippings from every newspaper circulating in New York in 1961 was annexed to the application. They showed that "the defendant was insidiously connected with other crimes of a horrendous nature" as a result of information "delivered to the newspaper offices by news releases from the prosecutor's office and Police Department in violation of the Canon of Ethics."

"The amount of publicity given to the defendant," the argument ran, "rivaled that given to a presidential candidate. The news media gave so much attention and play to prejudicing the rights of the defendant that legitimate news items, such as the international situation and the atomic bomb, were displaced by headlines concerning the defendant." Coupled with the court's failure to admonish the prosecutor about pretrial publicity and to question the jurors as to whether they had read these "highly inflammatory items," the media coverage had effectively deprived Joey of his constitutional rights. The application further contended that Tony Leone, "a co-defendant, was granted a stay of the trial on the consent of the District Attorney because of massive pretrial publicity." In addition, the media had consistently described Joey as "crazy," and he had himself admitted he was "confused." The court had, therefore, failed in its duty by not inquiring "as to the defendant's competency at the time of the proceedings against him."

The motion appeared on the calendar of the Supreme Court of New York on February 17, 1970, and Vladimir secured a quick, tactical advantage by getting Judge Sarafite disqualified from considering it. But his success was short-lived. On further consideration, the court found no merit in Vladimir's contention that, if a hearing were ordered, "Mr. Justice Sarafite would necessarily be required to give testimony," and, as a matter of judicial courtesy, passed the application back to him.

Sitting in judgment eight years later on his own conduct of the trial, Sarafite, not unexpectedly, found little to criticize. He upheld the District Attorney's view that Joey had waived his right to challenge the jury's impartiality, and that no evidence had been presented to show that the jury was prejudiced. The blunders in Joey's defense were again coming home to roost. "At no time did the defendant question the veniremen concerning any alleged prejudicial publicity," Sarafite wrote in the memorandum that accompanied his denial of the motion, "neither did the defendant on appeal of his judgment of conviction raise the issue that he was denied a fair trial due to adverse publicity. The defendant by remaining mute cannot now be heard to say that the jury was so prejudiced as to deny him a fair trial. . . . By his choice of the trial strategy of remaining mute, he lost his right to the relief sought."

Few of the annexed newspaper clippings had had anything to do with the trial itself, Sarafite continued, and the rest had mostly appeared while the case was in adjournment. Furthermore, the District Attorney had questioned the veniremen about what they had read or heard, and the court had several times instructed the jury to avoid outside influences. As for Leone, his stay had been ordered, not because of the publicity, but because his attorney was engaged at the time in a homicide trial.

The judge was particularly severe on the insanity issue.

. . . the defendant now for the first time suggests that there was a question as to whether or not he was competent at the time of trial. Nowhere in his petition does counsel allege that the defendant was in such a state of idiocy, imbecility or insanity as to be incapable of understanding the charge against him or the proceeding or of making his defense. Rather, he chooses now to raise the issue in an incidental manner. At no time while this case was pending did the defendant's retained counsel make any such claim. Neither was it raised at the time of sentence. Prior to sentence, the defendant was examined by a court psychiatrist. The records of the court psychiatric clinic reveal that on the advice of his lawyer, the defendant refused to answer questions except those relating to identification. The psychiatrist found no external evidence of psychiatric disorder. In the absence of any evidence that the defendant was incompetent during trial, his contention now is without merit. . . .

The defendant's motion is denied.

Destroyed might have been a more accurate term. It was the end of the line as far as the courts were concerned. Vladimir wrote to Joey on May 6, enclosing a copy of Judge Sarafite's decision, and informing him that notice of appeal had been filed in case he wished to take matters further. If he lacked the funds to do so, he went on, Joey could ask the Appellate Division of the Supreme Court to assign counsel on the grounds of indigence.

But Joey was not only indigent, he was indignant. After eight years of fruitless wrestling with this legal octopus, was he again to be saddled with assigned counsel? His last recourse was a plea for resentencing, a maneuver planned as early as 1966, but reserved while an alternative yet remained. By attacking the sentence rather than the conviction, it would inevitably have been construed as acceptance of the judgment against him, and thus have ruined his bid for a new trial. There being no guarantee of success in any case, it would have meant gambling the possibility of upsetting the original verdict against him on a fifty-fifty chance of halving his prison term, which made little sense at the time. Now, four years later, the ploy seemed hardly more attractive, although a well-argued brief was prepared for submission to the New York Court of Appeals by yet another attorney in his stable. Aside from being broke, Joey had already established that his conditional-release date (the day on which he would become eligible for parole) was March 10, 1971—

now less than a year away, assuming he could recover the "good time" he had lost in his war with the prison authorities. Even if his family had *had* the money to spare, the double-jeopardy issue might still be before the courts when he was paroled, which was clearly ridiculous.

In June, 1969, Joey had asked the chief clerk at Green Haven Prison, to which he had been transferred in 1966, to work out the figures and dates for him:

> DEAR MR. PARSONS,
>
> Approximately two years ago, I received a notification from the Prison Computation Board informing me of lost time returned. I seem to have misplaced said notice.
>
> On March 6, 1968, I wrote to you requesting my conditional release date and my maximum release date—you graciously answered my request, informing me that my conditional release date was 3/10/71 —no maximum release date was included.
>
> My present request is for a clarification of these three issues: (1) Computation Board's determination, (2) conditional release date, (3) maximum release date.
>
> Obediently,
JOEY GALLO

In reply, the chief clerk set out the situation for him on the back of his letter:

> Comp Bd 5/18/66:   220 LT plus 59 LC stand
> Restore 90 days
> Comp Bd 5/31/67:   45 LT plus 26 LC stand
> Restore 25 days.
> Max Exp Date: Jan 10, 1976
> Next parole appearance: Jan 1971
> You could earn 4 years 10 months off max, making a CR of 3/10/71 bearing in mind that lost time and lost comp time comes off the 4–10. Approx 6 mos before you are eligible for a CR release date, another Prison Comp Board will be held to determine how much time you will be allowed or withheld.

When Joey's final assault on his conviction was repulsed by Sarafite a year later, therefore, he decided to cut his losses and sweat out the months that remained, although the judgment was still technically under appeal at the time of his release. And if, in the end, his diligence in reading and research had come to nothing in the courts, it had nevertheless kept him alive and alert and engaged for nine otherwise sterile years. It had also provided him with an anthology of psychiatric definitions, of which these were his favorites:

Schizophrenia: A group of malignant psychoses characterized especially by a profound deficiency of the usual indications of normal emotion and capacity for "rapport," and an extreme preoccupation with ideas which are extensively symbolic, neologistic, unreal and intellectually incomprehensible, often accompanied by bizarre delusions, hallucinations and behavior. . . .

In dementia praecox, there is a . . . loss of objectivity; hallucination and reality are imperfectly distinguished, and every happening has a meaning and effect on the observer; the idea of an action produces the action directly, instead of offering a possibility of action, and this is interpreted as a compulsion from without. . . .

Paranoid psychosis: A psychosis whose most conspicuous feature is delusions that certain people are plotting, persecuting or disloyal, these delusions being highly systemized, intellectually rationalized and coherent.

14

Jeffie

Although Jeffie never stopped thinking of herself as Joey's woman, after nearly five years on her own she did stop thinking of him as her husband. This was partly Joey's own doing. Shut up in a daily nightmare that no one on the outside could even comprehend, much less share with him, he began to find Jeffie's visits with Joie more of a burden than a comfort. They reminded him of how much he had lost and had still to lose. They fed the rage that was always threatening to get out of hand and destroy him. With so little left over from the struggle to survive, it grew harder and harder to bear the thought of anyone's dependence upon him, emotional or otherwise. He kept urging her to go free, to find a life of her own.

Jeffie eventually took him at his word, although not with any great expectation of relief for either of them. She had been faithful to Joey because she loved him, and no other man had really interested her, but now she felt rejected, as she explained in her weekly sessions with Dr. Bruce. He still remembers how confused and uncertain she was.

"Jeffie used to talk about Joey as being in some ways totally anachronistic. For all his being a twentieth-century mobster, he was also a medieval knight-errant. You know—'I've been captured by the dragon, but you mustn't pine for me. You must go on, live your lives and forget about me.' She kept saying, 'He wants me to divorce him. He's pushing me and pushing me, and I don't know why the hell he's doing it. He's always saying, "You can't wait for me forever. Divorce me. Go ahead and make yourself a life. Forget it." ' Jeffie was very torn about this. She couldn't let go emotionally, but on the other hand, what was it doing to Joie? The message was getting through that Daddy was turning her off. She wasn't very old, but she was certainly at a critical period in her development. She was looking very actively for a male figure to attach to. How could she make sense of a relationship with someone she saw once a month in prison, particularly when he was not exactly trying to get close to her?"

The male figure Joie eventually attached to was the Canadian playwright, Ted Allan. Jeffie had met him through Georgia Brown, who had jointly rented a house for the summer of 1966 in Westhampton with Allan and several other friends. Jeffie spent several weekends there, and as she was beautiful and Allan amusing and both unpartnered, they inevitably paired off. "Ted had a great sense of humor, which was what drew us together. He was a warm, open, crazy, lovely guy—all you could ask for in a friend—but I doubt I could have made it with anybody just then. I had this fixed fantasy of Joey that nothing was going to alter. He was part of me. We had met on a level that was new to us both, although, thinking back, I probably needed Joey more than he needed me.

"Anyway, I started seeing Ted, and we immediately started fighting. One weekend, he invited me and Joie out to Westhampton —he was alone fixing up his play *Chu Chem*—and I couldn't understand what I was doing there if he was going to work all the time. Naturally, we had a row about that, and he said something like 'No Frenchwoman would behave this way.' So I said, 'When you're out with me, pay attention to me. Otherwise don't invite me out. Get yourself a fucking Frenchwoman,' and that was the end of that. I didn't want to hear about his writing or his fibrillating heart. I had troubles enough of my own."

One of them was the death of her mother that fall. By then, Jeffie's affair with Allan had jolted along by fits and starts to the point where they were discussing marriage. Everything was fine between them so long as Allan expected neither sympathy with nor interest in his problems. To Jeffie, a man was someone who would not only not bother her with *his* worries but also relieve her of hers. A man was someone like Joey. When she returned from California after her mother's funeral, she found Allan on the doorstep, broody and despondent because *Chu Chem* had been taken off in Philadelphia, and once more sent him packing.

They were back together, however, for Joie's fifth birthday, which they celebrated while on vacation in Jamaica, and although Jeffie was still reluctant to commit herself, she was coming around slowly to the idea of marrying him, despite the thought of having to break the news to Joey. She had never entirely trusted his insistence on setting her free, and while he continued to occupy such an unfillable place in her life, she was unwilling to risk losing him altogether. That summer, she confided in his family. They had already met Allan— he had rented a house for his daughter Julie and her children next to theirs on Fire Island—and Jeffie had made no secret of their relationship. Now she told Joey's sister Jacqueline that she was thinking of marrying him and moving to London, and this, too, came as no surprise.

"They all understood except his mother, who said, 'You can never leave him. It'll never work. You'll be back within a year.' She was right. It didn't work at all. Ted and I had got into an I-love-you-if-you-love-me kind of thing, and I guess that wasn't what I was looking for. I remember sitting him down and telling him, 'It may not look as if I have very much, but it has been a very secure little world for me. I am going to be very careful how I end it. Before we get married, you ought to know that you personally are going to pay dues for every man in my life since my father. Are you ready for that? You're taking me to a new country. You're taking an anxious, frightened lady into a whole new world, and you better keep standing on your feet. Give me a year. After a year I'll be fine, but for one year I'm going to be totally dependent, which is not something I do well anyway. Can you handle it?'

" 'Oh, yeah,' he says."

In June, Jeffie and Larry Gallo went to see Joey in Green Haven with her Mexican divorce papers. It was not an auspicious start to her new life. It was one thing for the captured knight-errant to release his princess from her vows, but quite another for the princess to take him literally at his word. Joey flew into a terrible rage, and refused her permission to take Joie out of the country. It was only after talking privately to Larry that he calmed down sufficiently to sign the papers and wish them well. On July 21, 1967, Jeffie and Ted Allan were married in Alexandria, Virginia, but it was a "betrayal" for which Joey never forgave her.

"Years later, after he got out of prison and we'd remarried, he said to me one day, 'Why did you marry him, Jeffie? Why didn't you just live with him?' I said, 'Because I thought it would look better. We had to go and live in England, and it was necessary for visas and things. And there was Joie. I thought it would be better for her if I ran off with a husband rather than a lover.' He just nodded. That was the only time we ever discussed it, but I think it was always in his mind."

As usual, marriage did nothing to calm Jeffie's impetuous nature. More worried than she cared to admit about Joey's reaction, she fought her new husband across the Atlantic for five days by boat, and was no sooner settled into his London apartment than she had the floor raised in the living room.

"It was a nice flat, overlooking the River Thames—except that when you sat down, you couldn't see it. So Georgia Brown and I decided the only answer was to raise the floor, and I had a carpenter come in and do it. Ted wasn't too pleased because we hadn't much money, but we were fighting constantly anyway, so it didn't make much difference. But he and Joie got on very well. He was marvelous with her. They would go on space trips and nature hunts together, and they really enjoyed each other. She was very happy with him.

But I wasn't. I used to lock myself in the bedroom and he would write me long notes and push them under the door. Such tumult was going on. In the end, it all blew up. He went to live at a friend's house until the dust settled. I told him I was leaving, but at *my* convenience."

Jeffie's departure was delayed for several months, partly because she didn't have the fare home, and partly because she felt guilty about separating Joie from her new stepfather. "In April, I went to Spain for a couple of weeks, and I remember writing to Joey from there explaining my plight. I had been writing to him every month about Joie, and he seemed to have gotten over the divorce. I told him how badly I felt at taking her away from something that was obviously so good for her, but that the marriage wasn't working out and I seemed to be living a lie. Joey wrote back saying I should give Ted a chance because, as we both knew, I wasn't too easy to live with. On the other hand, he said I should think of myself and not Joie, because Joie would be happy when her mother was happy. He really didn't seem angry any more, and that just increased the regrets I had about the divorce and getting married to Ted. I never lost my sense of dependence on Joey. He was my brother, best friend, lover, husband, daddy—everybody else just paled in comparison. I'd thought that maybe I could still have an adult, intelligent relationship with another man—with Ted—but we didn't make it."

As Joey had suggested, Jeffie went back for one last try with Allan after her Spanish trip, and they struggled through till July, when Joie, now six, finished with school for the summer. The three were together when the final break came. "I think my exact words were 'I am going to my embassy.' Then Joie said she was terribly sorry and she loved me very much but she was going to stay with Ted. 'You're going to stay with him, my ass,' I said. 'Get over here or I'll call a cop. You're my kid and you're coming with me.' She really would have preferred to stay with Ted, but as soon as he borrowed the money for our fares, we left. Just as Momma said I would, I came home with my tail between my legs to the apartment on Weehawken Street that I'd taken after Georgia finished her Broadway run in *Oliver!*"

Jeffie then picked up with her friend Dottie, a small, boyish, broken-nosed Sicilian beauty with a sense of humor no less lacerating than her own. The two had worked together for a while at Raymond's Exclusive Telephone Answering Service, before Jeffie met Joey, but seen each other only intermittently after that. While Jeffie had been oscillating between New York, Los Angeles and London, Dottie had been marrying, and leaving, first, a rich, middle-aged businessman, by whom she had two children (and no alimony), and then a much younger airline clerk, by whom she had another (and no alimony). When Jeffie returned from England with Joie, she found Dottie living with her three children, two dogs and a cat in Lyn Morgen's old house on Eighth Street, and with her usual ability to pick up a friendship years later as if she had never put it down, Jeffie teamed up with her for what turned out to be a splashy year on the town.

"We worked on the registers in McKay's Drugstore on Sixth Avenue until ten o'clock, two or three nights a week, and then we'd do the rounds of the discos. Dottie was going out with a guy who owned an after-hours club, and I sort of accumulated Scott. Scott was stark-raving mad. Some people thought he was gay, but he wasn't. He had a disdain for sex of any sort, and we liked each other right away. We had a Platonic affair—one of the closest relationships I ever had in my life. We never had any money, but I had a really good time.

"Of course, I had to be careful. I was not Mrs. Gallo any more, but I couldn't afford to go near anyone who was connected in any way with Joey's world. Ringside at the Copa was out. So was Jilly's, and all those places. The whole family must have known I was going out—it was no secret, God knows—but they'd taken me back in the fold. Whether that was on Joey's instructions or for Joie's sake I don't know, but they were always very good to me. No matter how much I goofed in their eyes, I always felt they accepted me. I used to take the kid out there just so Momma could clean her up, and we had great Sundays at the dinner table. She and I were both hollerers by nature. Momma was bright and alive and beautiful, and I think she envied me a little bit for being free the way she had always wanted to be. I got by by being the family nut. It was a sad time for them because Larry had just died of cancer in St. Vincent's Hospital.

"Joey took that very hard. First Ali Baba, now Larry—the two people who'd been closest to him, next to me. I took Joie up to see him, and he thought she was just fantastic, so bright and sure for a little kid. He teased her, of course—he had a whole series of examinations to put her through—but she understood him now. He was warm and welcoming, as if nothing had happened. In fact, it was the best visit we ever had. I really felt everything was as good as it could be while he was still inside. I expected nothing from him—there was just this contact with his being. And nothing changes that. Nothing."

In the summer of 1969, Jeffie took Joie to Los Angeles to see Aunt Ilma and Uncle Juan. As usual, she asked around for her first husband, Joe Barreras, and found him living at Hermosa Beach with his three kids, his wife having packed her bags one day and left. "Joie and I went out there and stayed with him a while. We sat and looked at the ocean, the sun shone down, we talked of old times and new times—it seemed like a very pleasant life. So when we got back to New York, I said to Dottie, 'Why don't you try California? *I* don't like it, but for you and the kids it should be great.' Couple of weeks later, we're all in Hermosa Beach. I rented a house and got a job as a cocktail waitress at Danny's, a sort of nightclub there. Dottie rented the house next door and went on welfare. Later on, I got her into Danny's as well, and we settled down nicely. After a year of screaming and raving in New York, I was very happy by the ocean."

With her eye for symmetry in such matters, Jeffie had thought to make a match between Dottie and Joe Barreras, but it didn't work out. She had to be satisfied that they became, and remained, friends. As far as her own future was concerned, since the Ted Allan episode, she had been disinclined even to consider risking another fiasco; when she wasn't waiting table at Danny's, she stayed home or sunned herself on the beach. But Dottie soon got bored.

"All I heard about was Joey—his letters and the endless phone calls to his family in Brooklyn. Her telephone bills were monumental. He wasn't writing too often then—he'd cut her off for a while. Then she'd get a one-liner—'Send a packet of provolone,' or 'See the

8th Street Bookstore sends this list'—and this would get her goat. She'd write back hostile, then beautifully, then tear it up. Nothing else seemed to mean anything to her. She was obsessed with him. Finally, I said to her, 'Hey, baby—bye, bye. If you want to lay up and eat and get fat and try to fulfill yourself that way—solid. It's cool. But me—I wanna go out and enjoy.' " And she did. She met and teamed up with a handsome ex-junkie from Synanon named Lou who played the guitar.

In the spring of 1970, Ted Allan's daughter Julie called Jeffie from New York to pass on a story she'd heard that Joey might be getting out soon. Rumors of this sort had accompanied every one of his appeals, and Jeffie put it down, at first, to the usual wishful thinking. But the source was more reliable this time, and a day or two later she called Joey's sister Carmella to check on it. "Carmella said she had heard nothing, and so I let it pass, but the rumors didn't stop. I kept picking up hints from all over, and I got pretty restless. Something about this wasn't sitting right. I was tired of Los Angeles anyway, so I decided it was time to get back."

Once again, she and Joie packed their bags and departed for Weehawken Street, and once again, fate took care of the rent. Among the friends she called on her return was Ruth Browne, designer for a major Seventh Avenue fashion house that needed a receptionist. "The job was pretty dull. You just sat there, well made-up, waiting for someone to call. But then the fabric buyer, Frank Balon, moved up from the plant in South Carolina, and when I heard he needed an assistant, I got him to try me out. I did well. It turned into the first serious job I ever had.

"That was around September. Soon after, I went to visit Joey in Auburn. I'd heard he didn't want to see me, but Momma encouraged me to go, and Roy-Roy drove us up. I was a bit nervous after hearing these stories, but when Momma and I sat down with him, he seemed fine. After we'd talked for a while, he suddenly turned to her and said, 'Give her an apartment out there.' Hit me like a kick in the gut. I didn't know whether to laugh or cry. He was not only getting out, he was saying, 'Come back.' But to *Brooklyn?* He knew it was the one place I never wanted to be, not ever, not as one of that group.

Right away I was going to have to pay dues. I was exhilarated and appalled at the same time, but luckily I didn't have to say anything because Momma was screaming, 'Oh, what am I going to do with my tenants? I can't get my tenants out.' 'Give her the attic,' he said. 'Take care of it. Don't bother me.' Nobody was asking for *my* opinion, but it made no difference anyway. If Joey and I were going to get together, it *had* to be in Brooklyn. One of the conditions of parole is that a guy can't live with a woman he isn't married to. But if we were both living in his mother's house, who was going to know? When they stopped yelling at each other, I told him we'd work it out. Nine years had gone by, but nothing had changed. I went back to New York feeling very strange.

"After that, I started commuting to work from Momma's house and visiting him regularly once a month. He knew he was going to be paroled soon, and we talked a lot about the future. He was going to write. He was going to get involved with prison reform. He was going to work with juvenile delinquents. I was very happy. He could have run for President for all I cared. I just wanted him back, although I knew it wasn't going to be easy. The beginning of February, he told me he was coming home March 10. I couldn't speak. I couldn't have been more breathless or eager or nervous. Monday morning, I told Frank, my boss. I'd been using the name Lee, but I figured he ought to know who he had working for him. Joey had always attracted a lot of publicity, and I couldn't see *that* changing any. Didn't care. 'No problem,' he said. 'There's no reason why anyone should know but me and Ruth.' He even gave me a couple of weeks off to settle Joey in."

In between fixing up the two-room attic apartment in Mary Gallo's house on East Fourth Street, dropping Joie off at P.S. 41 every morning on her way to work and buying new sets of lingerie in anticipation of the great day, Jeffie had spent hours on the telephone with her friends, trying to silence her qualms. She was concerned, for good reason, with Joey's true feelings about the divorce and her marriage to Ted Allan. Had he really forgiven her? She called Joyce about it in California.

"Jeffie was so full of doubts, and yet so full of hope as well. 'Can

I do it?'—like a little girl, desperately anxious to do the right thing. She had such a desire to make it work, you could hear her voice shake. 'It's worth everything I can give to it'—those were her exact words. But I knew the marriage to Ted *had* to be on his mind. Total dedication can't be split up, and he could never have settled for less. I warned her he would probably go crazy for a while. She couldn't expect him to come out and be a proper husband. He'd been away too long. But I thought there had to be a chance if she wanted it so much, because surely he needed something solid, too."

Jeffie was also worried about Joie. At nine, she was a tough, bright, spirited child with a higher regard for her independence than for a father she hardly knew. Lacking her mother's incentive, she could not be counted upon to make the same allowances for him, nor, with her fierce, protective loyalty, was she likely to forgive him any deficiencies as Jeffie's husband. To soften the confrontation, Jeffie brought in Dottie's daughter Pamela from the West Coast to stay with them. She was the same age as Joie, and her best friend.

"I figured it was going to be a crucial time for Joie. One night at Ruth's, I sat her down and told her, 'Daddy's coming home, and everything may *not* be all right. He's been through so much. So I'm asking as a favor—give me a shot with my old man. There's going to be tumult, but it won't be your fault. Just give me a year. I want to see if I can make us into a family.' So she said okay, and gave me a year.

"On the day he came out, Momma, the aunts and the women were in the kitchen, cooking up a storm, and the house was stuffed with people hanging around like Moses was coming to lead them out of the wilderness. Joie was hopping around on the porch as excited as the rest of us. It's her big moment, right? We've been living for this. So the car finally draws up outside the house, and he comes up the path with the guys that just fetched him from Sing Sing, where he's been since just after Christmas. And already he's looking right past her. He picks her up, gives her a peck on the cheek, puts her down again and carries on into the house, which is a mob scene. Shrieks, wails, tears, kisses, hugs, back-slapping—and Joie's outside, blinking. Is that *it?* That's it. Daddy's home.

"I'm not doing much better. The party goes on all day. In fact, it goes on for three straight weeks, and he doesn't shave or bathe for the first two of them. He was absolutely manic. He just sat at the table, looking worse than he ever did in prison, while literally hundreds of people passed through the house to see him and touch him, and hundreds more hung around outside waiting their turn. The king was showing himself to his subjects. I know why he had to do it, but that didn't stop us getting into a fight. I wanted him for myself, right? He knew how absurd it was, this godfather routine. Okay, so he couldn't just ignore all these people, but enough is enough already —now he's wasting *our* time. I had the whole scenario for our first night together worked out, right down to the soft lights and the background music on the record player. I'd had my hair done, and finally decided which one of the zillion nightgowns I'd bought I was going to wear.

"When I figured it was bedtime, I whispered in his ear and he said okay, he'd be up in a minute. So off I went to do all the things that blushing brides do to get ready on their wedding night, and still no Joey. I phoned down and the message comes back he'll be right up. Okay. I wait and I wait. Now I'm calling downstairs every few minutes, getting madder and madder. My hair-do is wilting, the nightie is beginning to annoy me, and I'm sick of listening to Sly and the Family Stone on the record player. Every time I call down, he's going to be up in a minute. Finally, when I'm about ready to blow my stack, he says to the guy who's answering the phone, 'Tell her I can't come up because it will violate my parole.'

"Aaargh! I ripped off the nightgown, threw on a pair of jeans and an old shirt and went downstairs again. For the rest of the night, I just sat between his knees and listened while he rapped with the family and the guys who were still awake. These people had kept him alive for ten years. He stayed down with them because he owed them something. He knew what he had to give and when. They'd worked very hard for him, and he had cost them. He was going to pay everybody back *his* way—and that trapped him. Nothing had changed. It was a lovely, romantic illusion to think that he could have accepted a woman as the basis of his life. He was too much of a warrior. He was too angry. He had to have tumult—I knew that. He was what he was and I loved him so much, but I sensed where he had to go.

"It was around three in the afternoon of the next day before we finally went up to the apartment. Then it was as if not an hour had passed, let alone nine years."

15

Dannemora to Auburn

Joey's nine years were less easily bridged. Where other prisoners yielded enough to get by, Joey never considered it. He was as he was, and the world still had the same choice: either give way or kill him. It was not enough merely to endure imprisonment. His nature required him to challenge the system to do its worst and *still* survive, still recognizably the man he was before. This he managed to do. He returned to Brooklyn neither broken in spirit nor totally poisoned with hate. But the unequal struggle had worn him down, and soured his hope for the future. He had won, but the victory had defeated him.

His three and a half years in Attica were the sternest test. With no constituency to work with, there was no chance to shorten the odds by playing prison politics. In solitary, he could only be a victim, a role for which he was temperamentally unsuited. Transferred to

Dannemora, he changed his strategy to suit the more promising goal of survival "in population," but again at a punishing cost. To the cautious hostility of the guards was now added the uncompromising hostility of the inmates. When the Department of Correction "boated" him on to Green Haven some sixteen months later, on October 21, 1966, it did so to save his life.

Even so, the run of events was turning at last in his favor. Throughout the prison system, and for some years past, the balance of power among the inmates had been tilting toward the blacks. With the alliances he had forged in Attica and Dannemora, this put Joey on the winning side. But that was not enough. Like a true disciple of Machiavelli, he saw in these changing conditions an opportunity to rise above the racial divisions in Green Haven and establish his dominance there as an independent power broker—most likely with the tacit assent of the prison authorities, who clearly had no answer of their own. The whites would come to him for mediation, knowing his influence with the blacks, and the blacks would look to him to advance their interests, knowing he had no cause to love the whites. A few months after his release, when he was discussing the possibility of a book about his experiences, Joey described how he came to take over the prison, referring to himself in the third person:

"The mentality of the guards is such that he is able to use a lot of psychology, because of his important position in keeping peace and harmony. He's allowed a lot of latitude because the guards fear him. One word from him and a guard could be on a guard tower. That's one of the most boring jobs in a prison—you sit up in a tower for eight hours at a clip, just by yourself—and he can have that done to a guard if he so wishes.

"Of course, he would have to have something to hang his hat on, but generally he has a pretty good run-down on every guard that he comes in contact with. His information on them is just as complete as his information on the prisoners. When the men in the block are in the mess hall or at work, he is usually answering the phone and doing the clerical duties. The guards hang out in that area—drink coffee and talk to one another about their outside lives—and he is smart enough to have them expose themselves without them being aware that he is listening. He knows of all the shenanigans that go on between the guards and their wives, and what guards are seeing other guards' wives, and what guards are drunkards, what guards are gamblers, what guards are homos. In the prison that we're speaking of, I'd say there was about fifteen overt homosexual guards, and maybe about sixty under cover—that would like to, but the job is of more importance to them.

"He uses this information in many ways. If a guard has a particular dislike for an inmate, and the inmate wants this guard off his back, he will contact Joey. And if his situation is one that Joey can capitalize on—either through money or getting this guy to do something for him—then Joey will check out that guard and tell him to cool it with this person, and he'll do it in a way that makes it seem like the guard is doing him a favor and at the same time himself a favor. They know he won't go to bat for someone unless it was righteous. He wouldn't go to bat for a troublemaker. He'd only go to bat for a guy that's a hustler, that's looking to do a quiet bit without no static from the prisoners or the administration. Some guards just don't like the way some guys look, don't like the way they talk or don't like their personal habits—they give them a rough time. That's where you see him come into play. There's never been a case where he's told a guard to lay off a particular inmate and then this inmate has done something embarrassing to him and the guard that laid off.

"An area where he don't involve himself is where there's violence —unless it's between races. Otherwise, if there's a violent situation, he usually backs off from that because the men usually tend to take sides—the prisoners tend to take sides in the situation and so do the hacks. They want a confrontation. They're all waiting for it to happen, and usually they discuss it beforehand, who will get the better of the situation. A few times, he has been approached to cool a situation like that, by friends of the individuals involved, and he's backed off because you would have to say who's right and who's wrong, and his whole philosophy is there's nobody right and there's nobody wrong. If he gets involved in anything, it's because he can gain something from the involvement and, at the same time, keep his record intact. In a violent situation, where violence is imminent, it's always been the case that you can straighten out a beef one day and it'll flare up tomorrow. The old animosity comes to the surface at the slightest provocation—or imagination, for many of these guys suffer from delusions, and he is aware of it.

"The only time he would get involved is if it's a white man and a black man, or a white man and a Puerto Rican, or a Puerto Rican and a black man—but not two of the same race. If it's different races, then he contacts the boss of the niggers, who is a good friend of his and more or less a working partner—he would contact this black tough guy of the prison and sound him out on how this situation can be resolved without it breaking into a racial conflict. Usually, anything that's brought to his attention of that nature is settled. There are battles between the races, but they're not known of beforehand. These battles take place almost instantaneously. Somebody steps on somebody's foot, somebody cuts someone off in a line, someone makes a breach of manners somewhere and they go slug, toe-to-toe. But anything that's brewing and he's made aware of it, where there's different races involved or nationalities, he'll always be able to squash a thing like that.

"No one in a prison is alone, not if he's worth anything. Everybody belongs to some certain group. You have a Muslim group, with a spokesman for that group. You have a Black Panther group, and a spokesman for that group. You have five-percenters, the Young Lords, the Nazi party, and spokesmen for those groups. Then you have the Mafia party—more or less, what they call the Mafia party, the Italians. And usually with the Italian group you'll find Jewish men mixed in. And then there's the Irish mob, and they're usually by themselves, the Irish.

"I don't think you could penetrate into any of these groups unless you come in recommended. There's no chance of you coming in on a draft, walking around the yard and just walking over and becoming part of one of these so-called groups. You have to be invited in. Somebody usually knows you, takes you in and vouches for you. He's responsible for any actions that you put down, and that makes it difficult for a person to get accepted, because no one wants to stick his neck out. Once you're with a group and for some reason they ostracize you, no other group in the yard worth any salt will pick you up. You just become a nobody in the prison, and you're fair game for ridicule and possibly assaults—sexual or physical, whatever. You're relegated to a certain part of the prison yard where all the nonentities congregate.

"Prison is a caste system—there's a hierarchy. Certain types of crimes that are abhorrent on the outside are highly respected on the inside. Molesters of children are the ones who are usually ostracized in prison, and murderers are on the top level. Guys that killed their mother and father, or just one of them, are pretty much on top. Guys seem to have a special regard for a guy that does that. I don't think they're proud of them or anything like that. It's just that they can understand why a guy would bump off his mother or his father or both. Then you have your armed robbers. And next, after the armed robbers, you would have your burglars and hijackers. These are in the groups I talked about—this is their status inside these particular groups. And the longer your sentence, the more you're on top.

"If you're a newcomer with a long sentence, there's a certain period everybody watches you to see whether you have control of the situation. It's usually a period of about three or four years before you see whether the man is in shock and whether he will come out of it. Usually you can't tell if a guy is in shock on a big bit because he's been in shock since the day he was arrested, and he's able to function and do everything. You might think he was normal, but when you find out is when he pops out of this shock. Then you see the real person, and that's when the shit is in the fire, because if he's wacky, it comes out then."

Dr. Bruce had seen Joey in Attica at around the three-year mark in his "big bit," when the shit was truly in the fire and everybody was watching to see if he would come out of it, but it had been a while longer before the question was finally answered in Green Haven.

Just how close Joey had come to disaster was afterward explained to the New York *Post* by "a white ex-con," Pete W., who knew him in Dannemora. Having brought their concept of "territory" with them, the inmates had been allowed to institutionalize it in a system of "courts." These were small plots of ground in the yard where they could raise vegetables, cook and mix with whom they pleased. "There are just so many courts, and they're registered in the names of certain individuals that have been there a long time, and you can accept anybody you want on your piece of property. The reason for that is there's less fights. You can stay with who you want and keep away from people you don't like, just stay with people you have something in common with.

"Gallo wasn't accepted by anyone. So, in other words, you walk the middle of the yard. He started hanging around with Puerto Rican and black guys. In Dannemora, the white inmates, the Italians, have a word for blacks. They call them *tuzune* or *melanzane,* the word for eggplant. And they used to call Joe Gallo a *melanzane*-lover and a *tuzune*-lover. They used to antagonize him all the time."

At first, the blacks and Puerto Ricans had merely tolerated him. "They tolerated him because he was spending like $40 a month in the commissary and getting a big package from home—salamis, tomato paste, cigarettes, fruit and things like that. But apparently he didn't get along with some of them for a while because he had about four or five fights with black and Puerto Rican inmates, and they probably figured it out logically, 'Well, he's not being protected by anybody; his own people don't want him,' so he really was a target within the prison.

"He was a small guy—Joe Gallo's about five-six. He's a very wiry guy. I'd say he weighs about 140. If you have to say a word, I'd say agile—he's very agile. He held his own. He probably won a few and lost a few, but he had heart. After a while, they accepted him because they couldn't rough him over. He'd fight back. He wasn't a patsy. Probably if he didn't fight back, then they would've taken everything from him."

With acceptance came a measure of authority. "He used to talk out of his cell to all the black cons, and he used to tell them about how all the crime in Harlem and the South Bronx and Bed-Stuy could be theirs if they had enough heart. All of us used to overhear it. But at the beginning, I think he really didn't believe what he was saying. It was just a way to belittle the Italian guys. He was saying that white guys bleed the same way as them, and they had to take a little heart and take what was theirs. But, like I said, I think he was just trying to get back at the Mafia inmates for outlawing him."

With authority came a measure of protection. The hostility of the white inmates was hardly diminished, but they left him alone after that, although Joey was several times in trouble with prison officials for fighting and possession of weapons. "By the time he left Dannemora, he was being accepted by the black guys because they wanted to get ahead in their so-called operations, and he could get them ahead. I mean, if I was a black guy and I met a guy like Gallo, I'd want to get tight with him, too. In prison, everybody wants to be a Mafioso. It's like playing minor-league ball until you get to the big leagues."

In spite of his black protectors, however, and, to a large extent, because of them, the animosity of the whites continued to fester, dividing the prisoners racially and building up so much tension between them that the Department of Correction decided to pull Joey out for fear of a riot. That eased the situation at Dannemora, but for a time it looked as if the Commissioner had merely succeeded in transferring the problem to Green Haven, as Pete W. heard on the grapevine. "There were two attempts on Joey's life there. Someone tried to stab him in the mess hall, and then they tried to set him on fire, douse him with gasoline in the cells. Why they tried to do him in was because he had given names of some high Mafiosi officials to some black and Puerto Rican guys in prison, and when these guys came out, they kidnaped a few of the Mafiosi."

Surviving this last sputter of hostility, Joey then rose above matters of day-to-day contention to become the "fixer" he described later. He could never adjust to prison life, but within its grinding limitations, he had found a role that restored a measure of self-respect. Now he *knew* he could make it, so that when Jeffie suddenly produced the divorce papers, he took her defection, if not in his stride, then well enough to recover his poise before she left and to tell his family to help her.

His instructions were given in a letter to Carmella on July 30, 1967, nine days after Jeffie's marriage to Ted Allan—and, indicative of his priorities, appeared as a footnote to a shopping list for one of the monthly packages that Pete W. remembered Jocy receiving in Dannemora:

Dear Cam,

The pillow is a blessing! The books a ball. Thank you.

Please prepare this package for next visit (if possible), one easel (for painting) 4 canvas on stretchers from 2 sq. ft. on up

black socks
Wildroot hair dressing (New Formula)
1 doz. lg. bars of Dove soap
Colgate toothpaste
2 boxes of C. Howard chewing gum
2 boxes of C. Howard violet mints
3 cartons Camel cigs
1 can of Half & Half pipe tobacco
1 box of White Owl cigars
3 grey short sleeve shirts size 15
1 can of shaving cream
1 fountain pen (the old type with the rubber tube reservoir)
2 doz mixed fizzies (all flavors)
1 doz bananas
1 doz loaves of Syrian bread, whole wheat (flat like plates)
Swiss Knight cheese
Sour pickles
Few cans of beef
1 doz Pastene tuna fish
4 small cans of bacala
½ doz cans vegetarian beans
1 lg. Calamata olives
1 head lettuce
6 tomatoes
1 bunch celery
1 Italian salad dressing
Some fresh fruit
No chicken, no cold cuts, no pastry
A few small cans of salmon
Few pounds of hard candy.

> Please send my best wishes to Jeffie and Ted. If there is any-
> thing I want, it is that they should be happy. Do whatever is
> necessary to give Jeffie her shot.

The order for easel and canvases marked his graduation to painting in oils. In art, as in everything else, an uncomfortable blend of
perfectionism and unwillingness to accept instruction drove Joey to
evolve his own techniques through experiment, and to assess the
results by criteria that owed no conscious debt to anyone. The results, though limited in scope, were thus intensely personal in both
content and idiom, and often, as his hand grew more practiced,
disturbing in their power. He produced a terrifying self-portrait, a
haunted green face ravaged by experience; a study of a stalking
leopard, oddly like him, which he gave to Joie; several gloomy ab-
stracts loaded with symbols of repression, and several dozen other
assorted canvases, none of which he felt were good enough to keep.
They were all lent out or given away to anyone who showed an
interest—and often reclaimed and awarded to someone else if the
original recipient fell out of favor.

Whenever he wished to send a picture home, he had to ask the
warden:

> To: *Deputy Warden Sawner*   2/2/70
> Dear Sir,
>   Your kind permission is needed for me to send two (2) of my
> paintings home with my family when they visit with me.
> > Obediently,
> > Joey Gallo #11916

Back came the note in due course with the word "obediently"
ringed around heavily in ink and a message at the foot:

> *Your to much!* [*sic*]
> The above gentleman has received the necessary materials which
> enable him to send his works of Art from the premises.
> > Your Humble Servant,
> > T. B. Baines C.O.

The byplay was amiable enough, but it had not always been so. He was now within a year of his appearance before the Parole Board, and it had already occurred to him that tactically it might be wise to move on, so that he could run up to his conditional-release date with a clean record in one prison at least. Although he had lost very little "good time" after establishing himself in Green Haven, there had been trouble enough in the early days, including several angry demonstrations against the authorities after permission had been refused for him to wear sunglasses in the yard and after he was told that his nephew Steven Gallo would not be allowed to visit him. Assuming, no doubt correctly, that the memory of these and other incidents might color the recommendations of Warden Harold W. Follette to the Parole Board, Joey applied in April for a transfer to Wallkill Prison, and was offered instead a place in Auburn. This was like asking for soda pop and getting Epsom salts, for Auburn had the reputation of a hell hole, but the chance of appearing before the Parole Board with a clean bill from another warden was too good to pass up. Joey decided to take his medicine. The last letter he wrote from Green Haven before moving to Auburn on May 13, 1970, was to Joie, who was then with her mother in Hermosa Beach.

Hello Joie!

Your letter knocked me out! Baby, I feel happy knowing you're doing so well in school, and at home with that Coo-Coo Pot Jeffie. You're the only one besides Olga that has had the pleasure of her company such a long time. That you have maintained your sanity (and liberty) is no small achievement. A lot of Indians have bit the dust!

I noticed Dotty and her kids in the photos. The boy (little monster) and the pretty little girl who was constantly at your side—that little girl loves you, Joie, and I love her and her brothers because they are like my Joie. You tell them kids that Joey will be their Daddy from now on.

Yes, I have read some good books lately, but none that would interest Jeffie. One would move you—"The Last Man Alive," A. S. Neill, from Summerhill, England.

I will paint something for you. I didn't write sooner because of the mail strike. Granma and Cam visited with me yesterday. They miss you both very much. Please write Granma a letter. She means so much to me. You know how kids feel about their Moms. Jeffie, do you remember the night I walked into your life? Tell Joie about it. Better still, use it as the beginning of the novel you promised to write. Damn gypsy!

Joey Gallo #11916

Joey's reputation preceded him to Auburn, as he had known it would. The days of having to fight for a place in the prison caste system were long gone. With an eight-year apprenticeship behind him, he arrived there as a statesman rather than a politician, having already earned the respect of prisoners and guards alike. In a matter of weeks, a court had gathered around him and he was exercising the kind of authority it had taken him almost four years to assemble in Green Haven. He needed all of it.

Auburn was primed to explode. Its 1,675 inmates outnumbered the guards by about 25 to one, and approximately half of them were black or Puerto Rican. Of these, at least 400 were militants—men who regarded themselves, not as convicted criminals, but as political prisoners, as black revolutionary victims of a racist society. Auburn to them was a concentration camp run by white racist pigs and Uncle Toms, a view shared to some extent even by those who were not prepared to commit themselves openly to the destruction of the system.

Many of their grievances were shared by the white inmates, particularly over prison clothing, rules on letter-writing, commissary prices, spending privileges, the food, the infrequency of Parole Board hearings and so on. When a five-man state legislative committee visited Auburn to investigate charges that the prison was unsanitary, that inmates were being brutalized by the guards, and that homosexuality and the use of narcotics were endemic, it found enough truth in these allegations to recommend that prisoners be allowed more than one shower a week, that correction officers work harder to relieve racial tensions, that Black Muslim and black nationalist ministers be allowed to visit with inmates "of these faiths," and that steps be taken to curb the traffic in marijuana.

Amid the turbulence, Joey needed all his ingenuity and eloquence to steer a course that neither cost him the respect of his fellow inmates nor alienated the prison authorities under Superintendent Harry Fritz. Despite his efforts at mediation, tension mounted sharply that summer, sparking a series of minor clashes between prisoners and guards and between black and white prisoners that led in August to a Cayuga County grand jury investigation. No indictments were returned, however, and the situation worsened steadily through the fall. On November 4, it erupted into a riot—a full-dress rehearsal for the Attica insurrection ten months later.

It began quietly enough on Monday, November 2, which the militants had declared Black Solidarity Day. When they assembled in the yard after breakfast, all but a handful of the prison's black and Puerto Rican inmates went on strike. They lounged around for five hours, talking, smoking and playing ball, before returning to their cells. The white prisoners went to work as usual, the guards made no attempt to intervene and, apart from a few exchanges of abuse, the demonstration passed off without incident.

Next day, however, fourteen inmates, said to be the organizers of Black Solidarity Day, were confined to their cells by Superintendent Fritz, with results that were later described in a signed statement by two white inmates, William Bitus and Marco Tedesco:

On the morning of November 4, 1970, leaders of the Black Solidarity Day Movement and their followers refused to go to work unless the men who were locked up for participating in the "No Work Black Solidarity Day" of November 2, 1970, were released from their cells. When they were informed that the men were not going to be released, they made up their minds to have the men released at any cost, and began soliciting the assistance of white inmates. This soon brought on some confusion among the whites.

Joey Gallo was asked to make a speech on his views of the matter. Gallo made it clear that it was the blacks' thing, stemming from their stand on Black Solidarity Day, therefore, the officers and white inmates should not suffer for it. This speech made many inmates look at it favorably. But the hard-core blacks continued to exert pressure wherever they could, and within an hour, word was out that hostages were to be taken, etc.

At this juncture, Gallo forced his way to the public address mike, with a lieutenant and sergeant standing nearby. Here, very emphatically, he stated that whites were not to participate, and if they did, to stay away from us; that if the officers ordered us to our cells, we would go; that we would die if necessary. We went to the block to have coffee amidst boos and curses.

In no time at all, all hell broke loose. We went to Polack (A-1-2) and borrowed knives. In a little while, Gallo and Tedesco went down front and I followed. Gallo and Tedesco took the officer out of the block. (Officer Pinkney, injured) Within a few minutes, orders were issued by the "new" administration to clear the block. In the yard, Gallo was telling all the whites there to stay together up against D block. We kept receiving messages from the blacks to play it cool.

An exact copy of the above was given to Lieutenant O'Connell on December 3, 1970.

Witnessed by: WILLIAM BITUS #48911
Witnessed by: MARCO TEDESCO #60–328

After Joey's second speech, the disturbance turned into a riot. Arming themselves with clubs and lengths of pipe, the black prisoners took thirty-six hostages, injuring six and dousing others in gasoline with threats to burn them alive. Then they overran the prison, except for the administration building, which by now had been ringed by state troopers. Urged on by volleys of revolutionary rhetoric over the public-address system, they cut the prison's telephone links and wrecked the kitchen and mess halls. Outside, meanwhile, two hundred more state troopers stood by, and in the city of Auburn, the Mayor declared a state of emergency and alerted the National Guard.

By late afternoon, however, the rebellion was petering out in a stalemate. When Deputy Superintendent Edward Morell agreed to discuss the rioters' demands and warned them that a large force of state and local police was waiting outside to restore order, the prisoners, both black and white, started releasing the hostages and drifting back to their cells. By five o'clock, they were locked in—most of them for the next three months—and it was all over.

Joey's part in all this was confirmed in a memorandum from Lieutenant O'Connell and C.O. Welch on December 3:

> HARRY FRITZ, SUPERINTENDENT
> SENIOR PAROLE OFFICER
> SERVICE UNIT
> Subject: Inmate Conduct
> On date of November 4, 1970, in the central yard of Auburn Correctional Facility and during the height of the insurrection by certain black inmates in quest of the release of some 13 Keep Locked constituents [sic] whom were being held for investigation of their alleged participation of November 2, Black Solidarity Day Movement, the following commendable acts were taken by inmate Joseph Gallo, number #62167, locking in A-1-13.
>
> Inmate Gallo strode to the center of the large platform occupied by a great number of the militant blacks who were using such to voice their campaign to the population, and spoke out on behalf of the white population stating that this was a black thing, that the whites were not involving themselves.
>
> Later on, when the rhetoric of the blacks was becoming more hostile and with a Sergeant and a Lieutenant standing by, inmate Gallo again took the microphone and asserted that the whites were not to participate that they were to group in a certain place in the yard and if any whites did choose to participate they were to stay away from the docile white group.
>
> Gallo continued by saying that if and when the administration ordered the population to their cells, all whites would abide and would not tolerate any black man preventing them and that he would die to support his claims.
>
> Still later, when the physical violence in support of the insurrection was under way and during the time when Correction Officers were being assaulted and taken hostage it was inmate Gallo with the aide of inmate Marco Tedesco who assisted assaulted officer Pinckney out of A-Block and up to the lower hall for medical treatment.

By taking this stand and rescuing a hostage, Joey had not simply blown his carefully constructed neutrality—he had earned the ineradicable hatred of the black militants, who now saw him as white treachery incarnate. Spotting a chance to wipe his slate clean at the expense of his former protectors, he had seized it without compunction. Indeed, he was very pleased with his official citation and showed it to everyone after his release. Though it would not have impressed a grammarian, it had worked like a charm on Superintendent Fritz. In his Good Behavior Allowance Report to the Commissioner of Correction and the Parole Board, he recommended the restoration of all Joey's outstanding lost time—380 days—and thus, in effect, the maximum remission of 4 years and 10 months from his sentence. Provided he lost no further "good time," Joey was now eligible for conditional release on March 10, 1971, a date less than three months away.

The long, grinding, destructive haul from solitary confinement in Attica to political mastery at Auburn had finally paid off. Starting with almost every possible disadvantage, he had wriggled, plotted, bartered, fought, connived, charmed and maneuvered his way out of the trap. His methods had been cynical, ruthless and brutally practical, but having achieved the influence his nature craved, he had again sought to use it wisely.

After his transfer to Sing Sing on December 28, 1970, he drafted a letter to the Commissioner of Correction:

> I've been in New York State prisons approximately 10 years. My Conditional Release Date is March 10, 1971, with five years' parole.
>
> I sincerely believe that I can be of some assistance as a counselor to juvenile delinquents, parolees or any group (except "The Fortune Society") that is involved in prison reform and security for inmates and correction officers alike.
>
> I've read a penetrating analysis of pioneering programs in the October, 1970, Bulletin, Number 20, of the Massachusetts Correctional Association, entitled, "The Involvement of Offenders in the Prevention and Correction of Criminal Behavior."
>
> Reading the Bulletin reinforces my belief that you, Commissioner, can make use of my extensive experience and profound desire to function as a worthy individual for the rest of my life.

Whether or how the Commissioner replied, or if, indeed, the letter was sent, is not known, since the Department has no record of it, but there seems no reason to doubt Joey's sincerity. With his release only weeks away, he had nothing to gain from dissembling. Nor had Little Andy, who wrote to Joey around this time to thank him for a kindness that clearly had no hidden purpose and showed the generosity of spirit of which Joey was capable once he felt secure. Found among his prison papers, the letter offers no real clue to Little Andy's identity, apart from a childish hand and copious misspellings, nor to the circumstances that gave rise to it. From the internal evidence it was probably written in Auburn just before Christmas, and, most likely, by a black prisoner who did not share the prevailing view of Joey's conduct in the riot:

Hello my friend,

hope this note can bring you a little cheer, under the circumstances. I would like you too know that, I for one think of you with the greatest respect. For when you let me eat at your table, after my own trouple, you proved too me what a truely great mind and compassionate heart you have. As for the court jesters that were around at the time, they were just following your example. In the event you put thumbs down, so would have been there sentiment. Therefore I am always in your debt. For that is how much you mean too me. Please, do not think me such a fool that I didn't understand how one in your shoes was leaving himself open for criticism taking such a stand. As you well know, public opinion does not sway my convictions one inch. Therefore, allow me too say you are my friend no matter which way the wind blows. Another words, I want you too understand that all the good you have done in my case anyway was not in vain. Do not my friend think all of us as dogs. Keep that good heart and keen mind that has brought you this far. May next Xmas be better for us all. Take care, keep punching. I am always in your cawner.

Respectfully yours
Little Andy
Please excuse my writing

P.S. The Kid says Merry Xmas.

Jeffie, though sad at the waste of life and the inroads on his strength and patience, was fiercely proud of Joey's achievement. "For nine years they'd had him pinned down in one place, with no boys, no guns, no reputation to protect him. He'd offended everybody, and everybody was out to destroy him. And who won? *He* did. He never behaved below the level he expected of himself. He survived. He emerged whole. They didn't get his mind. Body didn't matter—you couldn't hurt Joey. He had too many beatings in his life. Once they dragged him down four flights of stairs by his hair. Every time they arrested him, something like that would happen. I saw the scars on his body. But he never sold out. They couldn't do it to him. He had the whole fucking prison system crazy—from the Commissioner, to the wardens, to the hacks. He singlehandedly gave all those people more trouble than they gave him. If they got to him, they never knew it. For nine years, he fought like a bastard—and he *won*."

16

George, Laura and Mike

George Lloyd had not been looking forward to meeting Jocy. He had seen all he wanted to see of gangsters while growing up on the streets of Newark. He had no relish for the prospect of getting close enough to him to please Jeffie, and yet staying at a sufficient distance to avoid compromising himself and his family.

On the other hand, George had been the only really stable factor in Jeffie's life for more than twelve years, apart from Joie, and he couldn't abandon her now. Since their first meeting through Raymond's Exclusive Telephone Answering Service, where Jeffie had taken his messages, she had come to rely upon him for help, understanding and affection as daughter upon father, though they were much the same age. It was critically important to her that Joey should take to George, particularly now she felt him sliding back into the old life.

Like Joey, George had started out with every disadvantage and made his own way, but to a very different destination: a comfortable home in Short Hills, a settled family life, a housekeeper, two cars in the garage, two vacations a year and the vice presidency of a prosperous New Jersey business. If Joey could see himself in George, he might just see another way to go.

Laura Lloyd thought so, too. Unlike her husband, she was ready —indeed, determined—to see in Joey what Jeffie saw, which made her astonishment all the more extreme when he presented himself at their door. "Jeffie had had this dream. She believed Joey had come out for *her.* She was so excited. She bought all kinds of new lingerie and waited for him like a bride. Now he was home, and for days afterward, her voice was as high as a kite—you couldn't speak to her. Then suddenly I heard it. Crash! An ax had fallen. She said, 'Laura, I got to bring him out to you. Immediately. If I don't, there's no chance. I need help to talk to him. He's ambivalent, he's torn and I lose contact with him. We have moments together when it's beautiful. Then suddenly he's schizo and I can't reach him, he's into this tough-guy talk. I'm losing my own sanity. You got to get George to talk to him. I don't know how I'm going to get him there, but he must come to you. Plan on seeing us Saturday. I don't know what time, but we'll be there.'

"So naturally we got a bit keyed up. It was so important to her. And by the time Saturday came around, Jeffie was hysterical. She called about six times and said, 'Laura, I'm so nervous. I hope we get there. I don't know what's going to happen, but it's my last chance. I must get him to you. Please bear with me. If this doesn't go well, I will lose him forever.' She was pinning everything on this meeting, and she practically dragged him to us. They had a terrible fight coming out, first because he didn't want to come, and then because he didn't like the way she was driving, but she encouraged him to have a smoke in the car, and that calmed him down.

"Poor Jeffie—she was in agony. She really *did* think she would lose him if he didn't respond to us in the right way—and she was also terrified of maybe losing *us* if it didn't work out and he made an ugly scene. Anyway, this big black car pulled into the drive around four o'clock, and when I opened the door, I almost fainted. My feeling was 'Oh, Jeffie—you're kidding.' Out got this little man with his hat down over his face, and he sort of skulked in like something out of a joke gangster movie. I went weak in the knees. She'd never prepared us for *that.*"

George had the same reaction. "He hid in his hat. He sort of hunched up and came in sideways. If I hadn't been so scared, I would have laughed out loud—as a gag, it would have been hysterical. I looked, and I said to myself, 'I can't believe that's him. Or that that's Jeffie. And that she's with him and loves him.' He looked like an inmate of an institution for the destitute insane being taken out for the day by his sister. All the blood drained from me, and I thought, 'This is a nightmare. What, in God's name, are we going to do?' He wasn't sinister. He was pathetic. Bizarre. Laura saw him as a gangster; *I* saw him as a freak, a circus freak dressed in a gangster outfit. He was wearing the dumbest hat I ever saw. His suit didn't fit—it was much too big, and so were his boots. He sidled through into the den, rolling his eyes around, and said, 'What kind of a place is this? Looks like a Hawaiian restaurant.' That, I thought, was pretty funny, and it kind of jolted me back into gear.

"So then we had to case the joint for security. Nobody had come with them, but I kept glancing out the window to see if I could spot anybody lurking in the bushes. 'It's all right,' he said. 'It's an all-right place. It's got good vibes. What's over there?' He pointed at the fence and the screen of trees across the end of the yard. 'Nothing,' I said. 'Some open ground, a cliff and beyond that, a valley.' 'Good,' he said. 'That's good. You know, I never in my whole life sat with my back to that much window.' Well, that did a lot for our confidence, of course, with visions of half a dozen guys suddenly opening up on our Hawaiian living room with machine guns, and he didn't make me feel any better when I had to confess we didn't have a dog. 'Oh, you got to have a dog,' he said. 'Otherwise they're going to take you apart. This house is set up. You got no alarm system—nothing. I can show you fourteen ways to get in here. Got to have a dog. A dog is a pain in the neck if you're trying to bust in someplace. Even if you kill him, it makes a lot of noise, and some dogs are hard to shoot. They move pretty good. Then you got to shoot again, and pretty soon you've woken up the whole neighborhood.' It was wild. The following Monday, I went right out and bought a dog.

"Now he was starting to relax a little. 'Listen,' he said. 'First off, I want to thank you for everything you've done for Jeffie and Joie.' 'You're welcome,' I said. 'It was a pleasure.' 'Okay.' Then he got up, came over, pulled my pants out in front, stuck his hand in and patted me just above the pecker. 'You got a flat stomach,' he said. 'Yeah, it's all right,' I said, blinking a bit. 'It's been flatter. Am I supposed to do that to you?' 'I don't know,' he said. 'That's up to you.' 'Well,' I said, 'I can *see* that *you've* got a flat stomach,' and he laughed. 'Right on.' Took me a while to figure out what that was about. It was a symbol. Joey reaching for your balls sums up what he did in life. Some guys go for the throat; he went for the balls. It was nothing sexual. It was arm-wrestling. He was going to see what I was made of.

"Okay. So now it's drink time. He took Scotch. 'I have wine,' I said. 'Oh, yeah, that's right. I love your wine'—I'd sent Jeffie and him a case of stuff for his homecoming. 'Yeah, give me some wine.' So he finished his Scotch and I opened the first of about two dozen bottles.

"We're about fifteen minutes into this affair now, and I'm making with the light conversation because nobody else is talking. Laura is doing something in the kitchen; Jeffie's sitting in the corner like a shrunken skull, ashen green and speechless, and Joey's just listening to me prattle on. I was probably stiff as a board, but I'm trying like mad to help Jeffie out—to put him at his ease, to be relaxed and responsive and see what happened. And I suddenly got the feeling that Joey didn't know what the hell he was doing here. He'd thanked me; he'd had a drink; he'd felt my stomach and met my wife; Jeffie was wiped out, and I think he wanted to go home. I had a premonition there was going to be one of those long, awkward silences any minute. So I decided to take over and get into things, like what I was about and where I came from. I said, 'You know, my father was in vaudeville, and he grew up with a lot of guys in the streets.' 'Yeah, yeah,' he said. 'You knew a lot of those guys, didn't you?' And that's how it started. From then on came hours of truth and bullshit. When I ran out of truth, I made things up—I really talked that guy down.

"I told him about Longie Zwillman here in Jersey. I told him about Chicago in the old days, and he was fascinated. If anybody had come in then, they would have figured *I* was the gangster. I bullshitted on and on, telling him everything, and he told me nothing. Not a goddamn thing. But he was loosening up. He was drinking five glasses of wine to my one, and looked five years younger than when he came in. I was so pleased. I figured I was doing a masterly job in bringing the level of tension down by keeping the conversation on a very personal level. He had a brother; *I* had a brother, and I trotted out every family anecdote I could think of. I was working very hard to get accepted, and I still didn't quite know why. I didn't know my mission—except that he was in my house and Jeffie was sitting there waiting for me to do the ministerial bit. 'Now, my son, have you planned your life? I can help you. I shall be there to guide you when you reach the milestone marked Decision'—that's what she wanted me to do. And my ears were burning because the poor girl was hunched waiting in the corner and I was letting her down.

"She looked horrible. I'd never seen her like that. Her skin was all mottled. She looked skinny, sunken and gray, like she'd been through a war. She was listening to the words, and it just wasn't working out. The only time she'd move was when one of the kids came in. Then she'd jump up and take him into the kitchen. She was worried about them making a noise. She wanted a perfect setting for him—no interruptions, no distractions. And every once in a while she would burst out laughing at something we said. It was so sad. It was like going to see a comedy in which a dear friend of yours is playing, and it's lousy. No one else is laughing, so you laugh too much. Every little thing we said, either one of us, she roared—'Ha! ha! ha!'—and slapped her leg. Neither one of *us* would laugh, but *she'd* fall off the couch. Then she'd shrivel up again. She was dying.

"Anyway, after a couple of hours of this, Joey's fine—thawed out and loose—but I could use a breather. 'Listen,' he said. 'Could I ask you a favor? Could I take a bath?' 'Sure,' I said. 'Of course'—kind of bemused. But then I was very happy. I figured if he could take his clothes off and sit in a tub, he wasn't too worried about being murdered. 'Great,' he said. 'I haven't had a bath since I got out of the joint.' He was having a new hot-water system installed in his mother's house or something. So up he goes to the children's bathroom to take a long, leisurely tub, and that's when Jeffie broke down.

"I think Joey came because she had built me up over the years as a man who could accept him—and he trusted her completely, from the bone. She had this dream of him going straight and working for J. Walter Thompson or somebody. She believed there was still some hope if only he would see that things *could* be different, that the fury he had in him and the background he came from didn't mean he *had* to go back to the old life. She thought she was showing him a guy who felt what he felt but had gone another way. She was trying to show him he could choose. But the minute he went up to take a bath, she broke down and cried. 'It's hopeless,' she said. '*Hope*less.' It was a cry that tore me apart. 'Yes,' I said. 'It is.' And it was. It was tragic. She had deluded herself, and she knew it. That's why she was paralyzed. She knew it was a ruin. She turned to ice, and wept bitterly."

If they had been asked for their impressions of Joey at that point, both George and Laura would have been in difficulty. After the initial shock, they had striven so hard to make this first meeting a success that neither had had time really to consider how they felt about him. Laura had been impressed by his power and directness. Joey both pleased and frightened her. "Ten minutes after he came in, he said to me, 'You're really a powerhouse, aren't you? You're a strong dame.' " George, on the other hand, still found him "freaky and peculiar. He was certainly direct, but his contact was inconsistent. He wasn't so much perceptive as disarmingly frank. What he had said had been unadorned but so far unremarkable. He was blunt. He was a guy who didn't have to worry about what he said to us because he didn't really care what we thought."

Then water began to leak through the ceiling of the den, a trickle at first, dripping from the light fixture above the bar, and then a cascade, spilling freely onto the counter. This happened quite often. The grouting had crumbled away around the tub in the children's bathroom, and whenever they fought and splashed, the water would run down inside the wall and drain away through the rose in the ceiling downstairs. This time, Joey was the culprit, and, as usual, George bounded upstairs to try to stop the flow before it brought the plaster down or fused the power supply.

"He's sitting there soaking himself, this Public Enemy Number One, and when I tell him the water's coming through the ceiling, a look of absolute, incredulous horror crosses his face. He jumps up, naked in the bath, and says, 'Oh, gee whiz, George—I'm so *sorry!* What did I *do?* Oh gee, for*give* me. Did I do something wrong?' 'No, no,' I said. 'Happens all the time. Don't worry about it. Sit down. Have your bath.' To my grave I'll take that scene. 'What did I *do?* I'm so *sorry.* What did I *do?* '"

What he had done, apart from demonstrating an unwillingness to offend that George found heartening, was to break the ice. When he came down to inspect the damage, he and the Lloyds were friends.

George felt the change at once, though he kept his guard up. "He was relaxed, warm and affable. He took a look at the big red towel on the bar and said, 'Oh God, is that what I did? Gimme some more of that wine.' 'Yeah, yeah'—and we were laughing and giggling. I was in a state of controlled drunkenness by this time, and even beginning to enjoy myself in a painful sort of a way, although I still had to do most of the talking. 'Tell me more about your father,' he said. 'You like your old man, don't you?' 'I *love* him,' I said. 'He was a *real* tough guy.' 'That's great. But *why* do you love him? Why?' 'Why? Because he's such a goddamn honest man, that's why. My father couldn't steal. He was an orphan guy with the goddamnedest rage in the world—I never knew him to like *any*body—and yet he couldn't steal. Wouldn't even go into bootlegging, although he had several offers.'

"Joey really wanted to hear this stuff. I'd already told him a lot of anecdotes about my father, and how he'd taken my brother with him on the road, so now I told him more. 'Listen,' he said, I've got to meet your brother.' 'Yeah,' I said. 'Yeah, you'll like Mike. He's a big guy, like me. We'll have to arrange that.' 'Yeah. Does *he* like your father?' 'Well, to tell you the truth, he's got troubles with my old man. They kicked the shit out of one another.' 'Yeah, yeah'— that was something he could understand. 'Hey—get him on the phone.'

"It was an order, and now I had a problem. While Joey was in the bath, I'd called to see if Mike was free to come over that evening with his wife Stella in case I needed him to spell me, and he'd said he'd stand by. I was getting tired of talking. But if they came, it was going to be at *my* say-so, not Joey's. At that moment, I had to do something to establish myself. I had to stay even. I couldn't let him take over, so I said, 'I don't know if he's home.' 'Get him on the phone,' he said again, and this time a bit of the other Joey showed through. I knew I was in a jam, so I lied. 'No,' I said. 'He's not home. He's out'—and I went on to some other story about our childhood. But he knew what I had done, and he liked it. He knew I wanted Mike there but that I had to stay equal—I could tell from his expression. It was a point to me.

"So now we're talking about the neighborhood I grew up in. 'There were just a few things you could do,' I said. 'You could grow up and go to work in one of the factories for the rest of your life. You'd marry some fat Polish girl, she'd give you babies and get fatter. You'd drink beer and enjoy her getting fat, and you'd die when you were about fifty-five. Or you could become a ball player. A couple of guys would be good enough to make a living playing ball. Or you might make it as a prizefighter. A lot of guys became pros in those days. There were six clubs in town where they fought on Wednesday and Friday nights for fifty or a hundred dollars, and you knew them by their flat noses—that was the sign. Or you could go into the rackets.'

"Then he wanted to know if I'd ever thought of doing that, and I told him I could have. Longie Zwillman had been a childhood friend of my father's. I could have had a legitimate job with an illegitimate company—vending machines or something. Longie would have paid my way through college, and maybe I could have gotten to be president and married into the family. 'But I don't go for the rough stuff,' I said. 'I can get what I want another way. Why do I need all that grief?' 'No, no,' he said. 'That's right. You're not a tough guy.' 'You're damn right,' I said—and it was easy to say because there was nothing at all menacing in his manner. 'Believe me, I'm not a tough guy.' 'No,' he said. 'The difference between you and me is that *I* can kill you, but you can't kill *me.*' 'No, Joey,' I said. 'The difference between you and me is that I *know* you can kill me, but you *don't* know if I can kill you.'

"He hit the end of the bar, crash, with his fist. 'God*damn,*' he said. 'You're right. That is *right.*' From that moment on, we were soul mates. 'Put on some music,' he said. 'You pick some music. God-damn. You just hit me right between the eyes. Jesus Christ. Jeffie, he *is* smart.' He was giving me a medal, and Jeffie went crazy with joy. 'Oh, yes, he's smart.' I don't think she even knew what I'd said. She was still mourning in the corner.

"I put on some of my operatic records—Jussi Björling. 'I don't understand what they sing about,' he said. 'Is that good?' 'Yeah, that's good.' I told him what was happening, making it up when I had to as I went along. I did a ten-minute bit about the guy who's going to fight a duel and knows he will be killed, and Joey's saying, 'Right on, right on. Jesus, do I know how he feels! God, do I know! Georgie, do I *know!*' His shirt's open now, his hair's mussed, and as soon as he started Georgie-ing me, I knew we were pals. I was warming to him—I really was. He was so appealing when he was disarmed. His suit made an ass out of him. There was nothing on his body, and I was trying to make him laugh.

" 'Georgie, Georgie—that's good music.' He was grabbing my arm and I was grabbing his. 'Jesus Christ,' I said. 'Where the hell are the muscles? What's this? You're all bones.' 'I'm bones, I'm bones,' he moaned. 'I ain't a big fuck like you. I should have been as big as you. If I was as big as you—' 'If you were as big as me,' I said, 'you'd be a lawyer. You wouldn't be fucking Public Enemy Number One.' 'Hey, hey! Jeffie. He's doing a Lenny Bruce on me now. What is he doing to me? What is happening with my head around this guy? I love you, Georgie. I love you. I love being here with you and Laura. Will you come to see me?' Right away I lapse into a coma. 'Sure, sure, sure—how can I come?' 'Oh, we'll find a way,' he says. 'Don't worry.' Then I said, 'If ever you invite us somewhere, it has *got* to be safe. We'll have to have your word on that.' 'Listen,' he said. 'If ever I invite you, you'll be safe.' "

It was now about eight o'clock and time for dinner. "We had a housekeeper then named Pauline—well built and all woman. She was going to serve the meal, so naturally we introduced them. 'Pauline, this is Joey.' And once again he showed the kind of directness that either captures you or puts you off forever. Instead of just saying, 'Hello,' he looked her up and down admiringly and said, 'Built for work, Pauline. Built for good times.' She flipped. He liked her and he told her. He was a prince. 'You see, Jeffie?' he said. 'That's all right. Nice to have her here. *I* would like to have someone like that. I could use her.' Knocked her out. Pauline always liked to hear about him after that. He was bold with women. Not mean, not dirty—just very frank and almost ruthlessly affectionate. Most men are afraid to be that, but it was natural for him. So then we sat down—and he ate with his fingers."

Laura had prepared chicken Kiev, with rice and a salad. Joey had never come across this dish before and she saw him hesitate. "He wasn't sure if he was going to like it, or even try it, but he was hungry, so he took a bite—suspiciously—and then he loved it. Couple of hours earlier, I had brought out hors d'oeuvres, but he wouldn't touch them. 'No,' he said. 'I'm not ready to eat. When I talk, I talk; when I eat, I eat. I like to taste the food.' So now it was time, and he ate. With his hands. The rice, the salad—everything. But I didn't feel, 'Well, look at that pig.' He did it with great skill, using his fingers like chopsticks. I don't think he was trying to make a point. He just felt like doing it. I don't think he was trying to put the skids under middle-class gentility or anything like that."

George found nothing offensive in it either, but he was less convinced of Joey's artlessness. "I think he was testing us again. He never stopped testing people. I think he wanted to see how we'd react. If it had been a movie, I guess everybody would have ended up eating with their fingers, but I made a point of eating very neatly with my knife and fork. At all times I felt it was important to remember who I was. 'This is *my* house. *I* eat with a knife and fork. *You* eat with your fingers. Be my guest.' It was around this time that I said, 'Hey, I have a great idea. I'll see if Mike's home.' He picked it up at once. Drunk or sober, he never missed a signal. 'Yeah, yeah,' he said, marking another point to my scorecard. 'Think you can get him over? Boy, that would be nice.' I was doing okay, but I was tired and there was a long night ahead—which I didn't mind now. I was getting quite fond of this son of a bitch. But I felt I could use some help, so I called Mike, and he and Stella arrived as we finished our meal."

Neither Mike nor Stella was ready to be impressed. Like his brother, Mike already knew all he wanted to know about gangsters —in his youth, he had dated Longie Zwillman's niece—while Stella, a serious, concerned and well-informed student of politics, was prepared only to disapprove of Joey on principle. Both were very curious about him, however—indeed, the alacrity with which Stella accepted George's invitation quite astonished Mike.

"My wife never goes anywhere. But when I said, 'George just called. He's got Joe Gallo at the house and wants us to come over,' she said, 'I only need a minute to get ready.' Then we had forty minutes in the car to prepare for a stereotype gangster. We were all set to meet a rough, tough, uncouth, maybe frightening-looking guy —and what happens? This little, kind, friendly man jumps out of his chair to greet us warmly. 'You're the brother,' he says. I'm really disturbed. Where's the killer? Where *is* this brute? He was like up to my navel, this public enemy. It was a really disarming start to one of the greatest evenings we ever had.

"There was nothing frightening about him at all. He never once played the heavy. The only time I felt that tightness in the stomach was when a car backfired in the street. I don't think anybody else heard it, but he did a 180-degree turn in a 75th of a second. Made me jump. What the hell . . . ? Then I realized. This is Joe Gallo. I had *forgotten* he was Joe Gallo. So we got onto the subject of what we would do if someone came in through the door with a gun, and I said, 'I don't know. I guess I would just cooperate and do what he told me.' That's what George thought, too. He said he'd ask the guy what he wanted and tell him to take it and leave us alone. If the guy tried to hurt anybody, then he would have to try to do something about it, and I agreed with that, but Joey couldn't buy it at all. 'No,' he said. 'I don't stand still. When he came in that door, I got to go for him. Right off the bat. I'd get him and I'd kill him. Got to. Got to go for him.' And I believed him.

"Arising out of that, he told us a story about how in prison they had a contract out on him. 'This guy meets me in the machine shop,' he says, 'and he's coming at me with a wrench, and I know this is a contract. So you know what I did? I jumped on him and bit his tit off. I mean, what else can you do?' Stella's wide-eyed. Like most people, what do *we* know about prison? 'Like, I mean you make friends with a guy, right?' he says. 'You talk to him, you meet, you sit next to him—you're friends. But during the night there's a fly in his cell and maybe he doesn't sleep so good. That fly can bother him enough that he'll kill you next day. So I figured out a system. They ring the bell for breakfast, all the cell doors open up—but Joey Gallo don't go out and march down to the mess hall with a guy in front and a guy behind. He waits. I'm in no hurry. When everybody passed, *then* I go out. Because even though the guy's your buddy, you don't know—some morning you're going to bother him and he'll do you in.'

"Stella was fascinated with all this. There was a moment during the night that put Joey up somewhere in the top 2 percent of the world forever. She was making a point. She makes many points, and a lot of people don't listen because she sometimes gets lost in her points. He had already told us how he mastered speed reading in prison and had the warden going crazy because he couldn't get books fast enough—he was reading six or eight a day. 'I don't want to play football,' he says. 'What the hell is that shit? Those guys are crazy. You could get killed. I read. I go see the rabbi. I like the rabbi—he's a straight shooter. I don't bother with the priest—a bullshit artist— but I saw a lot of the rabbi.' And he recites all the Jewish prayers for us. 'Now Baudelaire,' he said, 'was influenced by that.' After all the gutter talk, to have a two-and-a-half-minute dissertation on Baudelaire in perfect English—my poor wife didn't know where she was. Anyway, she was making a point, and Jeffie started to say something like 'Isn't it getting cold in here?' and he turns on her and says, 'Jeffie, will you shut up? Stella didn't finish yet.' She could have kissed him.

"We were really thrown off base. The shift in speech patterns was like there was two men. Something would trigger off the real, tough kind of street talk, and the next minute it would be straight and scholarly. And he really listened. He really wanted to hear what you had to say. He enjoyed hearing people speak and reaching out to them. He was practically lying down in his chair—it was kind of a wild position—but the minute something interested him intellectually he'd sit up and lean into the conversation. He'd become deeply involved—all bright responses and understanding. 'I'll take issue with that,' he would say. Or, 'Right—that's the way I see it, too.' "

George, meanwhile, was taking a rest. "Though they didn't know it, Mike and Stella did just what they were supposed to do. They filled in superbly, carried it, and I just listened—I'd been working for hours. I remember they got onto the subject of surplus value, and Joey obviously knew what he was talking about. Then he discussed Machiavelli and the uses of political power. He thought Nixon knew how to use the system but that LBJ had been even better—a real tough guy. That took him on to the subject of leadership, and how to inspire the maximum loyalty in your people and soldiers, which led in turn to a discussion of the Catholic Church, the College of Cardinals and the Pope. He obviously hated priests. He had mixed views on asceticism, and felt purple was a particularly homosexual color. 'Priests!' he said. 'You see those movies where there's a war going on or something and everybody respects the priest. He always gets through, right? Everybody lays back when he shows up and listens to what he says. They always give him safe passage. Well, I got to shoot myself a priest someday. I want to see the look on his fucking face when he thinks he's so sacred and I blow his fucking balls off.' He admired Mao Tse-tung, though. He talked about the Long March and thought that was just superb. That was holing up like crazy—the maximum hitting the mattresses."

As the conversation with Mike and Stella broadened out into more general topics, so, paradoxically, did it begin to reveal more of Joey himself, though his professional caution never failed him. "How could I be any different?" he asked Mike. "I traveled with bums from the time I was nine, you know what I mean? At eleven, I got myself a crap game. When I was thirteen, I was running with the gang, and anything we couldn't steal, we busted. These were my people, and I lived on the street the way they did. So then they're giving me the slips. I'm running with the numbers, right? And people are getting to hear about Joey Gallo's floating crap game. They like the kind of action they get around me.

"One time we had Nicky Hilton in a game. He showed up with this big blonde chick—and she's built. Oh, man. So after an hour and a half, we own a hotel from him already, and he's really interested now—so interested he don't even notice all these guys dropping out of the game for a few minutes and going upstairs one by one to give this chick a bang. And where's it all happening? Safest place in Brooklyn. Downstairs in the building where the D.A. lives.

"That's the way I like to do things. Like the time I'm coming up in front of Judge Leibowitz. The night before I go to court I hear he's having dinner in a place up the street. So I go over there with a couple of guys, and there's a lot of bustling around when we come in the door, and I see him in a corner at a big table, eating his dinner with the Assistant D.A. So we give the other customers a couple of minutes to pay their checks, and then I go over to his table, and I notice when I walk up that his Adam's apple kind of gets jammed right in the middle of a swallow. 'Hiya, Judge,' I said. 'How are you?' 'Oh, hiya, Joe,' he says. 'What are *you* doing here?' 'What are you having?' I said. He says, 'I'm having the lobster thermidor.' 'Good,' I says. 'That's good here. Waiter, give us all the same thing.' So then we all sit down to eat and talk, but they don't seem so hungry any more. After a while he calls for their check. 'No, Judge,' I says. 'You're on *my* territory now. *I'll* pick up the tab. And you just take care, you hear? See you in court.' And that's the way I like to do things. I go right there—you know what I mean?

"Same as in prison. You got to go right to what it takes to get by. You got to do what you have to do to survive. There's no place to hide. Where can you hide? You know why I liked the rabbi? He told me a story once about some rabbi in a German prison camp who stayed alive because he took the job of pulling gold inlays from out of the mouths of the bodies. This was a rabbi! He understood you had to do that. He understood you had to stay alive. But it's got to be for a reason, right? I mean, it's not just to stay alive no matter what. If things don't work out or don't mean anything any more, then that's something else. What happened to Zwillman?"

George came back into the conversation at this point, partly because Joey, though drunk, was taking over as host; partly because Jeffie, though happier now, still wanted him to show Joey the light, and partly because Mike and Stella, though clearly enjoying themselves, were getting ready to leave. It was now around 1 A.M. " 'He hung himself in a closet,' I said. I'd never drunk so much wine in my life, and I never will again. 'That's what happened to Zwillman.' Joey nodded. 'It's the only way to go,' he said. 'By your own hand. I honor him for that. He was a brave man. When it's all over and there's nothing more, you kill yourself. He did the right thing.' Well, this upset Jeffie a lot. 'What do you mean?' she said. 'What are you talking about? That's ridiculous.' 'No, no—he did the right thing. Did you go to his wake?' 'No,' I said, and I was beginning to think I'd talked too damn much about Zwillman, creating an impression of far greater intimacy than was ever the case. 'But for every Longie,' I said, 'you got to remember there was a Leon Hess, who built a legitimate empire in oil. What about him? There was a brave man who *didn't* have to kill himself.'

"Frankly, I was beginning to think that half of what he said about himself was full of shit in any case. He'd told us a story, for instance, about a little fag he'd known in prison who serviced everybody. His specialty was fellatio, and one night the guards caught him at it. So he says to them, 'You can't get me on that. I'm the tailor, right? Well, I'd just sewn a button on his fly, and I was nipping off the thread.' I looked at Joey, and I said, 'You mean that actually happened? In prison?' 'Yeah,' he says. 'Absolutely.' 'Well, Jesus Christ, that's remarkable,' I said. He'd really let me down. That was one of my father's oldest jokes from his vaudeville routine. I suppose it could have happened, but now I felt that half of what he told us was a lie. As kids, he had been eating in his mother's restaurant, while I'd been on home relief. 'There's something more to why you are what you are,' I said. 'A whole lot more.' 'Hey!' he says. 'Something more. I love you, Georgie. It's a miracle.' "

Mike didn't *care* if Joey lied. "He wasn't lying when he quoted Kafka. With a 50 percent adjustment, this guy could have had a chair at Harvard. He reveled in the use of his brain. He didn't need it for the kind of life he led—he just needed to be crafty—but he was searching, and finding echoes of himself in unexpected places, in Kafka and Camus, in Sartre and Céline. In Camus, he found life is absurd and a pain in the ass. In Kafka, he found it arbitrary and hostile. Do anything you want—what's the difference? And I couldn't argue with him. I have a B.S. from Columbia, but he'd read a hundred times what I've read—and not because he had to. Because he *chose* to. It was natural to him.

"I don't think he was lying when he talked about his life. It may not have been the whole or the literal truth, but he was giving us its quality. 'Come on, Laura,' he would say. 'If I could tell you what I know about judges and senators—come on. You don't know. You take these people at their face value, but I'm with them in the backrooms. I know the deals they make. I've made them.' And I believed him. Gee, this guy is a student of our society. He's had insights we never had. He sees bums everywhere. Some are fancy, and drive in Cadillacs to well-upholstered offices, but he knows they're as phony and as crooked and evil as he is. I'm meeting a man who's *been* there, and you can't help walking away from that a little bit won over. He seemed to understand the times in which we live.

"I couldn't judge him. Survival was this man's guide to life. I got the feeling that, in prison, he filled in all the blanks. What do you do to survive? Bite off a tit? Rape a fag? Know the rabbi? Con the warden? Learn speed reading? Screw your buddy? Didn't matter. Whatever was necessary to come out standing erect, you did it. No problem at all. Maybe he was two men, but the one I saw could easily have been a friend of mine. When we left, around 1 A.M., we shook hands, and he slipped his left arm around me and drew me to him.

'We're going to see more of each other,' he said. 'As soon as we get a little place, I want you all to come up to my house.' And I would have gone. Willingly. Any time."

George and Laura had surrendered, too, although, drunk as he was, George never quite forgot who was clearing out his wine cellar. Not that there was anything in Joey's manner to suggest that his obvious affection for them was other than genuine, but, having succeeded in his aim of coming as close to Joey as Jeffie had wished, George could not entirely drown the uneasy thought that perhaps he had also opened the door to an association he neither wanted nor could safely sustain. It was one thing to enjoy the company of a warm, expansive, loving, drunken friend in his own living room, but quite another to imagine himself on some other occasion as a licensed jester in the court of King Joey, or, worse still, being forced to defend Jeffie or his family interests against the most notorious gangster since Capone.

"What Jeffie had been looking for us to do was establish some credibility for the myth, to show some cause why she had loved him so much all those years—and that *did* happen. There was contact with the man. In the last hours, he began to treat me as Jeffie treats me—'What do *you* think, George?' There was no audience. He didn't have to turn me on or off to prove anything to anybody. His collar was open, his pants were loose—he was really having a great time, and so were we. Nobody was expecting him to be anything but a fellow from Brooklyn with a runny nose. He was blowing and wiping it all evening. Okay—so he was a weasel, and destined to be killed. But I loved that son of a bitch for an hour and a half. He was delightful. I could have kissed him. We were two guys, pissed to the gills in the locker room, having just won the championship of the world. Jeffie's memory of that is legitimate.

"There was a moment when Joey said, 'How do you do it?'—as if on cue from Jeffie. It was the only time he recognized that our meeting had any sort of purpose, and I knew exactly what he meant. 'I tune out,' I said. 'You have to learn how to do it, but now I don't even have to think about it. I get up, I go to work, I take orders, I give orders—and if the going gets rough, I tune out.' He shook his head. 'I can't do that,' he said. 'I would like to know how. I don't know how to handle the energy in my body, how to turn it off. I feel like I'm jumping out of my skin. It makes me crazy.' And I think it did. Whenever his feelings were strong, he couldn't resist them. If he wanted something, he had to have it—right then and whatever the consequences. He couldn't handle frustration. It had to be all or nothing, which was why he was always in trouble. He wouldn't compromise. He lived alone in this world.

"The exception was Jeffie. He didn't love her; he was fatally attracted to her. 'Oh Christ,' he'd say, 'don't be intellectual. Just have that thing there so I can come into it. Don't talk so goddamn much. Just be there.' But he didn't really need her for that. And God knows he didn't need her for her cooking or housekeeping. He needed *her*. He was mad for her. An hour or two before they left, she went upstairs with Laura. Joey made a few pleasant jokes about her hoodlum quality—how tough she was—and I said something about how hard the waiting had been for her. 'She waited?' he said. 'She *waited?* She waited for shit. She don't wait for nobody. She didn't wait. She fucked her way around the world—that's how she waited.' I'll always remember that, though most of the rest is now a blur. Half of him needed her more than life, and the other half needed to get even.

"I also remember we both got a bit teary-eyed toward the end when I confessed to him that life was just a goddamn battle, a day-after-day battle. 'For you, too?' he said. And I said, 'For everybody.' 'Jesus Christ,' he said, shaking his head and blinking. 'You know something, Georgie? I'm going to live a year.' That was all he said about his gangster life all evening. He held his head then, and I think he said, 'I can't get out. There's no way out,' but I didn't want to see him like that, my new drinking buddy, so I asked him if he'd ever been to Europe. No, never. Then where *had* he been? Florida, California, Chicago, New Jersey. 'And one day,' he said, 'I would like to go to Italy.'

" 'Ah, Italy,' I said. 'We went there on our honeymoon—to Rome, Florence and Genoa'—which was true. It was just the usual Cook's Tour of Italy, but that didn't stop me telling Joey how well I knew and loved Florence. I rambled on in a kind of sentimental reverie, and he came right along with me. 'One day,' I said, 'one day, we'll go there together,' and we raised our clasped hands in brotherhood —we were so drunk. 'One day, we'll go together,' he said. 'Right,' I said. 'We'll roam and we'll be free.' I guess that was the high point of the night. We were going to leave the women behind. We really loved each other. And for Jeffie, considering what had been going on, it was like we were on Mount Olympus together. Uncle George and husband Joe had met and talked like men. She was home free. Our souls had touched. Now she really believed he could settle down to a normal life.

"Well, she was wrong about that, but not wrong in remembering how close we were at that moment. It never happened again, maybe because we never saw him again without an audience, but I think more probably because, deep down inside, in spite of his affection for us, he despised me. He thought I was a phony. He liked me, but he thought I was full of shit and he had to get me to admit it somehow. He wanted me to confess that I was playing a game, and that really his thing was better. He never wanted to go straight—never. Not for a minute. Never wanted it, never thought about it, never cared about it. He was just being sentimental for an hour or two, enjoying it as much as I did, but also setting me up as someone he might be able to use.

"There *was* a moment of soul, exceptional because I hadn't expected it, and in those last few hours, I never had a better time with a guest in my house. He was a remarkable man, and I don't quite know why. It wasn't because of his intellect or knowledge. I knew Camus better than him; he knew Mao better than me, and Machiavelli was a draw—I hadn't read him since the eleventh grade. Joey's political acumen was keen, but he was an archconservative. He thought black people were the scum of the earth, and he blamed Mayor Lindsay for crime on the streets, for allowing hopheads and junkies to beat the shit out of you for your money. He was dead serious about that. No, it had to do with his energy and the way it zeroed in to your core, raising the level of *your* energy, your own awareness. Nothing seemed casual or trivial in his company. He could make the most commonplace thing either wonderful or terrible. It was magic."

The magic worked on Laura, too. With her analytical bias, she also had an explanation for it. "Joey acted out our rebellious feelings for us—all our discontents and angers with society. That was his magic. It was exciting and stimulating to be with someone who did that. It was magical, but it was also terribly sad, because everybody used him —his friends, the guys—everybody. As much as Joey used people, so people used him. That one night we had when his guard was down I'll always remember. What followed, we could have done without. We carried on for Jeffie's sake, but it was no pleasure to see her so brutally hurt and debased in front of her friends."

To George, it was not only no pleasure, but a constant source of anxiety. Perhaps to please Jeffie, but more likely to test his sincerity, Joey had asked George during the evening if he could find him a job. A few days later, before taking it further, George discussed the matter with an attorney who knew the Gallos and who urgently advised him to break the connection at once. George then told Joey he had had no luck with his inquiries, and warned Jeffie privately that he didn't want any close social connection with them. "The minute the door closed behind them that night—it was around 4 A.M., and I sent them on their way with the last few bottles of wine we hadn't opened—the moment they left, I knew I had a hell of a problem on my hands, and it scared the shit out of me. Sooner or later, I knew there had to be a terrible confrontation with this guy. In front of me, he'd belt Jeffie in the mouth, or go too far with Laura, and then I'd have to do something about it and maybe get myself killed. He wouldn't *want* to kill me—I know he liked me—but he'd have to do it. Or maybe Jeffie would be unhappy and run away. She'd come to me, and naturally I'd take her in. But he'd have to come and get her in the end, and once again, I'd be in the way. It was a hell of a situation to contemplate, and sure enough, that summer, she ran off and came to my place on Fire Island alone.

"My heart sank into my boots. I knew he would have to make some sort of a move eventually. We had a house on the ocean front, and one night, Jeffie went over to Jacqueline's, leaving Joie behind with our kids and a sitter. It was twilight. They were asleep, and I was down on the walk with a friend of mine and his kid. As we turned the corner, my friend said, 'Who the hell is that running up on your porch?' Sure enough, there were three guys running up the path. So I sprinted after them, cursing under my breath like a maniac, and grabbed up the nearest weapon that came to hand, which turned out to be a pot of magnolias. I was going for the head of the guy in the middle of these three with their backs to me, when he turned around and I saw I was about to brain the Mayor of Seaview. He had run over with two of his men to warn off a truck driver who was making a delivery outside of official hours. That's how worked up I was.

"As it turned out, my fears weren't altogether wrong. The night after Jeffie went back, we had dinner with them. It was Momma's birthday, and the first time we'd seen Joey since he'd come to the house. He was very affable, but he said, 'You know, I have to tell you, George, that when she was out there, I had a bunch of guys in a boat on the East River ready to go and get Joie. The only reason I called them off was you and Laura.' 'Well, thanks a lot.' How long could it last? I didn't want to hear how close I came. I hadn't even wanted to be at the birthday party.

"Laura had come out of a group therapy session to tell me she had told Joey we would meet him at this restaurant in Brooklyn. 'You told him *what?*' I said. We had quite a fight about it. 'Well,' she said, 'I told him you would call.' So I go into a phone booth and call this restaurant. Some guy says, 'Hello?' I say, 'Hi! Er—is Joey Gallo there, please?' 'Who wants him?' 'Say it's George.' 'Jessaminnit.' Then another guy comes on. 'Hello? Who wants Joey?' 'Tell him it's George.' 'George who?' 'George, Jeffie's friend.' 'Jessaminnit.' Then a third guy comes on. 'Who's dis? How do you know Joey?' 'I was given the number. Tell him it's George, Jeffie's friend.' Then finally a fourth voice I recognize. 'Hey, George—how *are* you?'

"Not so good by this time. 'Look, Joey,' I said. 'Laura tells me you invited us over there, and I don't know where it is. I mean—well, good God, is it safe?' 'Listen,' he said. 'I promise you. It's safe. You come on. We'll have some good food. We'll talk, and I want you to meet my family and some of my friends.' 'Oh. Well. Okay. How do we get there?' 'You get on the West Side Highway, go through the Brooklyn-Battery Tunnel, make the first right and wait there. I'll send someone to fetch you. You'll be escorted.' When I told Laura this, she said, 'Oh. Now I'm scared.' 'Oh, good,' I said. 'Thank you.' Anyway, we followed his directions, and pretty soon we're parked on this empty street in a deserted warehouse area. It's pitch-black outside, we're sitting there in Gallo territory, they've got a war going on with Colombo mobsters, and I don't believe it. We've got three kids at home in Short Hills, and I'm sitting there with my wife, who is now giggling out of sheer terror.

"A couple of cars went by. Some kids looked in at us as they passed. Then finally a car pulled alongside, and a studious-looking guy with glasses wound down the window and said, 'Hello. Are you Mr. Lloyd?' I wanted to say, 'Not necessarily,' but I said, 'Yeah,' and he said, 'Follow me.' So I followed him through a maze of dark streets, getting completely lost, until we reached this restaurant, and there was the usual magic parking space outside with a kid waiting to put the car in it. From the moment we hit the street, our every need was attended to. The chef was at the door, our coats were taken, and as we went in, everybody rose to greet us, smiling. All except Jeffie, who was sitting there with a black eye. Joey kissed Laura warmly, and grabbed me by the neck. 'Oh boy,' he said. 'Am I glad you came—I really am. This is such a happy moment. It's beautiful.' He introduced us to everybody, and he was so lighthearted and proud that night to be showing us off. But I couldn't believe the way they were treating Jeffie. She was an outcast. Only Louie the Syrian was nice to her. He got her a drink. He fetched her another piece of veal. The others just mostly ignored her, including Joey.

"This was a family party, so for once Joey did most of the talking. Every other time we were together, especially when the guys were around, I would have to do about 80 percent of it, but that was from choice, and it wasn't as hard as it sounds. Whenever we went to a restaurant, I figured he was going to get it, so I would always have three big drinks, real fast, just to prepare myself for the coming bloodbath, and that sort of oiled my tongue. I remember once we were talking about the Army. One of the guys told a story about a fellow he knew who got pissed off with his lieutenant in Korea, and the next time he drew guard duty, he used that as an excuse to kill him—said he didn't answer his challenge or something. 'Well,' I said, 'I had a sergeant who was a *really* tough guy.' 'What do you mean, tough guy?'—they pick up on that at once. 'Well, he was at this reservoir in Korea, and the gooks had it surrounded and under fire. They had searchlights on our guys and were slaughtering them like fish in a barrel. And this sergeant, he went in there about fifteen times to bring out these kids, who were crying and sobbing.'

" 'Yeah,' they said. 'That's pretty tough. Except that he sounds like a schmuck. I mean, how many *times?* The guy wanted to die.' 'Okay,' I said. 'Then what about Patton—General Patton? *He* was a tough guy.' I realized that what had been lacking in the sergeant was real authority. 'Oh, yeah—*him,'* said Joey. 'What about Patton?' I found out he knew nothing about him. So I told them how he'd broken out across France with his armor and used captured German gas to keep going after he outran his supply lines, and it was all new to them. I could have made the whole thing up. As I finished, I said, 'But he was a general. He was having chicken and cognac before the battle while some poor fuck was getting dry rot and losing his toes.' 'Yeah, yeah, yeah,' said Joey. 'You're a liberal, huh?' 'Worse,' I said.

"Out of sheer compulsion to talk, to keep my head straight, I never gave him a chance to get at me. I was always trying to keep the initiative, steering the conversation all the time, because I never wanted to leave myself open when he was with the guys. If it got to be my turn to get kicked in the ass, he would have to do it, and then what? How strongly could I come back? Could I come back at all? I was determined never to be in that position, and I never let it happen. That was part of Jeffie's problem. She'd get in contention with him. With her big mouth, she'd put her foot in it, and when he turned on her, she'd put the other one in as well. She couldn't stop, and neither could he. But when she did it to him in front of his men, he had to kill her. They were murdering each other by degrees.

"But me—I told them stories about gangsters that had them captivated. They knew nothing about Prohibition, and when I described how Longie took over Newark after the shootout at the Kruger Auditorium, and then spread his authority over all New Jersey and wound up nominating the state's Attorney General, they were like my children at bedtime. Now they knew why Joey had me there at the table. Finally, when I figured I had done my bit, I'd announce it was time to go home—the kids and all that. Joey would jump up and say, 'Oh, yeah, yeah. Take care of the kids. Laura, go home to your babies.' Then he would smack me on the back and say, 'It was great, George.' And I would say, 'Thank you, Joey. It was terrific.'

"Sometimes it was. The first night was the best, and I shall never forget it, but there were moments after that—not many, but some— when, in spite of what he was, in spite of what he was doing to Jeffie, in spite of the danger we were in, in spite of the strain of trying to keep in with him for her sake and away from him for ours, there were moments when I loved him. This was an isolated, alienated, psychopathic, crazy, loving son of a bitch, but there were times when he felt like my brother."

17

Dottie and Lou

Dottie's debut was more painful than George's. For one thing, she was on trial. As Jeffie's accomplice, she had to suffer a little before Joey unbent. " 'Ah, the two of you running around—I can imagine,' he would say. 'Oh boy, can I imagine.' And always I'd tell him, 'Hey, Joey—she came back from London a fucking vegetable. And I'm single. All I like to do is dance. So we danced. Smoked a little grass. Hung out with different people—and no, she never fucked anybody. That's not Jeffie. She's contemptuous of that.' I think he believed me. Sometimes. But I'm Sicilian, and I know how Italians feel about their women, how suspicious they are. When she saw him in prison, he used to say to her, 'Don't make me have to do anything when I come out.' "

For another thing, Dottie and Lou were broke. They arrived in New York with three children, no money, no home and a totally misplaced trust in Joey's willingness to provide. "We came on the balls of our ass only because I knew this man was connected. My daughter Pammy was already there with Joie, and he called up one day and said, 'Look, Dottie, I know I can talk to you. I just came home. I want to relate to my daughter, but I've got two girls here and it's tough. Whatever I do with Joie, I got to do with Pammy, too, and it's hard enough with just one. But instead of sending Pammy home, why don't you all come in from the Green Death and settle down here in New York? I know Jeffie would like that.'

"Well, I wasn't so sure. When she first heard he was coming out, she used to say to me, 'No, no—you're too cute. You're not going to meet him. You stay away from my old man.' And when Joey put her on the phone, she wasn't encouraging. They were living at Momma's, she said, and she had no idea what he had in mind for us. But I didn't care. We were ready to leave California anyway. Nothing much was happening. Lou and I were making leather belts, just barely surviving, and after hearing about this man for twelve years, sure as shit it would have been a bitch not to meet him. My dearest friend's old man? I'd go in a minute. So we had a yard sale. We moved all the furniture out in the yard and sold pretty near everything to make the fare. Then we left, twittering with excitement, and walked in on a fucking dog act.

"That was some scene at the airport. Louie is in full beard, hair down to his shoulders, trying to look conservative. There are three grubby-looking kids and no luggage—just a guitar, the amplifier and a pile of cardboard boxes. One of the guys is there, looking us over. Jeffie is there, looking gaunt. And Joey is there, leaning against the railings with his hat on. They're all laying back. Holy shit! I mean, where's the red carpet? So I look at Jeffie. She rolls her eyes, and right away I know we're in trouble. But now the boxes are coming up on the conveyor, and as nobody makes a move to help, I start lifting them off. 'No,' says Joey. 'You don't do that. You!' he says to Louie. '*You* get those off.' Didn't lift a finger. Nor did his driver. All he did was get one of the airport security officers to look after some of the boxes. 'You got too much stuff,' he tells Louie. 'We're going to leave it here, and then you can come back for it.' "

None of this seemed strange to Lou at the time. Knowing little of Jeffie and less about Joey, his expectations were more modest than Dottie's. After Joey had made sure he was carrying no hard drugs, he was allowed to climb into the back of the limousine with Dottie and the children, and they were driven to President Street to have dinner at the Longshoremen's Rest. Then Joey proceeded to dispose of them for the night. Dottie was to take two of the kids to sleep at her sister's house in New Jersey, then return to President Street to pick up the other two and take them on over to his mother's house. Lou, meanwhile, would fetch the rest of their stuff from the airport. It took four round trips.

"I didn't mind that. They were my boxes, so it seemed logical I should go get them. The only thing I was a little uptight about was getting around—I'd never been in New York before. So one of the boys said, 'Don't worry about it. I'll take you. I'll show you how to sneak on the Brooklyn-Queens Expressway without paying the toll.' So I said, 'Dynamite, man!' And he did. It was a big thing with them. You had to go by the schoolyard and through a broken fence   very complicated. I guess it would have been easier to pay the dime, but it was more exciting this way. Sneaking on was better. I did it every chance I got after that. But now finally we're back at his mother's house, after all this running around, and it's been a long day. The kids are asleep, and we've just about had it.

" 'Do you have any weed?' he says to me. 'Yes.' 'Okay. Give me it.' I thought he wanted to stash it, that he was upset I had it in his pad and he wanted to put it away. I was wrong. He rolls himself a joint. 'Jesus,' he says. 'This is terrible shit,' and he gives it back to me. Then he breaks out some dynamite hash and goes through the whole ritual of chopping it up with tobacco. I didn't know then that this was unusual. Guys like him don't usually go for that—not even grass. Nothing. Joey never smoked when the boys were around. Only with us. With Jeffie and her friends. Joey had so much energy, smoking helped calm him down. Anyway, he gets me completely stoned. Suddenly it's Christmas. 'Listen,' he says, 'I'm going to get you a job driving a truck delivering *Screw* magazine. We'll get you a nice little place in Brooklyn with a yard for the kids, and that's it.'

And I thought to myself, 'Jesus. What a dumb fucking thing to do —to come to New York and get tied up with a maniac like this.' I was so mad I was shaking. And I was so stoned I thought I was going to say something terrible, but he had all these guys, and I knew I had to be cool. So I was cool, and things mellowed out a bit after that."

While Joey had been arranging Lou's future, Dottie had been working out the sleeping arrangements with Momma, who by now had gone to bed, and Jeffie, who was in any case cramped for space in her two attic rooms. "It's about two o'clock in the morning, and everybody's pretty well wiped out. Joey takes us downstairs to his mother's apartment—Joie's already asleep down there—and puts us in the big bedroom with the big bed. And I guess he must have disturbed Momma's sleep, because through the wall I can hear the sounds of a heavy beef in Italian. She's *mad*. 'What do you think this is?' she's yelling. 'A whorehouse? You bring these tramps to my house—'

"Louie and I are scared shitless. Joey's just got home and everything's going wrong. 'My kid ain't going to sleep in this house,' he yells back, which means he's now got to pick up Joie, who weighs almost as much as he does, and carry her upstairs. 'Come on,' he says to us. 'Let's go.' 'Okay, we're coming, we're coming.' Joie's sound asleep, of course, and dead weight, so he's banging off the walls, cursing as he goes, and Momma's left standing there in her nightgown.

"Well, there are now seven people in the attic, but somehow we sort them all out and finally fall asleep. In the morning, he's still a bit edgy, but when Lou tells him he's not interested in driving a truck, he just shrugs. He says, 'Swell. If you need anything and it's in my power, call on me.' And that was that. He gave us a mattress, and we all drove over to Weehawken Street in Jeffie's Chrysler.

"She was mortified. She had enough to cope with without having her friends' feelings hurt. Luckily, she hadn't given up her apartment after moving out to Brooklyn, otherwise I don't know what we would have done. Joey took care of Bill, the super there, who had always been sweet to Jeffie, and I remember she kissed Bill on the cheek. That made Joey mad again. As soon as he'd gone, Joey told her she shouldn't kiss fags. 'Yeah?' she said. 'Well, what have *you* been doing for ten years?' After that, Lou and I got the flu, and we didn't see either of them again until midsummer."

There were several reasons for this. One was that Jeffie's daily 6 A.M.–to–8 P.M. timetable made no provision for social life. Another was her well-grounded suspicion that Dottie would enjoy Joey's tormented readjustment as little as she did, and yet a third was the feeling, which Dottie shared, that he would permit no real intimacy between them until they had expiated the sin of having enjoyed themselves together while he was away. There were a few surreptitious telephone calls and one or two sneak visits to the Fourteenth Street apartment to discuss its redecoration and furnishing, but otherwise no contact between them until Jeffie ran away to the Lloyds on Fire Island. Meanwhile, Lou had moved the family upstate to Monticello, where he had found work as a counselor in a drug program, and Jeffie's apartment on Weehawken Street was now serving as their base for occasional weekends in the city. Dottie was surprised, therefore, when the telephone rang one Saturday afternoon, for they had told nobody they were coming down.

"Lou was in the shower; I've got a vomiting kid under my arm, and as soon as I hear his 'Hello?' I know it's Joey. And it scared me. Jeffie had called us in Monticello to say that heavy shit was coming down. 'The fucking guy's driving me crazy,' she said. So I asked her, 'What do you want to do? Can you come up here?' And she said, 'I don't know. I'll keep it in mind.' Now he's on the phone, and right away I'm thinking, 'What has he done to her? And how the hell does he know we're in town?' 'Listen,' he says, 'can you get over here?' 'Well, gee, baby, I don't know,' I says. 'Lou's in the shower and the kid's sick. Maybe in an hour . . .' 'No,' he says. 'Sooner. Like, in ten or fifteen minutes.' Now I'm *really* worried. 'Is Jeffie all right?' 'Can you get over here?' he says. Then I knew I had to go. With that man and that voice, I didn't dare say no.

"So I rushed into the bathroom to tell Lou, who gets mad. 'What do you mean, you got to go to Joey's? Who says so? Who the fuck is he?' 'Hey, don't holler at me,' I said. 'Call and holler at *him*. It's something about Jeffie, and I want to know what's happening.' I was really frightened. Ten minutes later, I was ringing the bell of their apartment. He answered the door himself, which was something he never liked to do. Fourteen bolts went back and there he was, wearing his airport face again. 'Where's your girlfriend?' he says. I says, 'Jesus, baby, I don't know.' 'Well,' he says, 'you're not going to leave here until you find her. She split, and I want her back. I want to know where she is, and she'd better get her fucking ass back here fast. So you get on the phone and you find her, because I've got things to do.'

"Well, things were not as bad as I'd thought. But first I wanted Joey to know that Lou was hot about my darting out like that while he was in the shower, leaving him with a vomiting kid. 'Get him on the phone,' he said. 'There's food—whatever. You're staying until I talk to her.' So then he tells Lou he's sorry to do this to him but to bring Timmy over in a cab, that everything's fine but I've got to find Jeffie for him. He was very uptight about it, but when Lou said okay, he relaxed a little. He even started teasing me. 'Come here,' he says. He leads me over to the coffee table, lifts up a newspaper, and there's a big, shiny revolver. 'This is what I've got for your old man when he walks in,' he says. 'Oh, Joey, please—come on. What are you going to do?' So then he giggled, and put the paper back, and I started making some calls.

"Joey knew Jeffie was on Fire Island, but he said he didn't know where. I figured she would go where the clothes would fit her, so I finally got through to the Lloyds, left a message, and after a while she calls—screaming at me. 'How dare you involve yourself in my affairs?' 'Listen,' I said, 'that's very fucking easy for you to say. You're a hundred miles away on Fire Island. I'm here with your old man breathing down my neck.' And he was. This cat was not playing games. He wanted her home. You don't leave the territory—you're not allowed to do that. You stay home and you take your lumps. And I'm hurting because I don't want her to be angry with me. The last thing I want to do is meddle in her affairs. So I gave him the phone and went to the bathroom. I didn't want to hear it. My best friend's hollering at me. She doesn't understand that this man's intimidating me. He doesn't want to know from shit. He wants his old lady home, and we're his hostages.

"Then one of the guys arrived to collect Joey and we were left alone in the apartment. I don't know, maybe he just wanted us there to answer the phone, because when he got back we were allowed to leave. I said, 'Look, I traced her for you. You know where she is, so now we got to go, baby. We got to get back up north.' 'Sure,' he said. He was very understanding, very appreciative. 'Okay, baby. Thank you very much.' Halfway back to Monticello, we bust out laughing."

Dottie and Lou were no longer on probation. From then on, they were welcome visitors to Fourteenth Street. When they moved back to the city after falling out with the director of the drug program, Lou would often drop in unannounced after work for a smoke and a chat. "Once I had on a very strange shirt—I mean, a groovy shirt, man, but like, from the Mafia's point of view, it was extreme. And I figured, well, he could handle the hair and the beard—he said to one of the guys once, 'You know, times are changing. I don't even *see* his beard any more,' and the guy said, '*I* see it.' But now I've got a shirt with a stripe on as well. They're not going to be able to take that. Maybe they'll kill me. So I walked down Fourteenth Street looking in the Puerto Rican stores, and bought one of those short-sleeved, white nylon shirts with a little collar. Ninety-eight cents. Made in Taiwan. I put it on, and when I got up there, he pretended not to recognize me. 'All you need now is a mohair suit,' he said. I told him they didn't have one for $2.95. He laughed. But I was very scruffy-looking. The boys would look at me and know in their hearts that I was a fag. And I guess he knew what they were thinking because he used to tell them, 'Watch out for big Louie. He's a bad-ass dude. That's a bad mother. Don't mess around with him.' He was protecting me.

"We got along good because we'd both been locked up and had a lot of stress. I was institutionalized once in a ward for the criminally insane, where most of the guys were too crazy to be in jail. We talked about that a good deal, and traded stories about different busts. He told me once they put him in a cell next to a real psychopath, and the guards had primed this cat to do away with Joey. When they locked up, they left these two cells open, and he knew immediately what was happening. He opened the door, and there was this guy—a real ape, according to Joey—coming out of his cell. But before he had a chance to do anything, Joey ran over to him, jumped up, grabbed him around the neck with both arms and bit off his ear.

" 'Now,' says Joey, 'the guy's screaming, and the guards think it's me, so nobody shows up for some time. Meanwhile, I'm back in my cell with the door closed and his ear in my mouth.' Finally, he said, the guards come, and he hears them talking outside. Then one of them comes in and says, 'Okay, Gallo. Where's the ear?' So Joey gets up, walks over to the toilet, spits it in the bowl and flushes.

"This came up because he was just going to have a lot of work done on his mouth. 'I'm very sentimental about my teeth,' he said, 'because they saved my life a few times.' Seems he also bit a guy's nipple off once, and a patch off the top of some other guy's head. Being small, he didn't have an awful lot to work with.

"We congratulated each other on having stayed alive. That was the important thing—to stay sane, stay on top of it, keep fighting. Like when you went to take a shower in the joint, he said, you had to stand in line with your clothes off. When it got to be your turn, you'd get under the spigot and they'd give you a shot of water to get you wet. Then you'd lather up, go back under the spigot and you'd get another shot of water to rinse you off. Then you're done. But when *Joey* went to take a shower, they'd give him a shot of scalding-hot water to start with, and he'd have to jump back. So how does he lather up? He has to go to the drain where the water's running away, get down on his knees and splash it over himself. Okay. Now he gets back under the spigot to rinse off, and down comes a shot of icy-cold water, right? But he knows it's coming, and he takes it. If he ever let on for an instant that anything was out of order, if he ever looked up at the guard working the spigot and said, 'Fuck you,' then *they* would have won. So he couldn't give in. He just had to pretend that his shower was fine.

"When other prisoners wanted something, they'd say to a trusty as he walked by, 'Hey, can you get me a pack of cigarettes?' and he'd get it for them. But when Joey called out, nobody stopped. He could sit there for a week without a cigarette—and he couldn't let them see he cared. If he did, they would win a little, he would lose a little. Like the radio. Every night he liked to listen to the news in his cell. But somehow, every time the news came on, his radio—it was piped in —would shut off. Nobody else's—just his. There was always something wrong with it at news time, but as soon as the news was over, it worked fine. For years he was subject to those pressures, plus all the time in solitary, and you can only torture somebody for so long. We understood each other because we'd both been through a lot of things.

"Once in a while, we'd go out alone to eat, and I would drive him. You were always under a little strain when you were out with Joey. There were guys looking to kill him, and neither of us had a gun. But forgetting that, I didn't want to goof because he was so competent. And he didn't make it easy. He wouldn't *tell* you where to go; he would just signal with his finger—right turn, left turn. If you missed one, you were in trouble. I remember once he was making so many hand signals that I suddenly realized I was going the wrong way down a one-way street. I said, 'We're going the wrong way.' He said, 'I know.' One of the guys told me he was driving him to a restaurant once and Joey was doing his finger number, so he starts to make a right-hand turn. 'Where the fuck are you going?' says Joey. 'You signaled,' says the guy in a panic. 'You schmuck,' says Joey. 'I'm putting out my cigarette.'

"I never saw him in action as a gangster, but there was no question his life was in danger. One time we went to an Armenian restaurant with some of the guys, and the moment we walked in, everybody just got up and left. So Joey said, 'Okay. I sit here. You sit there and you here,' and so on. They had a young kid on point that night with the gun—one of these huge automatic pistols—and he's sitting next to Joey, who doesn't like the way he's handling it. 'No,' he says, 'you don't do it like that. Move over a minute. Now here's what you do.' He folded a newspaper in half, put the gun inside, took the safety off and set it down on the table, pointing toward the door. 'All you have to do now,' he says, 'is pull the trigger.' While he's explaining this to the kid, I'm thinking, 'Wow, this is like fire drill.' And that's just

Dottie and Lou 325

what it was. 'Anything happens,' he says, 'This side of the table goes out the back door. This side goes out that way.' He had everything down pat, and he was dead serious. There was no one to do an act for that night.

"Except for that, I never heard a word about his business. The nearest he came to it was one night when I told him I was thinking of shaving off my beard. 'Don't do that,' he said. 'I may need somebody with a beard and long hair. Did you ever think about killing a guy?' 'Sure, I thought about it once or twice,' I said. 'Who hasn't?' 'Good,' he said, and that was the end of the discussion. It may have been a put-on, but being the kind of guy I am, I was in a great turmoil about it for weeks in case he made me a proposition. He knew I was as angry at everything as he was, but I'd learned to control it. I guess *he* never did—never wanted to. Anyway, I never heard another word about it after that.

"He was a tough little guy, but the rest was a sham. I watched him doing his gangster act for the rest of the world, and I knew he was a phony. And he knew that I knew. It wasn't such a tremendous secret, once you got to know him as a friend. That whole gangster bit was so laughable, so funny from one point of view, that I don't know how anybody could go for it—except that guys got killed. What made him different from other people was that he always did what he felt like doing. He acted out all his feelings. But by the time I knew him, he'd been through an awful lot of changes, and it was telling on him. It seemed to me that what he wanted to do more than anything else was just relax, only nobody would let him.

"We spent a lot of time talking about the girls, how they were hard-nosed and tough. You had to keep them in line or they'd kill you. I don't think he enjoyed hitting Jeffie, but you can't be under that kind of strain all the time in the streets, you can't have all those guys to look after, and their families, you can't watch out all the time in case someone kills you, and then go home and be insulted. Every once in a while, he had to give her a whack. He'd lost a lot of his life, and had a lot of bad times.

"We were trying to explain to her one night the difference between taking a position on something and standing by it through everything, and being adult enough to change your mind about a position you'd taken if the situation changed. Jeffie thought you had to stand behind your shit no matter what, but Joey and I thought you had to be able to bend a little. That way you stayed alive. We'd been talking about guys like George Jackson, who'd taken a position, wouldn't change it and are now dead. 'How useless, man,' he said. 'How pathetic. How valueless they are.' He thought Jackson was an asshole because he wouldn't give enough to stay alive and continue the fight. 'You can't let them win,' he said. 'You've got to give enough to survive, come back and carry on.'

"But he was so mad, and so torn by so many different things. He despised the system, but he didn't really want to change it. Change was bad for business. Maybe he thought along revolutionary lines, but he sure as hell didn't want the hippies taking over the country. That may have been the problem at the airport. I think he associated me immediately with the people that were trying to take away his numbers game. Joey was for anything that suited his purpose. He had a new way of being a reactionary, and the first rule was survival. That was why the Attica riot got him absolutely hypnotized. He thought the guys in there were stupid. That's not the way you do it. He could have gotten himself killed in the Auburn riot, he said, 'but what good am I dead to anyone?'

"That theme kept recurring in our conversations. Hang in there, man. Don't give up the ship. Don't let them get you. Don't let the broads get you down. Do what you've got to do. If you're a man, be a man. He kept saying, 'You can't believe this fucking broad, man. She's just like your old lady—a ball-buster. She's got the kid against me, too. It's an effort, man, just to keep them in line, to stay on top. It never ends.' He must have really loved her or else he would never have put up with all that shit. I think he must have loved Joie, too, even though he didn't know her that well. Must have hurt him a great deal to have her treat him like that. I thought it was a drag. I used to tell him, and tell all of them, that children should have some respect for their parents. It's nice to have an independent, intelligent little girl, but it's also a pain in the fucking ass."

Lou had been won over. As between Joey and Jeffie, there was never a doubt as to where his sympathies lay. Lou was for Joey. Dottie, just as naturally, was for Jeffie, although she, too, was often appalled by Jeffie's intransigence in what was rapidly becoming a do-or-die struggle for self-vindication. Being Italian, Dottie understood the weight of custom and responsibility pressing in on Joey. "She wanted him to see the absurdity of it all, but he knew that already. This was what he had to do, and he couldn't break away. He took us to dinner at the Queen Restaurant once—it was the first time we'd been out together. While we were eating, the cars started arriving outside. No one came in to disturb him; they just waited until we had finished, and then, there they were—the whole entourage. 'Hey, Pops, how are you? You okay? Everything all right?' Kisses, love, hugs. Louie with the beard—'Hey, I want you to meet my friend Louie.' They knew he was in there. They waited. And he couldn't turn them away. They'd waited for him. Larry was dead. Blast didn't want to make waves. But now the chutzpa-man was home, the man who created the tumult, and they were hungry for him, for what he could do for them. He knew it was all shit. The thing he'd set out to do originally he couldn't accomplish, and now it was too late to try again. They were old. The new kids were not like the guys he had before, the old Mafiosi. He had nothing to work with. It was doomed. But they had waited, and he couldn't let them down. He had an obligation to fulfill.

"Now Jeffie knew that, but she didn't understand it. I kept trying to tell her, 'Hey, Jeffie, ease up, man.' I was very sensitive to the fact that he'd been incarcerated for nine years. He had to have a chance to readjust. He'd come out to all these people who were panting for him. He had to figure out a way to satisfy them. The streets were full of enemies who wanted to kill him—I mean, the pressure cooker this cat had to be in. Then to come home to this—this banshee. I love her dearly, but she's a heavy. I begged her. 'Try. Keep your mouth shut. You don't have to win all the time.' But she had to play tough guy back—that's her nature. It was a tragedy. Because he *knew* that. He knew all about her. The thing he dug most was that she had the balls to fight back, that she wasn't a subservient little Italian. He loved it—but it was killing them. Inadvertently, somebody was going to get their head bumped against a wall, and the other would be up on a manslaughter rap.

"It was the same thing with Joie. Underneath it all, I'm sure he was prouder than fucking shit about that kid. What Italian turns out a kid like that? So together. So tough. So feminine. Such a tremendous lady. Jeffie did that for her, and I know deep down he wouldn't have had it any different, but he just couldn't cut it with the kid's behavior. I took Joie for the weekend once. I said, 'You guys have a honeymoon, and let *me* try to talk to her.' But all I did was make her cry. Joie couldn't understand what I was trying to say to her. 'But I don't like the way he treats me,' she said. 'And I don't like the way he treats my mother.' Well, I didn't either, so I couldn't argue about that. We got nowhere. When I took Joie home and asked Jeffie, 'How did it go?' she said, 'One hour can be a weekend for us,' so I guess it was worth it.

"It was such a shame, because Joey loved children, and children loved him. He won my daughter Pamela with a promise. He said to her, 'When you're eighteen years old, I'm going to take you to Florida, and you're going to be looking *so* good. I'm going to find out where your father hangs out, and I'm going to walk in there with you on my arm, and he's going to come up and say to me, "Hey, who's that great-looking girl you're with?" And I'm going to say, "You know who that is? That's your daughter." ' So then Pammy got very excited and said, 'You're really going to do that, Joey?' And Joey said, 'Sure. That's a promise.'

"He won my son Douglas with a trick. Douglas loves money, so Joey taught him this routine with a cup and a coin, and off he goes to the Laundromat with his older brother Adam as his shill. 'Hey, you want to see my brother do a trick? Okay. Put a quarter on the floor.' So the patsy shells out a quarter and Douglas covers it with the cup. 'I bet you can't remove the coin from under the cup without touching the cup,' he says, and the guy has to admit he can't. 'Okay,' says Douglas. 'You want to see me do it? Abracadabra. Now lift up the cup.' The guy lifts up the cup, Douglas takes the money. 'See?' he says. "I told you I could take the quarter without touching the cup.' They came back with eighty-four cents. I was so embarrassed.

"But Joey just couldn't seem to do that with Joie. Maybe part of it was because Jeffie wasn't always cool in front of her, so the kid was picking up a lot of *her* shit. I think Joie got confused. One minute, Jeffie's being very philosophical about mutual respect and the rights of the individual; the next minute, she's saying to her, 'You better shut up. Be cool'—things *she* couldn't do.

"There was one frightening night when she really flipped her wig. We were smoking, Joey was being pleasant and it was trying to be a nice evening, but Jeffie was in one of her black moods. I was picking up the vibes, but I didn't want to leave because I enjoyed him. It was great being with him. I loved him. And if she would only be nice and keep her mouth shut, we could all have a good time. But I guess things were catching up with her. She'd been attacked a lot. There were so many times for which she had to get even. I don't know what triggered it, what he said exactly, but from out of nowhere she suddenly let him have it. She sat on the couch and went absolutely insane. Hollered. Screamed. Cried. Frothed at the mouth. Whatever it was that he'd said, it really made her spew. But he didn't bat an eye. He just sat there and took it. He let her get it off. After a while, he walked over to her and handed her a joint. 'Here,' he said. 'Come on now—stop it.' At that point, *I* was ready to give her a crack in the mouth—that's how bad it was, how evil she was. For an hour straight she didn't shut up with her ravings, and he didn't budge. He was cool, but I figured he had to kill her. There's another man listening. There's another chick. Finally, she went into the bedroom, and I didn't want to have to say anything to Joey about it, so I followed her in there. 'I'm dying,' she said. 'You're at my funeral. I can't take it any more.'

"She'd been taking a lot. What she'd been trying to say to him was 'You can't abuse me like this. I'm too old to be hit. I haven't the patience.' The hunger they had for each other was as strong as ever —stronger maybe—but he couldn't turn that clicker off. She didn't open the door for him one night; she was asleep. He gave her a kick in the ass, man—kicked her right off the fucking bed. He had a key, but she had to get up to open the door. Okay, he was angry. She had

330   J O E Y

to be the punching bag. He'd had all that time in prison to think, 'What are you doing, whore? Now you're going to pay because people saw you in the street. You're going to pay because my mother says you were a whore. You're going to pay because you split, and ran all over the world. You're going to pay because you made me chase you. You're going to pay because I gave you a divorce. You're going to pay because you turned out a kid that won't do what I tell her.' Joey had to make Jeffie pay for a lot—I knew that in my guts, and told her so. A nice Italian girl in her situation would have sat back, crossed her legs and done nothing. Waited. She would have paid, but in a different way. Jeffie got it a lot harder. He could not get comfortable with her. She couldn't do anything right.

"Now and again they'd be happy together, these two strong people, and then you could see why they had to give it another try. They would exult in each other, and glow with fulfillment. You could warm your own life at that fire. Then some stupid thing would break the spell. All the shit would come down, and the pain of losing what they'd had would make them tear at each other worse than before. Toward the end, she was slipping him tranquilizers in his coffee, without him knowing, trying to keep him docile. One night, we were getting ready to leave, and he was sitting there in his bathrobe, looking like he was in Ward C—very nice, making no waves—and he looked at me and he said, 'You know, Dottie, she's going to have me on Thorazine pretty soon.' We all fell about laughing. He knew. He didn't mind. After that, she would feed him pills—'Here, honey, take this'—and he would take them.

"I always had this dream that they would go off together, maybe to Spain, and he would tap this creative resource he had, and write and be brilliant, and give life a shot. But she would always say, 'Oh, stop the bullshit. He's going to have to go down in a spray of bullets.' I didn't want to hear that because I knew how much she loved him, but she was right. I miss him. I always felt I was under his protection. I always knew I could reach out to him. He was like the brother I never had, like the daddy I never had. It was like, 'Here comes Tarzan'—for everybody who knew him. Now he's gone. Holy shit!

Are we in trouble! He's gone! I'll never see him smile again. I'll never enjoy those times when the two of them were happy together, when they'd run across the street, darting for a cab. The love affair went on so long, so long. It was part of my love affair, too."

18
Ruth

Jeffie's friends are of two kinds: those who, like Dottie, share her bold, romantic commitment to feeling as the only reliable guide to life and, in the end, its only reward, gauging the significance of every moment by the strength of their gut response; and those unwilling to gamble so much on so fickle a measure but who admire, perhaps envy, her freedom to do so. With the first, she enjoys an intimacy that can never be one-sided—for there are no sides—and which offers the reassurance of fellow feeling. With the others, she enjoys the perhaps more substantial comfort of having somewhere to go if her gambles miscarry—a surrogate family to whom she plays prodigal daughter, but whose protection, being based on more conventional values, requires some show of conformity from her. Having nothing to lose, the first were free to cross into Joey's world at will and enjoy him without constraint. Having nothing to gain, the others were often so preoccupied with keeping the two worlds apart that they scarcely enjoyed him at all. Ruth Browne was one of these.

Ten days after Joey's release, he and Jeffie went to dinner at Ruth's apartment in Greenwich Village. "My first thought on opening the door was that Jeffie was dragging a child behind her. I hadn't expected him to be so small and skinny. He was wearing a short leather jacket and, of all things, a cloth cap. He stood there with his hands in his pockets, looking at me with those pale, intent eyes of his, deep deep set in that skull-like face, and I was very disappointed. After all I'd heard from Jeffie, *this* was Prince Charming? But she was happy as a lark that night, and after we exchanged a little small talk, he said, 'Where's the music?' We were running out of conversation and he wanted music. So I explained that my son had taken the radio to school, and my daughter Marjorie had borrowed the phonograph. Sorry. No music. 'I'll go get the phonograph,' says Jeffie, and off she goes to Marjorie's house, leaving Joey alone with me. I could have killed her. I had a friend coming to make up four for dinner, but he hadn't arrived yet.

"I tried to keep the conversation going, but Joey was nervous, and sparring with me almost. He didn't like my place. Didn't like the way I had it furnished. He wasn't comfortable. He was moving around like a cat, which I found unsettling. Then the doorbell rang. It was too soon to be Jeffie. 'Who's that?' he said. He was looking around for some way of escape. 'Probably my friend Tom,' I said, keeping calm, and went to answer it. But he got there ahead of me, and positioned himself so that he would be behind the door when it opened. Then he motioned me to see who it was. But Tom had a key, and after ringing the bell, he decided to use it. Before I could stop him, he pushed the door wide open, and squashed Joey against the wall. I started to laugh—I really couldn't help it. But then I saw the look on Joey's face, and I quickly yelled out, 'It's okay. It's Tom.' I didn't know what he might do."

Ruth had met Jeffie some five years earlier, but it was not until Jeffie returned from England that the two became close. Ruth stayed with her in Hermosa Beach for a few weeks in 1970, and when Jeffie came back to New York later that year, prompted by rumors of

Joey's release, she got her a job with her company. As rumor turned to certainty, she watched Jeffie change. The apathy which had so worried Ruth a few months before gave way to a state of chronic anxiety. In a matter of weeks, Jeffie was as thin as she'd been fat in California. Her agitation was such that, the day before she was due to see Joey in Auburn to ask him to take her back, she went to the lengths of calling the prison to find out what kind of lighting it had, so as to be sure of using the right makeup, only to forget to take it with her.

It was not surprising, then, that a man capable of driving her strong-minded friend to these extremes should have aroused such lively expectations in Ruth, nor that their disappointment should have proved so comical, but as the evening wore on and Joey thawed out, she began to understand his fascination for Jeffie a little better. She still found it impossible to take him seriously as a gangster, however, despite his tough-guy talk at the dinner table.

Joey was full of stories about prison life. The guards, he said, were of low intelligence and often vicious or perverted, mainly as a result of generations of inbreeding. This was particularly noticeable at Attica, where most of them were cross-eyed, an inherited character-istic that drove him and his friend Willie Sutton, the bank robber, crazy because they could never be sure who it was a hack was looking at. Joey then capped this recital with an account of the various attempts on his life, and a particularly scarifying tale of a homosex-ual gang rape in which he participated. He described how, with several older convicts, he had spotted a pretty young boy among a new batch of prisoners and laid in wait for him. Dragging him into the Jewish chapel, they ripped his pants off and were struggling to hold him down when one of them heard the rabbi talking in the next room. A knife was immediately put at their victim's throat with a whispered warning not to cry out, and the rape proceeded in an orderly fashion, each man taking his turn in order of seniority. They wanted this kid, Joey said, while his asshole was still tight. Otherwise it would be as big as a silver dollar by the time everybody got through with him.

"Maybe he was just trying to shock us, but he told this story in a very matter-of-fact kind of voice, as if everybody knew that such things went on every day in prison, and that homosexuality there was normal, natural and unremarkable—which I suppose it is. This was going to be one of the themes in his book. Then Jeffie talked about her plans to get him away from President Street so that he could start to write, and he said yes, that was what he wanted to do. He had some things to straighten out first, but then he was going to sit down and write a novel, a black comedy about prison, based on his experiences. He thought almost everybody in prison was crazy and didn't belong there. Instead of being reduced to animals, they ought to be under psychiatric care. Instead of having their dignity taken away, they should be treated as sick people, because in most cases there was no rhyme or reason to what they'd done. The interesting thing was he excluded himself. He was a professional, he said. What he did was business. He took his risks knowingly, and could therefore cope with the prison scene.

"None of this was very original or very profound, but he was certainly a bright man. Very opinionated. He had a lot to say about everything, and you listened to him because of his manner of speaking, which was very Brooklyn and very direct. Sometimes he used words that he'd obviously read and understood but didn't know how to pronounce. He was very aware, very sharp. Street sharp. Survival sharp."

Several weeks then passed, with Jeffie reporting almost daily on her deepening crisis with Joey, before Ruth saw him again. She was at work one day when Jeffie's successor as receptionist rang through to announce a Mr. Joseph Gallo. "I said, 'Oh my God, send him up,' hoping no one else had seen him, and in walks Mr. Gangster in a huge hat and hoodlum overcoat. Jeffie had been buying him tons of clothes. When he first got out, she would stagger back to the office after lunch each day as though it were Christmas. A dozen shirts here, half a dozen pairs of narrow, straight pants there, sweaters, shoes—a whole bonanza of chic menswear. Jeffie has great taste. But as fast as she bought the stuff, so he would give it away. Jeffie told me he didn't like the pants because there was no place to put his balls. Wanted pleated pants. Didn't like the shirts because only fags wore things like that. In the end she gave up, and by the time he came to see me at the office, he'd reverted to type.

" 'I just happened to be in the neighborhood,' he said, 'so I thought I'd stop by. I'm in the furniture business now. I'm a salesman. Know anybody who wants to buy some good furniture?' And that's what we were talking about when Jeffie rang through with a query from purchasing. I told her who was in my office, and she was mortified. She refused to come up. He'd embarrassed her by crossing over from his world into hers. But now I'd gotten over the shock, I was beginning to enjoy the idea of having him watch me in action. I sat there making with the big executive decisions as people came in, and he seemed quite impressed. At one point, somebody brought in a couple of fabrics for me to choose from, and I asked him which he liked best. 'That one,' he said. So I said, 'That's it then.' Joey loved it. He was crowing. I also introduced him to Jeffie's boss, but Joey played the big shot with him, and talked a little too much—which made us both uncomfortable."

Having gauged Ruth's authority in *her* world, Joey now invited her to bring Marjorie to an Easter party on President Street so that they, in turn, could judge his. "He took us to the Longshoremen's Rest, which is owned by a lady named Frances. I went to look for my hostess, who was in the kitchen, naturally, and while I was talking to her and the women helping her out, Joey came in, very angry. 'Get out of here,' he said to me. 'You're not to talk to these idiots. You come out here with me.' If *I'd* been one of the idiots, I would have crowned him, but they just lowered their eyes and got on with their work.

"Then the other guests arrived, all of them very respectful, and Joey the king was completely in charge. 'You sit here. You sit there. No, no—you move down a couple of places.' When everyone was settled, I was sitting at the head of the table on Joey's left; Jeffie was opposite, on his right; then came the men, facing one another across the table, and finally the women at the far end. Now he was ready to begin, so they started bringing in the food, which was superb. Joey was a fine, attentive host—'You got to taste this—you're going to like it. Isn't that great? Have some more.' It was like a medieval banquet, with every dish being brought first to the king for his approval. Jeffie always said he looked down on these people, that he played this role only out of a sense of duty to them, but that's not how it seemed to me. He was happy with them. He *needed* their adoration. He enjoyed it. You could sense his pleasure in it.

"By the time coffee was served, everybody was very relaxed—even Jeffie. Then people started crowding in through the door, neighborhood people coming to pay their respects, pushing their children in front of them to say hello. The women hung back, but the men came forward and kissed him, first on one cheek, then on the other. Then they kissed *me* on both cheeks as well, which made Jeffie laugh. Everybody thought *I* was Joey's wife. It went on all evening, with more and more people coming up to him, kissing us, and then being told to sit down and take a cup of coffee or glass of wine. It was a royal reception for his subjects. No matter what Jeffie says, these were his people and they gave him his identity."

After the Easter Party, Ruth thought of Joey more kindly. He obviously liked her, and enjoyed showing her off, which he did in the course of further excursions to President Street. She, in turn, was entertained by his attentions, and stifled her occasional qualms with the thought that she was watching social history in the making. How many other "straight" people had a chance to share in the private life of the world's most notorious gangster? When he and Jeffie invited her in June to their second wedding, she accepted at once.

"I drove down with them in their car, and I only realized when we got to the courthouse that there were other cars in attendance because suddenly we were in the middle of a whole group of his people. As we walked through the building to the chambers of Judge Irwin Brownstein, who was going to marry them, we kept losing part of this escort. Men would drop out in pairs and station themselves at strategic points—in the lobby, on the stairs, by the elevators. When we got up to the judge's floor, there were two more already in the hall. Then we had to wait—the judge had somebody with him —so we went into an empty courtroom. While Jeffie and I sat talking, Joey was up in the judge's seat, swiveling around and opening all the drawers in front of him. We both groaned, and, sure enough, at that very moment, a cop walked in and caught him at it. So now, if they get married at all, I figure it will be in a cell—but no. 'Hello, Joey,' says the cop. 'Long time no see.'

"Joey was in a marvelous humor that day, and Jeffie was radiant. The ceremony was simple and lovely, and they seemed very happy together. None of the family was there, though, which I thought was a bad omen."

Just how untypical an Italian wedding it had been became clear to Ruth a week or two later. One of the boys was getting married in Brooklyn, and Joey asked her along. "I went over to their apartment, and found Jeffie doing one of her crazy numbers—putting her hair up, taking it down again, and then not knowing what to wear. 'The queen isn't ready yet,' said Joey—he kept calling her the queen. 'Will you see what the queen's doing?' Before she finally got herself together, I could cheerfully have killed her myself, but at last we were all set and Joey nodded to a couple of his men, who stood up and left. I got up as well, thinking we were all leaving, but Joey said, 'Now wait a second.' I guess something must have happened that day because security was tighter than I'd ever seen it. When we followed them down a couple of minutes later, we found them at the door, watching the street.

"Pete the Greek was driving, and we hadn't gone more than a few blocks before Joey warned him to go slow. He didn't want to attract any attention. Then he said, 'How many we got, Pete?' Pete showed him both hands, with his fingers spread out. 'Ten?' said Joey. 'What the hell do we need ten for? It's a friendly wedding. Six is enough.' Well, I just broke up when I heard that—this nice calculation of how many guns you needed for a friendly wedding. Joey laughed, too. He was very relaxed in spite of the precautions. 'The gang that couldn't shoot straight—right, Ruth?' And that's how it was—like something in the movies. I hadn't seen his mean side yet. I knew he and Jeffie were fighting, but they hadn't fought in front of me. They were just —competitive. Friends of mine said I was crazy, running around with them, but it didn't seem at all dangerous to me. It was funny. I was having a ball.

"When we got to this big hall in Brooklyn somewhere, there must have been four hundred people there, all in their Sunday best, singing and dancing and laughing and drinking. It was more like a block party than the kind of wedding I was used to. These were people of the streets having one hell of a good time, and they didn't care who knew it. But they cared about Joey. The moment we came in the door you would have thought *he* was the groom from the fuss they made. A table was set up for us by the door in two seconds flat, and two seconds after that, it was covered with bottles of wine and dishes of food. Meanwhile, some of his men are guarding the lobby and the others are working through the crowd to make sure everything's okay. And everything's fine. A lot of women are dancing with each other because their men are off drinking in groups; there are kids all over the place, getting underfoot, but everybody's very happy and very noisy. It's a great scene.

"Mary Gallo was there, and so was Joey's brother Blast—who I don't think approved of him bringing a stranger because he didn't say a word to me all evening. And it was like the Easter party all over again, only bigger. Everybody came up to Joey and kissed him. He was their chief, their leader and protector, and loving every minute of it. He even allowed Jeffie to dance, which was something he never let her do ordinarily. But he was in such a good mood that night, he was picking her partners for her. 'Dance with that one. Now dance with him.' She was having a wonderful time."

A few days later, Joe Colombo, peacemaker in the Gallo-Profaci war and titular boss of the Mafia family to which the Gallos nominally owed their allegiance, was gunned down in Columbus Circle. As the storm of publicity and speculation broke around Joey's head, Ruth was appalled to think of the risks she had run in the past three months, and it did little for her peace of mind when he dropped in two nights later to talk to her.

"I pulled him inside. 'Are you crazy?' I said. 'What are you doing here? Is there nobody with you?' He had been on television and in all the papers, and Colombo's men were supposed to be combing the city, looking for him. 'They won't recognize me like this,' he said. He was wearing a golf hat, a windbreaker jacket and moccasins, which certainly wasn't his usual dress. So I offered him a drink and asked him again why he'd come. 'Do *you* believe I did it?' he said. I didn't know what to say. 'Joey, what do you want me to tell you?' I said. 'All I know is what I read in the papers.' 'I'm not asking you that,' he said. 'Do you believe I did it?' 'Well,' I said, 'you're supposed to be a smart man, and I just can't imagine you shooting someone with all those women and children around.' 'Then you *don't* think I did it,' he said, but I just couldn't be sure. 'I don't know, Joey,' I said. 'I can't answer that. I don't know what your motives might have been.'

"Then Joey said, very emphatically, that he was *not* responsible for the shooting, and would give an eyetooth to know who'd done it. 'If I'm being framed for it—if it's the FBI behind it—I'm dead,' he said. 'I'm a dead man. But if it was an inside job, that I can control. And we'll soon know. If you read in the papers tomorrow that I got killed, you'll know it was a frame-up. You'll know the FBI used me as a patsy to get to Colombo and put us both away at the same time. You watch the papers. Every day I stay alive is good.' He went on like that for some time, and I still can't imagine why he would have wanted to come over and tell me about it. There was nothing I could do. Maybe he just wanted to talk to somebody— somebody who knew him but wasn't part of his world. I don't know. He said he didn't mind dying if he had to—he wasn't afraid of death —but he sure as hell resented the idea of dying just to suit the convenience of the government.

"And yet he didn't seem to be taking any special care of himself. He asked me if he could stay for dinner. There was nothing to eat in the house, so he went out to Bleecker Street to buy food and several bottles of wine. It was dark, but he had to be taking a chance. Over dinner, we got to talking about what might have been—how he might have turned out if his childhood had been different. But he would still have been the kind of guy who took his shots in life, he said. He began to compare my friends unfavorably with himself, which made me angry. He was strong; they were weak. He was a doer, and they were nondoers because they were frightened of paying the consequences. 'Well, you certainly paid some consequences, didn't you?' I said. 'Ten years. You wasted ten years of your life for being your kind of doer.' But Joey wouldn't agree it had been a waste. He was interested in power, he said. Didn't matter whether it was in New York City, the world or in prison—what difference did it make? The only thing that counted was taking your shots, getting on top, getting to be boss. If you didn't, if you just stuck to the middle of the road, you had to be a mediocre person.

"I resented this. 'I respect Napoleon for going for broke,' I said, 'or Alexander the Great, but every time *you* try it, you get wiped out. You don't even know if you'll be alive tomorrow, so don't talk to me about mediocrity. I think it's pretty mediocre just to be a moving target.' No, Joey said. Whether you won or lost had nothing to do with it. If you were a man, you had to take your shots, whatever the consequences. Soon after that, he walked back alone to Fourteenth Street."

As yet, Ruth still had no inkling of how savagely he and Jeffie were fighting. She continued to see them after the Colombo shooting—the furor soon died down, and Joey's fear of a frame-up appeared to be groundless—but they seemed just their normal, combative selves until that August, when Ruth left for Italy on business. Joey insisted on driving her out to the airport, which meant something was wrong because he was supposed to be on Fire Island with Jeffie and the Lloyds. "He was really mad about something that day, so I asked him, 'Why didn't you go with her, Joey?' 'What?' he said. 'And be on an island? Supposing something happens. How do I get away? How am I going to get off? I couldn't be comfortable there. That's why I didn't go.' He was really burning, and I guessed it had to be because of Jeffie. A week or so later I was on Capri when Frank Balon called from New York for some business information. Then he said, 'Of course, you know that Jeffie's not working for me any more.' But of course I *didn't* know. It came as a real shock. When I asked him what had happened, he couldn't even bring himself to mention Joey's name on the telephone. Said he'd discuss it when I got back."

The idea of Joey hitting Jeffie was more than Ruth could stand. Disillusioned, she saw less and less of them after that, keeping up her contact with Jeffie by phone. Though quite sure that Jeffie was as much to blame as Joey was for the now open warfare between them, Ruth could see no possible excuse for him breaking her ribs, or blacking her eyes, and she told him so. "I was alone late one night when the doorbell rang, and I found the two of them standing there. 'You son of a bitch,' Jeffie was screaming. Her face was all swollen and puffy. 'You lousy son of a bitch—I'll kill you for this.' He was trying to calm her down, but she was hysterical. So I got them inside before they woke up the building, and I went into the kitchen to make an ice pack. He followed me, trying to justify what he had done. 'Let me explain, Ruth,' he said. 'You don't know what she's like. She asked for it.' 'I don't care,' I said. 'As far as I'm concerned, she's right—you're a son of a bitch.' They sat on the couch, and he tried again to talk her around, but she wasn't buying it. She was going to kill him. 'Get me a doctor, Ruth. That bastard. Look what he did to me. Do you know a plastic surgeon?' He seemed genuinely upset it had happened. He really believed she'd forced him to do it. The only reason he'd come with her was because he wanted to make her see that. He wanted us to understand that she'd given him no choice."

It was now clear to Ruth that the two of them had to separate. When Jeffie announced just before Christmas that she was ready to go back to work, it seemed a sensible first step for her to take. "She told me that Jack Mario, the sales manager of one of our suppliers, had promised her a job anytime she wanted it—if Joey would let her. This was news to me, although he was a good friend of ours, but I said I would mention it to him. 'Better still,' I said, 'why don't you ask him yourself? I'm going to a business party tomorrow night, and Jack'll be there, so come with me.' Well, she thought that was a good idea, and the next evening she put it to him. But, according to Jack, she'd got it wrong. He'd only said he would discuss the possibility of getting her a job if Joey changed his mind. He was sorry, but there was nothing he could do. So then Jeffie blew her stack. He'd lied to her and led her on. He'd promised. And the more he denied it, the angrier she got. By the time we got her home she was raving. I was sorry about it, of course—for her sake—but there was nothing *I* could do. That was the end of it as far as I was concerned."

But it wasn't the end of it as far as Joey was concerned. Ruth's final disillusionment with him set in next day. "I had to go down to Jack's place to look at some samples. I walked into his office, and found him there with two of Joey's boys. When I saw them, I felt sick. It wasn't a friendly visit. So I got to a phone and called Jeffie. 'It's nothing,' she said. 'Don't worry about it. It's business.' Business? *What* business? She didn't know. So then I called Jack to find out what was happening. The two men had gone by then, and he said they had threatened him. Either he gave Jeffie a job or they'd break his legs and fire-bomb the office. 'Oh my God,' I said. I'd had a terrible feeling it might be something like that. And it was my fault. Jeffie would never even have met him if it hadn't been for me.

"But something didn't ring quite true. I could tell from the way he was speaking there was more to it than that, and finally he told me. There had been a dock strike, which had tied up a huge shipment of his merchandise on the piers. So Jack had decided to play hero and get it off. He had met Joey once or twice through Jeffie, and he'd gone to see him about it. 'Sure,' Joey said. 'I can do it. But it's dangerous. My men might get hurt. It'll cost you ten thousand dollars.' 'Okay,' said Jack. 'Don't do anything yet. I'll call you tomorrow. I got to get permission from my boss to pay that kind of money.' And, of course, he didn't get it. He worked for a company that didn't do business that way. Next day, Jack had to call Joey and tell him never mind. He couldn't get the money. The deal was off. But Joey evidently figured that Jack owed him something for his trouble. On top of that, Jack had now broken his promise to give Jeffie a job. So unless Jack kept his word—which he swore he never gave—he was going to get his legs broken. And Jack didn't like that idea, not at all. He was also Italian. As he calmed down, he began to think about his own connections. Unless they left him alone, he said, he would have to speak to some people he knew.

"So I told him that would just make matters worse. I would see what I could do. Around six o'clock, I took a cab downtown to talk to Joey. We argued till 1 A.M. 'He put my wife down. That's an insult to me.' 'He put her *down*?' I said. 'Look who's talking. *You* beat her *up*. All *he* did was tell her he couldn't give her a job.' 'He owed me

344   JOEY

that favor.' *'What* favor? You didn't *do* anything for him, Joey. The deal didn't go through. And even if it had, he would have paid you for it. You would still have been all square.' 'No. He was obligated to me.' *'How,* Joey? Explain it to me. I don't understand. Maybe that's the way it is in your world, but it doesn't make sense in mine. A deal is a deal. If it goes through, both parties benefit. If it doesn't, nobody benefits. Either way, nobody owes anybody any favors.' No, he was obligated. And Joey's manhood was also at stake because Jack had insulted his wife.

"Then I got mad at Jeffie. Though she had never dreamed he would send the boys up to his office, she had started this whole horrendous mess by telling Joey that Jack had broken his promise. Now, instead of helping me cool it, she was reveling in this scene. I told her to cut it out. 'Jeffie, while you're prancing around, here's a man who's going to end up in the hospital. And here's somebody —a friend of yours—who's morally responsible for Jack's safety.'

"No. Joey didn't see it that way. This was between him and Jack. Had nothing to do with me. And now I was getting frightened because I could see he was dead serious. 'Forget Jack,' I said. 'He should never have gone to you. It was stupid. If he promised Jeffie a job anytime she wanted it, that was stupid, too. *He* swears he didn't, *she* swears he did, but consider the facts. Joey, this guy works for a living. It's not *his* company. *He's* not the boss. *He* can't take her in whenever he feels like it—he doesn't have the power. He's a working man with kids to support.'

"No. If Jack wanted to play big shot, that was *his* problem. If he'd made a promise he couldn't keep, all the more reason why he should take his lumps. If I wanted to involve myself, that was up to me. As far as Joey was concerned, it was a matter of honor—and I could tell from the way he was talking that he thought he was doing me a favor even by discussing it. I was desperate at this point. 'Joey, how *dare* you walk into my world like this?' I said. 'So *what* if she was told she couldn't have a job? Worse things than that have happened to me. In my world, all you can do is beat your head against the wall, tell them off or walk away. That's all I have in my power. That's all *she* has in *her* power if she wants to work in *my* world. So how dare you use these tactics? Would I break the rules in *your* world?'

"I could see that wasn't doing much good either, but thinking in terms of *his* world had given me an idea. 'Okay, Joey,' I thought. 'You walk into my world, I'll walk into yours.' I would try to convince him that he owed *me* a favor. 'Listen,' I said. 'When I got Jeffie a job with my company, it was just something I wanted to do. I didn't think of it as doing her a favor or doing you a favor. But now, after listening to you, after hearing you explain how Jack is obligated because he asked you to do something for him, even though he changed his mind, you've convinced me. You owe me something. In your terms—by your own admission—I did you a favor by getting Jeffie a job. So now you owe me a favor in return.' 'Don't ask me that,' he said, but I knew that I'd gotten to him. 'But I *am* asking you,' I said. 'I'm asking you to leave Jack alone—as a favor to me.' That was the turning point. He went on arguing, of course, but I just hung in there, sticking to that one point, and in the end he said, well, maybe he *did* owe me something. He'd have to think about it. And with that I left, limp with exhaustion, after the worst seven hours of my life. Next day, Jeffie called to say it was okay. It was all over."

With anyone else, it might have been all over with their friendship, too, but Ruth understood what Jeffie had been going through, and her anger soon subsided. Though she stayed away from Fourteenth Street after that, she kept in touch with Jeffie by phone and did her best to persuade her to leave, both for her own and for Joie's sake. At the end of January, Jeffie arrived at Ruth's apartment with Joie one evening and announced she had left him. A few hours later, she took Marjorie back with her to Fourteenth Street to collect a few things, and the following morning, she and Joie flew out to California.

With Jeffie's departure, Ruth did not expect to hear from Joey again. They had exchanged hardly a word since their marathon debate before Christmas, and as the weeks went by, she was reminded of him only by what she read in *Women's Wear Daily* about his new career as a socialite. Then, without warning, about a month later, he turned up at Ruth's apartment one night, alone and unannounced, with a portrait he had painted of Wilhelm Reich under his arm. "He couldn't stay long, he said. He was on his way over to a literary agent's house. 'Brilliant dame,' he said. 'Brilliant. I'm taking her this picture as a present. Do you mind if I call her?' 'No, go right ahead,' I said. He got on the phone, and went through a whole seductive routine in his sexiest voice. 'Don't go away, sweetie—I'll be right over.' Obviously for my benefit. I was supposed to call Jeffie as soon as he left and make her jealous.

"He told me he was meeting some fabulous people. 'I'm finished with President Street,' he said. 'I'm never going to go back there again. It's a new life. It's a whole new world.' So I said it was a pity he hadn't thought of that a year ago. It was what Jeffie had always wanted. 'Your girlfriend's no good,' he said. 'She left me, and I'm divorcing her.' I was surprised to hear that, and even more when he said he was planning to marry Sina, this girl he'd met at the dentist's office—although I knew from Jeffie he'd been seeing her. Then he left, very up and manic, and that, I figured, was that. He'd stopped by to tell me the end of the story. But the next night, he came back —and this time he was depressed, and half drunk. It was Jeffie. She was to blame for everything.

" 'She's always let me down,' he said. 'She has everybody convinced that it's my fault, Ruth, but it's not true. It's not my fault alone. Think back on the times now. Whenever I need her, she disappears. Remember when she went to Fire Island? I was in terrible trouble then. When I'm in prison, she's off dancing instead of coming up to see me. She divorces me when I need her and goes off to England. Whenever I'm in trouble, Jeffie packs herself up and leaves. I'm in trouble now, and she's done it again.' When I tried to defend her by saying she hadn't blacked her own eyes or beaten herself up, he said. 'Ruth—listen to me. Your girlfriend's not what you think she is.' By now he's completely drunk, and I'm wondering what to do. Altogether it's a charming evening and I'm glad to see the back of him. Having got it off his chest, maybe Joey will now leave me alone.

"He did. For twenty-four hours. Back he came for the third night in a row. I didn't even look to see who was there; I just opened the door and said, 'Come in, Joey.' He was tortured with indecision. He had this possibility, or thought he did, of a whole new life as a writer, with a new wife and a new daughter—but he loved Jeffie. It was as simple as that. They'd been killing each other by degrees, but without her he was dying anyway. 'She's no goddamn good, Ruth,' he said. 'I'm not a bad guy. If I had a woman who stuck by me, I'd look after her—a woman like you. *You'd* stick by me. But *her!* Jesus Christ. As soon as there's trouble, she's gone. So what can I do? I got to divorce her. I've got this woman who can be good to me. I'm going to marry her. I'm going to make a new life for myself. She's not Jeffie. There'll never be another Jeffie, but I got to do it.'

"He was terribly torn and confused. It crossed my mind that he wanted me to urge him to give it one last try with her. He was waiting for me to suggest it, and maybe even sound her out for him, so that he wouldn't appear to be making the first move. I could almost feel him willing me to say it, so I did. I asked him if he wanted Jeffie to come back. 'I don't know, Ruth,' he said, playing it cool. 'I don't know if I can make it with her. Call her.' 'Don't ask *me* to call her,' I said. 'There's the phone. Use it.' 'You dial,' he said.

"So I dialed her number in Los Angeles, and she was home. 'Joey's here,' I said. 'For the third night running. He wants to talk to you. I think he probably wants you to come home. He feels you ran out of reach—that you knew he couldn't come after you to California because of his parole.' And immediately she began to scream, 'You're damn right I ran out of reach,' so I asked her if that meant she wasn't interested in coming back. That slowed her down a little. 'Well, does he really want me?' she said. 'You'd better ask *him* that,' I said, and gave him the phone.

"Then they had a long argument, and, as usual, they ended up yelling at each other. 'Goddamnit, Jeffie,' he said, 'you're always leaving me. You shouldn't have gone like that. You knew I couldn't come after you'—telling her all the things he'd been saying to me for the past three nights. Then it would be her turn to yell back at him, and at one point he put his hand over the mouthpiece and said, 'I'm sorry it had to be *your* phone, Ruth.' Finally, he said, 'Yes, I *do* want you to come back. Come back tomorrow,' and he handed me the phone again.

" 'Do you think he means it?' she said. 'I don't know,' I said. 'Well, if you can get the money from him for my fare, we'll *both* know he means it.' So I told Joey she didn't have the money to get back, and he could either give it to me or make out a check and I'd wire it to her. No, he couldn't do that. He didn't have enough on him and he hadn't brought his checkbook. I should call him in the morning. He gave me a number, and that's how we left it."

When Ruth telephoned next day as arranged, the number turned out to be Sina's. Joey was there, but sounded embarrassed. He said he couldn't speak to her then, but promised to call right back. While she was waiting, Jeffie rang through from Los Angeles, and when Ruth told her what had happened, she said she had pretty well decided not to return in any case. Some hours later, Joey called to say he'd been thinking things over and had decided it would be best to leave things as they were, although he left Ruth with the impression that he simply couldn't raise the money. He thanked her for her trouble, and wanted to know if there was anything he could do for her.

Ruth told him there wasn't, and never saw or spoke to him again.

19

The Colombo War

Even the FBI had awaited Joey's homecoming with the liveliest anticipation. The day after he returned to Brooklyn, the New York *Post,* welcoming back its once most prolific source of gangland copy, reported that "Federal authorities have expressed the fear that Gallo's release may touch off renewed underworld violence."

The Colombo family shared their alarm, although its boss was then too busy picketing the FBI's office at Sixty-ninth Street and Third Avenue with his Italian-American Civil Rights League to confide in the newspapers. Joey had never made a secret of his distaste for the Versailles-type treaty that Larry had accepted from Colombo in the winter of 1963–64, letting it be known from Attica, as Hitler had from Munich, that he refused to be bound by its terms. With Larry dead and the old troublemaker on the loose again, it took no great powers of imagination to foresee a new trial of strength.

And yet the general air of expectancy probably contributed as much to the reopening of hostilities as any deliberate intention on Joey's part. The evidence suggests that, upon his release, he had nothing much more demanding in mind than to rest awhile and catch up with life after nine embattled years. Exhaustion alone would not have kept him quiet for long, of course, but he was also out of tune with the old days. The letter he drafted to the Commissioner offering to help with young offenders was apparently sincere, as was his expressed determination to write about his prison experiences. Left to himself, he might well have taken time out to experiment with these possibilities, and the early rapture of his followers could hardly have survived the realization that they were not the sole, or even his first, concern. But he was not for a moment left to himself. The guys on President Street never doubted that he had returned to show them the way. When Jeffie pleaded with them to give him a break, to let him relax and unwind, they told her they couldn't. They had waited too long, and invested too much. There were too many mouths to feed. They needed him, and Joey couldn't deny them.

He couldn't deny his enemies either. He was no sooner home than Joe Colombo and Joe Yacovelli sent word for him "to come to a meet," offering $1,000 as an inducement to keep the peace. Provoked by this insulting offer, as they must have known he would be, Joey replied that he would accept $100,000 as an inducement to negotiate —a rhetorical flourish that was at once taken as a declaration of war, as he must have known it would be. With the Parole Board, the New York Police Department and the FBI also breathing down his neck, the pressures were more than his pride could bear. Since everybody expected an underworld spectacular, Joey was not the man to disappoint his public. On June 28, Joe Colombo was shot down in Columbus Circle.

What hand, if any, Joey had in this has not been established and probably never will be. In public, he, of course, denied all responsibility for it, and if he said anything else in private, we are not likely to hear about it. But, as he suggested to Ruth Browne, the obvious beneficiaries of the shooting were himself, J. Edgar Hoover and the other New York families, each of which stood to gain from ending

Colombo's deliberate provocation of the FBI before it brought down unwanted heat on everybody. If Joey *didn't* do it, and if the black gunman Jerome Johnson, who actually fired the shots, was *not* a stray psychopath, then somebody probably *was* out to frame him, for they would not otherwise have had a reason to stage the execution attempt in such a flamboyantly Galloesque manner. Colombo was accessible. He could have been disposed of more discreetly. But with the blame pointing at Joey, all the other beneficiaries gained a double advantage. They were not only rid of one substantial nuisance in Colombo, but his vengeful followers would now quite likely rid them of another in Joey Gallo. Not for the first time, organized crime and organized law enforcement had similar aims where he was concerned.

On the other hand, whether Joey planned it or not, the botched assassination did clear the way for him to make a second bid to enlarge his territory. With Colombo out of action, and Joey's old enemy Carmine Persico having just arrived in Atlanta Federal Penitentiary to begin a fourteen-and-one-half-year sentence for hijacking that had hung fire through appeals and delays since 1960, there was no one left of sufficient stature to hold the family together. If Joey was to lead his people into the promised land, it had always been clear that he would first have to split up the larger force opposing him—that he would have to get rid of Colombo. And since Colombo's men were certain to hold him responsible anyway, it hardly mattered if he was discreet or not. Indeed, if he *did* plan the shooting, there was an argument for staging it in just the way that it happened. With everything pointing at him so obviously, people might say that not even Crazy Joe Gallo would be crazy enough for a stunt like that —which is, in fact, exactly what several newspaper accounts *did* suggest at the time, and what some law-enforcement officers still believe to this day.

The only positive link between Joey and the murder attempt was the presence at Colombo's side that morning of Gennaro Ciprio, a thirty-one-year-old restaurant owner and a trusted Colombo bodyguard. After the shots were fired, Ciprio charged into the frightened crowd, lashing out at every black man he could reach until he was eventually subdued by the police. No evidence was ever produced to connect him with the killing of Johnson, who was gunned down so swiftly after he had fired three times at Colombo's head that the volleys seemed to overlap, but Ciprio was certainly in the right place at the right time. He might also have had a motive for killing Johnson besides the obvious one, for, as it turned out, he was working under cover for Joey Gallo. Ten months later, when Colombo's men discovered this, they killed him outside his restaurant on Eighty-sixth Street, Brooklyn, on the day of Joey's funeral.

Apart from that, there is nothing to connect Joey directly with the events in Columbus Circle on June 28. Some play was made with the fact that Johnson was black, which reminded the press that Joey in prison had often identified himself with black causes, and it was widely reported that he had been recruiting black gunmen for his gang. But only the *Daily News* seemed aware that Joey had forfeited the goodwill of the black underworld by his actions during the Auburn riot, and the Pizza Squad detectives watching the comings and goings on President Street could certainly have confirmed that no black man had ever been seen with the guys on the block. Detective James O'Brien and his colleagues had been instructed to check on these rumors thoroughly, since they might have foreshadowed a dangerous shift in the balance of power. "The word had come down that Joey was lining these black guys up as they got ready for parole and we were to watch for them, but there was absolutely nothing to it. In the old days, the Gallos had a bookie joint on Vanderbilt Avenue that was run by colored guys, but we saw nothing like that after Joey got out of prison."

Detective O'Brien also happened to be on President Street when Colombo was shot, and although there was "a lot of back and forth and whispering" after the news came through, the surprise seemed to him, as an experienced Gallo-watcher, genuine. "My opinion is that I don't think Joey was responsible for the shooting—I don't buy that. I didn't see him there that day, but I could tell from the reaction of the guys. They weren't expecting it. I think they figured right away that they were going to be blamed for it anyway, so they'd better regroup, but I don't think they knew it was going to happen ahead of time. Not that Joey seemed worried. A couple of weeks later, he's making jokes. He was telling everybody—and he got a big kick out of this—that he heard Joe Colombo had come out of his coma and asked for some food and drink. When he opened his eyes, there's this bottle by his bed labeled Gallo wine, and he goes right back into a coma again. Joey thought that was just the funniest thing. He got a big boot out of that, and told the story two or three times in *my* hearing."

Amid a storm of speculation about a new gang war, Joey pushed ahead with his program of expansion as quietly as the newspapers and Parole Board would allow. In July, the Waterfront Commission reported that he had successfully displaced Colombo's men from most of the South Brooklyn waterfront, and he was also said to be moving in on Colombo's gambling and vending-machine interests in Bedford-Stuyvesant. By doing so he was also forcing a quick resolution of his opponents' leadership crisis. With Colombo out of the picture with irreparable brain damage, the influence of Carmine Persico, as leader in absentia of the most powerful faction in the family, was clearly decisive. Since it was equally obvious, however, that he could not fight a war in Brooklyn from a cell in Atlanta, not even with his brother Alphonse (Alley Boy) Persico acting as proxy, and as most of his business interests were in Manhattan anyway and not immediately threatened, he acquiesced in the promotion of Vincent Aloi, whose claims were supported by Joe Yacovelli, as acting head of the family. These two then proceeded to plot their counterattack against Joey's forces from a hideout they rented at 101 Gedney Street, Nyack, New York.

Remembering Joey's fondness for the Luna Restaurant on Mulberry Street, Aloi was said by informer Joseph Luparelli to have ordered a permanent stakeout there by a hit squad headquartered in an apartment chosen for this purpose on Baxter Street. Two men were to keep watch on the restaurant, and if Joey showed up, "they would go in and kill him, no matter who was there." But Joey never did show up—he was not ready to die just then—and, according to Luparelli, after several months of fruitless vigil, they put out an "open contract" on his life, which meant that "anybody in the

Colombo family who had the opportunity to kill him without getting caught had the right to do it."

These conditions were not satisfied until Joey himself finally decided they should be—on the night of his forty-third birthday. Besides his own very adequate security arrangements, he also enjoyed police protection—so much so, indeed, that the New York *Post* complained in August that it was costing the taxpayers $20,000 a week to keep him alive. The Police Department naturally refused to confirm or deny this figure, but Deputy Commissioner Robert Daley did admit that "we're all over him at all locations." The reason for this, he said, was not so much Joey's safety as averting another gang war. "We're trying to keep confrontation and violence in a state of arrest," he added in a suitably policemanlike turn of phrase.

The salaries of Detectives O'Brien and John O'Flaherty were included in the *Post*'s estimate. Like the other members of their squad, they had viewed Joey's return with the gravest suspicion, for Brooklyn had been relatively quiet for years. In his absence, the Gallos had attracted little attention once the Profaci war was over, and then only in the worthiest of contexts. In 1966, for instance, they were twice called out by the city's Youth Board director to cool racial tensions between black and Italian teenagers in East New York—an effective, if unorthodox, ploy which the Brooklyn District Attorney, Aaron E. Koota, roundly condemned as "a deplorable abdication of official responsibilities." But in Joey, Detective O'Flaherty detected an immediate ambition to settle old scores.

"You got to remember how well that peace was going. When Larry died, everybody came to the funeral, including Joe Colombo. It was held in Prospero's Funeral Home, and, supposedly, Colombo's the man that owns it. There was a real good peace, and as far as we could see, everybody was living well. Now Joey comes out, and nobody's going to tell *him* it's settled. His brother Al was for live and let live, but Joey was always a thorn in everybody's side. He'd break up a High Mass if he felt like it. Inside of a week, that guy could destroy everything that had been done over a couple of years—just by going here and going there and saying things. People were afraid of him.

"But Joey didn't *start* the trouble with Colombo. That was there when he got out. When Colombo started the Italian-American Civil Rights League, the guys down there were right behind him. They went around recruiting members and collecting money for it. Then there came a time when they began to think, 'Well, this money coming in isn't being used the way it was meant to be used. We're just promoting one guy's issue here, and he's bringing down a lot of extra heat on us. Who needs it?' And that's where the trouble started. Joey came out to that, and he found most of the guys were ready for him."

Unconfirmed reports had it that there were at least five clashes between Gallo and Colombo supporters in the weeks preceding the League's second Unity Day rally, including an incident on May 22 involving Colombo himself. In what was variously described as harassment, an attempted assault and a thwarted kidnaping, he and his bodyguards brawled inconclusively with a group of "house painters" on a street corner in Bensonhurst. On another occasion, Rocco Miraglia, Colombo's most trusted bodyguard, was personally intercepted by Joey while distributing Unity Day posters on Gallo territory. All accounts agree that Joey ran him off, but some also say that he threw Miraglia out of a second-story window and his ripped-up posters after him. What is certain is that Joey and his men toured most of South Brooklyn warning storekeepers and bar owners to stay open on the day of the rally lest they incur his severe displeasure.

But the iron fist still had a velvet touch. Despite his preoccupation with the problems of building an empire while appearing to meet his parole conditions, Joey never neglected the true source of his power —the affection in which he was held by the people who lived on his territory and enjoyed his protection. He ordered a whole series of neighborhood improvements, of which the most notable were a covered barbecue-picnic area with tables and chairs, and a sizable swimming pool on a vacant lot opposite Gallo headquarters on President Street. "Yeah, we made a gazebo for the kids on the block with a Hawaiian motif," said one of the boys proudly—an amenity which not only proved extremely popular, but also provided Detective

O'Flaherty and his watching colleagues with a certain amount of light relief.

"This wasn't just for the Italians. It was for everybody in the neighborhood, which has gotten predominantly Puerto Rican with a touch of some black through there. It was this kind of thing that makes these guys seem like Robin Hood. They cleared the lot, poured concrete on it, set up this pool, which is a good size—twenty feet or more across—and then serviced it all summer, along with the barbecue right next to it. It was comical sometimes, watching them mix cement in their hundred-dollar shoes. But they have something going with these people. That Thanksgiving, though I don't think their finances were too great, I know they bought a load of turkeys and distributed them through the neighborhood."

There was certainly not much else to report at the end of 1971. Once the hubbub died down after the Colombo affair, Joey's drive to enlarge his territory petered out in stalemate. It had not been a shooting war—in spite of at least one abortive attempt on his life—so much as a pushing and shoving match. Nervous about his parole, since to be caught out in even a minor violation could mean another five years in prison, Joey found himself with very little room for maneuver. Too many people were watching, including Detective O'Brien.

"Ten years before, when he went inside, Brooklyn was wide open compared with what he found when he got out. Now it wasn't just *us* he had to contend with—and *we'd* made life pretty difficult for them even in the old days. Now there were other agencies from within the Police Department on the job as well, like the Organized Crime Section, and the FBI was also very active. We had a fairly free exchange of information between us, so Joey and the guys had to be very careful. They never knew who the hell was looking at them, which is the only way you can beat these people or stay on top of them. Being here, there and everywhere, they're going to think twice before they pull anything. They know that there's law around some-where. Driving around, they're constantly being stopped for license checks and registration checks, and if we find a reason to take them in, then we can search them. They know we're just waiting for them to put a foot out of line so we can lock them up. It's real cat and mouse. They're forced to meet people they don't want us to see in other places—a lot of people are very reluctant to go on the block knowing we're going to see them—and that's got to hurt them financially. Gambling is still their biggest moneymaker, but when we're around, the *gambler* is afraid, and then he goes elsewhere. Of course, when they leave the block and shake their tails, who knows how many trucks they may be hijacking, but with enough harassment, maybe they can be forced into doing something legitimate."

By the winter, Joey didn't need much forcing. Partly because the pickings were poor, but as much from boredom and disillusion with the old life, Joey was already thinking of something legitimate. Just before Christmas, he had several meetings with his present biographer, first to discuss the possibility of collaborating on a book about his prison experiences, and then to rough out its general outline. But that was as far as he could take it, he said. There was too much on his mind just then. He had to get his head straight before settling down to work. The book would have to wait until he'd taken care of a few little domestic and business problems, and also until he'd finished with the dentist. Three months later, he signed a collaboration agreement with Marta and Jerry Orbach which, he said—with more feeling than accuracy—had nothing to do with the serious work he had in mind. A month after that, all his literary ambitions were blown away by three .32 caliber bullets.

They had also been doomed from the start, for Joey was broke. Though he gave up the apartment after Jeffie left with Joie for California, he still had to send her money to live on. On top of that, the divorce was expensive—he sent one of the boys out to Los Angeles with the papers—and there was several thousand dollars' worth of dental work to pay for. Worse still, as he saw more and more of the Orbachs and less and less of President Street, his followers grew more and more disgruntled, and Joey, correspondingly, less and less free to command their financial support, even if his pride had allowed him to, which it did not. His expenses were rising, his income falling, and as yet there was nothing to show for the literary life. It was not until after his death that a contract was signed with Viking Press, to advance $40,000 in three installments for a sixty-thousand-word memoir by Marta Orbach on her two-month association with Joey, the money to be split fifty-fifty with his estate.

Disillusioned again, this time fatally, Joey turned once more to Brooklyn in the last few weeks of his life. At once, rumors began to fly about a new attack on Colombo interests, and even about his alleged complicity in a bakeshop burglary. On June 4, 1972, quoting anonymous investigators who had been "extremely close to the case," Fred J. Cook wrote in the *New York Times Magazine*:

> Three weeks prior to Joe Gallo's getting killed, he, Frank (Punchy) Illiano and John (Mooney) Cutrone went out to the San Susan night-club in Mineola, L.I., in which John Franzese [another powerful capo in the Colombo family]* is reported to have a hidden interest. Joey is reported to have grabbed the manager and said, "This joint is mine. Get out." In other words, he was cutting himself in.
>
> This was the first sign we had that Crazy Joe was acting up again. Then we come to Easter week, and a lot of things began to happen. On Easter Sunday night or sometime into Monday morning, there was a safecracking at Ferrara Pastry Shop on Grand Street in Little Italy. It was reported that the safecrackers got $55,000. Now Ferrara's is a legitimate business, but Vinnie Aloi is always hanging out around there. It's reported that he does a lot of his shylocking in the immediate neighborhood.

This, according to Mr. Cook's informed sources, was the final straw. Their theory was that Aloi knew the job had been pulled by Gennaro Ciprio and one Richard R. Grossman on instructions from Joey Gallo, who thereby traded his birthright for a mess of cannoli.

On Tuesday, April 4, Aloi called an emergency meeting at Carmine Persico's farm in Saugerties, New York, and next day, Alphonse Persico flew out with his bodyguard, Jerry Langella, to confer with his brother in Atlanta. On Thursday, Gennaro Ciprio was seen on President Street, talking to Joey, and in the early hours of Friday morning, April 7, Joey was shot down in Umberto's. Twenty-

---

*Franzese had just begun to serve a fifty-year term for bank robbery.

four hours later, the police found Grossman's body in the trunk of a car abandoned in the Sheepshead Bay section of Brooklyn, and on April 10, the day of Joey's funeral, Ciprio got his from a rooftop sniper, thus neatly rounding off the pattern of revenge, and, apparently, proving to the satisfaction of Mr. Cook's informants that while the attempted assassination of a gang boss is an acceptable act of war, to tamper with his pastry supplies is deemed to be dirty pool.

As an alternative explanation for Joey's murder, this theory commended itself as little to Detective O'Brien as it did to the boys on President Street, although the sequence of events is not in dispute. "The Ferrara bakeshop burglary? That's a joke down there. They laugh about that. But nobody was laughing the day Joey got shot. We saw them watching the TV while the news was on and going through the Crazy Joe career. When the newscasters started speculating about who did it, whether it was Joe Colombo's retaliation or because Joey was moving in on this or that, there wasn't one change of expression on any one of their faces. They would never let you know what they were thinking. One of the guys said, 'Bullshit,' at something he heard while they were watching there, and Al Gallo stared him right into the ground.

"You'd think they would have shown some emotion, but nothing. It was like they were looking in a mirror. No other group behaves the way they do. They got great control like that. When I talked to Al that day about his brother's death, he said, 'Well that's the way it is. That's the way he lived. But not in front of the family.' That was the only thing that had him upset. The fact that Joey got hit— well, that's the game. But don't kill in front of the family. That was a bad one. We know for sure there was irritation between the brothers. The guys didn't want Joey messing around with those other people over there. I think they felt he wasn't minding the store. But how far or how deep that irritation went, we have no idea."

On Joey's forty-third birthday, there was little sign of it. He arrived on President Street like a king returning to court, confident of his welcome. As his car stopped outside the social club at No. 74, a kid ran up to open the door. Joey stepped out, smiling and nodding, and slipped him a dollar.

The kid stood his ground. "So what about my brother?" he said boldly, jerking his head at the slightly older boy standing at his elbow.

Joey gazed at him without surprise. "Get lost," he said pleasantly, and started across the sidewalk.

"Fuck you," said the kid, and at once staggered back from a slap on the cheek. Curious now, Joey waited to see his reaction. "Don't get smart with me," he said, prompting him almost.

Uncowed, but unsure of himself, the kid glared back for a moment, then glanced sideways at his brother and hung his head. Joey laughed. He ruffled the kid's hair and fished another dollar from his pocket.

"Go ahead," he said. "Take it"—and went inside, smiling again.

20

Jeffie

Jeffie never had enough patience to keep a diary, but she did occasionally record her thoughts in an engagement book she used while working for Frank Balon. On January 31, 1971, she wrote: "Life returns to my body. It is hard to wait." February 3: "Called Ted. He's happy for us. He will help." (The help required was a quick divorce. Ironically, Jeffie had thus far refused all Ted Allan's entreaties that she should release him from their ruined marriage, deriving a perverse pleasure from "punishing" him in this way.) February 18: "Signed divorce papers. Final June, hopefully." Then the great day. March 10: "We begin." And exactly one week later, March 17: "It ends."

In her wretched disappointment, Jeffie wrote that as a grim joke; she didn't really believe it, although she had read the signs correctly. As far as the life she had dreamed of was concerned, she and Joey had as much chance of pulling it off as a pair of wildcats tied together by their tails. Besieged by his family and followers, he saw at once the futility of any hopes he might have entertained of following a different course. And so did Jeffie, although she forced the thought from her mind.

Jean Lerner saw it, too. She drove out to see him with Al Lettieri and two bottles of Dom Perignon on Joey's second day home. "Al called me because he was in town to do some work on *The Godfather,* so we went together, and there he was in the middle of this celebration, this block party. He'd changed a lot. He was smaller. Shriveled. He couldn't talk much with all those people around, but I'd gone there certain in my mind that he had no idea of ever going back to the rackets. He was home free. He'd paid his dues. I said, 'You must write a book while it's fresh in your mind.' 'Sure, sure,' he said, smiling and nodding at everybody like he hardly heard me. So then I began to wonder, but I went on insisting he had to write this book, based on his letters, on his ideas of art, his philosophy, his social ideas, prison reform. He had to write a book having nothing to do with crime. 'Yeah,' he said. 'Yeah. I'll do it, I'll do it'—humoring me. He was gaunt with fatigue. Then I had to make way for some more of his subjects, and that was the last time I saw him."

Joyce never saw him at all, but he called her in San Francisco. "When I answered the phone, he didn't say, 'Hello.' He said, 'Is this the singer that used to sing the truth to me, a long time ago? Can you still do it?' Then it dawned on me it was Joey. He sounded like he had been in Bermuda for nine years. We wanted to see each other, and he said, 'Why don't you come to New York?' I said I couldn't right then, so why didn't he come to us instead? I knew he and Jeffie had to get away, just as I knew it that evening before the trial. I knew in my bones they'd never make it in Brooklyn, not with all that pressure from the family and the boys. But all he said was 'Listen, I've got a feeling we're going to see each other. Soon. It'll all be good, you'll see. Everything's going to work out the way it has to.' And I guess it did at that."

The pressure was, indeed, acute. Despite their many kindnesses, Jeffie never had any illusions about the family's underlying attitude toward her—she was "the stranger." And now she was competing for Joey's time and attention under Momma's own roof, their feelings toward her hardened. "Everybody had led this rigid life and kept themselves in check. They'd followed the rules, like good Italians, so who deserved him? How come *I* wind up with their king? How come I can *divorce* him yet, get married to somebody else, and *still* he takes me back? There *had* to be resentment. Logically, understandably and rightly so. Had I been in their position, I would have felt it, too. I understood, and never really took offense. They used to say, 'You can't insult her,' and they couldn't. They were very good to him. They loved him. I used to say to him, 'Thank God for your sisters and your brother and your mother, because if it was left to me you'd starve to death before I'd start with the baccala out of season. I'm incompetent.' Years went by, and they serviced his every need. As someone who loved him, I was only grateful for this.

"The second night, all the young guys came in. I'd never seen them before. They were funny and cute, all dressed up and doing godfather numbers. Joey knew them when they were kids on the street of fourteen or fifteen. Now he's home and, oh God, they don't know what to do. They're in awe. The magic man is back. And nobody knows how to explain me. One of the older guys comes up to me and says, 'See, if you hadn't have divorced him—I don't even know how to introduce you.' I didn't have a name. I'm Jeffie, Joey's er-um-ah-hmm. I said, 'I know. I did a terrible thing. What can I tell you?' I had to apologize constantly, just to shut them up. Anything they'd say to me, I'd say, 'I know, I know—I'm so *lucky*. It must be because of the baby.' Anything so long as they didn't think that Joey *loved* me, because that would have upset them terribly. But the young guys were great. I used to walk through the house throwing lines about Joey, and they'd die, trying not to laugh. I had such fondness for some of those boys. I still do.

"Joey was hell on wheels when he came home. Three weeks he was up, and his mother had had it by then. She was cooking around the clock for hundreds of people. I was lucky. After the second week, I went back to work—but she was still in the kitchen, muttering under her breath. I really felt bad for her. I'd say to him, 'Listen, baby, why don't you cool it? She's an old lady. She's tired.' 'Oh, she loves it.' 'She loves it, my ass. She doesn't love it so much. She's cooked for you guys all your lives. As much as she loves you, she's tired. Give her a break.' No, no, I didn't understand. This was what she liked to do. Meanwhile, he's turning the house upside down and driving her crazy. Momma was notoriously skimpy with hot water, so he has a boiler installed in the basement big enough for an apartment house. And because the blacks were now out to get him for what he did in the Auburn riot, the house has got to be made secure, with new fences, locks, bolts, bars—and nothing is getting done fast enough to please him.

"To start with, he had had a new scheme every day about who he was going to be, but mostly he was going to write, relax, take it easy and be cool. 'You and the kid, you and the kid'—he doesn't need anything but his wife and child. Great. Joey, Blast and I, *we* would decide his future, the three of us. Nothing was going to happen unless it was approved by all. Fine. That lasted a fat two weeks. By then he was going around saying, 'Jesus, I have to do everything myself,' and Blast and I were off the list. It was all over. He was back in it again. He couldn't go to President Street because of his parole, so all the guys would come up to the house. I can't say for sure what he was doing because I used to leave at six in the morning and get home exhausted at eight in the evening. All I know is I wanted him with me when I was home, and we fought about that every night. 'I'm available from eight till midnight,' I said. 'Isn't there any way of talking to these people some other time?' No, there wasn't. He always managed to be very busy until about two in the morning. Then I would have to wake up."

That was just the beginning. Tied down by a parole officer who was clearly determined to enforce the conditions of his release to the letter, Joey decided to exchange him for someone more amenable by moving to Manhattan. To Jeffie's other duties he accordingly added the job of finding an apartment and furnishing it in her lunch hours.

The first part was easy. She found one with two bedrooms on the eighth floor of a West Fourteenth Street apartment house. Fixing it up took longer, however, and while she was collecting tickets for double-parking outside furniture stores, Joey continued his campaign to wring concessions from the Parole Board. A standard provision was that he could not associate with anyone who had a criminal record. Strictly observed, this meant that only two or three of his least experienced men were eligible to act as his bodyguard or, indeed, be seen in his company. Trading on his Auburn exploits, therefore, Joey argued that this condition endangered his life. The "schwartzes" were out to get him as a result of his meritorious services, and he needed his men for protection. If he could pick the right guys to look out for him, he could save the taxpayers a lot of money.

Evidently the Parole Board found this reasoning persuasive, because after he moved to Manhattan, there were no apparent restrictions on his freedom of association, nor on his movements to and from President Street. But he continued to report regularly, and, to fulfill another condition, took a job as a salesman with a Brooklyn manufacturer of ornate, reproduction furniture. His duties were undemanding, however, and became nominal after the shooting of real-estate salesman Joe Colombo on June 28.

Joey and Jeffie had then been married almost three weeks. Not only had his family again stayed away from the ceremony; there were no wedding presents. "I used to get very annoyed about that. Everybody else had big envelope parties, and collected lots of money. But me—I'd been married, divorced, married again, had a kid, and no one ever gave me an envelope party. They didn't even give me any help with the move. The only time they came to the house was to bring food. They thought I was starving him, and I *was*. They would run out to the stores, buy food, bring it back and get busy in the kitchen, mumbling under their breath. And I would say, 'Good, good. Cook more. Cook enough for a week.' "

There was no honeymoon, although Joey had asked his new parole officer for permission to spend a few days on Fire Island. This was granted, but at the last moment, he changed his mind. He was too busy—too busy even to inform the Parole Board that he wasn't going after all. His sister Jacqueline, who was already out there, told Jeffie later that on the day they were due to arrive, it looked as though the

Marines had landed. There were more cops than vacationers in Seaview; helicopters shuttled back and forth along the beaches, and even the Coast Guard had turned out to patrol the waters offshore.

Meanwhile, back on Fourteenth Street, Joey and Jeffie were settling into a pattern of domestic guerrilla warfare. The essential difference between life now and life as it had been before Joey went to prison was that then they had always managed to resolve their difficulties in bed, but now they simply put them on and off with their clothes. "He'd obviously taken over from his brother, but it seemed such a bore and a waste of time. We fought about that a lot. I wanted to know what the hell he wanted—of himself. I'd lived through years of this cops-and-robbers routine. None of it was new to me or particularly interesting. Nobody was bothering us much—not until after the Colombo shooting anyway. He would do his wary, alert numbers on the street, but we quite often went out alone and walked uptown to the movies. Now and again we'd be tailed, very noticeably, by a bunch of cops in a white car, but they didn't seem especially diligent. And Joey didn't seem especially nervous. He used to look out of the window a lot, watching the street, and I would say, 'Listen, I don't want to upset you, but I don't think anybody's following you today.' So when Colombo got shot, I thought, 'Well, that's nice if it's what everybody wants,' but the thing that bugged *me* about it was that the maid quit.

"I was at work when it happened, but Joie got home from school around three, and was doing her homework when the cops came by to pick Joey up for questioning. He was out, so she asked them if they'd care to wait, sat them down in the living room, made them coffee, and generally had a nice time playing hostess. Meanwhile, the maid is flipping out in the kitchen. She left that night and never came back. By the time I got home, Joey was there, we were all over the newspapers, and now everybody at work was going to know who I was. He didn't seem alarmed or unusually concerned about the shooting—nothing made Joey nervous, except me—but all my friends were. Whether he was involved in it or not, they figured Colombo's guys were going to think he was. Georgia Brown called me from London as soon as she heard the news. She wanted to know if I'd like to hide out with her until the bullets stopped flying. 'What are you talking about?' I said 'I'm on my honeymoon.'

"By this time, I was coming apart from lack of sleep. Joey's nocturnal habits were finishing me off. If he decided to have company at three in the morning, it would be, 'Jeffie!' 'Wha'? Huh? Wassamatter?' 'Get up and make coffee.' Make coffee. It was my nemesis. The only way I could work all day and cope with that was by taking pills. After three days without sleep, I'd take a Dexie to keep going, and then he'd scream at me for doing it. I kept asking him, 'Are you *sure* you want me to work?' And he kept saying, 'It's absolutely necessary. We got to show income.' So then I'd say, 'Well, if you want me to work, why don't you let me *sleep?*'—but it made no difference. I'd take another Dexie. Then he'd start yelling that the pills were unbalancing my mind, and that's why I was behaving irrationally. 'For Christ's sake,' I told him, 'why do you keep telling me to work and then never let me get my rest? God sent you to torture me? I don't understand. Tell me what you want.' But we never came to terms with our beefs. He was just very angry, and anything served. If he wasn't in the right mood, whatever you did had to be wrong.

"One morning, I got in the car, absolutely manic after another sleepless night, and drove over to see Joey's father. It was very early. I woke him up, and he came to the door with his teeth out. 'Listen, Pop,' I said. 'Give me some money. I want to go buy some records for Joey.' Well, that impressed him like horseshit. After all those years of expenses, the thing he most wanted me to do was go buy Joey records, right? But he pulls out all he's got—almost a hundred bucks or so—and off I go to the record store. I wanted to get him a good cross-section of all the music he'd been missing while he was inside. It was supposed to be a treat.

"Instead of that, he has visions of me dancing away nine years of his life. Our tastes in music were the same, but he wouldn't admit he liked it. I'm playing this stuff only because it reminds me of the nine happy years I spent fucking around while he was away. He got especially mad over a Byrds album called 'Chestnut Mare' that I wanted him to hear. 'Listen to the lyrics,' I said. 'They're so pretty, and so well done.' 'I don't want to hear any fags singing about any fucking horse,' he says—and he's really venomous. 'It's not about a fucking horse,' I said. 'If you'll listen, it's about life.' But he doesn't want to hear about life either, and goes to take a bath. Okay, I love 'Chestnut Mare.' I want him to like it, too, and I figure that now he's in the tub, I've got him where I want him. I'll play it low. Maybe he'll catch a bit of it subliminally and change his mind. So I put it on low. Next thing I know, he jumps out of the bathtub, snatches the record off the machine, stomps out in the hall stark-naked and pitches it down the incinerator."

These spasms of anger often had nothing to do with Jeffie at all. She was a convenient lightning rod for his general frustration. Both of them needed a rest. If they were to stand a chance of weathering their readjustment to one another after so long a separation, Jeffie felt they had to get away together, however briefly, and she had ten days' vacation coming in August. With this in mind George and Laura Lloyd had rented a summer place on Fire Island with a separate guest house. When Joey agreed to go, Jeffie booked a helicopter to fly him from Twenty-ninth Street and Second Avenue to the door-step, and waited out the interval, impatient for sleep and a last chance perhaps to save their marriage. Then, a few days before they were due to leave, Joey casually let it drop that something had come up, and they might not be able to go after all. Jeffie was incensed.

" 'Hey, come on, man,' I said. 'It's my vacation.' No, no, he wasn't sure we could go. Either there was something going on he couldn't leave, or else he simply wasn't going to indulge me. He blew hot and cold, and kept me guessing right up until the night before we were supposed to leave. But I wasn't taking any chances. I didn't care *what* happened. I was going to get my rest on Fire Island. Joie was already out there, and, just to be on the safe side, I'd been sneaking my things out of the house, bit by bit, for a week. So now I'm sitting in my office, debating what to do. It's 8 P.M., and the cleaning ladies are looking at me strangely. If I call home and say, 'Are you coming?' like as not he'll say, 'Sure, I'm all ready. Come home and collect me.' But I have a nasty feeling that as soon as I get in the door, he's going to say, 'I just had a call. We can't make it,' and then I'll be stuck. I *know* him, and I don't want to risk it. So I picked up my bag and left. I didn't call home, and I didn't *go* home.

"I caught the last train to Bay Shore, waited hours for a water taxi, and because it was so late, went to Jacqueline's house instead of George's. Naturally, she's not all that glad to see me at five o'clock in the morning. 'Where's Joey?' she says. 'Fuck Joey,' I said. 'He's home doing whatever he's doing. I don't care. I'm so tired. He's driving me crazy, and I have to rest. He's driving his kid crazy, too. I don't know what to do with him.' Then she said something completely unexpected. It really made me stop to think. She said, 'You know, Jeffie, if you really loved Joie, you never would have gone back to him.' I looked at her. I didn't want to believe it, but Joie was certainly having a rough time."

The next day, enraged by her desertion, Joey took Dottie and Lou hostage until they ran her to earth. When she defied his orders to return, George and Laura spent an unhappy weekend waiting for the gunmen to call, but nothing happened, and they went back to the mainland as usual on Monday morning, leaving Jeffie unrepentant. "Whatever I got, I would get—it was worth it. I figured he wouldn't come out himself because he had his parole to worry about, but I really didn't care. The scales were out of balance. I was too old, too tired, too bored, to take any more of his bullshit. I wanted out. I loved him, but I couldn't stand him. All his shit about loving me was just—shit. That's not how you love somebody. I wanted out, out, out, but I didn't know how or when I'd be able to do it."

Jeffie was not exactly looking forward to going home. She had heard that after his ploy with Dottie had failed to bring her back, Joey had run amok among her friends, and even made a heavy-handed pass at Ruth's daughter Marjorie. Joie was terrified at the thought of what he might do. She was so tense she could hardly speak when her mother left for the city on the following Saturday morning. "I thought it might be smart to phone him first, so I called from Saks Fifth Avenue. 'Where are you?' he said. 'I'm at the office,' I said. 'You want to talk to me? Meet me someplace.' If he was going to kill me, he wouldn't do it in public. I'd have a chance to talk him down. But he didn't even answer. He just hung up. So I took a helicopter right back to Fire Island. George turned white when he saw me, but

I figured I still had a day and a half to come.

"Sunday night, I tried again. I always keep a few spare keys, so I went to Marjorie's apartment and called him from there. 'You'd better get your ass home,' he said, 'or I'm going to come and get you.' I didn't like the way he said it, but I figured I had no choice. I was due back at work next morning. I put on one of Marjorie's miniest mini-skirts, took a cab over and flounced into the apartment, twitching my ass in the air. He was sitting there in the dark. 'Yes?' I said. 'What do you want?' And pow! I got it. Right in the eye.

"He was so fucking mad he was going to kill me. He didn't know what to do. 'I wasn't going to touch you,' he said, 'until you came in with that attitude, but now you're going to get it'—and with that, I threw myself into his arms, crying. When in doubt with Joey, you always had to do that, otherwise you couldn't be sure he'd know when to stop. So I threw myself at him, screaming, 'I love you, I love you. I'm sorry, but I was so tired. I didn't mean to cause you such pain and unhappiness'—and on and on like that until he finally forgave me. We stayed up all night while I cried in his arms, and he carried on about what I'd done to him. 'You'd leave me alone for ten days? How could you do that? You ran out on me without saying a word. I'm alone here and going crazy. Last night, I had a couple of the boys on a boat. I was going to send them out there to get you.' 'I know, baby, I know. I'm sorry, I'm sorry.' "

Jeffie was sorrier still in the morning. Instead of going to work, she had to listen in silence while he called her boss. "Frank? This is Joey. I know you'll understand. I need my wife at home from now on. You know how it is. Okay?" There was nothing she could do about it, but Jeffie grieved for her job. She had finally taken her mother's advice. She had really applied herself in a more demanding situation than any she had known before, and found that she enjoyed making decisions of greater consequence than whether to add a twist of lemon. She also grieved for her Fire Island suntan. She had a Technicolored eye that put her behind dark glasses for a week.

The only consolation was that, following her involuntary retirement, she became a lady of leisure. For three weeks, nothing was asked of her. She was allowed to sleep as late as she liked; she was relieved of all domestic duties, and there were periods, lasting sometimes for two or three days, when she and Joey were as close as they had ever been. He even painted the hallway brown for her, as a surprise, while she and Joie were at a Donny Osmond concert. But neither of them could hold the mood. When they made love, it was like resting between rounds in a fight to the finish. Afterward, Joey would at once revert to what had become his normal suspicious self, and Jeffie, who had previously been able to hold off long enough to cushion the shock of his withdrawal, now found herself matching him blow for blow. Within a month, she was again being kicked out of bed in the middle of the night to make coffee, and was again expected to attend to his every need, from matching his socks to preparing him for the dentist.

"I'd been nagging him to get his teeth fixed. All during prison, they'd wanted to do things—pull them or cap them—and he'd always said no. He was right. I used to say to him, 'Please, Joey, unless it's medically necessary, please don't come home with a mouthful of teeth. If there's anything you don't need, it's lots of sparkling white teeth.' But now there was bone damage, and it turned out there was a dentist who specialized in treating that condition downstairs in our own building. So Joey started going to him three times a week, which didn't improve his temper any because he was in a lot of pain all the time. I wouldn't let him in the door until he'd taken Miltowns, Darvon—whatever I had handy. Then one day he came up and said he'd been talking to the woman who ran the dentist's office. Her name was Sina Essary. She had a cute little girl of Joie's age whose name was Lisa. They also lived in the building, and he'd arranged for the two girls to get together.

"When I met Sina, I liked her right off. We're very different, but we found we had a lot in common. She told me she'd been divorced for ten years, and had raised her child alone. I said I'd done the same, although Joie's father and I had just gotten back together, and if she really wanted to know, I said, I thought she was probably better off. Having a man around the house was not all it was cracked up to be, so she shouldn't feel bad. After comparing notes about men in general, we both decided we hadn't had much luck with them. It was just a casual conversation, but it planted a thought in my mind.

"Joey and I were still obsessed with each other, but neither of us had any use for each other. I was as close to being an adult as I was ever likely to be, and I couldn't take this kind of treatment any more. For four days out of seven, he was an absolute monster, and I didn't know why. When he came in the door, instead of feeling joy, I felt, 'Oh God, here he is. Who has he got with him *this* time?' I was resentful now. I was like him. The moment he switched off, *I* switched off—and with both of us switched off, we're in a lot of trouble.

"I also had a kid in the house to think about. Joie and Joey had been cat and dog from the start. I'd spent nearly ten years trying to raise her on the basis of mutual respect, and here he was being the autocratic father. She would respond every time he said to her, 'Okay, Joie, this is the score, and I want you to do this or that.' She would be a lovely hostess for him. She would make coffee, and cook eggs and bacon for the boys, but it depended on how he approached her. If he was demanding, and ordered her to do it, she would say to him, 'No, Daddy, I'm not your servant.' She was singularly unimpressed by big shot Joe Gallo. Once we were waiting for the elevator in the hall. It was taking even longer than usual for one to come, so Joey was pacing about and muttering. Joie looked at him and said, 'Hm! I wonder if they know who you are.' She did try very hard to understand what he wanted, but her dignity was involved. He would turn on and off with her, as he did with everyone.

"When he was on, he'd be very protective. One day she came home from school and told us about a problem she was having with a much bigger girl in her class. Right away Joey says he'll go down and take care of it. I'm not so sure this is a good idea, but next morning he walks into the office of P.S. 41 and asks to see the principal. Well, they say, there's a teachers' conference going on with the principal and vice principal, but if he'll just sit down and wait a few minutes, they'll see what they can do.

"Now, Joie's with him, which means his reputation's at stake. So after waiting for about thirty seconds, he walks around the desk and straight into the principal's office. 'Excuse me,' he says, holding up his hand as all these people look at him. 'Just a minute. Would you excuse me, please? Are you the principal? How do you do. My name is Joe Gallo. This here is my daughter, Joie Gallo. I've been in prison for nine years, and I'd like to introduce myself. I'll just take a minute of your time, everybody—so if you'll just relax, I won't keep you long. My daughter seems to be having a lot of trouble with a girl named Laura in her class, and I would like them separated. I would like them separated today. Will *you* take care of it, or shall I?'

"I said to Joie afterward, 'Weren't you embarrassed?' She said, 'No. I thought it was funny.' But she didn't think it was so funny when he and I fought, which was now most of the time. At first, it frightened her, but after a while it became part of the daily routine. I explained that I knew it was ugly and unpleasant for her, but I *had* said a year and I still wanted to make it if we could. After that, she figured it was *my* business and sort of let me get on with it. I remember once she came out of her room singing a Carole King tune, and when she found me crying on the couch—he'd just gone out after one of our better scenes—she patted me on the head, said, 'Take a couple of Miltowns, Mommy—you'll feel better in the morning,' and went back inside without missing a note of the song. But it wasn't doing her any good, this endless fighting.

"Luckily, the apartment was well laid out from her point of view. The two bedrooms, each with its own bathroom, were separated by the living room, so she could use her side of the house, including the kitchen, and come and go without ever having to see us. She didn't have to hear us either. If there was trouble brewing, she'd put on her earphones, close the door and get on with her homework. We were three strong egos in the same house, and she understood the problem as well as anyone. Once she sat us down and said, 'Listen, the three of us cannot live together. I can live with you. You can live with Daddy. Daddy and I can live together. But the three of us are never going to make it.'

"Joey was fascinated by her grasp of the situation. She was only nine. He gave her five hundred dollars once, just to make her feel important. He meant it—the money was hers. But later on, when we were broke, she gave us enough to pay the rent, and he loved that.

When he was being human, he loved to observe her character; he was very pleased with it. But when he was doing his dog act, he didn't want to know from character. All he wanted was his own way, and then there'd be trouble, because she was as hard a bargaining agent as he ever came across. When it came to logic, she could always hold her own. At times, I used to say to her, 'Please, Joie, I know he's wrong, but maybe if we indulged him a little bit, it might make things better.' Then she'd try, but it was hard. When Joey was in the house, you didn't get a chance to pee. He couldn't do anything himself. He had to have help even to dial the phone—and if he didn't get it, he could be really malicious and unkind to her.

"When he first got home, he bought her a cat—Marie—and Marie had a relationship with Joey that I wished I could have had. When he was home, she never left his lap. Then their relationship dissolved and it was Joie's cat again—she became very fond of it. And one day Joey was especially mad at Joie about something, and when I got home, I couldn't find Marie anywhere. Joey's in the kitchen washing the dishes, which generally means he's done something; one of the boys is standing there in the living room with red eyes, and I can't find the cat. 'What's the matter with your eyes, Tony?' I said. 'What is it?' Then a terrible thought came to me, and I started screaming. 'He made you do it, didn't he? You killed the cat—I know you killed the cat. Tony, it's not you—*I* understand. He made you throw it down the incinerator, didn't he? That's why your eyes are red. She clawed you.' I'm wailing like a crazy woman, and he just sort of hangs his head. So then I ran into the kitchen to yell at Joey, tears running down my face. 'You made him kill the cat, you bastard son of a bitch. Why did you kill the kid's cat? What are you trying to do to her? You know how she cares for it. What did you want to kill her cat for?' But Joey doesn't say a word either; he just gets on with the dishes. P.S. Five minutes later, I find the cat sleeping in the closet. Tony's eyes were red from an allergy."

Jeffie's worst fears were not always turned against her quite so comically. Her anxieties about Joie were real enough, and not a bit diminished when Joie showed her the lyric of a song she had written, as much from her mother's standpoint as her own, entitled:

Have a Little Heart and Consideration

Cours
Have a little heart and consideration or else you'll wind
up without a friend.
Have a little heart and consideration, and don't blame me
in the end.
One morning I felt you pulling me you see I work at night
so I try to sleep to 3 you said get up you bum, it's past
the sleeping hour, it's a quarter to 1
Cours
When we're having company you're always knocking me you're
so busy being so concited you can't see
Cours

The nature of their life together had inevitably encouraged in Joie a sense of being united with Jeffie against a hostile world. From the age of four, she had always been tigerish in defense of her mother, never, for example, permitting a word of criticism to pass unanswered when Joey's family discussed Jeffie behind her back, which they did very often in Joie's presence. Now, with her mother under almost daily attack, and not just verbally, the strain on Joie was almost more than she could deal with. Her natural, partisan hostility toward Joey, as the agent of Jeffie's unhappiness, provoked not only ever more arbitrary displays of parental authority from him, which was bad enough, but also the increasing displeasure of her now desperate mother, who had problems enough with Joey without having to take her daughter's part as well. Under fire from both sides, therefore, Joie found her best line of defense was to tune out and withdraw from them both, a course that Jeffie felt was almost equally damaging for the child and which proved yet another source of anguish to her. It was a vicious triangle. And there seemed no obvious way to break out of it, for Joey's attitude toward a separation had been made very clear to Jeffie after her flight to Fire Island for ten days.

Under severe and increasing pressure, therefore, Jeffie watched

Joey's growing interest in Sina with a calculating eye. "I knew how his mind worked. I'd told him up front that, as far as I was concerned, he'd been away for ten years, and if he wanted to make up for lost time, I wouldn't be jealous. What Joey and I had was not something he was going to have with anybody else. I was not possessive at that point, and he knew it. But Sina was different. She wasn't a broad. She was a lovely woman with a nine-year-old daughter, and if there was anything he thought he could do to punish me it would be to play around with someone who looked a bit like me, who was ten years younger and who had a nine-year-old daughter. I *knew* Joey. But what he didn't understand was that I really wanted out, and she could be *it*. No broad was going to get me off the hook, but Sina just might. He was now seeing her practically every day at the dentist's, and there were times when I knew he was in the building although he certainly wasn't home. So I decided to remove myself as a possible obstacle. I had a very long, very frank conversation with Sina on the telephone.

" 'Listen, Sina,' I said. 'I love Joey very much, but it's been six months now, and I'm very well aware that our relationship isn't going to work. I don't know anything about you or him and what he's doing or isn't doing, but if you have any feeling for him, if he's attractive to you, I want you to know that as far as I am concerned, you have nothing to worry about or feel guilty about, because I want out. If you like him and he likes you, you would be doing me a great favor. Of course, I don't want to put any ideas in your head, and I may be completely out of line, but I know him and I know you. If there's any woman he would like, it would be you.'

"I just wanted her to know that if she dug him, she had my blessing. And while I didn't want to talk her into anything either, I tried to tell her some of the lovely things about him. I wanted her to know that he was capable of something else besides being hours late for his dental appointments and coming in with a crew of twenty people to disrupt everything. So she listened, but I don't know that she really understood. People who don't know me don't always believe I mean what I say. She certainly wasn't embarrassed or insulted—just noncommittal. She said she thought our problem was probably because we were readjusting, that it would probably work out, but she didn't indicate what her own feelings were toward Joey at all. I think maybe she wasn't too sure of them herself at that point because for a time she tried to avoid him. She'd be out of the office when she knew he had an appointment.

"Meanwhile, I'm trying to make Joie's life bearable. I kept telling him there were three people in the house to consider, and if that wasn't a livable situation for him, then he shouldn't be in it. He should go someplace where he *could* be happy. We were not happy. And if we were not happy, what were we doing together? 'Go. Do what you have to do. Be happy.' Then he would stay out—overnight, two days, three days—and I would think to myself, 'Well, maybe he's with Sina. Maybe the nightmare's over at last.' Then he'd come home for days on end and be sweet, which was certainly better than all the tumult, but I knew it wouldn't last. It was finished, and the sooner it was finished, the better. I didn't love him less. I loved him enough to figure that if it wasn't working with me, then it ought to be working with somebody else. I was sad, but I didn't have time to worry about that. I'd be sad about it later. We were having such screaming battles about everything and anything that I just wanted to get it over with. 'Get out, get out, *get out!* Why don't you GET OUT?'

" 'How are you going to live?' he'd say. 'What are you going to do without me?'

" 'I don't know,' I said. 'Go away and I'll find out. Don't worry about me. Just—get—OUT!'

"Joie was asked to a Halloween party. Naturally, we didn't do anything about her costume until the last minute, so the day before, I asked him, 'Please, Joey, as a great favor, may I have a few hours to think of something beside you? Will you please stay out tonight so I can get the kid ready for her party?' Sure, he said—and I made him promise not to come home. Great. At about eleven o'clock that night, I've got her costume spread out all over the floor and I'm sprinkling sequins on it when, all of a sudden, he walks in with his father and four guys carrying boxes and boxes of food—seven dozen steaks, twenty-four dozen chops, eighteen bags of fruit. . . . I went crazy. I ran up to his father, who had been over maybe three times since Joey got out, grabbed him by the lapels and started wailing and crying. 'I can't, Pop. You don't understand. I can't take it any more. I can't—he's going to drive me insane. I don't want it. Where am I going to put all this fucking food? You don't know what I'm going through.'

"His father looks at me like I was a complete maniac. He says, 'What's so hard to put away? A few lamb chops?'

" 'No, you don't understand. He's driving me crazy. You got to take him away from me.'

"I went totally ape-shit. Joey had promised me. Now to walk in with all this food on my night off seemed like the most hostile, brutal thing he could have done to me. I just grabbed everything, threw as much in the garbage as I could, shoved the rest in paper and slammed it into the freezer. Months later, you couldn't get a steak because they were all stuck together. I had a complete, hysterical nervous break-down—and nobody took any notice. I was running around like a lunatic, but Joey would never get mad at me when *I* was mad. I was always allowed to rant and rave and scream. He poured everybody a drink, and they sat down and talked and stepped all over the sequins and just kind of ignored me.

"I was beside myself. I didn't know who to kill first. I kept running over to his father, kneeling at his feet and begging him, 'Please. I can't stand it. You've got to get him out of here, Pop. I can't take any more. Please.' But his father was used to Joey's mother, I guess, because he'd just look at me with this blank stare, shrug his shoulders and carry on with the conversation over my head. I dragged the costume into the other room, and stomped around like an insane lady until they finally left. Later on, when I was off the boil, I got a pretty good slap, but not because I'd made a scene. He never smacked me when I did anything. Well—hardly ever. He'd smack me if the venetian blinds went up wrong. I never knew when I was going to get hit."

Although certain that her life with Joey was over, Jeffie was finding it impossible to let go. At one moment, she would be doing her best to throw him out or fix him up with Sina, and in the next, she would find herself clutching at the first sign of a peace overture and believing in miracles. Through November and December they battled on, with Jeffie certainly getting the worst of their physical exchanges, but, angry as she was, she never seriously considered leaving *him*. Once, he packed his things and left—for three days. Then, after a further wounding campaign, he said he was leaving again—but Joey couldn't let go either.

"We're discussing it, calmly but with a finality. 'Okay,' he says. 'This is it. This is what you really want?' 'Yes.' 'You're *sure* this is what you really want?' 'Yes, I'm sure. I don't really want it, but it's the best thing because—well, you know, I love you very much and everything, but it's not working out. I really think you should leave, yes.' So he's finally convinced, and I collapse on the bed. I remember this very well because *Mildred Pierce* was playing on television that night, and I'd been looking forward to it for weeks. It's one of my favorite movies. But he was coming back for his stuff so I couldn't look too happy. I had the room dark, and I was lying down so that when he came in, he'd think I was bedridden after our terrible scene. Sure enough, he comes home right in the middle of *Mildred Pierce,* turns down the television and sits on the bed in his hat and coat, just looking at me in the dark. I don't say a word. No matter what I say, I'm in trouble, so I just sit and stare sadly into space, with the occasional tear running down my cheek.

"This time, I really thought he was leaving. He poked through the closets, went into the bathroom and generally futzed around for a while. I didn't dare turn up the sound, so I was trying to read Joan Crawford's lips. Then he sits down on the bed again, still in his hat and coat. 'Are you sure?' he says. It's one of his tricks. If I'm happy he's leaving, he won't go. 'Are you sure this is what you want?' I shake my head. 'No, Joey. It's not what I want, but I think it's the best thing. I think you should give yourself a chance to see what else there is for you. I love you. I'm not going anyplace. I don't care *who* makes you happy—just get happy. Give yourself six months. See what's out there. Try. Maybe you'll find some happiness. If you don't, I'll still be here. Let's have a trial separation—anything you want. Stop driving me crazy. Stop driving *yourself* crazy. Just be happy.'

" 'You know your own mind, now—you're sure?' he says. 'This is it. If I leave, you won't see me again, you *know* that.'

" 'Yes, yes, *I* know. It's my fault. I'm no good for you. I tried, and I'm sorry, but I can only do what I did, and it didn't work out. . . .' And on and on. He's torturing me, but I hold out and in the end he leaves.

"Two hours later, he's back. 'Well, you know,' he says. 'I can't—er—the parole. I can't leave because of the parole. I got to leave my clothes here.' Not only hasn't he gone, he's ruined *Mildred Pierce.* "

He also ruined Christmas. It had been arranged that George and Laura Lloyd and George's brother Mike would meet Joey and Jeffie at their apartment on Christmas Eve and then go out to dinner, but Joey had disappeared. When Laura arrived early, Jeffie was dressing and prepared for the worst, having trimmed the tree without him and labeled two of the presents underneath it to Joie from her father in case he failed to show up or to give her anything. Just how wise these precautions were Joey then demonstrated by telephoning to say he couldn't make it; he hadn't slept. Later on, Jeffie was to wish she had left it at that, but instead she reminded him that he had promised Laura a present, knowing his pride in meeting even the most trifling obligation, and generally shamed him into coming home. Unshaven, unkempt and slightly drunk, he arrived with three of the boys a few minutes ahead of George.

"Joey's not very happy, and now he's home, I can't sit still. It looks like we're in for an embarrassing evening. One of the guys then hands me my Christmas present, and Joey had either goofed or bought it for somebody else because it was a zodiac charm with a little diamond in it—very nice except that it wasn't my sign. Still, I didn't say anything because George and Laura were there. I just said, 'Oh, isn't that beautiful'—trying to keep things as pleasant as I could while wanting to stab him through the heart. But then he starts in on me—for no reason. Half the time, the trouble between us was my fault, I know that. My big mouth. But I was really trying that night to bite my tongue. We'd never fought in front of George and Laura, and I didn't want to put them through it, especially not at Christmas. But the more I tried to pacify him, agreeing with everything he said, the more he hollered at me. He was really trying to pick a quarrel, and obviously to give himself an excuse to leave. I figured he had some other engagement—probably with Sina—in which case he was going to go anyway, so finally I answered him.

"It was an ugly display. He's stomping through the house. We're screaming at each other, and George is saying, 'Why don't you just try and keep quiet?' He's telling me to cool it, but I can't any more. So in the end, I just looked at him and said, 'I don't know what the fuck to do. The fucking guy is out of his fucking mind, and I've had it. Fuck you, and fuck Christmas.' And with that I went into the bedroom to have hysterics, which was just what Joey wanted. He became reasonable in a minute, complained to George about me, man to man, and then left, saying he couldn't cope with me at all and that was why we couldn't have Christmas dinner together. I found out later he went straight upstairs to Sina.

"Well, George and Laura eventually dried me off and took me out to dinner, but it wasn't exactly a festive occasion. About an hour and a half later, they left me downstairs, I went up to the apartment— and there he was! Back again. And acting like he was terribly preoccupied with the world's problems. It's incredible. *'Why are you home?'* So naturally we have another big fight, and he decides to make his second exit that night. 'See what you're making me do?' he says. 'You're making me go into the streets.' In other words, it was my fault he was going to go out and get shot by four black guys because I was aggravating him. 'You *made* me do it'—that was a standard line of his. 'You made me love you.' 'You made me hit you.'

" 'Jesus,' I said. 'You're really negating yourself completely. I didn't realize I had such great power. What are you? My puppet? I don't make you do *shit.*' So then he took back his Christmas present and left, which I thought was very funny. But Christmas Day wasn't so amusing. Joie had gotten everybody a present, including Daddy. She sat by the tree all day waiting to give it to him, but Daddy never showed up. And I thought to myself, 'How unlike him.' It was another one of the things he had done since getting out of prison that were really beneath him. Joey had never been petty or small-minded. I couldn't understand it."

Jeffie understood it better later on, when she came to compare notes with Sina. Joey's behavior at this time was not so much an exercise in calculated malice as a display of helpless ambivalence worthy of a Feydeau farce. Having more or less successfully courted Sina, he now found himself torn between two women in two households in the same building, each with a nine-year-old daughter expecting him home for Christmas. And since to be with one was, in either case, to be racked with guilt about the other, in the end he simply settled for the more peaceful option, hoping to balance things out later. Joie left early next morning to stay with her Grandfather Lee in New Orleans so that settlement of *her* account had to be delayed, but his chance to mend fences with Jeffie came later the same day, when she was admitted to New York Hospital for an operation on her nose, which she had injured a couple of months earlier in a car accident. Within a week, in spite of her anger and accumulated resentment, in spite of her resolve to drive him out and have done with their unhappy life together, he had not only won her around but rekindled her hopes of their marriage. She was no longer interested in smoothing his way with Sina or sharing him with anyone—and all it had taken was a little sympathy, a little tenderness and three dozen roses.

"I deserved half the belts I got—and I got a lot. It was my mouth. I would get him so angry I knew I had to get it, but I didn't care. I deserved the bop in the eye after Fire Island. At Thanksgiving I got a goody, too. And he broke my ribs when he threw my purse at me, only that was an accident. He used to say, 'I don't know what to do with her. You hit her, and she comes up talking. She'd only shut her mouth.' But there was no way he could make me. I'd start a sentence, he'd throw a punch, and then I'd finish the sentence. He always held back, of course, otherwise he could have really hurt me, and I know he didn't enjoy it. It was just that everything in his life was pushing him beyond words. All he could do was lash out. But he was lovely to me in the hospital, and on New Year's Eve, when

I was due to come home, he sent two of the boys to fetch me.

"Bobby came up to my room and said, 'Er, Joey didn't give me enough money. They want six hundred bucks for the kid—you still owe them for the kid.' Sid Slater, that son of a bitch, had pocketed half the money he was supposed to pay my bill with when Joie was born, and for ten years they'd been lying in wait for me. So I sat down on the bed, and said, 'Oh my God, what are we going to do?' I knew they wouldn't let me off the floor without a paper from the cashier. You give the head nurse the paper, and everybody waves good-bye. Now we had to figure out how to get down without one because I wasn't about to stay there, so Bobby goes off to case the exits. He comes back and says, 'Okay—this is the plan. I'm going to walk by the nurses' room very fast with the bags. You're going to be right behind me, with Stevie between you and the door. Don't look right or left—just keep going. Before we get to the regular exit, we make a right through an unmarked door and down the stairs—okay?'

" 'Oh my God,' I said. 'Let me see if I've got it straight' I was *dying.* I'd been there five days and everybody had been so good to me. I had to get out, but it was so embarrassing. 'How can they keep records for ten years?' I kept asking him. 'What'll happen if they catch us?' But Bobby didn't seem to hear that. He was already walking very fast down the hall with the bags. So I took Stevie's arm and we followed. I knew that if anybody said a word to me, they were going to have a cardiac arrest on their hands, but we made it to the door okay and onto the stairs. I started breathing again. And then we got lost—totally lost! We were wandering around in the bowels of this hospital, and we couldn't get out. It was a Mack Sennett comedy. 'All right, Ollie—what do we do now?' Laugh? We had to hold each other up, we were so weak from laughing. In fact, I was about ready to turn myself in, just so I could get back to bed, when we sort of fell through another door and found ourselves out on the street.

"Well, the boys took me home, put the bags in the hall and left. They didn't think Joey was there, so I didn't either, but he had waited for me, and he was still in the same kind, gentle mood he'd been in all week. He asked me what I wanted to do, but now I didn't feel so good from all the Demerol and stuff they'd been giving me. I said, 'Forgive me, baby, but I'm really not up to anything. I just want to go to bed.' No problem. He fussed around, sat on the edge of the bed, talked like the Joey of old and it was all very pleasant. Then he said he had to go to President Street, and I said, 'Great. But it's New Year's Eve. You'll come back?' 'Yeah,' he said. 'I'll call you' —which meant I probably wouldn't see him for three days, but that was okay, too. I had a good feeling about everything now.

"Except for the way I looked, of course. After he left, I inspected myself in the mirror a lot. I hadn't looked too wonderful when I went in, but right then I couldn't have won a beauty contest with Judy Canova. I had tape over my nose, I was swollen and bruised—I was definitely the victim of an accident. I was going to have to get by on what people remembered and my winning personality. I took a bath to freshen up, washed my hair, and by about nine o'clock, I was beginning to feel I'd like some company. So I called downtown and got Joey himself, which was unusual. Generally you had to pass a message, and if he wasn't too busy, like drinking a cup of coffee, he'd maybe come to the phone.

" 'Yeah, what are you doing?' I said. He says, 'Uh, having a few drinks.' So I say, 'What do you want to do?' And he says, 'You want to eat?' 'Yeah,' I says. 'Okay,' he says. 'Well, why don't you come down?' 'Oh yeah?' I says. 'You want to come home?' He says, 'No. Come down. You feel all right?' 'Yeah, I feel all right,' I says. 'I don't know how long I'll be.' 'That's okay,' he says. 'Take a cab.'

"Telling me to take a cab was a nice gesture. It meant I was a whole person, of equal standing, who didn't have to be picked up and delivered like a piece of luggage. Being allowed the freedom to walk downstairs and hail a cab exhilarated me beyond belief. Also, I could take my time getting ready, so it was around ten before I arrived— and there was nobody there except men. Not a wife, not a girlfriend. Just me and forty-seven guys. Wow! I figured maybe I was going to be sworn in. The whole place rises. 'Have a seat. What do you want to drink?' Soon I'm showing everybody my scars and telling them about my escape from the hospital and we're all very jovial. But I still couldn't get over these guys being here on New Year's Eve without their old ladies. It obviously wasn't a party party, although *I* was having a very good time.

"Joey and I sat together at a table for a good hour talking about a house that was soon coming vacant on the block. We'd discussed it before, on and off in our saner moments. I wanted to open a children's boutique there called Crazy Joe's, and we would live over the store. Joey wouldn't have anything to do with the business. *I* was going to run it *my* way. All I wanted from him was for the boys to ferry my Park Avenue clients to and from Manhattan in their limousines. 'Yeah,' he says, jumping up and down with excitement. 'Let's do it. Hey, Pop—come and listen to this.' It was great. It was like coming home. He was so full of ideas and enthusiasm. And he adores me—after all these terrible months. Doesn't leave my side.

"But more people are coming in now, including some neighborhood chicks, and he has to be social. So the guys sit with him, and these little girls sit with me and I notice they're looking at me like I'm supposed to say something. They've got the same sort of expectant look as the guys have got around Joey. Well, I'm not used to that, but I tried to say something in young, and I could see that even a belch would be a big moment for them. I thought to myself once again, 'My God, how does he *cut* this?' This was just one evening, and he'd been doing it for years. I was appalled at all the time he had given to these people. But a happier guy there never was, and I am the belle of his ball. 'There's nobody in the world to compare with my wife,' he's telling everybody. 'Listen to the funny things she says,' and he takes me from group to group so I can throw them lines about different people. Everyone's laughing, everything's lovely, and then midnight comes. It's the New Year, and for once it really feels like a new start. We kiss. I'm transported. He's as hungry and urgent as ever he was. Without a word, he leads me into the kitchen by the hand, locks the door and we make love. After all our terrible troubles, we're whole again.

"I'm so happy I'm crying. I'm also rather drunk. But I know Joey doesn't go for sticky sentiment, so afterward I stepped out into the yard to look at the stars. It was such a romantic, magical night. 'Come inside,' he says. 'I want to shut the door.' 'No, baby,' I says.

'Not yet. It's so beautiful out here. Come and have a look.' He says, 'No. I want to shut the door. It's cold.' So I hold out my hand to him, and say, 'Just for a minute. Come see the stars. It's not cold.' He looks at me. Then he closes the door and locks it. I'm shut out in the alley. And it *is* cold. So I tap on the door. 'Joey?' I'm trying to laugh, because I know it's just his little joke. 'Joey, will you let me in, please?' No answer. 'Joey? *Joey!* I want to come in.' Nothing. 'Joey, unlock this goddamn door—do you hear me?' Silence. 'YOU SON OF A BITCH! LET ME IN!' Not a word. He's gone back to the party.

"Now I want to kill him. I'm freezing out there in just a dress. I'm going to get back inside and kill him. So I start climbing up the fire escape, shouting and hollering fit to rouse the neighborhood. I'm looking for a way in, but everything's locked up tight. Now I'm on the roof, and talking to myself. I'm going to kill them all. Every one. With my bare hands. But him first. 'YOU'D DO THIS TO ME, YOU MOTHERFUCKER? YOU WAIT. I'LL GET YOU FOR THIS. BASTARD SON OF A BITCH!' Lights were coming on in people's windows, and it suddenly crossed my mind that clambering over the rooftops of President Street might not be too healthy. I could not only catch pneumonia, I could also catch a bullet maybe. So I climbed down the building again, still bawling and beating on the windows like a madwoman, and attacked the door again with my shoe, fists, everything. I was hoarse by now, but still making enough noise for a police raid.

"Well, Joey's brother Blast was expecting some friends to drop in for a drink, and he didn't want to embarrass them. So finally he says, 'Let her in.' They open the door, and the kitchen is full of people, but the first person I see is Joey. I don't have a weapon to kill him with, but there's a loaf of French bread on the table, so I use that. There was a bottle as well, but something told me not to. Then Blast came between us, and told a couple of the guys to take me home. 'No, you can't do that,' I'm yelling, as they carry me out. 'You'll hurt Joey's feelings. Take me back and let *him* throw me off the block.' "

Jeffie was home and in bed when the phone rang at 5 A.M. It was Louie the Syrian, inviting her back to the party. This she took to be the equivalent of an apology, and, after declining the invitation, she went back to sleep somewhat mollified. When Joey eventually arrived home around noon on New Year's Day, they both started to laugh. But underneath nothing had changed. The mood of the previous week soon faded. When Joie returned from her visit to New Orleans, Joey made good his desertion at Christmas by turning up unexpectedly at her sleep-over birthday party on January 11, but by then he and Jeffie were once more at each other's throats.

In her savage disappointment, Jeffie now seriously proposed for the first time that if he wouldn't leave *her,* maybe she should leave *him*—and he agreed. Taken aback slightly, Jeffie went out and rented an apartment, but two days later he changed his mind, and once again she allowed herself to be persuaded.

"He couldn't leave me. 'You can't leave me?' 'No, I can't leave you. I love you. You're my woman. You're the only one for me.' 'Well, if you can't leave me, why do you act like this? What kind of love is that?' 'I know. I'm sorry. I know I'm wrong. I've got all these problems. You have to understand. I can't let you go.' 'Yeah, yeah —we've been through this a dozen times already.' 'No, no, it's different now. I really mean it this time.' Okay, so he really means it. He really loves me. He's going to be cool. 'All right—but no fooling around now. If you've got any more wild oats to sow, you're more than welcome to sow them—but not in *my* bed. Take six months. I don't care what you do. I'll be right here.' No, no—we'd made up forever. There'd be none of that. He even showed me a special key on his keyring—probably Sina's—and made a big show of throwing it away."

Unconvinced, yet anxious to *be* convinced, Jeffie told herself it was the last chance she would give him. She wanted to get away, not just for Joie's sake now, but for her own. Joey was making a mockery of twelve years of her life, and his behavior didn't improve much after this latest assertion of undying love. But the peace was still more or less holding when, in mid-January, Joey announced one evening that a detective he knew, Eddie Lambert, had told him that the guy who played the character based on Joey in the film of *The Gang That Couldn't Shoot Straight* wanted to meet him. His name was Jerry

Orbach, his wife was Marta Orbach, and did Jeffie know them?

By an odd coincidence, she did—indirectly, through Dottie. All three had children at P.S. 41, and Dottie had mentioned how kind the Orbachs had been to her kids while she was living alone in the Village—taking them to the circus, and backstage to *Promises, Promises.* When Joey heard this, he told Jeffie to get Dottie on the phone, and, having satisfied himself with this character reference, instructed Dottie to call Marta and say it was all right—they could meet him. And as he and Jeffie already had a dinner date coming up with George and Laura Lloyd at the Queen Restaurant, he suggested that Dottie and Lou and the Orbachs should all meet at his place and tag along.

But when the evening arrived, Joey had already repented his offer. "I gotta meet these actors?" he grumbled to George, who arrived first with Laura. "Why do I want to meet these fucking people?" He was in an awkward mood, and his temper wasn't sweetened any when Jerry Orbach and his wife both turned out to be bigger than he was. He complained about it as he rode down in the elevator between George and Jerry, who looked like basketball players beside him. "Jesus, I'm really getting nervous in here with these two. They could fall on me." To even things up, he then said to Jerry, "Hey, tough guy, you better look out when we hit the street. Who knows who's waiting for us down there?" George, recognizing the signs, stepped in quickly to head him off. "Hey, Joey," he said, in mock alarm. "I'm here, too, don't forget. Don't say things like that. You promised me." Joey laughed and let it drop, but left George with no particular desire to be in Jerry's shoes that night. The Orbachs would not be the first to pay dues when applying to join Joey's circle.

On the street, Joey elected to go with George, although he disapproved of his Toyota. "What *is* this thing?" he asked. "A guy like you—get yourself a car, George. A big, black car. Take Laura's Mercedes. Give *her* this." Slightly unnerved, George set off across town, joined the traffic on the West Side Highway and got off too soon for the Brooklyn-Battery Tunnel. Realizing his mistake as he did so, he drove straight back up again on the facing ramp and pretended the whole maneuver had been intentional. "How's *that* for driving?" he said. "I shook everybody." In fact, he had shaken nobody. Both the Orbachs in their car and the police tail behind them had dutifully followed George down the exit ramp and up again on the other side.

Entering into the spirit of the thing, when they reached the toll booths, Joey made George pay for all the cars, including the police, who were now obviously in trouble. They had stopped in the roadway just clear of the tunnel and were frantically kicking the front of their car to make the headlights come on before Joey got away. George asked him if he should wait, and Joey said no. The cops knew where they were going, and he waved to them as they drove off. But the kicks had been shrewdly aimed. When George pulled into the parking space outside the restaurant, their police escort was already inside eating dinner, having been advised by Joey's reception committee that he would be settling in there for the night. As always, Joey had elected to follow a highly circuitous route, while his tail had driven over directly.

He at once took charge of the seating arrangements. Jeffie, who was having difficulty with a loose cap on one of her teeth, was banished to the far end of the table, where she set up an immediate clamor for clams. There she was joined by Lou, whom Joey evicted from the chair at his side, by Dottie and by the detective Eddie Lambert. Joey then seated Louie the Syrian's girlfriend in the place vacated by Lou, and made Pete the Greek move down to make room for George on his other side, an honor that Pete clearly did not believe George deserved. Next came the Orbachs, sufficiently removed for Joey to observe them, and talk to them or not, at his convenience.

After ordering for everybody, tasting everything and drinking several glasses of wine, he relaxed, losing the edginess that had alarmed George earlier. When Louie the Syrian arrived, he mellowed still further, for they loved each other, and were always warmed by each other's company. Joey seated him next to George, and turning at last to Marta Orbach, began to question her, in a faintly jeering though not unfriendly tone he sometimes used with strangers. "Okay, so you finally got to meet me," he said. "You wanted to meet the star, the star gangster of America, and now you got your chance. So where are you from, big Italian girl? You're an Italian girl, right? Where are you from?"

Uncertain of his mood, Marta did the best she could while Joey listened in the same spirit of genial condescension and George, on behalf of the straight world, squirmed with irritation. Jerry said very little. He laughed at the jokes, and when anyone spoke to him he displayed a wealth of what looked like white plaster between his teeth, for he, too, was undergoing dental work. It was his turn next. Punchy Illiano came in, eying the strangers at the table with undisguised suspicion, and was told to sit down and pour himself a drink.

"Hey, Punchy—you see the one over there? With the white?" said Joey, pointing at Jerry. "That's the guy that played me in the movie. You know what? We should have broke his legs. Just to teach him to be a better actor." With a great laugh, Jerry took a pull at his drink. "And you know what else pissed me off?" Joey went on, pleased with the general response to this sally, for the whole table was now listening appreciatively, except for Jeffie, who had just spilled wine down her dress. "About you doing me?" Jerry shook his head. "You ain't good-looking enough." Everybody roared, and Jerry nodded eagerly.

"Now, Joey," said George. Although it was funny, he knew how easily the teasing could get out of hand. "You got to understand, Jerry, Joey's no Bosley Crowther, but that's his review of the movie."

"Oh Jesus, George," said Joey, slapping his leg. "Do Abba Eban." Louie loved it, too. "Oh, Pops," he said. "You got a fucking mouthpiece on you. Let's hear it." So George did his imitation of the Jewish statesman with the British accent, which always amused Joey, and the moment passed. Jerry refilled his glass and sat back. Then Marta stepped into the breach.

"Mmm-mm! Is this good food!" she said. "And *I* know. I'm a cook. My momma taught me to cook like a good Sicilian girl."

"Hey, are you from *Sicily?*" asked Joey, as if about to greet a long-lost relative.

Marta beamed. "I'm Sicilian, Joey," she said. "You betcha."

"Yeah?" he said, nudging Louie. "Well, I'm from Naples." And

Louie exploded. "Oh, Pops," he said, slapping him on the back.

Once on the subject of spaghetti, Marta kept going with it, on and off, for the rest of the evening. But George still mistrusted Joey's intentions toward the Orbachs, and did his best to monopolize the conversation. He had also sensed another kind of tension in the air. Joe Iovine, Joey's lawyer uncle, was prowling about by the bar with a worried frown, and Pete the Greek was not joining in the fun either, but watching the door. In the middle of another spaghetti recipe, he said suddenly, "There's some fucking kid outside, looking through the window."

"Well, check it out, Pete," said Joey, with no perceptible change of tone, and Pete, Louie and another of the boys immediately left the table. George reached for the bottle of Dewar's and poured himself an enormous drink. Then Louie came back to report they were neighborhood kids. "They're all right, Pops."

"Yeah, well," said Joey, turning back to Marta. "How much spaghetti do you put in the pot?"

"Hey, Joey," said George. "Do you mind not talking about spaghetti while I'm eating?" Louie slapped him on the back cheerfully. "Jesus, Pops," he said. "Who is she? An actor?"

Realizing that Louie hadn't been listening earlier, George explained that she was the wife of the guy who played Joey in the movie, and he pointed Jerry out to him. "He stinks," said Louie. "He stinks. You—hey, you! I didn't enjoy that movie. You weren't so hot in that." Jerry laughed uproariously and took another drink. "You stir and you stir," said Marta. "You got to do it with feeling. You're making it for your man."

"You're right, Joey," said George. "Mao Tse-tung is great. You remember that picture of him in the *Times* swimming in the Yangtze River? With all his body showing from the navel up? Do you suppose he really swims like that? I bet there were ten guys underneath holding their breath and holding him up."

"Oh, Jesus Christ, George," Joey spluttered. "Listen, Italian girl, someday I'm going to come over and I'm going to eat your goddamn spaghetti. Will your actor be there? Will you be there, actor? Listen, what are they doing to your mouth?"

"Okay," said Marta. "That's a date. Anytime you say. And you'll have to show me President Street. I would love to see your headquarters."

Joey shook his head solemnly. "We've been hitting the mattresses for years," he said. "You come down there and who knows what could happen to you—right, actor?"

"Ha, ha, ha," said Jerry.

"So what are you working in, actor? A musical? How can you sing with that shit in your teeth?"

"How about Sunday?" suggested Marta. "For brunch. We can get rid of the kids upstairs."

"I *love* kids," said Joey, injured. With George's help, he reviewed all the children he knew. "Hey, Dottie," he called down the table. "What does Pammy want more than anything?"

Surprised by this sudden attention and drunk, Dottie couldn't think. "I don't know, Joey—what *does* she want?"

"She wants money, right? Loves money. She's going to be a hooker, your daughter."

"Oh, my poor baby," said Dottie.

Meanwhile, Jeffie had lost her cap, and in between hearing about the French connection from Eddie Lambert, was blowing kisses at George and mouthing, "I love you. Keep him busy."

"Come down here," said George. "I can't hear what you're saying."

"Oh, am I missing something?" she asked.

"No." George's guard duty was over. The Orbachs now seemed to be safe. There was too much hubbub, too many open bottles on the table, too much joviality amid the wreckage of their meal for Joey to be interested in resuming his inquisition. He was now reminiscing with the boys, swapping fantastic stories of derring-do in which they were always as brave as lions and the cops ineffably stupid.

George knew most of them by heart. "How many times have you heard that story?" he asked, as they all doubled up at a special favorite.

"Laugh a little," said Joey. "Laugh with them. What else have we got to talk about?"

On January 24, Marta Orbach set about sponsoring his debut in the show-biz, table-hopping cheek-peckers' club. Writing to thank him for the most exciting evening she and Jerry had ever spent, she offered to return the favor in any way that appealed to him: dinner in or out, with or without other people, some Sunday with the kids or another day without them—whatever Joey would like the best. She also reported that Ben Gazzara wanted to meet him, that Buddy Greco had asked her to bring him to his opening at the St. Regis, and that Elaine's, which she described as a haven for movie stars, writers and other major celebrities, would give them the best table and VIP treatment any time Joey wanted to go *there*. All he had to do was pick a night and give them a call.

It was an error in protocol. Princes may graciously consider specific invitations from their subjects, but rarely respond to questionnaires. A few days later, she made another approach. This time, she invited Jeffie, Joey, Joie and Tony, Joey's bodyguard, to an early dinner at her house on Sunday, February 6. She also reminded him that a table had been booked for the Greco opening for a party of eight—the four of them, the Gazzaras, Tony and Pete the Greek. And Joey was not to worry about the cops. If necessary, she would get them a table, too. He had to remember that, so far as she and Jerry were concerned, he was worth whatever trouble there might be in knowing him.

Their acquaintance had ripened as a result of an intervening dinner party at the Gazzaras. Although Jeffie was lukewarm toward the Orbachs, and turned off completely by the idea of hobnobbing with "major celebrities," she was mortified by Joey's willfulness. "He was so erratic in his social behavior. When Marta called to invite us to dinner at Ben Gazzara's house, he told me to accept, and then, on the night, just as I was getting ready, he said he didn't want to go. 'Call them up and say we can't come.'

" '*I'm* not going to call them,' I said. 'You want to insult people? *You* do it.' 'Well, I'm not going to go with you,' he said. '*Me?*' I said. 'If *I'm* the obstacle, sweetheart . . . If you think *I* want to go, you got to be kidding. You're the one that's starting with these people —not me.' No, he didn't want to go. So then I went into the bedroom again to get undressed, and he told Tony to go home. Fine. The cops see Tony leave, assume Joey's in for the night, and they go home, too. Ten minutes later, he says it was just a ruse to get rid of Tony. *'What?'* 'Yeah, I want us to go alone.' 'Oh, fucking hell,' I said, and went back to the bedroom to get dressed again. Still, I have to admit he was in good form that night, although not in a way that made me proud. It was a great performance. He did exactly what was expected of him. Joe Gallo, boy gangster. Not tough—just overpowering. Alone on alien territory, he dominated everybody until 5 A.M., and they all had a wonderful time.

" 'What are we having for dinner?' he wanted to know. Ben said, 'Roast beef.' 'Roast beef? What kind of an Italian has roast beef for dinner? Who's cooking it? The shine?' 'Oh my God,' I thought, 'he just blew their maid.' But no. They loved it. Then Buddy Greco came in, wearing knickers. 'Jesus Christ,' said Joey. 'You've been singing for thirty-five years. What kind of an outfit is that?' Beamed. Adored it. Then he told Janice Rule how much the boys in the can enjoyed her movies. Charmed. Ate it up. He was masterly. It was fascinating to watch how he handled them all, and kept them interested. He would come out with a dese, dem and dose line, and then follow up with some esoteric, erudite reference that would throw them completely. He played in and out. He was marvelous at verbal games.

"I had to take my lumps, of course. Ben brought out some special brandy, and I don't quite know how it happened because I'm certain I didn't open my mouth, but Joey somehow got the impression I was trying to pretend I knew about brandies, and turned very hostile. 'Don't be a wise guy,' he said, and started hollering at me in front of everybody. 'Oi, vai,' I said. 'Please. It's enough. Don't make a scene.' I then had to sit with my eyes lowered for a good half-hour. 'He *is* outrageous, isn't he?' said Janice, and I agreed.

"The most I could hope for was to get through the evening without a disaster. We could never enjoy ourselves in places where I might possibly have been while he was in prison, or with people I might possibly have known. By now he'd probably convinced himself that I'd slept with Ben Gazzara, Buddy Greco, Janice Rule *and* the shine. So I played it safe. I talked to Janice, rolled my eyes occasionally and went to the bathroom a lot. It was snowing that night. I remember we went out on the terrace, and the snowflakes fell on our lips. It was the last of our social engagements."

Two days later, they both went too far to draw back. Despite his most recent vows of fidelity, and the ceremonial disposal of his "special" key—she discovered later that Sina had changed the lock on her front door at about this time—Jeffie realized that Joey was again deceiving her. But she was still unwilling to make the final break unless he forced her to it. When Sina, in an effort to protect herself, invented a story that Joey had been seen visiting the apartment of a Miss Zukor in the building, Jeffie swallowed the news and said nothing. Then, some forty-eight hours after leaving the Gazzaras, Joey went out with one of the boys at four o'clock in the morning. That in itself was not unusual, and Jeffie went back to sleep. She got up early, went shopping, and then remembered that Joey had to report to the Parole Board that day. Thinking he might have forgotten, she called home, and when no one answered, spoke to the doorman of the building to ask if he had seen him. Oh, yes, he said, Tony had come over to pick Joey up. Okay, she said. How long had Joey been home when Tony arrived? The doorman didn't understand the question. "What time did Joey get back?" she demanded. "He's still out," he said. "No, no," she said, "I'm talking about the *first* time you saw him this morning. What time did he come in?" "The first time I saw him this morning," the doorman said patiently, "was when he went out with Tony."

Jeffie slammed down the phone. When he'd left her at 4 A.M., he had obviously stayed in the building. Breathing hard, she took a cab to the apartment, confirmed that no one on the door had seen Joey after he had arrived home the previous evening until he had left with Tony, and then found the remains of breakfast in the kitchen. He had not only spent the night with someone else, he had come back for coffee and eggs. He had gone too far. So Jeffie went too far as well. Stepping outside their private battleground for the first time, she called his parole officer.

"I said, 'This is Mrs. Gallo. May I speak to my husband?' And as soon as he said hello, I let him have it. All those months when

I wanted him out and he wouldn't go, all the promises he'd made and broken, all the beatings, all the humiliations sort of rose up in my throat and spewed down the phone. So he hung up. I called back, afraid for my reason. 'Put my husband on again.' 'I'm sorry, Mrs. Gallo,' the guy said. 'He just left.' Obviously, he was lying. There hadn't been time. Joey had told him to say that. 'Well,' I said, 'if you *should* happen to see him, just tell him he'd better get his ass home quick or I'll *really* blow the whistle on him.' I figured *that* should get some action. It was all over. I'd had it. Now he was shoving his crap in my face, and I couldn't sit still for that. I wasn't going to let him destroy what we'd had together. I wasn't going to sit and watch him be an asshole. If he was going to be an asshole, he would have to find another audience."

She heard nothing from Joey for four hours, and went berserk. First, she called everybody she knew to find out if they'd seen him, and to announce, "He's up for grabs, ladies." Drawing blank, she then raged through the building from Sina's penthouse to the dentist's office, convinced he was hiding out there somewhere, bawling obscenities in the hallways until she was hoarse, and hammering and kicking at apartment doors. At last, he came home, in a fury equal to hers. She flew at his throat, and he knocked her down. Picking herself up and holding her ear, she eyed his impassive bodyguards. "I take a pretty good punch, right?" she said, and returned to the attack.

"We chased each other in and out until we finally ran short of hysteria, and then he said, 'Okay, this is it. Where's Joie?' It was going to be another of his siddown-and-listen declarations. I told him she was at ballet school and wouldn't be home until six. 'Then we'll wait,' and we sat there immobilized. 'You know, I've gotten myself into something,' he said, 'and you're not giving me a chance to get out of it.' 'You bet your ass,' I said. 'You told me that last time, and you've had long enough. If *you* can't get out of it, *I* can.' He may have meant Sina, but he didn't say. Then a delivery boy came from the cleaners with some of his stuff, and I got off the last immortal line in our marriage. 'Take it upstairs,' I said. 'The name is Zukor. First name, Cock.'

"When Joie came home, she took one look at our faces and turned to go out again. But he sat her down next to me—like two criminals awaiting sentence—and explained to her that he could no longer live with us. He was leaving. And it was my fault he was leaving. And it was my fault Joie and he hadn't gotten along because I'd turned her against him. And it was my fault this and my fault that—and by this time, we were yelling at each other again, and that was my fault, too. 'Listen,' I said. 'I just blew my cool. And however bad you feel, you're not supposed to do that in public. But I just blew it all over, so obviously I can sustain no more of this. You're going to leave, you're not going to leave—fuck *you!* When are you *leaving?* And I mean, *with* your clothes. I don't want *you* and I don't want your clothes. I just want you *OUT!*'

"Oh, no—the parole . . . his problems . . . can't be alone . . . got to keep this address . . . I don't understand. . . . 'Joey,' I said, and I've got a terrible pain behind the eyes now, like I was going to have a stroke. 'Joey—what do you want? *What* do you *WANT?* You want a furnished apartment, is that it? You want to be comfortable? Is it possible that this whole thing is going on because you don't want to be inconvenienced? You want a furnished apartment—right?' And he started to nod. 'Yeah,' he said. 'Right. That's what I want.' So I took a deep breath, and said, 'Honey—you got it. I'm out.' 'Yeah?' he said. 'How fast can you make it?'—and I didn't like his tone. 'How about an hour?' I said, and he starts toward me. 'Yeah, make it an hour,' he said. 'And don't let me find you here when I get back.' With which tender word, he gave me a belt in the stomach and walked out with the two guys. The year was up. I never saw him again."

Jeffie took Joie to Ruth's. Later that night, she decided they should go to her aunt's in Los Angeles—not permanently, but until the crisis blew over. If she stayed in New York, she knew Joey would find her, and they would simply pick up their murderous game where they'd left off. Even now, she never doubted that he loved her as she still loved him. During the night, she and Marjorie ventured back to the apartment to collect her papers, pictures and a few other belongings, and as soon as the bank opened next morning, she drew out every cent she possessed—some $400. Before boarding the plane, she telephoned Sina from the airport to say she was leaving, in haste, but five months too late. Concerned, as always, Sina wanted to know if she needed money or any other kind of help, and when Jeffie said no, promised to keep in touch.

They had scarcely arrived at Aunt Ilma's house before Tony called from New York to say that Joey was sending everything out after her —virtually the entire contents of the apartment, including the wall-to-wall carpet, which he had ripped up with his bare hands. Tony wanted to know what he should do with Marie the cat. Utterly astonished, because it had never for a moment occurred to her that Joey would give up the apartment, nor had she the slightest intention of staying in Los Angeles, and even if she had, there was nowhere to receive the furniture, Jeffie managed to talk Tony into having everything stored for the time being, and to call Dottie to collect Marie. And she had barely recovered from *that* shock before Joey's sister Carmella called next day to announce that he wanted an immediate divorce.

"Even in the break-up of his own marriage, he can't do anything himself. Tony has to send the furniture; Carmella has to arrange the divorce. 'What do you want?' she says. I said, 'I don't want anything, Carmella. I only want to make him happy. And as I have no way in the world of knowing what *will* make him happy, I'd be glad of your advice. I know you love him, so tell me what he wants and he's got it. I mean it. The guy's been away ten years, and I'm not about to rain on his parade. Whatever he wants, he can have. Name it.' Poor Carmella, I think she was disappointed. She wanted to fight to rescue her brother, and nobody was trying to keep him. 'Oh,' she said, 'all right. I'll take care of it.'

"About a week later, Joey himself called. We had a nice, calm, friendly conversation. He said he was taking Sina out. 'Good,' I said. 'I'm glad. I like her. Be good to her—she's a nice chick.' 'Well, she likes you, too,' he said. Then he heard the dog barking. 'Oh, you have a dog?' 'Yes, Joey, I have a dog.' 'Oh. Good. And how's Joie?' 'Fine,' I said. 'I've got her into school here.' And he said, 'Well, you know, I'm glad you're all right. Don't worry about anything. I'll take care of everything. You know—money, and that.' So I said, 'I know, Joey.

I'm not worried. I'm shocked I'm now living in California, which wasn't what I had in mind, but other than that, I'm fine. Be well. And enjoy your dinner with Sina.' I was angelic. After that, he called me quite often."

Then Tony flew out with divorce papers for her to sign, and they entertained each other hugely trying to decide what counteraccusation she could make to Joey's allegation that she was "unsafe to live with." In the end, she charged him with "excessive drinking," and when Tony went back next day to report her reaction, Joey was furious. "When he got the papers in his hand, when he saw the divorce as a reality, he called me in a screaming rage. 'You bitch . . . you fucking cunt . . .' I said, 'Joey, what's the matter *now?* I did what you wanted. Why are you mad?' He said, 'Well, we're divorced, you dumb, stupid broad.' 'I *know,*' I said. 'You just divorced me. And so what? When did that mean anything? What are you hollering about?' He was really angry, and even three thousand miles away, I had to worry about that. He had connections in California. 'I've no money,' he said. 'And if you think I'm going to support you for the rest of your fucking life . . .' He was yelling so loud, I couldn't put the phone to my ear. I was holding it out at arm's length, waiting for him to slow down so I could get a word in, when he suddenly hung up. Next day, he called again, and was as sweet as pie.

"Two nights later, he phoned from Ruth's at about five in the morning. He'd been telling her for hours how he couldn't live with me because I was crazy, but that I was his woman, and he'd never love anybody else. He wanted her to agree that he'd done the right thing. But he's not sure, so now he wants me to come back and talk. 'Yeah, you should come in,' he says. 'We got to talk before—well, I'm going to do something. I'm going to make a stupid move. And I love you.' 'Listen,' I said, 'are you drunk?' 'Do I have to be drunk to say I love you?' he says. 'I want you back here. We can't talk this thing out on the phone.'

"So, more to get him out of Ruth's house than anything, I said I'd go if he sent a ticket, and we left it at that. And Joie, who'd woken up and overheard the conversation, got out of bed and said, 'Mommy, if you go back to him now, you're crazier than he is.' 'Oh, shut up,' I said. 'Leave me alone. Go back to sleep and mind your own business.' But lying awake, thinking about it afterward, I had to admit she was right. I'd been ready to go back the first time he crooked his finger, and for what? So he could give me three more good slaps? Or kill me? Sina had called at one point to say she'd overheard him planning to send two of the guys out to take care of me, but I hadn't paid much attention to that because I knew he'd said it for *her* benefit. People only overheard what Joey wanted them to overhear. But even so . . . After brooding on it for a while, I called Ruth back to say I wasn't coming, and if he bothered her again like that, to call the cops if necessary. But later on, she checked with him at Sina's, and he'd changed his mind anyway, so that was that.

"Then he and Sina called a few days later to say they were getting married—and that surprised me. I was shocked she was going to go for it. But she was obviously anxious that everything should be on the up and up, so I was gracious, and even after that, he kept calling me, so I really couldn't be sure he meant to go through with it. Nor could Sina. Finally, she phoned and said, 'Joey doesn't know I'm calling you. Before anything else happens, Jeffie, you've got to tell me how you feel. Do you want him? Do you love him?' I said, 'Sina, those are two very different questions. I love him. I will always love him, but I will not tolerate his behavior. The fact that I love him is *my* problem. It's got nothing to do with what can be. We cannot make it together. I love him enough to want him to be happy. So if you think you've got a shot, take it. All I want is for him to send me something every week, because I don't have shit money, and I'm a little old to be a cocktail waitress.' 'Oh, sure,' she said, and from then on I got his two-hundred-dollar paycheck every week from the furniture company.

"But that didn't last long. Right after they got married, he quit, and there were no more paychecks. Now he's calling me to say he's a struggling writer, and I'm going to have to fend for myself, and Sina's calling me on the sneak to say not to worry. She'll see he meets his obligations because it's her obligation, too, and she knows what it's like to bring up a kid with a father who never sends any money. So she got him to call again, and I told him what my expenses were, and he promised to do what he could. He said he was writing a black comedy about prison, and Marta Orbach was going to help him with it, so I wished him the best, and assured him that, apart from our money worries, we were fine.

"After that, there was a two-week gap when I heard nothing, and I figured they were settling into married life. Then he called to talk about Sina. He was very subdued, very wistful, and I knew something was badly wrong. Joey never lacked purpose in anything he did; even in repose, he was always in charge—of himself and everyone else. But this time, he sounded beaten. I'd never heard defeat in his voice before. 'Do you love her?' I said to him. And he said, 'I married her, didn't I?' 'No, that's not what I asked you,' I said. 'If you love her enough, you'll make it.' So then he sighed. 'Sure. Just the way *we* made it, right?' There was no Joey-Jeffie bullshit that day. He was reaching out for a friend to talk to. And if I was anything, he always knew I was a friend. A couple of mornings later, George called me early from New York, and woke me up. He said Joey had been killed. And as I lay there, hearing that, *my* life ended, too."

21

Joie

"When I was small, I didn't think about my father much. The first time I actually remember seeing him in prison, I must have been about four. All those hours in a hot, stuffy car, and then this guy behind bars who didn't really mean anything to me—it was so boring. There was nothing to do but walk around, and make forty trips to the water fountain. Later on, he used to give me a kiss, and ask me about school and the books I'd read, but I got that all the time from everybody, so that wasn't so thrilling either. He seemed pleased to see me, but when you're sitting in a cell most of the time, I guess you'd be pleased to see anyone. Once I saw him in the library, where I was allowed to sit on his lap. He had a paper cup with water in it, and he asked me if I was thirsty. I said I was, but I didn't want to drink out of the same cup that he'd been using. I remember that sort of annoyed him. He didn't feel like my father at all.

403

"Then we went to England, and I had a marvelous time with Ted. It was just Mommy and Ted who didn't have a marvelous time together. He spoiled me a little—I had a big allowance and he took me around a lot—but my mother was always pretty tough, and I never got away with anything. I loved Ted. I used to think *he* was my father, but it was still Mommy and me against the world. Once they were having a fight, and he just casually grabbed her arm. It wasn't much, but I thought he was hurting her, so I bit his leg like it was a piece of Southern fried chicken. Poor Ted. I'm glad I didn't have braces then. Later on, when he and Mommy broke up, I wanted to go with him, but she threatened to call a cop.

"Joey was in Green Haven when we got back, but otherwise the visits were pretty much the same old thing. He looked just the same. We'd talk a bit, and he'd slip me a violet mint or some gum, but I still didn't feel like his daughter. I'd never written to him or anything, and he never really wrote to me, so we weren't close. I just felt obligated to go up and see him, although I knew I could get out of it anytime I wanted to. I used it a lot in school. 'My father, Joe Gallo—he's in prison,' I would say, just to impress the other kids. Finally, Mommy had to tell me, 'You know, Joie, it's really not that important that your father's Joe Gallo. He has the opposite effect on some people.' When he came out, I found that out for myself. There were times when I felt like changing my name—except that I didn't see why I should have to.

"We were living in Brooklyn then. When we heard he was coming home, Mommy got excited—and I caught on to it, too. I was going to have a daddy, so I got excited as well. When the car drove up, he got out with a very nice smile on his face, and I was suddenly sort of nervous. It felt like a big moment. Things were going to be different now. But all that happened was he picked me up, looked at me, gave me a kiss on the cheek and disappeared. For two weeks, he was swamped with people, and I hardly ever saw him. It was very disappointing. The nicest thing he did was when he took me and Pammy out, and we could have any animal we liked so long as it was a cat, because that was all we could keep in a small apartment. That's how I got Marie.

"Then the trouble started. I didn't like the way he was treating my mother, and I didn't like the way he was treating me. We were just his servants. 'Joie, get me a cup of coffee.' 'Joie, do this and do that.' Sometimes, when he was nice about it, I'd say, 'Oh, yes, Daddy. At once, Daddy.' Other times, when he wasn't so nice, I'd say, 'Get it yourself, Daddy,' and then he'd start yelling. I'd forgotten that *he* was the star and that I was his slave. Once, I was really fed up with him, so I started emptying my drawers into a big green plastic garbage bag. I was going to move all my things downstairs and live with my grandmother. It was very dramatic. I had my winter coat on, and this big plastic bag across my shoulder, and I told Mommy, 'I'm leaving home. Now you two can be alone.' *She* was upset, but Joey acted very cool, like he knew he was calling my bluff. 'Okay, Joie, what are you waiting for?' Luckily, Mommy talked me out of it, because I really didn't have the nerve to go through with it.

"That was funny, but another time, he slapped me and I was mortified. I remember we were having dinner with Grandma, and she fell down the stairs and hurt herself. 'Now you've ruined my appetite,' he said, and I thought he was making a joke. I laughed, and he slapped me. Then I got slapped again for something else. We'd just left President Street, and this car was following us—a station wagon. Suddenly, it zoomed by, missing us by inches, and squealed around the corner. 'Joie, what color car was that?' he said. 'Blue,' I said, and he said, 'Very good.' He'd been teaching me things with flash cards—you know, flash! 'What did you see?'—and it was also very dark. Then we saw this car was following us again, so we drove back around onto President Street, and stopped. He said, 'Joie, stay in the car,' and he got out with the guy who was driving us. The driver of the other car stopped, too, and tried to pull a gun, but our guy was quicker. He stuck *his* gun at the other guy's temple, and Joey went over to talk to him.

"By this time, I was out in the middle of the street with my mouth hanging open. I couldn't believe what was happening. Then the girlfriend of this man who'd been following us ran out, saying, 'Please don't hurt him,' and Daddy took her by the hair and banged her face down on the car. Now I got very scared and started to cry, and he scolded me for getting out. In the end, he let these two go, and when we got home that night, I told Mommy what had happened. I started to cry again, so she cuddled me in her arms and Daddy got very angry. He said he'd told me to stay in the car, but instead of that I'd been a nuisance. I'd cried and distracted him. So he gave me a slap. And when Mommy tried to protect me, he gave *her* one as well. But not very hard.

"After we moved to Fourteenth Street, things got a little better for a while. He and Mommy used to sit up to all hours, playing soft music, drinking white wine and keeping me awake. Whenever he wanted coffee, he would knock on the wall. Mommy could yell and scream, and I'd never hear her, but all he had to do was knock and I'd be right there. 'Yessir? Take your order, sir?' He was good sometimes. I didn't mind that. One lazy Sunday, I remember we sat around all day listening to records. He was a Bing Crosby fan. He liked that kind of music, and also jazz—Charles Lloyd and Miles Davis. I got so sick of those records. But I laid on the couch all afternoon with my head in his lap, and he stroked my hair. I think that was the closest we ever were.

"At other times, we had roughhouse fights. He used to slobber me and kiss me with his bristly beard, which I couldn't stand. So then I'd punch him, and he'd wrap me up in a blanket so I couldn't breathe and throw me up and down, or throw me on the couch. That was fun, but then I'd put on an act and start crying to Mommy, who would come to my rescue and get in a fight. Poor Daddy. He'd be wondering, 'What the hell is that kid *doing* to me?' I was sort of teasing him. We were very competitive. Mommy was like a lollipop we were both after. 'Gimme.' 'No, *I* want her.' I was used to having her, and *he* was used to having her. He'd never known what it was like to have a kid in the house, and I'd never really known what it was like to have a father. It had just been Mommy and me, and we'd enjoyed life together.

"He never took me out much. We went to President Street a few times, and once to Central Park zoo, but I specially wanted to go to Coney Island. Finally, after I'd worked on him for three months, he said okay, and we went with Mommy, my friend Ida and Tony. The first thing I wanted to do was go on the Cyclone, which is the biggest roller coaster in the world. Daddy played it cool, and we went on with Tony, who didn't enjoy it much, although *we* thought it was fantastic, and wanted a second ride. So we asked Daddy to come with us. Well, he didn't want to, but he wasn't going to have his daughter think he was a coward, so he got on with us. And he nearly died. We were screaming and holding on to him, and he was shaking and turning green and purple. When we got off, he could hardly stand.

"Then he got his revenge. We wanted to go on the big wheel, but we didn't know that some of the cars swing right out as it goes around, and he put us in one of those. Now it was *our* turn to think we were going to die. Every time the car swung out, we got hysterical —and down there was this little dot holding his stomach from laughing. We were throwing popcorn at him, and he was jeering at us. He always liked to pay people back. I like to as well, and I guess he had a right to get me that time. After that, we went on all the other rides, and he bought me a lot of pistachio nuts, which he knew was my favorite thing in the world. He was in a good mood that day, and we really had fun. On the bumper cars, I hit him in the side about fifteen times.

"There weren't too many days like that. I guess he was too busy. I remember Mommy saying once, 'Joey, try to go out with her more. Pay more attention to her.' And he said, 'If I did what you wanted me to do, it would take twenty-four hours a day, and that's impossible.' So sometimes he bought me things instead. Poor Daddy—he didn't know. Once he bought me a pants suit. Red pants with a plastic leather vest and a white shirt. I hated it. So did Pammy. He used to say to me sometimes, 'Why don't you wear it, Joie? Don't you like it?' And I'd say, 'Oh, sure. Oh, I love it, Daddy.' But finally I had to tell him, honestly and truthfully, that I hated it, and although he laughed, I could tell that maybe he was a little hurt.

"The only other time we went out together was when he took me to see *Bonnie and Clyde*. I was horrified, and had nightmares afterward, but it was just ordinary, everyday life for him. Most of the time, I really couldn't have cared less what sort of business he was in. Didn't bother me—not even when I read about him in the papers.

Sometimes they'd ask me in school, 'Are you *really* Joe Gallo's daughter?'—like they wanted my autograph or something—but the only time I ever worried about what he did was when Mommy and Daddy had fights. I'd think, 'Oh God, this is it. This is where Mommy gets it,' and then I'd say a Hail Mary. Otherwise, I never thought about it.

"The day Colombo got shot, Mommy was at work and Daddy was out somewhere when I came in from school. I remember I was doing my homework, and the doorbell rang, and there were these three detectives asking to see him. 'Sorry,' I said. 'He's not here right now. Would you like to come in and wait?' So they did, and I made them coffee and we talked for a while, and then, about fifteen minutes later, he came in, looking at me like I was some sort of traitor. So I took my homework into my room and left them to it. I wasn't that interested anyway. But after that, we had a special code. Daddy kept his hash on the bookcase near the window, where he used to sit. And he told me that if anyone came in and he called my name in a special way, then I was to eat the hash, or throw it out the window. We worked out another code in case anyone was using me as a decoy when I came home from school or wherever. He would always say, 'Who's there?' before opening the door. If I then said, 'Joie,' it was all right. But if I said, 'Joie Marie,' then that would mean someone was behind me. Luckily, I never had to say, 'Joie Marie.'

"Things were getting pretty bad though by this time. He was a very demanding person. When he was home, nobody else was supposed to do anything but serve him. While the Attica riots were on, he was just unbearable. He sat glued to the television, and I couldn't walk across the room without him getting hysterical. 'Sssh! Are you crazy? Can't you see I'm trying to watch this? Look what's going on here.' So we'd have to sit and watch for hours while he turned to different stations, just so he could see it all over again. Mommy said to him once, 'You just did ten years. Are you trying for twenty?' I remember Ruth came over one night to teach her needlepoint, but Mommy wasn't even allowed to look down to see what she was doing with the needle.

"Our worst fight was because I distracted him while Attica was on, but we were fighting a lot now because I kept saying no to him. He would come home and say, 'Make me some coffee.' And I would say, 'Daddy, I have homework. Can I do it later?' 'No. Now.' It was like I was refusing him, and nobody ever did that. He was the king, and I couldn't stand it. I wanted to take him and choke him and kill him. I respected him for stopping a riot, but enough is enough. He never knew when to get off. He used to abuse Mommy terribly, and I resented him coming between us. He broke her ribs once. He got mad and threw her purse at her. There was something heavy in it, and it hit her in the side. I used to have to strap her up terribly tight with this white tape. And then the black eyes. Oh, what we used to go through!

"I blamed him for everything bad that happened. I used to complain to Mommy about him, and bug her to leave him. 'What a man you picked,' I'd say. 'Who'd want to live with that maniac? You've got to be crazy to put up with this.' So then I'd divorce him as my father. I'd take a piece of paper and draw a very fancy certificate that said, 'I, Joie Gallo, hereby divorce Joey Gallo as my father.' Then I'd make him sign it, and Mommy and Tony would sign as witnesses. I divorced him so many times, in the end I had some Xerox copies made so I didn't have to keep copying it over.

"Mommy and I were always ganging up against him, although we never let him know it. But I remember once that he and I ganged up on *her*, and *she* never knew it. Ida and I had gone down to the basement to do the laundry, and, by accident, we put the whites and colors together in the same machine. Everything came out purple from my tie-dye blouse. We nearly had a fit. Mommy's brand-new orange sheets—everything. Ruined. So we took this stuff up to Daddy, and said, 'What are we going to do? Mommy will kill me when she gets home.' So he laughed, and said, 'This is what you do. You take everything back down to the basement and hide it behind the machines. She'll never know the difference.' And he was right. I was so scared, but it was weeks before she missed them, and then she thought they'd gotten lost at the send-out laundry. He never said a word. And always, if Mommy and I had an argument, he would say, 'Oh, stop it, Jeffie. Leave the kid alone'—which was nice of him, but she'd generally get me anyway.

"It was a funny situation. I knew that if I was alone with him, I'd soon become his little Smiley-Smiley and his robot. I didn't want that, but we could have gotten along. I also knew that if I was alone with Mommy, I could stay the way I was. And I could see that if Mommy and Daddy were alone together, they would probably get along, because she liked to serve him—to a certain point. But the three of us were never going to make it. We couldn't live together. One of us had to go. And, obviously, it had to be him! But he just couldn't see it that way.

"They had big fights about him staying out, and Mommy made him sleep on the couch once. The next day he started getting his stuff together. He's had it, he says. He's leaving. And he's going to take the leopard he painted for me. 'No,' I said. 'I'm sorry. You can't have it.' So I hid it. Then I told him what I thought of him. He sat there for an hour with his hands folded, listening to my complaints, and when I finally got through, he just got up and strolled out. He didn't say a word in his defense. He didn't even say good-bye. He just collected half his things and left. The next day, while we were out, he moved the rest, and when we came home, it was 'Ding, dong, Daddy's gone.' Mommy and I were both so happy.

"Two nights later, we came home and found all the lights were on. He was sitting by the window. He was back. He said he was sorry and things would be different. He was in a very good mood, so Mommy forgave him, and I started rehanging his pictures, though we were still in shock from finding him there. I kept saying, 'Mommy, do you think this one should go here?' and she kept saying, 'Joie, shut up,' because they were kissing on the couch. But that didn't last long. A few days later, she was reading aloud to him from her astrology books, and Daddy didn't like it because what she was saying matched his personality to a T. So he snatched them away and threw them out of the window onto Fourteenth street. Only *he* could predict his future.

"By now, Lisa and I had met each other and become instant friends. I'd already seen her in the building, and I knew she was Lisa Essary, actress—which was what I had always dreamed of being. She was making commercials, and trying out for plays, and I was terribly jealous of her for a while, but that passed. We went to the same dance school, so we walked home together, and I started going up to their apartment quite a lot. That's how I knew Daddy was seeing Sina, but I didn't mind that at all. If Sina could handle him, then God bless her, and please take him away as soon as possible. Mommy knew about it, too, of course, because she and Sina became friends as well, although Daddy didn't know that. As far as we were concerned, Sina and Lisa were welcome to him.

"Sometimes, he would take Lisa and me out to dinner together. We were the Gallo girls. He favored *her* a bit, but again I didn't mind. At that point, it was 'Listen, Lisa, you can have him. He's all yours. Take him. But don't say I didn't warn you.' He liked Lisa, and Lisa loved him. He was the king, and she was the princess. He made *me* feel like a peasant, but I was happy for Lisa if she could get some pleasure out of him. It made me sad sometimes that I wasn't getting on with my own father, but I knew it wasn't *all* my fault. He was just unbearable to live with. Like at Christmas. He stayed out the whole day. I was terribly angry, so we opened our gifts without him, and the next day I left to see my Grandpa in New Orleans.

"But he made up for it on my birthday. I really loved him that night. I had arranged a sleep-over party with about eight or nine of my girlfriends from the fifth grade at P.S. 41. No adults were invited. We had frozen pizza in the refrigerator, and I knew how to use the stove. My mother was confined to her room, and not allowed to come out for any brownies or anything. So we were having a great time, playing records and dancing, when this lady comes up from downstairs, rings the bell and says, 'What do you think you're doing, making all this noise after eleven o'clock at night? Don't you know people are trying to get some sleep?' So now I'm thinking, 'Well, that's the end of the party,' but then Mommy breaks the rules and comes out to see what's happening. And right away this lady starts yelling at her, 'I'm going to call the police.'

" 'Okay,' Mommy says. 'You go right ahead. When they get here, you tell them to come up here, and maybe they can have a piece of cake with us. This is my child's birthday. If she can't have a birthday party once a year and make a bit of noise, then *I* will call the police.' And she closes the door in her face. So then we start screaming, 'All-American mother—yeh! yeh!' and dance harder than ever. Now it's getting pretty late. Mommy's back in her room. Some of us are making forts with the pillows and having fights. Some of the others are throwing water out the window and screaming at people on the street, and one or two of us are falling asleep. So then, at about 3 A.M., we hear someone trying to get in the front door.

"Panic. We switch out the lights and hide. There are people under each couch, between the couch and the wall, and me and Pammy are under the radiator. It can't be Daddy, because he said he wasn't coming home. Then the lights go on, and a voice says, 'Hey, what's happening here?' And it *is* Daddy. 'What are you doing home?' I said. 'You told me you were staying out. You promised me.' But my girlfriends start fussing over him in the kitchen, making him coffee, and I can see he's in a very good mood, so maybe it will be all right. And it was. He was great. He gave everybody two dollars, and started playing blackjack with us. Pammy was his partner. They were the bankers, but she got all the money. And she was winning a lot until my friend Tina bought the bank from them. It was fun. We played until about six, and took him for maybe fifty dollars between us. Then we slept for an hour, and got up at seven to make breakfast. He made one unkind remark about me when I was asleep, but except for that, we really had the greatest time with him.

"Otherwise, things went on as before, and I knew it couldn't last. It was too hard on everybody. So I wasn't really surprised when I came home from dance school one day and found them both sitting there waiting to talk to me. I sat down next to Mommy, and he said, 'Let me get you a cup of tea'—and already I knew something was wrong because Daddy had never done that before. 'Your mother and I have decided to get a divorce,' he said. 'We think it's the best thing.' Then he started going into the reasons why, and soon there's a big argument. I'm getting good and scared, and also wondering how they can discuss such private business in front of his personal bodyguard. Finally, they're into a hushed, screaming sort of thing, and I can see somebody is going to get killed, so I burst out crying on the couch.

Mommy comes over to hold me, and, as he's walking out the door, he changes his mind, comes back and punches Mommy in the stomach as she's sitting there.

"Now I'm really in a complete state of hysteria, but Mommy is saying, 'Don't worry. It's all for the best. It's all going to work out.' When I calmed down a little, she got a couple of things together, and we went off to spend the night at Ruth's. I still didn't think we had left for good, but while I was sitting on the bed that evening, doing my homework and watching TV at the same time, Mommy was figuring in her bankbook, and all of a sudden she said, 'Joie, what do you want to do? Do you want to go to California?' And I said, 'Yeah. Of course. I'm ready. Let's go.' But then I remembered I wasn't ready, and I started to cry. I'd left all my pictures and Donny Osmond posters back at the apartment. But Mommy got Marjorie to go with her in the middle of the night, and she came back with them, and a lot of other stuff, so everything was all right.

"I only talked to Daddy once after that, when he called us from New York. He wanted to know how I was getting on in school out there—the usual thing. Then one morning, as I was ready to leave, I heard Mommy say on the phone, 'Is he dead?' and I knew it was Daddy. Mommy started crying, but I didn't really feel anything until later in school, when it suddenly struck me. I told my two boyfriends in class—nobody else—but it soon got around. And as soon as people started asking me about it, I started to cry and got real upset. I missed him much more than I thought I would. I still do.

"A couple of days later, I went with Lisa and Sina to the funeral in their limousine. I even had my picture in the paper, although the reporters didn't know who I was, and I'm sort of glad. Uncle Blast said Mommy could go, too, and she was in the last car with Grandpa Gallo. I thought it was all disgusting. There were tons of flowers, and I wanted to take the carnations, but I wasn't allowed, although I know Daddy wouldn't have minded. And that beautiful, bronze-gold casket—it was velvet-lined, and terribly elegant. How could they put such a beautiful thing in the ground? Mommy said it would have made a good planter. And Daddy had always said he wanted to be cremated.

"He was a completely different person around the family. He was relaxed with us, when we weren't fighting, but with them he was always on his toes, trying to show everybody how tough he was. I don't think he was so tough. I think he was an old softy. He couldn't stand to see a stray cat on the street. I thought he'd come to tears sometimes. Once I fell on my roller skates and gave myself a real good cut—the blood was gushing out—and when I went up to Daddy to get a Band-Aid on it, he had to go into the bathroom. He looked really sick. He wasn't so tough. He was an old softy trying to be something he wasn't."

22

Joey

Joey, if I asked how you got into the rackets, would I get the old soft-shoe shuffle about the slum kid from Brooklyn who never had a chance?

You want I should apologize, right? I'm sorry I was such a stupid kid, but now I see the error of my ways, I'll try to be as good as you —that what you want?

No, no. I didn't mean it like that.

Sure, you did. You're a condescending limey son of a bitch. But that's okay. It's not your fault you're full of shit. You're just a victim of your environment.

Let me rephrase the question.

Don't bother. I heard it every which way. It's a free country, right? They told you that. Everybody's free to choose. Jesus! I could have been a dentist! I could have been a nice person. But I didn't do that. I chose to run a crap game, and make you feel superior. Schmuck.

Thanks. But did *you choose? That's all I'm asking. Was there a moment when you said, "Okay, I've taken a look around, and all things considered, I'm going to be head gangster"?*

Listen. I did what I had to do.

Yes, but was it what you wanted? *No, wait. What's wrong with that? I want to find out if you knew what you were doing. I'd like to know if you made a conscious choice, that's all.*

I know what you're saying. I understand English. Nature or nurture, right? Well, let me tell you something. I *always* knew what I was doing. Always. I accept that responsibility. But what *you* don't understand—because you got no way of knowing and because you're the kind of guy who does all his living inside his own head—what *you* don't understand is that your mind works different in that situation. You don't think about it. You *live* what you are. You know what I mean? You don't hang around waiting for no career counselor to walk up to you and say, "Listen, I've been watching you. I see you got a head for numbers, so I figure you'll do good on Wall Street or maybe running a policy bank." Never happens. You don't think about choice. You do the best you can with what there is.

And if it's against the law?

Look. Try to understand. Legal, illegal—people do what they think they can get away with. It's not the law that cramps them up. It's fear. You got two ways to go. You need money or nerve. You wanna new suit? You don't have the money? Steal one. Looks just the same. Feels even better, if you don't get caught. These fucking kids today, they want to opt out? Great. They're free to do that. But when I was a kid, we weren't never allowed to opt *in*.

And didn't want to anyway.

Never thought about it.

Well, some of you did. Some of those kids came in from the street and got to be dentists. And lawyers and politicians. Cops, even.

Not too many cops. Not in my neighborhood.

All right. But how come they did it, and you—

Not too many dentists either. That's a Jewish thing. But you wanna know why those guys got off the streets? I'll tell you. There's family reasons, and there's personal reasons. The family reason is their *mommas* wanted them to be a dentist. How many kids you know wanna be a dentist? They wanna be ball players, right? Or airline pilots.

Or gangsters?

Okay, I'll buy that. But it's the family decides. If you're Italian, and your momma's got ambition for you, then, brother, that's it. If you don't shape up, you don't know the heavy shit that's gonna come down. If she wants you to be a dentist, then you better start learning to say, "Wider, please," because that's what you're gonna be.

And your mother wanted you to run a crap game?

Don't get smart. My mother had a restaurant. I used to help her out in there, fixing fifteen-cent hamburgers for greaseball truck drivers. Okay. So I could have worked my way up to head soda jerk at Whelan's Drugstore, but what kind of a life is that for a guy like me? That's where it gets personal.

Your pride was involved.

Sure. That's part of it. But you know the real reason why a lot of those kids got off the streets? Because they couldn't cut it. It was too tough for them. So they listened to Momma. They knew they'd get their heads busted out there if they didn't.

But you could handle yourself.

You bet your ass. I was comfortable. I knew what to do. I knew what the other guys were going to do before *they* knew it. And you know the best thing about it? There's no bullshit. If you want to do something, you don't sneak around, kiss the boss's ass. You *do* it. Straight out. And if you're a little smarter, and a little tougher, and a little quicker than the other guys, then pretty soon you got it made. You're boss in the only way that means something. You're *better* than they are.

Well, that goes for the straight world, too, doesn't it? I mean, if you've got that bit extra, chances are you'll make it.
Oh, come on. You kidding me? The best man *never* wins. Step out of the crowd, and they'll kill you.

It's different on the streets?
It's more honest.

What?
Sure. You don't pretend you're doing a guy a favor when you kick him in the ass. People know where it's at, so they can watch out for themselves.

Yes, but hold on, Joey. You lost me. Leaving your mothers out of it, you're saying the big difference between you and the dentist is that you *knew you could make it on the streets and* he *knew he couldn't.*
Yeah. More or less.

Then both careers were equally acceptable? I mean, pulling teeth or running numbers, nobody was drawing any moral distinctions between the two? You're just two guys trying to make a living.
Right. Who eats morals?

Fine. But now you're going beyond that. You're not just saying it doesn't matter what you do—legal or illegal, it's all the same. You're saying illegal is better.
Not better. More honest. You call things by their right names. If you steal, you steal. You don't charge a guy a dollar for two cents' worth of merchandise and act like you were doing him a favor. And stop saying legal and illegal like you meant moral and immoral. That's a whole different thing there. Gambling's illegal, right? But it's not immoral—not to me. Somebody wins a bet with me, I pay off. That's moral. Now take the dentist. Pulling teeth is legal. But if

you're in pain on a Saturday, and he charges you double to take care of it, that's immoral. I'm honest. He's a hypocrite.

Don't bookies sometimes welsh?

Sure. And they wind up dead. But the dentist, he gets to join the country club.

Okay. So the system's corrupt. It's hypocritical. Absolutely right. But that doesn't make everything morally neutral, does it?

I don't know what you mean.

I mean, if a dentist kills a patient in his chair because he won't pay his bill, and makes it look like heart failure, he's a hypocrite, sure— but it's murder, right?

Listen. I'm in the chair three times a week. I owe the guy a lot of dough. What are you trying to do to me?

Okay. Forget the dentist. But let's suppose—just for the sake of argument, of course—let's suppose you do in a bookie who welshed. Okay? Nobody can pin it on you, but you let everybody know you did it. Does that make it better? Because you're not a hypocrite?

You want to know something? If the D.A. asked me, I'd be a hypocrite. Believe me.

I do. Because it's still murder. Just because people know about it doesn't make any difference. And anyway, dentists don't usually kill patients who don't pay their bills. Isn't that the difference? I'm not talking about legal or illegal. I'm talking about right and wrong. Good and evil.

Dentists are good, and I'm evil. Right?

Now you're just trying to intimidate me. I mean good acts and evil acts. Distinguishable by their nature.

Yeah, but how do you tell? We're getting in deep here. How do you judge an act out of context? You wanna know my definition of morality? I got one rule in life.

Thou shalt not get caught?

Look after your friends, and take care of your enemies. You'd be surprised how that simplifies everything.

Maybe for you. But it doesn't do much for me—not if you think I'm an enemy. Where's my protection? Are there no moral absolutes? How about "Thou shalt not kill"?

Who says so? Jesus Christ? Fuck Jesus Christ. Look what happened to him!

I think it was Moses, actually.

Well, fuck Moses, then. Look. Forget the bullshit. It's simple. Think of it as a war. I'm in a war, see. Italians? When I was a kid, they were nothing. Dumb greaseballs. Good for humping garbage and delivering ice. And waiters—they were good as waiters. You know why? They were meek. Very meek. They took orders. When they weren't humping garbage, they shuffled off back to their slum so the nice people didn't have to look at them and get that greaseball stink in their nostrils. You understand what I'm saying? They were white niggers. Okay. Now I don't like this so much. Neither do the kids I'm going with. So we start moving around a little, making a little noise, just so people'll know we're there. We're not meek. Like you say, it's a free country—so where's *our* piece of the action? No place. Everything's sewn up tight. And not only that, nice people don't wanna know from Italians. They're getting nervous. Hey, what's going on here? The natives are restless tonight. We better send in the cops. So pretty soon, it's a war. They don't *call* it a war. They're hypocrites, right? They're enforcing law and order. Nice people's law, and nice people's order. Fuck what happens to them greaseballs. What do they know? Fuck the niggers. Fuck the Jews —the poor ones anyway. They gotta protect the rights of the individual—so long as he's a nice person and belongs to the Rotary Club. Well, okay. Only from where I'm standing, it feels like a war. They're taking the Statue of Liberty, and they're ramming it up my ass. So what do you want me to do? Say I'm sorry for getting my ass in the way? Fuck you. If you want a war, I'll give you a war. Don't tell me, "Thou shalt not kill." Tell that to the nice people.

Okay. But is that all?

All? Listen, creep—

I mean, are you sure you're not just using that to justify things you were going to do anyway? Plenty of other Italian kids must have got it up the ass as well. And some of them turned out to be judges and senators and corporation lawyers.

Yeah? Well, they were for sale, and I wasn't. It was a war. Maybe I *like* war, but I didn't invent it. You wanna talk about politicians? How many been caught with their hand in the till? You wanna talk about cops? Who's handed out more beatings, them or me? You wanna talk about lawyers and judges? I'll buy you one for Christmas. You wanna talk about business? You short-change the world and call *me* a thief. You wanna talk about Wall Street? Congress? The President of the United States? Tell me what you wanna talk about. Is that *all*? Jesus Christ. I'm just a skinny kid from Brooklyn. You want I should set an *example?* Fuck you. Things are not right or wrong any more. Just smart or stupid. You don't judge an act by its nature. You judge it by results. We're all criminals now.

Maybe so. But it's still a very convenient rationale, isn't it? I mean, for every antisocial move you ever made or felt like making, you could always point to something worse, and that got you off the hook. That makes it okay.

So?

So it's not more honest. It's just another kind of hypocrisy.

Listen. What do you want? I gotta deal with things the way they are. Plenty of people have said to me, "You know, Joey, if you'd gone another way, you might have made something of yourself. If you'd put your brains and your energy into something legitimate, you could have gotten to be President." And you know what I always say to them? "Bullshit. I couldn't be that crooked. I don't know how to lie and cheat and double-cross that bad. I'd never make it in politics. I'm too honorable."

Now who's full of shit? I think it's strictly personal with you. Okay, so you're in a war. That's because you enjoy it—you said so. You don't want to overturn the system. You like fighting it, that's all. You don't have a cause. You just use other people's.

No, I've got a cause.

You have?
Yeah. Me.

Ah.
Now you're happy, right? But don't go too quick. Because that's the kind of a cause that gets tied in with other people's causes. Remember that. Sometimes you can't tell 'em apart.

Are they causes you would die for?
You crazy? What for? What can I do for anybody dead? That's such a dumb thing. When I die, I'll die for *me*. Death don't scare me. We're all dying. But it's gonna be when *I* decide.

Well, then. You're saying the same thing. You follow a cause for as long as it suits you. The only ideas you believe in are those that serve your purpose.
Wrong. I don't *know* my purpose till I know the ideas.

Joey, you're a self-educated man. You only know what you wanted to learn. That makes a difference. There's still nothing beyond you. So how can the world trust that?
You don't understand. And maybe if I could explain it, I wouldn't have to do it. I don't know. Things exist when I feel they exist, okay? *Me. I* am the world. The world is in *me*. Good, bad, ugly, beautiful —it's all there. Everything. And it's all legitimate. It's gotta be. If it exists, if I feel it, it's legitimate. I am alive. I feel it, therefore it exists. And if it exists, it's not good, it's not bad. It just *is*. You know what I'm saying?

Yes. You're saying you're going to do anything in the world you feel like doing whenever you feel like doing it. And you're saying the rest of us have got to rely on your goodwill. And, Joey—I don't know that it's enough.
No? Then kill me. Because *I'm* supposed to rely on *your* goodwill, right? I'm supposed to trust all you nice people? Well, I got news for you. It ain't enough for me either. So you wanna kill me now? You're bigger than me.

No, I don't feel *it.*

Okay. But don't pretend you're different. All I know is my *self.* That's *real.* I'll listen to that. And it's the same for you. You just need the guts to go through with it.

We don't live in a vacuum, Joey. The world's not going to end with me. It didn't start with me either. I've no right to pillage it.

Pompous fucking limey. You should have thought of that four hundred years ago. Now it's my turn.

Not if you want to survive.

Jesus Christ. *You* are going to tell *me* about how to survive?

Well, maybe I could tell you a little something about self-control.

I don't think so. I don't think you got anything *there* to control. You locked yourself in, and you won't come out, so it's easy. What can you tell me? You've gone dead inside. I know a lot of people like that. All they can do is watch guys like me and jerk themselves off. No, you got nothing to say to me.

Maybe you're right. If we're going to talk about jerking off, what can I say to an expert? What can you say to a guy who deliberately brings the whole world down on himself and his family just to show off his powers of manly endurance? You're right. That kind of jerk-off is out of my league altogether.

Hey, hey! What's this? Are we blowing our British cool just a little bit? Do I see a bit of the old animosity sticking out there?

Could be. I'm in there watching all right, but I'm not locked *in.*

Yeah, well, I guess that's the difference. I'm a doer. You're a watcher. Maybe you'll live longer, but you won't live as much.

Bullshit. I don't call that living. It insults the mind. You give it nothing to do but make up alibis for what you've done already or mean to do regardless. Degrade it like that, and we're just clever animals. That's not living.

Let me ask you something. Did you ever rape a woman?

No. I never did. I never watched it either.

Didn't you ever want to?

Not since I was about fifteen, no.

You never wanted to grab a hold of some juicy little broad, and throw her down, and tear her clothes off, and get it up there and give it to her while she's wriggling and moaning? You never wanted that?

I prefer a little cooperation.

How do you know you wouldn't get it?

How do I know I wouldn't get fourteen years?

You don't. That's it. You'd like to, but you're afraid, right?

Well, it's not much of a bargain at those prices, is it?

No. And all that shit you been giving me about morality—that ain't such a bargain either. You'd do it—if you thought you could get away with it. So would I. We're no different underneath.

Joey, it's what's on top that counts. That's the part people have to live with. You know something? All your problems are problems of excess. You never know when to stop.

Yeah? Well, let me tell *you* something. It's guys like me that make the world go round. Nobody wants to write a book about *you,* wise guy.

There you got me.

Right. And I'll tell you something else. You really wanna know what my problems are? Time and place. That's all. If I'd have been born at the right time and the right place, they'd have put my statue up in the streets.

I think that's very likely true. But what's the difference? They look at a statue, and what do they see? Stone and pigeon shit.

Yeah? Well, what will they see in a book? Paper and bullshit.

Maybe not. Maybe we'll be holding up a mirror.

23

Sina

Joey made so slight an impression on Sina the first time they met that even when he described the circumstances to her later, she still had no clear recollection of ever having seen him before he offended her one day in Dr. Schuchman's office. According to Joey, some weeks before, he and Tony had by mistake taken an elevator going up instead of down, but had stopped bitching about it when this beautiful brown-haired woman got on at the penthouse floor with a cute blond kid around Joie's age. He had tried to make conversation with her on the way down, failed and, on reaching the lobby, had asked the superintendent who she was. On hearing that she worked for the dentist in the building, Joey immediately called him to make an appointment.

Sina was then working part-time because Lisa was still on vacation from school. They had just returned from Europe after spending much of the summer there, and visiting relatives in Italy. When Dr. Schuchman told her that Joey Gallo had signed on as a patient, she looked at him blankly. They had been away when Joe Colombo was shot, and by the time she and Lisa came home, the fuss had died down. Schuchman then explained who Joey was, adding that he lived in the building and generally showed up with a retinue of body-guards. Sina was horrified. She said she would not come to work when he was expected. Somebody in the office could call her when he had gone, and she would then come down.

Sina had an old-fashioned, middle-class, Middle Western aversion to gangsters. Born in Akron, Ohio, in 1941, she had lived there until she was twenty-eight. Her father, of German-English stock, owned a grocery store, her mother was Italian, and both shared a comforta-bly orthodox outlook on life. At eighteen, Sina married her child-hood sweetheart, Lambert Essary, and she was twenty before she first defied convention. Before their daughter was born, she separated from her husband and went home to her parents. Divorce followed a year or so later, by which time she was working as a dental assistant in Akron, where she might have remained for the rest of her life had it not been for Lisa.

Her daughter had shown early a talent for the stage. In 1969, Lisa's dancing teacher arranged an audition for her with John Ken-ley, a well-known producer of summer stock, who immediately of-fered her the part of Baby June in a touring production of *Gypsy*. She was then seven. Sina, of course, accompanied her, and by the end of the year, Lisa Essary was well enough launched on a theatrical career to make it essential to move to New York. Encouraged by Allan Jones, who later sang at Sina's wedding, and by John De Main, the young conductor who accompanied him on that occasion, she rented an apartment on West Fourteenth Street in June, 1970. But they were no sooner installed than they left again, for Lisa now had a part touring with Gig Young in *Nobody Loves an Albatross*. When they returned home at the end of the summer, Sina went to work for Dr. Schuchman downstairs, and, pending a Broadway offer, Lisa em-barked on a soap opera and a profitable series of television commercials. Nothing could have been more remote from their lives and experience than Joey Gallo.

A year later, after avoiding him for a week or so, Sina received a letter from the relatives she had just visited in Italy. Not reading Italian, she needed someone to translate it for her, and so made a point of being in the office for Joey's next appointment. When he arrived with Carmella, however, Sina gave it to her to read instead. The news was most upsetting. Sina had doted on her grandfather, who had died shortly before she moved to New York, and the main purpose of her European trip had been to see his only surviving brother, who lived in Bari. The letter was to inform her that a few hours after she and Lisa had left for Rome to fly back to New York, the old man had died of a heart attack.

Sina was distraught. She retreated into Schuchman's private office, and refused to be consoled. Joey, who had left the dentist's chair to see what all the commotion was about, went in to see what he could do. On hearing through her sobs what the matter was, he said, "No wonder the old goat had a heart attack. They don't see many broads like you in Italy." This made her so furious she stopped crying.

Though Joey had given her little cause to revise her opinion of gangsters, he was certainly not a terrifying figure, and it seemed silly to go on avoiding him after that. In the course of subsequent, less emotional conversations, he arranged for Joie to meet Lisa, and then, early in September, for Sina to meet Jeffie, who was rather abrupt, although Sina at that stage had no unprofessional interest in Joey at all. He was charming, polite and just another patient. By now, she completely discounted what Schuchman had told her.

The weekend after school reopened that fall, Lisa invited a friend to sleep over, and Sina decided to take them out to dinner at a nearby Chinese restaurant. As they were leaving the building, they met Joey coming in with two of his bodyguards. He asked them where they were going. When she told him, he professed to be horrified that she should think of venturing out after dark with two little girls, and insisted on escorting them. Successfully negotiating the hazards of a three-minute walk on Fifth Avenue, he then seemed equally unwilling to abandon them to the perils of Cantonese cooking, and over Sina's token resistance, all six sat down to dinner.

As always, Joey was a delightful host. Jeffie often said that he was the only man she had ever known who could have entertained his mother, his wife and his mistress at the same table and kept them all equally happy. Although Sina had no thought then of any such intimacy, she was sufficiently charmed at the end of their meal to invite her escorts up for a nightcap. But as she opened the door, the telephone rang. Excusing herself, she took the call in her bedroom. When she emerged some minutes later, she found Joey had sent his bodyguards home.

Wary now, Sina poured him a drink, but Joey just wanted to talk. He talked until six the next morning. He told her about his life in prison, and the horrors he had seen there. He talked a lot about Jeffie, and how they were getting a divorce because they were so unhappy together. He said he was hurt by Joie's attitude toward him, but blamed this on her mother. Between them, he said, they acted like they were doing him a favor by letting him back in their lives. And yet he spoke without rancor or bitterness. Indeed, for much of the time, he seemed to be talking to himself, as if he simply needed someone to sit with him while he struggled to work things out in his mind. And if he was also bidding for Sina's sympathy, he got it. When he appeared not to notice her yawns and hints, she hadn't the heart to order him out. It was getting light before he stirred himself to go, but even then, Sina felt nothing but pity and admiration for him. He was still not attractive to her—or rather, she had still not considered him in that light—but she believed him to be a good man, and the lurid stories she had heard about him seemed more absurd than ever.

A few hours later, her former brother-in-law telephoned. He and his wife and their five-month-old baby were passing through New York on their way home to Akron from Maine. Delighted with this unexpected opportunity for Lisa to meet her new cousin, Sina invited them to lunch, and, a few minutes before they were due, went downstairs to meet them with an umbrella, as it was now raining heavily. While she was waiting at the door, Joey's Cousin Tony, who often accompanied him to the dentist's office, saw her standing there and wanted to know what she was doing. When she explained, he gallantly told her to stay in out of the rain. As soon as her guests arrived, he would run out and tell them to park in the garage. And so he did, to the alarm of her brother-in-law, who, when he saw the tall, rather sinister-looking Tony racing toward them, suddenly believed all he'd heard about New York muggers. But his consternation was nothing to Sina's when she took her visitors up to the apartment and found Joey in the living room. Lisa had let him in while her mother was downstairs.

Speechless with shock, Sina quailed at the thought of what they would make of this in Akron. Though Joey was again on his best behavior, she ignored him until he got the point and left. But that night, just as she was getting ready for bed, he stopped by again. This time he wanted to know if she would like to go to a wedding with him. When she refused, he asked if he could come back later, and Sina gasped. A little frightened now, she told him not to think of it, and closed the door in his face. Undaunted, he returned the next evening to tell her what a good time she had missed.

From then on, for about a month, Joey stopped by to see her almost every day, often around dinnertime. Unless she fed him, he said, he would starve to death, because Jeffie never cooked. Though he took his welcome for granted, and sometimes embarrassed her in front of her friends with his prison stories and street talk, Sina did nothing to discourage him. He was gentle, warm and kind—and her daughter loved him. But then he took to calling, often very late, with groups of people she had never seen before and never saw again. On one such night, she had gone to bed after a dinner party without clearing up because the maid was coming in the morning. Roused by the persistent ringing of the doorbell, she found Joey outside with a group of strangers. He led them in and offered them drinks. As she stood watching, in utter disbelief, Joey caught her eye. Instantly contrite, he broke off in mid-sentence and bundled everybody out again, which must have left Sina with the uneasy feeling that she was on display for some reason, that she was being maneuvered into a situation she didn't really want but couldn't really avoid. And her suspicions deepened when Jeffie called soon after to say that, as far as she and Joie were concerned, if Sina wanted Joey, she could have him with their blessing.

Then his family took a hand. Carmella already approved of Sina as a more suitable match for him than Jeffie, and evidently his mother did, too, on the strength of what she had heard, because she began sending presents of food. Sina came home one evening from visiting friends in Riverdale to find Joey pacing up and down outside the building with a dish of baked peppers. Grabbing her by the arm, he demanded to know where she'd been. He'd been waiting for her out there for two hours, at some risk to his life, he said. Sina shook him off angrily, with a warning never to lay a hand on her again, but there was no mistaking his increasingly proprietorial air. Nor was there much mistake about her response. To her dismay, almost, she found herself resenting his attitude less and less. She was falling in love with him, and when she finally realized this, Joey acknowledged it, too.

Sina loved him, but, at the same time, she didn't really want him. For one thing, the thought of deceiving Jeffie and Joie downstairs was very unappealing. Never having taken Jeffie's offer of her husband very seriously, Sina had the distinct impression that Jeffie was still trying to make the marriage work. Then again, she had no real desire to change the pattern of her life. She had lived alone with Lisa from choice, not from any lack of suitors. She also strongly objected to Joey's behavior around the house. She had spent practically every cent she possessed on fixing up the apartment, and from the moment he began to treat it as his own, she found herself in a running battle to protect it. Her housewifely instincts were continually affronted by the cigarette ash he ground into the wall-to-wall carpeting, by the nails he banged into the bathroom wall, and the hooks he hammered into her brand-new bookcase. She only narrowly prevented him from sawing the back off an $1,800 armoire to accommodate the television set.

Sina hardly knew what to think. When Joey was there, and he would sometimes stay for two or three days before going home, he could hypnotize her into believing that the half-life they were leading was unavoidable. The last thing he wished to do, he kept saying, was to mess up her life, but his parole was a serious problem. He was afraid that Jeffie would have him "violated" if he left her. He even suggested she might harm Sina and Lisa in some way if he acted precipitously. But the moment he left, all Sina's doubts would stream back. She then no longer wanted him to break with Jeffie, who was still telephoning her from time to time, often while Joey was there in the apartment. The sense of guilt and her distaste for the petty deceptions she had to practice were getting her down.

But Joey had a powerful ally in Lisa, and another in his mother. When they at last met, Mary Gallo, like Carmella, behaved as though Sina were already his wife. After that, he took her and Lisa to Brooklyn once or twice a week—they were now part of the family—and the only discordant note was the Gallo women's incessant criticism of Jeffie: how she had failed Joey in prison, and failed Joie by not looking after her properly. But even this served Joey's purpose in a way, for it helped salve Sina's conscience about her. By Thanksgiving, she and Lisa were close enough to his mother and sisters to celebrate the holiday in Brooklyn without Joey. Kid Blast was there instead.

Like Jeffie, Sina was resolutely incurious about Joey's life away from Fourteenth Street. In their first long conversation, he had told her he had been questioned about the Colombo shooting, and he sometimes referred to other crimes of which he had been accused, including fourteen killings, but she always refused to listen. Talk of this kind had nothing to do with the kind of man he had shown himself to be. It was necessary for her to believe that she had fallen in love with an ex-gangster who was now going straight, who went around with the boys from President Street because they were his people, and whose orders were obeyed because this was his due as head of the family. Besides, he spent too much time in the building to be very active elsewhere. For the same reason, she found it hard to believe his life was in danger, though he often told her it was.

Meanwhile, in sharp contrast with the tranquillity he found with Sina, Joey's battles with Jeffie were becoming more frequent and violent—a fact that Sina could not dismiss so easily. A week after Thanksgiving, Joey came up to her apartment to announce he was moving in. He had broken with Jeffie for good. As he spoke, the boys began to carry in his paintings and belongings. The rest of his stuff was going to his mother's, he explained, so that the Parole Board would think he was living there. On Monday, when he had to report, he would tell them he was getting a divorce.

Sina panicked. It was one thing to live with the distant possibility of perhaps marrying Joey someday, and quite another to have him move in, bag and baggage, without warning. But, as always, she was unable to refuse him directly. Instead, she began to lay down a series of conditions she knew he could never accept. The first was that he would have to give up smoking. He was ruining her carpets. She even pinned a notice to the door to remind him: "No smoking inside my apartment"—and by Monday morning, she had achieved her object. They were drinking coffee when he suddenly got up from the table. "I can't live here," he said. "It's your apartment, not mine. Everything in it is yours. I could never feel comfortable here." Then the phone rang. While Sina was answering it, he put on his hat and coat, collected his things together, and moved back downstairs for yet another reconciliation with Jeffie.

As the door closed behind him, Sina started to cry. The apartment, she realized, had become an obsession with her. It now seemed ugly and empty. She felt she had made a terrible mistake, and probably lost him forever. After several days with no word, she was sure of it, but she had also begun to think that, while she might have ended the affair more honestly, it was nevertheless right to end it. Early in December, she flew out to California with Lisa, planning to stay with her brother and sister for a while before driving down the coast to Acapulco for the Christmas and New Year holidays. A vacation seemed a more sensible way of trying to get over Joey than remaining in the same building and perhaps running into him two or three times a week at the office. But Joey had no intention of being gotten over, and circumstances once more played into his hands. Lisa took sick, and Sina's trip ended in Los Angeles.

When he learned where she was, Joey began to call her from the apartment every day, begging her to come back. Anxious in any case to get Lisa home to her own doctor's care as soon as she was well enough to travel, Sina caved in completely when Carmella called to say that her husband had died suddenly. She and Lisa took the first plane back to New York, and went straight to Carmella's house.

When Joey arrived there next day for the wake, they left at once without speaking to him and went home to Fourteenth Street. That night, some friends stopped by to welcome her back, and midway through the evening, Joey burst in on them, annoyed that she had avoided him, and furious she had taken a taxi when there were thirty men there who could have driven her home. He had not seen her for two weeks, but it might have been two minutes for all the difference it made. He not only stayed the night, but hardly left the apartment until after Christmas, when Sina ran away again.

This was not because Joey had spoiled the holiday. In fact, it was one of the most enjoyable she had ever spent. He sent Lisa out with Tony to buy the biggest tree they could find, and they spent the afternoon of Christmas Eve decorating it while playing carols on the phonograph. He then went downstairs to pick a fight with Jeffie, so as to get out of having to dine with her and the Lloyds, and later that evening, drove over to Brooklyn with Sina and Lisa for a meal with his father. After dinner, Joey astonished everybody by taking them to midnight Mass, putting up with some good-natured mockery from the boys as a result, and on their way back to Fourteenth Street he told Sina and Lisa that they would celebrate every Christmas Eve that way for the rest of their lives.

On Christmas night they were expected at his mother's house, but, as the day wore on, Sina became increasingly fretful about Joie. She told Joey that he really ought to be with her instead, that the thought of a little girl being cheated of her father on Christmas Day was spoiling their own pleasure in his company, and in the end he agreed to go downstairs. They didn't see him again that night, and all Sina's ambivalence returned in strength. His continuing dishonesty with Jeffie was getting to be more than she could stomach, and although he kept saying that Jeffie would rather see him dead or in jail than with another woman, Sina was neither convinced of this nor prepared to carry on if it was true. Summoning up her courage, she told Joey she had met someone else in California, and was going back there. She had the locks changed on her door, telephoned Jeffie to say she was bowing out, and left with Lisa to spend the New Year holiday, not, as she had told him, with an admirer in Los Angeles, but with her family in Akron. When Joey went up to the apartment and found his key no longer worked, he flew into such a passion that he almost broke down the door. But he then returned to Jeffie to declare another truce.

Sina was away five days. When she returned, Jeffie called her down to her apartment to say how happy she was at the way things had worked out, and to tell her about their plans for a children's boutique on President Street. Sina was happy, too. She was going to miss Joey badly, but it was all for the best. Although Lisa was very upset, she would soon get over it—she had a part coming up in *Voices* to distract her.

But Joey was not to be denied. A week later, on January 12, the day after Joie's tenth birthday party, he bumped into Sina in the elevator and once again overwhelmed all her doubts and objections. He was going to tell Jeffie the truth and get a divorce. Sina was not to worry. He would handle everything.

He then borrowed her last $500 to go toward a surprise party on President Street for *Lisa's* tenth birthday, on January 18. He had the social club carpeted and refurnished for the occasion and brought in a firm of caterers.

Lisa was delighted. Joey gave her a solid-gold roach-holder and a knife that had once belonged to Ali Baba, and she was allowed to stay up until 7 A.M. Joey's brother was rather less impressed, however. Although he was on the block and said he would come, Blast preferred to remain next door rather than endorse the latest in what was now a very long list of extravagances.

By the end of January, the rift with President Street had become quite evident, although Sina was past caring. In spite of his protestations, Joey had continued to shuttle back and forth between herself and Jeffie, who was apparently still under the impression that he had returned to her. Sina had had enough. Exhausted and ill with worry, she told him she was resigned to whatever he chose to do, but choose he must. She couldn't cope any longer. Until he decided between them, she had no further wish to see him.

She didn't have long to wait. A few days later, Jeffie called her at the office, crying hysterically. Joey had left her in the middle of the night, and gone to some girl's apartment in the building. As usual, Sina tried to console her, but this time Jeffie was beyond reach. She was so in love with this man, she said, but he had finally pushed her too far. She had called him at the Parole Board, and when he had hung up on her, she had called back and told the guy who answered that Joey should start coming home nights instead of going straight to his parole officer from God alone knew where. Knowing Joey's sensitivity on the subject of parole, and having heard, incredulously, about the beatings he had given Jeffie, Sina tried all the numbers she knew in a vain effort to reach him before he got to her. She was afraid for Jeffie's life.

In the early evening, as Sina and a girlfriend came home to Fourteenth Street after picking Lisa up from rehearsal, she met Joey with two of his boys in the garage. He was just leaving, in an evil temper, after his final battle with Jeffie. She was obviously still alive, but Sina's relief was immediately swamped with fright. Bundling them into the back of the car, Joey himself took the wheel, though he had no license, and drove like a madman to Brooklyn, weaving in and out of the pillars supporting the West Side Highway with such recklessness that he reduced Sina and her girlfriend to tears. Even Lisa fell foul of his mood when they sat down in the Queen Restaurant for dinner. For the first and only time in the six months she knew him, Joey scolded her—for eating bread and spoiling her appetite before the meal. Stung, she snapped back at him. He called her a brat and promptly told Tony to take them all home. Then he changed his mind. It was not a happy evening. When they got back to the apartment, he kept Sina up all night while he went over and over his troubles with Jeffie, seeking to justify what he had done.

Next morning, Jeffie surprised her by calling from the airport. She said she thought her absence for a few weeks in California might bring Joey to his senses. Sina was not so sure, but she agreed Jeffie was doing the right thing. There seemed no possible future for the two of them together. Joey's first reaction on hearing that Jeffie had left town was also one of surprise—shock even—but he recovered quickly enough to move in with Sina and give up the apartment downstairs that same day. The boys were set to ferrying the furniture over to his mother's—though they soon tired of that and brought in a removal firm to finish the job—and Joey superintended the operation as if he couldn't wait to wipe out every last trace of his life there.

But he now had to find another answer to the problem he had faced on his release. He was still not free to live with Sina or any woman but his wife. There was nothing to prevent him living alone, except that he didn't want to, or with his mother in Brooklyn, except that he had already done that, and neither was anxious to repeat the experiment. If he was to move in with Sina, he needed somebody with a place in Manhattan to cover for him, somebody who would hold enough of his clothing and personal effects to make it look as if he were living there.

As luck would have it, he and Jeffie had accepted an invitation to have brunch with the Orbachs that Sunday. Joey toyed with the idea of taking Sina instead, but eventually decided to go alone to explain what had happened and to see if they would help. He had no wish to continue the acquaintance if they refused him, and, in any case, promised Sina to come home early. But it was 5 o'clock next morning before he returned, in high excitement, to report that Marta Orbach had not only agreed to cooperate, but would also ask an influential friend to speak to Governor Rockefeller with a view to getting him pardoned.

Later that day, Joey tried to set his thoughts in order by jotting them down on a yellow legal pad:

Short Stops
Released from Sing Sing after serving 10 years of 15 year sentence on 10 March 1971—Writing these thoughts on Jan 31 1972.

Sitting on soft warm couch listening to WLIB

Malcolm speaks—Gregory bores—two cops shot dead in East Village—Sol Hurok bombs! British soldiers kill 13 in Ireland—Mass graves in Bangladesh—Harlem 5 win hung jury—

Enough! No end—but a beginning is theoretically necessary and understanding start will entitle the bearer to be progenitor of life.

Willowbrook! pornographic—obscene—insane—

Only sensitive application of euthanasia from this point on should be legal —let the abominations that have plagued our planet and infected our atmosphere live out their miserable deaths.

Who are the abominations? Individuals—groups—who has the power has the opportunity—Bullshit! But what about the Bad Guys? Play safe— don't get involved—take a position—Why? Because you want to help— Why? Money? The need to be recognized? Man's healthy need to create from his contact with his experience of his practicality into an art form that offends no one is acceptable—but any form that supposes direct intellectual action is met with hostility and eventual murder—

Keep your eyes on the absurd—not to be understood—just delight— Keep your circle small—eat together—live openingly with one another— dig music, ideas, faces, places, shadows, forms and silence.

That evening, Joey took Sina to meet the Orbachs, and they all went on, with David Steinberg, to Buddy Greco's opening at the St. Regis. Significantly, Joey's bodyguard was Punchy Illiano, who was there for old times' sake rather than as paid protection.

From the moment Joey took up with his new theatrical friends, the already wavering support of the gang fell steadily away, leaving only a handful of the faithful to share the responsibility of driving him around and carrying the gun. But security was of small concern to him that night. Though courteous, polished and at ease, he was reserved to the point of reticence in comparison with his normal social self. When they got home, he demanded to know from Sina if he had behaved properly. Had he done anything wrong or embarrassed her in any way? On being assured that he had not, Joey then kept her awake till dawn, telling her he had never thought he could be so happy or ever deserve a girl like her. Now he was going to write, he said. He was going to write a comedy, a black comedy about prison revolving around a character named Slick, and Marta had said she would help him with it. Everything was going to be different now. A whole new world was opening up for them. Grimly aware that she would soon have to be at work to pay the rent, and knowing better than Joey how empty the promises of theater people could often be, Sina was rather less enthusiastic.

For several weeks, however, his bubble refused to burst. At brunch with the Orbachs on Sundays, he introduced Sina to the Gazzaras, to the Bruce J. Friedmans, Harold S. Prince, Neil Simon, Joan Hackett and her husband, Richard Mulligan, the John Barry Ryan IIIs and the Thomas H. Guinzburgs, among others. Joey was having a grand time, in spite of Sina's warnings that some of his new friends might be exploiting him for the thrill of having a real live gangster empty their ashtrays and talk about life and art. When Marta Orbach told him that Viking Press was interested in publishing his work, he could hardly contain himself. For about two weeks, Joey saw her for an hour or two almost every other day, either at her house or at Fourteenth Street, to tape his prison reminiscences.

With the crystallization of his literary ambitions, however, his early enthusiasm began to fade. Originally, Marta had offered to help him write a prison comedy, but by early March, there was talk of Joey helping her write, not a humorous work of fiction, but his authorized biography, and splitting the proceeds, fifty-fifty.

In the old days, Joey would probably have taken care of the problem in his usual, direct fashion—at one point in their negotiations, he did, in fact, tell several people that he had threatened to blow Jerry Orbach's head off—but he was now too deep in the toils of his brave new life to do more than brawl with him verbally. There was not only the matter of his parole to think of—the divorce was not yet through—but he was also in debt to Marta, having borrowed from her in anticipation of the riches to come.

This was particularly upsetting for Sina. From the very beginning she had told Joey repeatedly that he should not get involved with the show-biz world on her account. Though there was no more money coming in from President Street, and his paychecks from the furniture company were going out to Jeffie every week, they could still live very comfortably on what she was earning. But Joey's pride was involved. It was not that he had any qualms about spending Sina's money, or, indeed, anybody else's. He was simply incapable of stepping back from any situation before he had mastered it.

Some four weeks after they had first met, Jerry came around one evening to explain to Joey in considerable detail the terms of the fifty-fifty deal they had in mind for him. He began by telling Joey what a splendid job Marta was doing in negotiating a contract with Viking Press, and how she had already saved them 10 percent by dispensing with the services of an agent. He then proposed that Joey should bind himself to them for three years, in the course of which he would collaborate with them exclusively in the preparation of various literary properties based on his life, assign them the exclusive right, and an irrevocable power of attorney to negotiate and act on his behalf, and also forbear from speaking to reporters or other media representatives without first obtaining their permission. In return for these undertakings, Joey would receive 50 percent of the net proceeds of their collaboration, after the deduction of all expenses, but excluding any share in the money that Jerry Orbach might earn from performing in any of these properties.

Joey listened without change of expression, but once Jerry had left, he could hardly contain himself. "What the fuck is going on here?" he hooted. "Since when did it become a life story with pictures? I'll give 'em pictures. And who said she was going to get half? Jesus Christ. If and when I ever do my life, it'll be when I'm so old and so rich it doesn't matter." A few nights later, both the Orbachs stopped by to discuss the matter. With Sina and Joey's father sitting as an unwilling jury, Joey and Marta reconsidered the proposals in an exchange in which, to the surprise of their audience, Marta successfully countered all his objections, and retired with the tapes he had made thus far.

By now, Sina had had enough of all of them. *Voices* had already opened in New Haven, and moved on to Philadelphia, its last stop before Broadway. Unwilling to neglect her daughter any longer, she left early one morning to spend the day with Lisa, promising to come home after the performance that night. But it was such a relief to escape from the uproar on Fourteenth Street that she purposely missed the last train back to New York, and stayed on for a second day. Returning late that afternoon, in some trepidation, she walked in on a scene even more bizarre than any she had seen so far.

She was partly prepared for it by Joey's Cousin Tony, whom she noticed waiting in his car across the street. She had not seen him for almost a month. He told her that Joey had called President Street, in a wild mood, and asked John (Mooney) Cutrone, the most respected member of the group, next to the Gallos themselves, to sit in with him at a meeting with Marta Orbach and two people from Metro-Goldwyn-Mayer. But before Sina even opened the door, it was obvious from the bedlam inside that their discussions had long passed the point of coherence. Everybody was shouting at once, nobody was listening, and the apartment was littered with liquor bottles, glasses, coffee cups and overflowing ashtrays.

Joey, it seemed, had had an offer to appear on the *David Frost Show*. Though he had no intention of accepting it, he had used the invitation to prod Marta into action, into producing something tangible, some earnest of what he might expect if he bound himself to her as she proposed. He wanted a movie contract. He wanted money for the movie rights to the book they'd been talking about. Accordingly, Marta had managed to persuade a friend of hers at M.G.M. to bring along a top production executive to talk things over, whereupon Joey had prudently asked Mooney Cutrone to hold a watching brief for President Street lest anyone get alarmed at what might otherwise appear to be an appalling indiscretion.

Dismayed by the din and the havoc in her apartment, Sina tried to clean up around the contestants. The M.G.M. executive said later that she seemed to be the only sane person in the room. The story has since gone around that, in the end, Joey was so overcome with disgust at the proceedings that he suddenly jumped up from the couch, unzipped his fly, pulled out his penis and said amiably, "See? I'm Jewish."

Marta Orbach and the others were too busy talking to each other to notice the evidence for this unlikely claim. The meeting then broke up. Marta stayed behind, however, and followed Joey into the bedroom when he went to change, so anxious was she to assure him that she had his interests at heart. They were still talking when Sina finished tidying up and sat down for a breather. So far, nothing had been said about her two-day absence or her failure even to call Joey from Philadelphia, and she was beginning to think that perhaps she might get away with it in all the confusion. But then he came out of the bedroom alone, took her by the throat and forced her head back until she was looking up into his eyes. "Don't you ever leave me again," he said softly. "Not for one hour." Then he kissed her, and went back to resume his discussions with Marta.

Some hours later, he showed up at Ruth's for the third night in succession, called Jeffie and asked her to come back from California before he did something stupid.

Next day, March 10, he went downtown to complete the divorce proceedings against her, and on March 13, he signed the collaboration agreement with the Orbachs, making only very few changes. They had convinced him that without this proof of their exclusive right to his literary output they could not get a concrete offer of any kind, not even from Tom Guinzburg of Viking Press. But as far as Joey was concerned, neither document weighed on him heavily. He was simply keeping his options open. He was now free to marry Sina whenever he wished, and the Orbachs would continue to sponsor his society debut. Of the two, the divorce was strategically more important. By marrying Sina, and thus acquiring the legal right to live with her openly, he would no longer have to rely on the Orbachs for an address.

After signing the agreement with them, he and Sina took their blood tests and went on to City Hall to pick up a marriage license, with Joey cursing at President Street because no one had shown up, as instructed, to drive them around in the snow. Next day, Tuesday, he sent Jerry Orbach out to buy a ring—a thin gold band, Sina told him. He returned with a fat gold one from Cartier, which Marta agreed was all wrong. She took Sina back to the store, where they bought a $400 ring with diamonds, and charged it. Joey, Marta said, would be happy to pay her back when the money from the book came through. She was also anxious that they should be married at her house, although Joey had still to name the day.

On Wednesday, out of the blue, Sina's former husband telephoned and asked to speak to Lisa. Sina got rid of him by saying she would have her return his call when she came home from Philadelphia, which made Joey indignant. Nobody was going to make Lisa do anything she didn't want to do, he said sternly. *He* was her father now—an idea so potent that he decided then and there not only to marry Sina next day, but also to claim blood paternity of her daughter.

On Thursday morning, the first person to hear that it was Sina's wedding day was her cleaning woman. Then, just in fun, Sina suggested that he should call the Orbachs and tell them she had run away, leaving a "Dear John" note on the pillow. Marta rose to the bait with gratifying dismay, and then rose as readily to the occasion when he tired of the joke and told her they wanted to get married that afternoon. In little more than two hours, she found a minister —the Reverend William Glenesk, of the Village Presbyterian Church—ordered a wedding cake and flowers, invited a dozen guests and persuaded Earl Wilson to send Tim Boxer from the New York *Post*. Sina, meanwhile, had called Lisa in Philadelphia, who was upset she couldn't be there, but urged her mother to grab Joey before he changed his mind, and John De Main, who promised to come, and to bring Allan and Maria Jones as well, if they were free.

Joey, however, was having a little trouble with *his* guests. Mary Gallo and his sister Jacqueline spent the day looking for something to wear, found nothing suitable and, in the end, stayed home. Carmella, who had promoted the romance from the beginning, was at first to be matron of honor, but, by the time she arrived, with one of his aunts, Joey had decided to make David Steinberg his best man instead of his bodyguard Tony, and Marta then seemed a more logical choice. When Tony called an hour before the wedding to find out what time he should collect the bride and groom, he was so annoyed at the thought of being displaced by a comedian that he, too, stayed home.

By four o'clock, the survivors had assembled in the Orbachs' townhouse on West Twenty-second Street and the proceedings were about to start when Joey discovered he had left the license at home. While someone went to fetch it, John De Main worked out the musical arrangements. He would first play a few bars of "Here Comes the Bride" to get Sina on, and then, as part of the service, accompany Allan Jones at the piano in a setting of the Lord's Prayer.

Forty-five minutes later, the license arrived, and the Reverend Glenesk, whose prior claim to fame had been to marry Tiny Tim and Miss Vicki on Johnny Carson's television show, at last got under way with the ceremony.

As Earl Wilson and Tim Boxer reported next day to the nation, the minister "was going good when there were gasps from the 20 wedding guests because he said, 'Do you, Nina, take this man . . .' 'No, no, not Nina! SINA, SINA!' several people called out. The minister, considerably shaken, buried his head in his prayer book, then turned meekly to the bride-to-be and said, 'Let's do it again.' The bridegroom mumbled, 'Are we married yet?' and when somebody said, 'No, not yet,' Joey exclaimed, 'God is a tough customer!' "

He enjoyed Allan Jones's singing though, and sought him out when the service was over with tears in his eyes. "You made a Christian out of me," he said. "I got religious, hearing you sing that." His conversion, however, did not extend to telling Tim Boxer the truth. In all seriousness, and with Sina at his side not daring to deny it, Joey invented the story that was widely reported by Earl Wilson as though Sina had told it: "My grandfather owned a grocery store in Akron, and he used to buy olive oil from a man in New York who was a friend of Joey. Joey and I met when Joey came to see my grandfather. He was sent away to prison. I married and have a ten-year-old daughter. It's strange how we met again. Six months ago, I moved to an apartment on West Fourteenth Street. One day, I was taking my daughter to do a film commercial. We were in the elevator going down from our penthouse when Joey got in on the seventh floor. Were we surprised!"

They certainly would have been if he had gotten in on the seventh floor because he lived on the eighth, but apart from that, the real surprise was felt by her friends when they read the Wilson-Boxer story in the *Post* next day. As openly as he dared, Joey was suggesting that Lisa was his natural daughter, but the only particle of truth in his account of meeting Sina eleven years earlier was that in those days he did indeed know a man who dealt in olive oil—and his name was Joe Profaci. But if it was not the literal truth, it was at least a metaphorical truth. Joey certainly *felt* like Lisa's father. He even told his mother and his aunts that she was his, and they seemed to believe him.

At dinner with the Allan Joneses on the evening after the wedding, John De Main asked Sina and Joey, "What's this bullshit in the paper about Lisa and you two?" Joey looked him in the eye. "We *did* know each other eleven years ago," he said. "Lisa *is* mine. She's my own little girl." There was no suggestion that this was simply a story he and Sina had agreed to tell the world outside. Joey wanted it to be so, and therefore it *was* so.

He was in a strange mood that Friday night—calm, content, but somehow removed. He spent a lot of time staring silently at the magnificent view of the Hudson River from the Joneses' apartment, and when his host joined him at the window, spoke wistfully of the years he had lost looking out on a prison yard. Sina, who had seen very little of her friends for weeks, was enchanted that Joey was getting along with them so well. That Thursday and Friday were the happiest two days they ever spent together.

By Saturday, it was business as usual. They went to hear Jimmy Roselli sing at the San Susan nightclub in Mineola, Long Island, an excursion that unidentified sources, quoted by Fred J. Cook in the *New York Times Magazine,* later described as an attempt to take over a business owned by John Franzese, a Colombo capo serving a fifty-year stretch for bank robbery. If so, it was the first recorded instance in the annals of organized crime when a mobster, bent on a shakedown, moved in with his mother, his sister and his bride of two days. The only muscle he had with him that night was provided by Pete the Greek and Bobby Darrow.

On the other hand, it was certainly no ordinary social occasion. On entering the club, Joey objected to being led across the floor in full view of everyone, and there was a brief scuffle with the waiters that badly frightened Sina, who had never seen him in action before. With his two bodyguards, Joey then disappeared behind the scenes for about twenty minutes, leaving the women to cover their uneasiness with small talk. When they returned, his manner discouraged curiosity, and he proceeded to get very drunk.

Some time later, to the evident surprise of all concerned, a contingent of the boys from President Street arrived to catch the show. For a while, they pretended Joey wasn't there, but when that became impossible, some of them stopped by the table to say hello. Nobody referred to the wedding, much less congratulated him on it, and all escaped as soon as they decently could. To Sina's acute embarrassment, Joey then subjected Roselli to a running barrage of insulting comment throughout his act. Still less in character, he interspersed his heckling with bouts of demonstrative affection toward Sina, hugging and kissing her in public for the first and only time—not, she was certain, out of any desire to impress those watching, but out of the turmoil he was in that night. When he finished his act, Roselli joined them at their table, and later followed Joey into the bar, where they joked, danced and generally carried on with the musicians. This worried Pete the Greek and Bobby Darrow almost as much as it did Sina, and both were visibly relieved when they got him home. It was then broad daylight.

It was also Sunday. As usual, Joey was due at the Orbachs, but he stayed in bed all day. Next morning, Marta showed up on Fourteenth Street with her notebook and pencil, but was sent away. In the three weeks that remained to him, he saw her twice more to Sina's knowledge, once at the Broadway opening of *Voices* on April 3, and once by chance at the Copacabana on the night of his death. Frustrated by his refusal to keep the appointments she made for him with her attorney, Marta called Sina at one point, wondering if the Parole Board might help. Sina managed to dissuade her from that approach. It could hardly have made Joey's position much worse, for, a few days after their marriage, Sina had lost her job. They were broke. Joey's options had expired.

He could no longer count on President Street. Even if he had wished to reassert his authority there, his followers were not likely to forget his desertion, and any extra effort to win back their allegiance would inevitably have put his parole at risk. Besides, he had outgrown the old life. To allow himself to be forced back into it was unthinkable—a submission to circumstance, a confession of failure.

As for his new life, the prospect was hardly less humiliating. It entailed another kind of surrender—to show-biz society and public opinion. His self-esteem would depend, not on his power and sovereign will, but on how long an ex-gangster could stay in fashion. Like an ex-prizefighter, he might even be reduced someday to making yogurt commercials.

Forward or back, Joey was in check. He had sacrificed most of his pawns, and the queen was in California. But then, a week before he died, Joey thought he saw a way out, a way not only of recovering the loyalty and support of President Street without having to go back there, but also of keeping his glamorous new friends without having to depend on them. He had lunch with former Congressman Alfred E. Santangelo, president of Americans of Italian Descent.

"Joe called me about working for AID," Santangelo told the *New York Times*. "We met in a restaurant . . . and had a nice talk. He said he wanted to work for the Italian people. He wanted to know about our organization. He wanted to know if I was controlled by outsiders."

Founded in 1965 as the American-Italian Anti-Defamation League, the organization had begun its drive to disassociate Italian-Americans from the stigma of organized crime by appointing Frank Sinatra as its first national chairman. Whereupon, the Anti-Defamation League of B'nai B'rith had disassociated itself from AIADL by means of a lawsuit that forced the new group to change its name to Americans of Italian Descent, and in 1967, many of the original board members—including Sinatra and Tammany chieftain Carmine De Sapio—disassociated themselves from AID amid rumors of Mafia infiltration. Leadership in the campaign to brighten the image of the Italian-American community then passed to Joe Colombo's Civil Rights League, which he started in 1970 after Joe Colombo, Jr. had been picked up by the FBI on charges of conspiring to melt down coins for their silver content.

With Colombo now out of the way, it seemed to Joey that if he could recover the initiative for AID, he might also recover for himself a position with all kinds of interesting possibilities. And while Santangelo was afterward at pains to discount Joey's claims about his status within the organization, it was clear that they hit it off together, for, on parting, they exchanged wristwatches and agreed to meet again as soon as Joey had checked him out with the FBI. That was on Friday, March 31.

On Monday, *Voices* opened on Broadway after a week of previews. Knowing that his best man, David Steinberg, was standing in for Johnny Carson on television that night, Joey had asked him some time before if he would have Lisa on the show, never doubting that he would agree. When Joey phoned him during the day to confirm it, Steinberg said he didn't know if there would be time on the show for Lisa. In the middle of the call, Joey lost patience. His disillusionment was complete. The Orbachs had booked a table at Sardi's for an opening-night party that evening, but Joey refused to go. Barely civil to them as they sat together during the performance, he waited outside the theater afterward with his back to the wall while Bobby Darrow brought the car around.

On Wednesday, less than forty-eight hours before he was killed, he went back to see Santangelo in his law office at 299 Broadway, and told him that he appeared to be running an "honorable" organization. "I got a clearance from the FBI," he said. "I asked them if they had any objection if I worked for Italian-American groups. They said they were only against the League, and would have no objection if I worked with you."

Whatever misgivings Santangelo may have entertained, as one of AID's original board of directors, at the prospect of enrolling another Gallo, he evidently felt that this was an offer he couldn't refuse, particularly as Joey had also brought in "eight men who were going to help." Santangelo designated them all as "recruitment representatives," assigning several of them to AID headquarters at 400 Madison Avenue. But he and Joey were still clearly at cross-purposes. Talking to Detectives O'Brien and O'Flaherty on President Street on the afternoon of his birthday, Joey told them he planned to reactivate AID by recruiting a panel of important Italian-Americans, but Santangelo later denied this. "Gallo wasn't even a member yet," he said. "He came to work for us. He volunteered. He had no control at all, no position in AID at all."

If this was true, if Santangelo had made it plain at their meeting the day before that he was not about to hand over the organization to him, then Joey might well have suspected that his last hope of escaping the trap would prove as illusory as the first. That night, as though reminding himself of the old days, he had gone back to Mulberry Street for the first time in over ten years to dine at the Luna. And if, on his birthday, the reaction of his own people had in any way echoed the polite skepticism of the police, then at last Joey would have had to have conceded defeat, for there was nowhere else to turn. At any rate, in the early hours of April 7, after a farewell public appearance at the Copacabana, he went on to Little Italy and offered himself up to his enemies.

Jeffie is convinced of it. "He *had* to die. When he knew he was in a corner and couldn't beat it, then he said, 'Fuck it. I'll die. I'll die before I say I'm sorry.' Life or death, it always had to be *his* way. He could never fall down in his own eyes. We had terrible arguments about it. 'If you want to do James Cagney, you gotta do Yankee Doodle Dandy, too,' I used to tell him. 'Who made you God? I want to see a paper. Show me a paper that says you're God. If you want to be God, you'll get nailed to the cross.' But he never sold out. He wouldn't 'Yessir' nobody. Never did it—never in his whole life—so he *had* to die.

"Joey was an artist. He was a poet, an actor and an anarchist—not good traits to live a long life. He was a prince before the kingdom, which no doubt was torment. I respected him. I respected him enough to go down with him, I think he knew that. But I had a child. She didn't understand, and I couldn't put her through it. If there had been no Joie, and he'd said, 'Come on. Tonight we got to get killed,' I would have gone with him. I didn't want to die, but I never found anything in the world to believe in but Joey. He knew me better than I knew myself, that son of a bitch. Now he's sitting on my fucking shoulder and won't get off."

His brother Blast made arrangements for Jeffie and Joie to attend the funeral on April 10. About one hundred relatives and friends went to the private service at the Guido Funeral Home on Clinton Street, Brooklyn, where his body had been on view for two days. Afterward, thirteen limousines followed the flower-laden hearse to

Greenwood Cemetery, where many more people were waiting to pay their respects. And among those who cried to see that Joey dead could command a following he had looked for vainly in the last few weeks of his life was his ten-year-old stepdaughter Lisa. In her grief at losing him so soon, she tried to put her feelings into words. Some days later, Sina found what she had written:

> I hate. My thoughts don't seem to be really real. They just float in and out of my mind. Like cobwebs really, their there and then sweep sweep, dust dust, and thier gone. Friends come over and try to make things better, but it is over for me. Why didn't they come before? So many questions unanswered, so many people who never come when you need them the most. It seems that no one really realizes his great love for another until thier dead, that I'll never understand. I hate what I am. Where I am and what I am. I hate.

But on the other side of the piece of paper, Lisa had drawn a picture of herself smiling, sitting on the ground among spindly flowers. And underneath she had written: *"Things pass."*

Envoi

This is Jeffie's book—not just because she made it possible, but because she was recklessly truthful. She wanted the truth about Joey. She wanted his story told, without constraint, apology or adornment, and without thought for her pride, which she otherwise values as highly as her privacy. The cost to both, as it turned out, has been considerable, and my debt to her is one I can only humbly acknowledge since it is quite beyond my ability to repay.

I am also considerably indebted to Jeffie's friends, who, taking their cue from her, provided me with material of a candor and intimacy that has rarely come a biographer's way, and never before, to my knowledge, about such a man as Joey. In some cases, to spare them the risk of embarrassment, I have changed their identities, but little else, for they, too, see this as Jeffie's book. *Her* satisfaction with it is the measure of ours.

D.G.

450